250 True Italian
Pasta
Dishes

RISTORANTE

QUARTINO

PIZZERIA • WINE BAR

APERTURA
DALLE 15.00
ENGLISH SP

ARIA
IZIONATA

250 True Italian

Pasta

Dishes

Easy & Authentic Recipes
Inspired by Quartino Ristorante
Pizzeria Wine Bar

John Coletta with Nancy Ross Ryan

Robert
ROSE

Location Photographs (Quartino Ristorante, Chicago): 2, 52, 96, 138, 164, 176, 200, 218, 236, 278, 304, 340 © Tyllie Barbosa.
Other Photographs: background texture on chapter openers © iStockphoto.com/Laura Eisenberg; 7 © iStockphoto.com/Kelly Cline; 26 © iStockphoto.com/ShyMan; 362 © iStockphoto.com/Julien Bastide.

Dedication

To Steve Lombardo, Hugo Ralli and Larry Shane — alla tua saluta!

For complete cataloguing information, see page 375.

Disclaimer
The recipes in this book have been carefully tested by our kitchen and our tasters. To the best of our knowledge, they are safe and nutritious for ordinary use and users. For those people with food or other allergies, or who have special food requirements or health issues, please read the suggested contents of each recipe carefully and determine whether or not they may create a problem for you. All recipes are used at the risk of the consumer.

We cannot be responsible for any hazards, loss or damage that may occur as a result of any recipe use.

For those with special needs, allergies, requirements or health problems, in the event of any doubt, please contact your medical adviser prior to the use of any recipe.

Design and Production: Daniella Zanchetta/PageWave Graphics Inc.
Editor: Judith Finlayson
Copyeditor/Proofreader/Indexer: Gillian Watts
Recipe Testers: Julie DeRoin and Audrey King
Illustrations: Kveta (Three in a Box)
Food Photography: Colin Ericson
Food Styling: Kathryn Robertson
Prop Styling: Charlene Erricson

Cover image: Penne with Vegetables and Aromatic Herbs (page 68)

We acknowledge the financial support of the Government of Canada through the Book Publishing Industry Development Program (BPIDP) for our publishing activities.

Published by Robert Rose Inc.
120 Eglinton Avenue East, Suite 800, Toronto, Ontario, Canada M4P 1E2
Tel: (416) 322-6552 Fax: (416) 322-6936

Printed and bound in Canada

1 2 3 4 5 6 7 8 9 TCP 17 16 15 14 13 12 11 10 09

Contents

Acknowledgments

Without the encouragement, help and expertise of the following, this book would not be:

My partners at Quartino — Steve Lombardo, Hugo Ralli, Larry Shane, Greg Horan, Bob Kanzler and Matthew Graham.

Quartino's entire staff, from the front-of-the-house managers, servers, bus staff and bartenders to the kitchen full of chefs, sous-chefs, cooks, apprentices and dishwashers. I just wrote a book; you make the restaurant run.

Lucia Bove Coletta and the late John Coletta, my mother and father, in whose kitchen and home I first tasted, learned the nuances of and began my lifelong journey in great Italian food.

Jenifer Kisgen, my wife, and Olivia Foy and Christian Bernard, my two children, whose patience and unqualified support gave me the time and the inspiration to write.

Julie DeRoin, the book's recipe tester, who worked tirelessly to test and tailor each and every recipe for the home kitchen.

Nancy Ross Ryan, the writer who captured my voice, understood my intent and put both into words.

My publisher, Bob Dees, of Robert Rose, Inc., who after dinner at Quartino said, "How about a pasta cookbook?"

My friend and agent Lisa Ekus-Saffer, who answered for me, "Yes!"

The entire team at PageWave Graphics, especially designer, Daniella Zanchetta. I'd also like to thank food stylist Kathryn Robertson, prop stylist Charlene Erricson and photographer Colin Erricson. This group has gone the extra mile toward making this such a beautiful-looking book.

Judith Finlayson, the editor at Robert Rose who painstakingly and skillfully turned the manuscript into a book.

John Coletta

Introduction

Why did I write this book? Not because the world needs another cookbook, much less another Italian cookbook. I wrote it because I want to inspire you to begin cooking one of the finest forms of Italian gastronomy: pasta.

Home cooks are often challenged and frustrated by their inability to prepare high-quality restaurant food in their own kitchens — perhaps not realizing that cooking that kind of food usually demands a large staff, specialized equipment and purveyors who deliver a world of ingredients to the door. However, there are some things you can make at home and produce better results than most restaurants. Pasta is one of those dishes.

The pasta that my mother and father cooked for me when I was growing up in New York City, as a first-generation son of Italian immigrants, and the pasta I have eaten in Italy bears little resemblance to pasta served in most restaurants in America. My Italian friends, who prepare and enjoy pasta at home, refuse to eat it in restaurants simply because it is not as good as what they make themselves. In part, logistics are to blame. Restaurant customers don't want to wait for pasta to be freshly cooked for them, so most restaurants precook the pasta, then reheat it by dipping it in hot water. That means pasta rarely arrives at the table properly cooked. Not only are the sauces often overcooked and too salty, there is usually too much of them. Pasta should be lightly coated with sauce rather than drowning in it. And the ingredients are all too often mediocre. For all those reasons, I strongly believe that pasta is best made at home.

The sole purpose of this book is to give you, the home cook, all the skills you need to produce delicious pasta for yourself, your family and your friends. I've also included an abundance of recipes for many different kinds of pasta — fresh and dried, festive and everyday. Most are very easy to make and don't take much time, but some are more complex and time-consuming, suitable for special occasions.

Italy's history makes it very difficult to write about "Italian" food because, until 1861, when Italy became unified, the country was a collection of 20 separate kingdoms ruled by a disparate group of foreign invaders. (If you want to know more about this subject, you might enjoy reading *Italian Cuisine: A Cultural History*, by Alberto Capatti and Massimo Montanari, Columbia University Press, 2003.) These occupiers brought their own food traditions with them, which is why you'll find marzipan (originally from Persia) in Sicily, crespelle (which resemble French crepes) in Tuscany, and sauerkraut soup in Trentino. And yet, despite this foreign domination, a strong internal culinary regionalism and rivalry emerged in Italy. Each of the regions developed its own ingredients and cooking styles. For centuries recipes were passed on from mother to daughter and from father to son, and prepared only in the immediate area because many of the ingredients were not available elsewhere. Interestingly, this practical reality also influenced social attitudes.

For instance, at the turn of the twentieth century, if a Tuscan man married a woman from Alto-Adige it was frowned upon as a "mixed marriage."

While the recipes reflect the regionality of Italian cooking, they also speak to simplicity, approachability, our lifestyles and our palates. Most are simple and quick. A few of the sauces, such as Bolognese and some of the other ragùs and sugos, are time-consuming because they take a long time to cook, but they are not complicated to assemble. I have kept these recipes to a minimum.

The ingredients called for are readily available. Yes, anyone can get white truffles from Alba, bottarga (cured fish roe) from Sardinia, and buffalo burrata from Apulia. But because many regional Italian foods are intended to be consumed in season and within their region, by the time they have been transported you will likely find yourself overpaying for products past their prime. I believe you should use the freshest seasonal ingredients you can find, locally grown if possible, and my recipes are written to accommodate this.

At the end of the day, a dish of pasta is a simple, affordable pleasure that is easy to execute in the home kitchen. It's informal and meant to be shared — brought to the table in a big bowl or on a platter, to be served by the host or presented so that everyone can help themselves.

I grew up eating Italian pasta as it was meant to be prepared and enjoyed. I hope that with this cookbook I can pass on that experience so that you too can fully appreciate this delicious food. Enjoy!

John Coletta

All About Pasta

In 1861, when Italy became unified, it became a country primarily in the legal sense. Regional traditions and rivalries persisted, which means that even today a great deal of confusion exists about the names and preparation of traditional Italian dishes. If the same shape of pasta varies by a less than a centimeter it may be called by a different name — for instance, spaghetti, spaghettini, vermicelli and angel hair, or capelli d'angelo. Although these long-strand pastas decrease in thickness by less than $\frac{1}{8}$ inch (0.25 cm) from spaghetti to angel hair, which is the thinnest, each thickness has its own name. And, oh yes, there is also thick spaghetti — less than $\frac{1}{8}$ inch (0.25 cm) thicker than regular spaghetti — which also goes by a different name.

And no two Italians will agree on food nomenclature. This year I was honored to have two Italian food and wine experts dine in my restaurant. For dessert I served them zeppole, listed on my menu as "hot Italian doughnuts." These two gentlemen were born in the same hometown and grew up together. Not only did both call the zeppole by different names, each insisted he was correct.

These differences notwithstanding, there really *is* an Italian cuisine. It is characterized by a dedication to — almost an obsession with — the finest and freshest ingredients. Italy is about as big as the state of Florida, and the Italian market basket is very limited. But from those limited resources Italians have created an enormous variety of dishes. Pasta is an excellent example. It is made from flour and water and sometimes eggs. But from these simple ingredients Italians have created dried pasta in 700 different shapes and sizes and fresh pasta in many different forms. And then they developed the hundreds of sauces and many, many fillings to accompany them.

Pasta Gastronomy

All the world has noodles, but only Italy has pasta. In my opinion, pasta as we know and love it is Italy's gift to the world. The word *pasta* is Italian, but many other cultures claim it for their own — the Chinese, Etruscans, Greeks and Arabs, to name just four. It is not the purpose of this book to delve into the history of pasta, but if you want to know more about the subject, please read *Pasta: The Story of a Universal Food*, by Silvano Serventi and Françoise Sabban.

However, I do want to lay one myth to rest: Marco Polo did not introduce pasta to Italy after returning from his travels to China in 1295. Pasta was already there. The oldest surviving recipe appears in *De arte coquinaria per vermicelli e macaroni siciliani* (The Art of Cooking Sicilian Macaroni and Vermicelli), written around 1000 by Martino Corno, chef to the patriarch of

Aquileia, then a powerful city-state in northeastern Italy. In 1279 a Genoese soldier listed "*una bariscella plena de macaronis*" (a basket full of dried pasta) in his estate inventory. Polo wrote about the Chinese eating "macaroni or other sorts of pasta" in his memoirs, but Italians had been cooking and eating pasta long before that. When an Arab geographer named Al-Idrisi collected existing geographical knowledge in the 12th century, a flour-based product in the shape of strings was not only being produced in Palermo but was also being exported to other countries.

What's Pasta Without Sauce?

The amazing variety of sauces for pasta blossomed fully in 19th-century Italy. Tomato sauces were not invented until long after Spanish explorers had brought the tomato from the New World in the 16th century. By the early 1800s outdoor vendors in the south of Italy were boiling tomatoes with a little salt and some basil leaves and using the sauce to season macaroni. The first recipe for pasta with tomatoes — *vermicelli con le pommodoro* — was written in 1839 by Ippolito Cavalcanti, Duke of Buonvicino. Today residents of Buonvicino, which is in Calabria, claim that their town is the birthplace of *pastasciutta*, which means pasta with sauce — in this case tomato sauce.

During the 19th century, pasta production spread as factories for mass-producing the product were built throughout Italy. Pasta-making technology developed to include machines that mixed, extruded and dried pasta, and by the 1900s Italy was exporting pasta to the rest of the Western world. However, it wasn't until the 20th century that the different pasta shapes really began to proliferate — on one level to compete in the marketplace and on another because the technology existed to support manufacturers' imaginations. If a shape can be visualized and a die can be cast to create it, then why not make pasta in the shape of a wheel (ruote), a radiator grill (radiatore) or a tree (spighe)?

Fresh or Dried, It's All Delicious

Let me be clear from the outset: there's no such thing as bad pasta. There is fresh pasta and there is dried pasta. These are two different forms of the same product, and each has its own texture, traditions and uses. If pasta is properly cooked and sauced, it's good whether dry or fresh. But that's a big *if*, because most non-Italians

Whole-Grain Pasta

If you prefer to use whole-grain pasta, feel free to substitute dried whole-grain pasta, preferably imported from Italy, or Fresh Whole Wheat Pasta (see recipe, page 222) in any of the recipes in this book.

don't understand the fundamentals of cooking and saucing pasta.

Basically (with a few exceptions: see "More or Less Al Dente," right) both kinds of pasta should be cooked, just before serving, to the al dente stage. The literal translation of *al dente* is "to the tooth," which means the pasta should be firm and supple, not soft and mushy. After it is cooked, the pasta is drained but not rinsed. It should be tossed in just enough sauce to evenly coat and cling to the pasta. When it comes to sauce, less is more. Pasta is the star. It shouldn't be thick and gluey, or swimming in sauce, and it should be served immediately.

With the exception of some of the long-cooking ragùs and sugos, in the tradition of the Italian market basket, pasta sauces should focus on a few well-chosen ingredients. Some examples of simple pasta sauces that appear in this book include

- cheese, cherry tomatoes and fresh basil
- cheese and butter
- squash and sage
- egg yolks, cream and cheese
- broccoli rabe, garlic, olive oil and cheese
- pancetta and spring peas

However, because the ingredients are so limited, they must be of excellent quality — otherwise the dish won't live up to its potential. With very few exceptions the ingredients in my recipes are not expensive, which means that the price differential between an ordinary dish and one of extraordinary quality will likely amount to just a couple of dollars. But there is more to quality than cost. Produce is best in season and when harvested closest to market. So despite the year-round availability of most ingredients (strawberries, tomatoes and asparagus in December!), I am, like any true Italian, a great believer in seasonal, local produce. The payoff is that when produce is abundant, it is usually more reasonably priced.

More or Less Al Dente

In most situations both fresh and dried pasta should be cooked to the al dente stage, firm but supple. But because this is Italian cooking, there are, of course, exceptions. When preparing pasta in meat sauce (page 97) or baked pastas (page 279) and a few other dishes, the pasta should be cooked slightly less — that is, firmer — than al dente because it continues to cook in the sauce or in the oven after it has been sauced. Also, when preparing pasta salads (page 177), the pasta should be cooked slightly more than al dente — softer — because pasta tends to harden at room temperature and when cold.

Non-reactive Pans

I recommend cooking in non-reactive pans, ones that are made of materials that won't react with certain ingredients, specifically acidic foods: tomatoes, citrus, wine, pickles and cranberries are a few examples. An interaction between the pan and any of these can impart a metallic taste to the ingredient or darken it. Among the reactive metals are aluminum, cast iron and unlined copper. Non-reactive materials include glass, stainless steel, glazed ceramic, unglazed clay and porcelain-surfaced cast iron.

Pasta Quality

While dried and fresh pasta are equally good, there are quality differences that distinguish all pasta, whether it is fresh or dried. The quality of fresh pasta depends largely on the skill of the maker and the quality of the flour used. While you can produce good fresh pasta using unbleached all-purpose flour, you'll produce a superior version if you use Italian Tipo 00 flour. Both methods are described in Making Fresh Pasta (pages 219 to 235).

Dried pasta is a little more complex. In my mind, there are three different grades of dried pasta: good, benchmark and superior. The quality reflects the type of flour, how it is mixed, the kind of die used to cut the pasta, and the drying technique. Most pasta is made from durum wheat semolina. Durum wheat is a hard wheat that is very high in protein and gluten. Semolina is part of the endosperm, the inner part of the grain. Durum's high protein and gluten allow dried pasta to be boiled without turning to mush, and to hold its shape and texture. The golden durum gives pasta its attractive color, and the wheat in general gives pasta its good flavor.

Good Quality:

Good-quality dried pasta is generically branded and commercially made, usually in the United States. It is produced from durum wheat semolina and mixed and extruded by machines fitted with nonstick plastic or bronze dies, which give the pasta its different shapes. Nonstick plastic dies are easy to clean but they give the pasta a uniform smooth surface, which isn't optimum for sauce. Good-quality pasta is dried quickly in a hot-air drying tunnel at temperatures of up to 120°F (49°C). Be sure to read the label for ingredients — durum wheat semolina (and vitamins, because the flour is enriched) should be the only ingredient listed. The cost per pound is quite reasonable.

Kosher Salt

Kosher salt, one of several different types of sodium chloride, is the salt that many chefs prefer for cooking. Salt comes from two sources: it is harvested from seawater by evaporation or mined from inland deposits left by prehistoric oceans. During the refining process, the different textures from coarse to fine are created. Kosher salt should not have any additives and has larger crystals or flakes than the very fine-grained (usually iodized) table salt. However, some but not all brands of kosher salt may, like table salt, contain an anti-caking substance. The brand I use does not. I prefer kosher salt for its purity of flavor. It is easy to control in cooking because coarse-grained kosher salt weighs less than fine-grained table salt, and I can really add it in "pinches." It also dissolves faster than table salt. Although chefs often use kosher salt, bakers prefer table salt because it's uniformly refined, and 1 teaspoon (5 mL) always equals 1 teaspoon.

Benchmark Quality: Benchmark dried pasta is also commercially made from durum wheat semolina, but it is imported from Italy. It is shaped and cut by machines fitted with bronze dies. Bronze dies produce a rougher, more textured surface than those made from plastic. The unevenness helps the sauce to cling. More care is taken in the manufacture: the mixing may be slower and the drying time is most likely longer than that for good-quality pasta. The slower mixing and drying help to develop and preserve both the flavor and the protein in the flour. Pasta manufactured in this way can cost twice as much per pound as good-quality pasta.

Other Kinds of Pasta

Having said that good pasta contains only durum wheat semolina, I am now going to contradict myself. As previously noted, because of its intense regionality, Italian cuisine is full of contradictions. In Italy, dried pastas are made from whole wheat, spelt, farro and Kamut as well as from durum wheat. In North America, pastas are made from brown and white rice, quinoa, artichokes and corn, usually for people who have difficulty digesting gluten. In addition there are nutritionally enhanced pastas made from durum and other wheat and grains that have higher protein and fiber content than traditional pasta.

Superior Quality: Like its relatives, superior dried pasta is made from durum wheat semolina and shaped and cut by pasta-making machines fitted with bronze dies. However, this is where the similarity ends. Many small pasta factories in Italy produce superior dried pasta with great attention to excellence. They choose freshly milled durum wheat that they custom blend for a signature mix. In some cases the wheat is grown especially for them. The bronze dies on the machines are often unique to their factory, and they often limit the number of shapes they make. The pasta is dried very slowly at a low temperature (as low as 40°F/4°C), often taking up to three days to dry. As little as an hour of that time may be spent in an automatic drying tunnel; the rest takes place on screens or, in the case of one manufacturer I know, in drying closets — small enclosed rooms equipped with fans to slowly air-dry the pasta on screens. Pasta that is dried slowly dries uniformly and remains porous throughout. (When pasta is dried at high heat, the protein content may be reduced and the delicate flavor compromised. Moreover, high heat forms a hard "shell" on the outside of the pasta that reduces its ability to absorb sauces and flavor.) Manufacturers of superior pasta like to call it "artisanal."

How to Cook Pasta

Cooking the pasta is the most important step in my recipes. All my recipes serve four to six people and use 1 lb (500 g) of pasta. When cooking that quantity of pasta, I use an 8-quart (8 L) pot and 6 quarts (6 L) of water. The general rule of thumb is to use at least 1 quart (1 L) of water for every 4 ounces (125 g) of pasta.

No matter how good the sauce, if the pasta is overcooked, the final result will be somewhat diminished. In general terms, pasta should be cooked al dente, which literally means "to the tooth." It should still be a bit firm when you bite it — not soft and mushy. This being Italian cooking, there are, of course, exceptions. In some of my recipes where the pasta is simmered longer in the sauce, it is cooked to just under the al dente stage. When making pasta salads (a popular non-Italian dish) the pasta should be cooked to slightly more than al dente because pasta tends to harden at room temperature, especially after being refrigerated.

Timing

If you are cooking fresh pasta, this will take from three to six minutes, depending on the size and cut of the pasta. The thicker pastas and filled pastas take slightly longer than thin strand pastas. If you are cooking dried pasta, use the time suggested on the package as a guideline.

Testing and Draining

As the end of the cooking time approaches, whether you're cooking dried or fresh pasta, you should taste a piece by fishing it from the water and biting it. When pasta is cooked to the preferred stage, scoop off about a cup (250 mL) of the cooking water and set aside, then drain the pasta in a colander. Do not rinse it. The starch remaining on its surface helps the sauce to cling and is important for producing the best-quality dish.

Blanching Vegetables

In many recipes I call for blanching vegetables before they are added to the sauce. I do this to set their color, flavor and texture. To blanch vegetables, place them in a large quantity of lightly salted boiling water for about 3 minutes. Drain, chill in ice water or under very cold running tap water to halt the cooking process, then drain again. Blanching temporarily stops enzyme activity during cooking, which causes vegetables to loose flavor, color and texture.

Equipment for Cooking Pasta

You need only four basic pieces of equipment to cook most of the recipes in this book. They are standard and available at any cookware store.

- One 8-quart (8 L) tall pasta cooking pot with insert or a separate colander. You can use a larger pot if you have one, but a smaller one won't work to cook a pound (500 g) of pasta. If you use a smaller pot, after the pasta is added to the rapidly boiling water, it will boil over onto your stovetop.

- One 6-quart (6 L) 12-inch (30 cm) heavy-bottomed stainless steel sauté pan. A large sauté pan is necessary to accommodate the quantity of sauce plus the cooked pasta in the recipes.

- One large, sturdy wooden spoon. While a wooden spoon is useful for stirring sauces while they cook, it is necessary for tossing shorter or more delicate fresh pasta with the sauce.

- One 12-inch (30 cm) pair of stainless steel cooking tongs. You'll need tongs to toss long, stringy pasta, such as spaghetti, with sauce.

In addition, if you're making a ragù or a sugo, which cooks slowly in the oven, you will need a 3-quart (3 L) heavy range-to-oven casserole with a tight-fitting lid. I recommend enameled cast iron, because it cooks slowly and evenly and holds the heat well.

Preparation Notes

As written, my recipes assume the following:

- Vegetables and fruits have been trimmed (of stems, roots and woody ends), seeded, washed and drained or patted dry.

- All vegetables (except mushrooms) and fruits are peeled unless the recipe says "skin on" or "unpeeled."

- Recipes requiring pasta cooking water to be added to the sauce (a few don't add water) specify the initial amount. I suggest that you scoop or ladle out at least a cup (250 mL) before draining the pasta, just to make sure you have enough. When adding additional pasta water to the sauce, use your judgment. The pasta should be moist and lightly coated in sauce, not wet or drenched.

When to Add Salt

I prefer to add salt to the boiling water in which pasta will be cooked just before I add the pasta. The kosher salt I use dissolves quickly, so the pasta will be able to absorb it, and it allows me to use exactly the amount I prefer. If salt is added before the water comes to a boil, evaporation may increase, however slightly, the saltiness of the cooking water. And because I use small amounts of pasta cooking water just like stock — to add to sauces — it's important that it not be too salty.

Pairing Pasta and Sauce

Much has been written about matching the sauce — thick, thin, chunky, creamy — with the pasta shape. Delicate pastas such as angel hair can't stand up to the weight of thick, heavy ragùs such as Bolognese. And hardy pastas such as penne need more than a little garlic and olive oil. In general, flat long, thick pastas such as fettuccine go well with ragùs and sugos, and short tubular shapes such as penne, ziti and rigatoni go well with chunkier meat and vegetable sauces. Certain pasta shapes such as spaghetti and farfalle are extremely versatile and go well with all but the heaviest of meat sauces. Some pasta shapes, such as manicotti and giant shells, are meant to be stuffed and baked, while others such as lasagne sheets are meant to be layered and baked. In my opinion, about 85 percent of these theories have some merit, but then the theory breaks down because of the nature of Italian cookery.

The pasta sauce recipes in this cookbook were created to match the traditional pasta shapes with which they are paired — at least, 85 percent of them. The remaining are nontraditional recipes that I have created for today's tastes but are still not too far outside the Italian market basket or cooking traditions. I believe they go well with the pasta shapes I recommend. If you have difficulty finding a specific shape, or are making pasta as a quick dinner solution and are reaching for pantry ingredients, you can always substitute spaghetti for any long stringy pasta and penne for the short tubular ones.

Pasta Glossary

Types of Pasta

- **Shaped Pasta:** This type of pasta comes in many different sizes and shapes and is most often dried. Examples of small shaped pasta include orzo (rice-shaped pasta) and pastina (tiny stars). Medium shapes include farfalle (bow ties or butterflies) and orecchiette (little ears), and large shapes include conchiglioni (jumbo shells) and farfallone (a large version of farfalle).

- **Tubular Pasta:** This type of pasta is hollow in the center. It, too, is available in many different sizes and shapes — long and narrow (bucatini), short and narrow (pennette), short and wide (paccheri). Tubular pasta can have a smooth or ridged exterior and the ends can be cut straight or at an angle. Some of the largest tubes with the widest hollows are stuffed and baked.

- **Strand or String Pasta:** These are long rods of pasta, round like spaghetti or square-cut like chitarra. String pastas can be extremely thin (angel hair, barbina, capellini), thin (thin spaghetti, vermicelli, fedelini), or a little thicker (spaghetti, perciatelli, bigoli, spaghettoni, vermicelloni). Although strand pastas are usually dried, a few, such as chitarra, are made fresh.

- **Ribbon Pasta:** These flat strands come in different lengths, widths and thicknesses. Some are short and wide (mafalde), some are long and narrow (fettuccine, linguine, tagliatelle) and others are long and wide (pappardelle). They can be fresh or dried, and the edges can be straight or fluted.

- **Pasta Sheets:** These are flat, thin sheets of pasta, either fresh or dried. Lasagne is a good example. You can make the sheets from fresh plain or whole wheat pasta dough, or you can buy dried, ready-to-bake (also no-boil) lasagne sheets. Fresh pasta sheets can be cut into long strand pasta or short square pasta, or into small squares or rounds of pasta for filling.

Al Dente

Al dente means "to the tooth" or "to the bite." When you bite into the center of pasta, it should offer a slight resistance or firmness. The reason is twofold. First, pasta continues to cook a little from the residual heat after it is drained. Second, if you finish the pasta with a hot sauce or in a skillet, it will cook even further. Ideally, by the time the sauced pasta arrives at the table, it's perfectly cooked. Although al dente is your goal, whatever you do, don't make yourself frantic trying to figure out what the perfect al dente is. Experience with cooking pasta will be your best teacher.

Extra-Virgin Olive Oil

It is important to use extra-virgin olive oil when cooking my recipes because of the authentic flavor it adds to the dish. Olive oil can vary in color — from pale gold to green — depending on the time of year and the type of olives. It can also vary in flavor from mild and fruity to peppery and pleasantly bitter. Taste is really a matter of personal preference.

Olive oils are graded according to their levels of acidity. Extra-virgin olive oil has the lowest acidity. The best Italian oils are labeled "first cold-pressed extra-virgin," meaning that no heat has been used to extract the oil and no refined olive oil has been added. Labels, however, can be misleading when it comes to country of origin. A label that says "imported from Italy" does not necessarily mean the oil was extracted in Italy from trees grown in Italy; it could have been bottled in Italy from Spanish olive oil and then exported. The best assurance of good authentic Italian olive oil is a label that not only reads "first cold-pressed extra-virgin olive oil" but also has the name of the farm or estate in Italy where the olives were grown and the oil was produced. Olive oil tastes better fresh, that is, within the first year it is produced; after that it loses flavor.

Granulated Cane Sugar

Plain white granulated sugar comes from one of two sources: sugar cane or beets. I prefer cane sugar because it has a better, cleaner flavor. Sugar made from sugar cane is always labeled "cane sugar."

Finely Grated Cheese

Use finely grated, not shredded, cheese for cooking unless otherwise called for in the recipe. To grate finely, use the finest side of a three- or four-sided metal box grater.

Cooking Wine

I specify Italian wine in my recipes because you will have the best chance of producing a successful result if you use ingredients from the Italian market basket. In general, Pinot Bianco or Pinot Grigio are good all-purpose white Italian cooking wines. Chianti is a good middle-of-the-road red Italian cooking wine. In certain recipes I have suggested other, more regional wines that are produced in the same region where you would find the traditional dish.

Pasta Cousins

In this book I have included three typically Italian dishes that, while not technically pasta, are treated like pasta because they are sauced and baked the same way. They are also served, like pasta, as first courses or main dishes.

- **Crespelle (see recipe, page 359):** Crespelle are thin pancakes similar to French crepes. They are wrapped around various fillings and baked in the oven, and they can also be layered and baked like lasagne.

- **Gnocchi (see recipe, page 344):** These are little dumplings usually made from potato and flour, although they can also be made from semolina, bread or cornmeal. They are poached and sauced or baked in a sauce.

- **Polenta (see recipe page 352):** Polenta is slow-cooked cornmeal. It is served hot as a side dish or as a main dish with different sauces. It can also be chilled until set, then cut into shapes and fried, grilled or baked.

A Caveat

It's a given that someone will argue with any definition of any given pasta. Some will say that bigoli is made only of whole wheat flour. Some sources say that tagliatelle is thicker than fettuccine, while others claim that the names are interchangeable. And so on and so on. My purpose here is not to debate such issues but rather to use as many readily available pasta shapes as possible to give you a sense of this incredibly versatile food.

Pasta Shapes

There are many glossaries of pasta shapes. This is not intended to be an encyclopedia of shapes but rather an inventory of those I have used in this book.

agnolotti

A

Agnolotti: fresh crescent-shaped or rectangular pasta with fluted edges that is filled.

Anolini: fresh small, half-moon-shaped pasta that is filled.

anolini

B

bigoli

Bigoli: dried long, thick tubular pasta made of buckwheat, whole wheat or durum semolina. The most available type is made from durum wheat.

Bucatini: dried long, hollow tubular pasta that is thicker than spaghetti.

bucatini

C

Cannelloni: dried large round pasta tubes or fresh pasta squares rolled into tubes that are usually stuffed and baked.

cannelloni

capellini

Capellini: dried thin string pasta that is thicker than angel hair (capelli d'angelo) but thinner than vermicelli.

Cappelletti: fresh small triangular pasta shaped to resemble a cap and filled.

cappelletti

caramelle

Caramelle: fresh medium pasta shaped like a wrapped caramel candy and filled.

Cavatappi or cellentani: dried short, ridged spiral tube pasta.

conchiglie

cavatappi

Conchiglie: dried conch-shell-shaped pasta.

Conchiglione: dried large conch-shell-shaped pasta, often filled and baked.

Crespelle: freshly made small pancakes, often filled and baked (not shown).

conchiglione

D
Ditalini: dried tiny, short pasta tubes traditionally used in soup.

ditalini

F
Fagottini (also called borsetta): fresh square pasta packets shaped to look like beggar's pouches and filled.

fagottini

Farfalle: dried pasta shaped like butterflies (*farfalla* is Italian for butterfly), often called bow ties in America.

farfalle

Farfalline: dried small farfalle.

Fettuccine: flat, narrow ribbon pasta that can be fresh or dried.

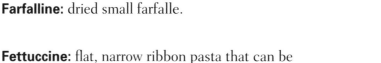

fettuccine

farfalline

Fideo: dried thin pasta strands, sold coiled in bunches or cut.

Fusilli: dried corkscrew-shaped pasta.

G
Garganelli: dried penne-like ridged pasta. It differs from penne in that it is a diagonally rolled square, creating a very pleasing shape.

fideo

fusilli

Gnocchi: little dumplings made from semolina, bread, cornmeal or — the most traditional — potato and flour, served poached and sauced, and also baked.

gnocchi

garganelli

L

Lasagne: flat, wide pasta sheets that can be fresh or dried, used for layering and baking. Dried lasagna can be smooth or ridged, short or long, no-boil or traditional.

linguine

lasagne

Linguine: narrow, flat ribbon pasta, narrower than fettuccine, that can be fresh or dried.

M

Maccheroni: dried tube-shaped pasta cut straight at the ends and about 2 inches (5 cm) long.

Maltagliati: "badly" or irregularly cut triangles, dried or fresh.

maccheroni

Manicotti: dried hollow pasta tubes. In America cannelloni are often called manicotti (see cannelloni).

maltagliati

O

Orecchiette: "little ears" — small hollowed-out semicircles of pasta, fresh or dried.

orecchiette

orzo

Orzo: dried pasta that resembles grains of rice, used for soups and as a rice substitute.

P

Paccheri: dried large, smooth tubular pasta from Naples, similar to rigatoni.

pappardelle

Pappardelle: flat, wide (¾-inch/1.5 cm) noodles with straight or ruffled edges, fresh or dried.

paccheri

Penne: dried, usually ridged, relatively short tubular pasta. Penne rigate is 2 inches (5 cm) long and cut diagonally at the ends to resemble the point of a quill pen. It can also be smooth, in which case it is called penne lisce.

penne

Pennette: smaller penne.

Perciatelli: dried thick, long bigoli-like tubular pasta from southern Italy.

perciatelli

pennette

Polenta: slow-cooked white or yellow cornmeal or buckwheat (not shown).

Q

Quadrati: fresh large pasta squares (about 3 inches/7.5 cm) cut with a straight or fluted edge.

radiatori

R

Radiatori: dried short, deeply ridged pasta that resembles the grills of radiators.

quadrati

Ravioli: fresh filled pasta pillows in a variety of shapes: square, round, triangular.

Rigatoni: dried short tubular pasta from southern Italy, usually ridged, cut straight at the ends.

rigatoni

Rotini: dried spiral twists like fusilli, only shorter.

ravioli

rotini

Ruote and rotelle: dried pasta shaped like cart or wagon wheels. Rotelle are "little wheels."

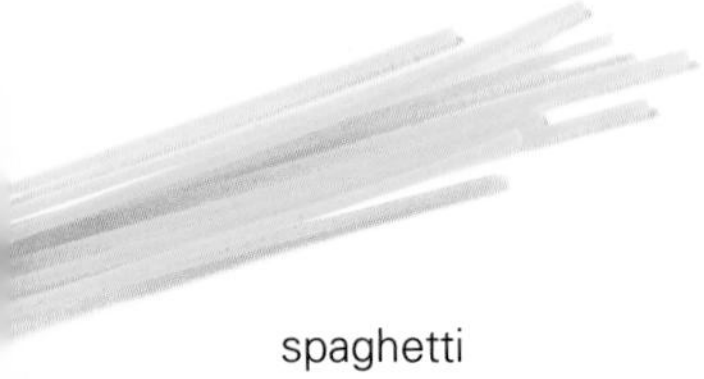

S

Spaghetti: dried string pasta, the oldest and most famous shape.

spaghetti

ruote

Spaghettini: dried thinner spaghetti.

Stracci: long, wide (2 inches/5 cm) pasta ribbons with straight or fluted edges, dried or fresh.

spaghettini

stracci

Strozzapretti: "priest stranglers" — a short twisted, very attractive tubular pasta, dried or fresh.

strozzapretti

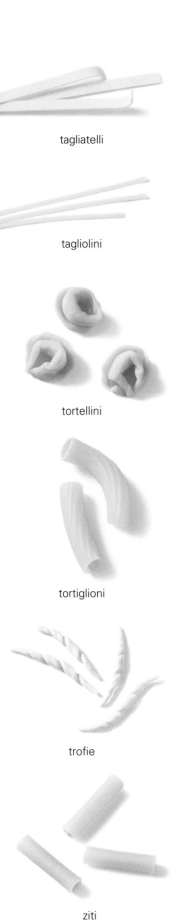

tagliatelli

tagliolini

tortellini

tortiglioni

trofie

ziti

T

Tagliatelle: fresh ribbon pasta about $\frac{1}{8}$ inch (0.25 cm) wide from Emilia-Romagna.

Tagliolini: fresh long, thin, delicate strands slightly thicker than angel hair and thinner than tagliatelle.

Tortelli: fresh medium-sized filled pasta in half-moon shapes.

tortelli

Tortellini: fresh medium-sized, filled, cap-shaped pastas similar to cappelletti but bigger and shaped from rounds rather than half-moons of dough.

Tortelloni: large tortellini.

tortelloni

Tortiglioni: dried twisted, curved tubes slightly larger than rigatoni, cut straight at the ends.

Tripolini: dried tiny bow ties with rounded ends.

tripolini

Trofie: rolled ribbon pasta that twists as it rolls and finishes with tapered ends, fresh or dried.

V

Vermicelli: dried string pasta thicker than angel hair but thinner than spaghettini.

vermicelli

Z

Ziti: dried tubular pasta. Ziti means "bridegrooms," which applies to the long ziti traditionally served at weddings in Campagnia and Sicily. Short ziti are usually called cut ziti.

Pasta Express: By the Time the Water Boils

Some pasta sauces, such as my mother's meat ragù, took six hours to cook. Her cavatelli, the fresh pasta she made to go with that sauce, took another two hours. She started cooking early in the morning so dinner would be ready by evening. But even my mother, a traditional Italian woman who came to America (before I was born) from Campobasso, the capital city of the Molise region in southern Italy, cooked that way only on weekends.

Today almost nobody devotes that much time to preparing a meal. We simply don't have the time. I'm a chef, and even I don't cook that way at home. Given the pace of our lives, next to good health, time is our most precious possession. We never seem to have enough. Still, we like to eat good food and we enjoy entertaining and getting together with friends, so unless we want to eat at restaurants or order takeout every day, somebody has to cook at home.

Authentic and Quick

This chapter is a doorway to authentic Italian pasta that is quick and easy to make. How quick? Well, it takes about 20 minutes for 6 quarts (6 L) of water to come to a rolling boil in a proper pasta pot. In the time it takes for the water to boil, you can make almost all the sauces in this chapter. It takes about 9 minutes for the dried pastas in this chapter to cook to the al dente stage. When the pasta is cooked, drain it, combine it with the sauce, and serve it. So, all told — 30 to 45 minutes, everything inclusive, from prep to plate. The dishes are flavorful and satisfying, serve four to six people, and show that good cooking and quick cooking are not mutually exclusive.

I have specifically used pastas in this chapter that are quick-cooking, but the recipes are varied for two reasons. Not only do the different kinds of pasta add variety — pasta is both long (strings, ribbons and tubes) and short (tubes and shapes) — the combinations of ingredients in the sauces further differentiate the results: cantaloupe and Marsala wine, walnuts, salmon, crab and peas, cream and cheese, to name just a few. While I have suggested specific pastas in the recipes, feel free to substitute spaghetti for any long pasta or penne for any short tubular pasta, if that's what you happen to have on hand.

I am confident that the recipes in this chapter will deliver a big return in enjoyment for a small investment of time and money. And I hope they will inspire you to cook, enjoy and share good pasta *a casa* — at home. *Buon appetito!*

Pasta Express

To speed preparation when making pasta,

- Always put the pot of pasta water, covered, over high heat to boil before you do anything else. That way the water will be boiling and ready for the pasta when you are ready to cook it.
- Be sure to have all your ingredients assembled and prepared before you start to cook (see *Mise en Place*, page 15).
- Cook the sauce while the water is coming to a boil. The recipes are written to incorporate this efficiency.

Spaghetti con pomodoro piccanti

Spaghetti with Spicy Tomatoes

This is a very simple pasta dish sauced with a tomato and fresh chile sauce. It's not too hot, but you can always increase the heat by adding more black pepper and more fresh red chile to suit your taste.

Serves 4 to 6

Tips

The Italian red chile, which is medium hot and slightly sweet, is not available here, but a good substitute is the California-grown red finger chile (also called Dutch or Holland chile) or the red Fresno chile. In a pinch you can use a ripe jalapeño or a cayenne chile, both of which are much hotter. If you're using one of these, mince it and reduce the quantity to about $\frac{1}{4}$ tsp (1 mL).

Use finely grated, not shredded, Parmigiano-Reggiano cheese. The fine teeth on a standard box grater produce nicely grated cheese for cooking. In the interests of time, particularly when making recipes from this chapter, purchase good-quality pre-grated cheese.

3 tbsp	extra-virgin olive oil	45 mL
3	garlic cloves, quartered	3
	Salt and freshly ground black pepper	
5	fresh ripe tomatoes, skin on, diced	5
1 tsp	thinly sliced fresh red finger chile (see Tips, left)	5 mL
1 cup	dry white Italian wine	250 mL
1 tbsp	salt	15 mL
1 lb	dried spaghetti	500 g
6 tbsp	grated Parmigiano-Reggiano, divided (see Tips, left)	90 mL

1. In a covered pasta pot over high heat, bring water to a rapid boil.

2. Meanwhile, in a large sauté pan, heat oil over medium heat. Add garlic and salt and pepper to taste and cook, stirring, until garlic is translucent but not browned, 2 to 3 minutes. Using a slotted spoon, remove and discard garlic. Add tomatoes and chile and stir well. Cover and cook until tomatoes are soft and tender, about 5 minutes. Stir in wine and simmer, uncovered, until wine is reduced by half. Remove from heat if necessary.

3. While sauce is simmering, add salt and spaghetti to the boiling water and cook, uncovered, over high heat until pasta is al dente. Scoop out about 1 cup (250 mL) of the pasta water and set aside. Drain pasta.

4. Add 2 tbsp (25 mL) of the reserved pasta water to tomato mixture and raise heat to high. Add the spaghetti and, using pasta tongs, toss to coat evenly, adding more pasta water if necessary. Add half of the Parmigiano-Reggiano and toss well.

5. Transfer to a large serving platter and sprinkle with remaining cheese. Serve immediately.

Variations

If you are a heat seeker, use black pepper liberally and/or increase the sliced chile to 2 tsp (10 mL).

If you're interested in increasing your consumption of whole grains, use whole wheat spaghetti.

Substitute bucatini for the spaghetti. It will take a little longer to cook.

Pennette with Fresh Cantaloupe

Although cantaloupe and pasta may seem like an odd combination, in botanical terms tomatoes are also a fruit, and pasta with tomatoes is a classic combination. The flavor and color of fresh ripe cantaloupe lend themselves to pasta, especially when it is combined with a little Marsala — Italy's famous fortified wine — and a touch of cream. I believe you will be pleasantly surprised by this sauce.

Serves 4 to 6

Tips

Always use a large pot and plenty of water when cooking pasta. To properly cook 1 pound (500 g) of pasta, you'll need a pot with a volume of at least 8 quarts (8 L) so you can use 6 quarts (6 L) of water.

Because this is a short, sturdy pasta, it is easier to toss using a wooden spoon rather than pasta tongs, which work best for longer pastas.

3 tbsp	extra-virgin olive oil	45 mL
3	garlic cloves, quartered	3
	Salt and freshly ground black pepper	
1½ rounded cups	diced ripe cantaloupe	375 mL
½ cup	dry Marsala wine	50 mL
2 tbsp	heavy or whipping (35%) cream	25 mL
1 tbsp	salt	15 mL
1 lb	dried pennette (see Variation, below)	500 g
3 tbsp	grated Parmigiano-Reggiano	45 mL

1. In a covered pasta pot over high heat, bring water to a rapid boil.

2. Meanwhile, in a large sauté pan, heat oil over medium heat. Add garlic and salt and pepper to taste and cook, stirring, until garlic is translucent but not browned, 2 to 3 minutes. Using a slotted spoon, remove garlic and discard. Add cantaloupe and Marsala and cook until wine is reduced by half, 4 to 5 minutes. Stir in cream and simmer for 3 minutes, reducing heat as necessary to prevent burning. Remove pan from heat and set aside.

3. While sauce is simmering, add salt and pennette to the boiling water and cook, uncovered, over high heat until pasta is al dente. Scoop out about 1 cup (250 mL) of the pasta water and set aside. Drain pasta.

4. Add 2 tbsp (25 mL) of the reserved pasta water to cantaloupe mixture and raise the heat to medium. Add the pennette and, using a wooden spoon, toss to coat evenly, adding more pasta water if necessary. Add Parmigiano-Reggiano and toss well.

5. Transfer to a large serving platter and serve immediately.

Variation

Substitute penne for the pennette (pennette are small penne).

> ### Al Dente
> Al dente means "to the tooth" or "to the bite." When you bite into the center of pasta, it should offer a slight resistance or firmness. There are two reasons for cooking pasta to the al dente stage. First, after it is drained, it continues to cook a little from the residual heat. Second, if you finish the pasta with a hot sauce in a skillet, it will cook even further. Ideally, by the time the sauced pasta arrives at the table, it's perfectly cooked. But don't make yourself frantic trying to figure out what the perfect al dente is. Experience is the best teacher.

Penne al prosciutto e asparagi

Penne with Prosciutto and Asparagus

Served on a large platter lined with prosciutto, this pasta is a bit of a conversation piece. Serve it with a fork and spoon so you can include a little of the prosciutto in every serving. Simply delicious!

Serves 4 to 6

Tips

Prosciutto is best eaten at room temperature. At the restaurant we serve a similar presentation, allowing the sliced prosciutto to sit at room temperature, covered with plastic wrap. Do not allow the prosciutto to sit uncovered for longer than 30 minutes, or it will begin to oxidize and dry out.

I recommend seasoning the asparagus only with pepper just before serving, because prosciutto is salty. The pepper adds flavor but doesn't increase saltiness.

Any dry white Italian table wine will work fine in this recipe. Here I'd probably use Pinot Bianco, which is a good basic dry white wine for use in Italian cooking.

12 to 15 slices	paper-thin prosciutto (about 7 oz/210 g)	12 to 15
3 tbsp	extra-virgin olive oil	45 mL
1 cup	sliced (2 inches/5 cm) pencil-thin asparagus	250 mL
	Salt and freshly ground white pepper	
½ cup	dry white Italian wine	125 mL
1 tbsp	salt	15 mL
1 lb	dried penne (see Variation, below)	500 g
¾ cup	grated Parmigiano-Reggiano, divided	175 mL
	Freshly ground black pepper	

1. In a covered pasta pot over high heat, bring water to a rapid boil.

2. Meanwhile, line a large platter with prosciutto slices. Set aside.

3. In a large sauté pan, heat oil over medium heat. Add asparagus and season to taste with salt and pepper. Cook, stirring, until asparagus is tender but not browned, about 3 minutes. Add wine, raise heat to high and cook for 6 minutes, until wine is almost evaporated. Remove from heat and set aside.

4. While asparagus is cooking, add salt and penne to the boiling water and cook, uncovered, until pasta is al dente. Scoop out about 1 cup (250 mL) of the pasta water and set aside. Drain pasta.

5. Return asparagus to medium heat. Add 2 tbsp (25 mL) of the reserved pasta water and bring to a simmer. Add cooked penne and, using a wooden spoon, toss to coat evenly, adding more pasta water if necessary. Add half of the Parmigiano-Reggiano, season to taste with pepper and toss.

6. Transfer to prosciutto-lined platter. Sprinkle with remaining cheese and serve immediately.

Variation

If you can find it, substitute garganelli, a square, ridged egg noodle rolled diagonally into a tube, for the penne. Except for the overlapping end, it looks just like penne. Garganelli is indigenous to Emilia-Romagna and is frequently available in gourmet Italian markets and online. This pasta looks particularly attractive on the prosciutto-lined platter.

Linguine with Pancetta and Broccoli

This is very simple: pasta, meat and broccoli. It's the kind of pasta you would find in Central Italy — Lazio, Molise, Marche and Tuscany. It's quick and easy and very rewarding.

Serves 4 to 6

Tips

Pancetta comes in two forms: thinly sliced or in a chunk. To dice thinly sliced pancetta, first stack the slices, next cut them into thin julienne strips and last, dice the strips. To dice thick (chunk) pancetta, slice it ¼-inch (0.5 cm) thick. Julienne the slices, then cut into ¼-inch (0.5 cm) dice.

Pancetta is salty, so you may not need to add salt, just pepper, after adding the first portion of cheese.

When you combine the sauce and the linguine, be sure to toss well and for as long as it takes to coat the pasta evenly with sauce.

3 tbsp	extra-virgin olive oil	45 mL
¾ cup	finely diced pancetta (see Tips, left)	175 mL
¼ cup	finely diced onion	50 mL
2 cups	quartered broccoli florets	500 mL
1 cup	dry white Italian wine	250 mL
1 tbsp	salt	15 mL
1 lb	dried linguine (see Variation, below)	500 g
¾ cup	grated Parmigiano-Reggiano, divided	175 mL
	Salt and freshly ground black pepper	

1. In a covered pasta pot over high heat, bring water to a rapid boil.

2. Meanwhile, in a large sauté pan, heat oil over medium heat. Add pancetta and onion. Cook, stirring, until onion is soft and translucent, about 3 minutes. Add broccoli and cook, stirring, until tender, 3 to 5 minutes. Add wine, raise heat to high, and cook until reduced by half. Remove pan from heat and set aside.

3. While sauce is simmering, add salt and linguine to the boiling water and cook, uncovered, over high heat until pasta is al dente. Scoop out about 1 cup (250 mL) of the pasta water and set aside. Drain pasta.

4. Return sauté pan to medium heat. Add 2 tbsp (25 mL) of the reserved pasta water and raise heat to high. Add linguine and, using pasta tongs, toss to coat evenly, adding more pasta water if necessary. Add half of the Parmigiano-Reggiano and toss well. Season to taste with salt and pepper.

5. Transfer to a large serving platter and sprinkle with remaining cheese. Serve immediately.

Variation

Linguine is a narrow, flat ribbon pasta. Substitute spaghetti instead.

Pennette all'Arrabbiata

People outside Italy are familiar with this "angry" (a literal translation of the name) pasta — so named because of the hot chiles in the sauce. Many restaurant versions are heavily sauced and use dried red chile flakes, which make for a harsh flavor, rather than fresh red chile pepper, which supplies heat without harshness.

Serves 4 to 6

Tip

This dish comes from Rome and southern Italy, where its heat comes from fresh, thinly sliced Italian red chiles, or *peperoncini*. The Italian red chile, which is medium hot and slightly sweet, is not available here, but good substitutes are the California-grown red finger chile (also called Dutch or Holland chile) or the red Fresno chile. In a pinch you can use a ripened red jalapeño or a red cayenne chile, both of which are much hotter. If you're using one of these, mince it and reduce the quantity to about $\frac{1}{4}$ tsp (1 mL).

3 tbsp	extra-virgin olive oil	45 mL
1 tbsp	thinly sliced garlic, packed	15 mL
1 tsp	thinly sliced fresh red finger chile, packed (see Tip, left)	5 mL
	Salt and freshly ground white pepper	
2 cups	canned crushed Italian tomatoes	500 mL
2 tbsp	packed hand-torn fresh basil leaves (see Tips, page 37)	25 mL
1 tbsp	salt	15 mL
1 lb	dried pennette (see Variations, below)	500 g
$\frac{2}{3}$ cup	grated Parmigiano-Reggiano, divided	150 mL

1. In a covered pasta pot over high heat, bring water to a rapid boil.

2. Meanwhile, in a large sauté pan, heat oil over medium heat. Add garlic, chile and salt and pepper to taste. Cook, stirring, until garlic is translucent but not browned, 2 to 3 minutes. Add tomatoes and basil and stir. Reduce heat to very low and simmer while pasta cooks.

3. While sauce is simmering, add salt and pennette to the boiling water and cook, uncovered, over high heat until pasta is al dente. Scoop out about 1 cup (250 mL) of the pasta water and set aside. Drain pasta.

4. Add 2 tbsp (25 mL) of the reserved pasta water to tomato sauce and raise the heat to high. Add pennette and, using a wooden spoon, toss to coat evenly, adding more pasta water if necessary. Add 3 tbsp (45 mL) of the Parmigiano-Reggiano and toss well.

5. Transfer to a large serving platter and sprinkle with remaining cheese. Serve immediately.

Variations

To increase the spice level, double the amount of chile.

Substitute penne or cut ziti for the pennette.

Penne al salmone e porri

Penne with Salmon and Leeks

This is a contemporary, not traditional Italian, pasta. However, true to Italian tradition, no cheese is used, because it is made with seafood. Sweeter than onions, leeks are a delicious but underutilized vegetable that nicely complements the salmon. Most people enjoy salmon, and nutritionists praise its health benefits. The combination of leeks and salmon prepared with a little olive oil and white wine makes this quite healthful. Your heart will thank you.

Serves 4 to 6

Tips

Leeks can be gritty, so be sure to clean them well before using. To clean leeks, trim off and discard the root end. Cut off top, leaving about 6 inches (15 cm) of leek. Trim off and discard dark green outer leaves. Use the white and pale green parts only. Cut trimmed leeks into 2-inch (10 cm) lengths and cut in half vertically. Immerse in a large bowl of cold water, separate leaves, and rinse well to remove sand and grit. Save the trimmings for making stock.

Never rinse pasta after draining it. The surface starch helps the sauce to cling and is important to producing the best-quality dish.

3 tbsp	extra-virgin olive oil	45 mL
3	garlic cloves, quartered	3
	Salt and freshly ground white pepper	
¾ cup	diced leeks, white and green parts (see Tips, left)	175 mL
1¼ cups	diced skinless, boneless salmon (10 to 12 oz/300 to 375 g)	300 mL
1 cup	dry white Italian wine	250 mL
1 tbsp	salt	15 mL
1 lb	dried penne (see Variations, below)	500 g

1. In a covered pasta pot over high heat, bring water to a rapid boil.

2. Meanwhile, in a large sauté pan, heat oil over high heat. Add garlic and salt and pepper to taste and cook, stirring, until garlic is translucent but not browned, 2 to 3 minutes. Using a slotted spoon, remove garlic and discard. Add leeks and salmon and reduce heat to medium. Cook, stirring, until leeks are tender and salmon is opaque, about 5 minutes. Add wine and cook until reduced by half. Remove from heat and set aside.

3. While sauce is simmering, add salt and penne to the boiling water and cook, uncovered, over high heat until pasta is al dente. Scoop out about 1 cup (250 mL) of the pasta water and set aside. Drain pasta.

4. Add 2 tbsp (25 mL) of the reserved pasta water to salmon-leek mixture and raise the heat to high. Add penne and, using a wooden spoon, toss to coat evenly, adding more pasta water if necessary.

5. Transfer to a large serving platter and serve immediately.

Variations

Increase the amount of salmon to 2 cups (500 mL) for a more substantial dish.

Penne is used in this recipe because the tubular shape helps capture and hold sauce. Substitute cut ziti or pennette for the penne.

Conchiglie con granchio e piselli

Conchiglie with Crab and Peas

This dish reminds me of the Veneto region of Italy, where spider crab, a species of hard-shell crab found in the Atlantic and the Mediterranean, is plentiful. In North America the most readily available crabmeat is pasteurized lump crabmeat from the blue crab. You don't have to catch it, kill it, clean or cook it — all the work is done for you.

Serves 4 to 6

Tips

I usually season my sauces in the initial stages of cooking so the flavors have time to bloom. I always taste the final product and, if necessary, add more salt and pepper just before serving.

Because this is a short, sturdy pasta, it is easier to toss using a wooden spoon rather than pasta tongs, which work best for longer pastas.

6 tbsp	extra-virgin olive oil, divided	90 mL
2/3 cup	defrosted frozen peas, preferably organic	150 mL
2/3 cup	pasteurized jumbo lump crabmeat	150 mL
1/2 cup	dry white Italian wine	125 mL
	Salt and freshly ground white pepper	
1 tbsp	salt	15 mL
1 lb	dried conchiglie (see Variations, below)	500 g

1. In a covered pasta pot over high heat, bring water to a rapid boil.
2. Meanwhile, in a large sauté pan, heat 3 tbsp (45 mL) of the olive oil over medium heat. Add peas, crabmeat and wine. Season to taste with salt and pepper. Cook, stirring, for 2 minutes. Cover pan, remove from heat and set aside.
3. Add salt and conchiglie to the boiling water and cook, uncovered, over high heat until pasta is al dente. Scoop out about 1 cup (250 mL) of the pasta water and set aside. Drain pasta.
4. Add 1/4 cup (50 mL) of the reserved pasta water to crab mixture, return the pan to high heat and bring to a simmer. Add conchiglie. Using a wooden spoon, gently toss pasta with the sauce to coat evenly, adding more pasta water if necessary. Simmer until liquid is reduced by half. Drizzle with remaining olive oil and toss again. Taste and adjust seasoning, if needed.
5. Transfer to a large serving bowl and serve immediately.

Variations

If you have time and fresh peas are in season, it is worth the effort to shell and blanch them to use in place of frozen peas in this recipe. The flavor of fresh peas is incomparable.

In summer I often add 1/3 cup (75 mL) coarsely chopped pea tendrils, packed, to the olive oil in Step 1. Pea tendrils are young leaves and shoots of the snow pea plant, and when they are fresh, they are quite delicious. Increasingly available in supermarkets, they add a nice flavor and texture to this recipe.

Conchiglie are small pasta resembling conch shells. Substitute penne if desired.

Spaghetti al burro e basilico

Spaghettini with Butter and Basil

Pasta doesn't get any simpler than this: pasta, basil, butter and cheese. This is a dish from la cucina povera, *the kitchens of the poor, but it is fit for a king — as long as the butter is sweet, not salted, the basil is fresh and hand-torn (not cut or sliced, see Tips), and the cheese is very good. Spaghettini is thin spaghetti, and because the sauce cooks so quickly in this recipe, the pasta is cooked first.*

Serves 4 to 6

Tips

I like to use unsalted butter in my recipes because it contributes fresh flavor without adding extra salt.

I think that tearing the basil leaves by hand rather than slicing them makes them look and taste better.

When you combine the pasta with the sauce, be sure to toss well and long enough to coat the pasta evenly with the sauce. Don't be afraid to add more pasta water if you feel the results are too dry.

1 tbsp	salt	15 mL
1 lb	dried spaghettini (see Variation, below)	500 g
2 tbsp	lightly packed hand-torn basil leaves	25 mL
6 tbsp	unsalted butter	90 mL
6 tbsp	grated Parmigiano-Reggiano, divided	90 mL
	Salt and freshly ground black pepper	
6	fresh basil leaves	6

1. In a covered pasta pot over high heat, bring water to a rapid boil. Add salt and spaghettini and cook until pasta is al dente. Scoop out about 1 cup (250 mL) of the pasta water and set aside. Drain pasta.

2. In a large sauté pan, heat 2 tbsp (25 mL) of the reserved pasta water over high heat. Add torn basil and butter and cook, stirring, until butter melts, about 1 minute. Stir in half the Parmigiano-Reggiano until well mixed. Season to taste with salt and pepper. Add the spaghettini and, using pasta tongs, toss to coat evenly, adding more pasta water if necessary.

3. Transfer to a large serving platter and sprinkle with remaining cheese and whole basil leaves. Serve immediately.

Variation

Spaghettini is thin spaghetti. If you don't have it, substitute spaghetti, which will take a couple of minutes longer to cook.

Grated vs. Freshly Grated Cheese

I prefer the flavor and texture of freshly grated cheese. However, when time is at a premium, by all means use already grated cheese, but please use the very best Italian Parmigiano-Reggiano or Pecorino Romano you can find. If you have access to an Italian market or gourmet cheese shop, purchase cheese from them. Better still, buy it by the piece and have them grate it for you. If you don't live in a large city with lots of shopping options, search the Internet for purveyors of imported grated cheese who will ship. Buy in small quantities. A quarter of a pound (125 g) yields about 1 cup (250 mL) finely grated cheese; a half-pound (250 g) yields about 2 cups (500 mL) finely grated cheese. Store the cheese in an airtight container in the refrigerator. Portion out the quantity you need and bring it to room temperature before using.

Spaghetti al sugo di borlotti

Spaghetti with Borlotti Bean Sauce

Pasta and beans is a very Tuscan combination — people in Tuscany were traditionally called mangiafagioli, *or bean eaters, because so many of their dishes include beans. This is good hearty pasta for autumn and winter.*

Serves 4 to 6

Tips

Also known as cranberry beans, borlotti beans are cream-colored beans with red streaks. They have a mellow, nutlike flavor. They are available fresh in summer, dried year-round and also in cans, which are great for convenience. You will need about 1 can (14 to 19 oz/398 to 540 mL) of beans for this quantity. Save any excess for another recipe.

Always drain and rinse canned beans well before using.

When reducing the heat from high or medium to low on an electric range (which responds to changes in heat more slowly than a gas stove), it is better to switch the pan to a different burner set at the new heat level, because the burner won't cool down fast enough.

¼ cup	extra-virgin olive oil	50 mL
3	garlic cloves, quartered	3
	Salt and freshly ground white pepper	
2 tbsp	diced onion	25 mL
2 tbsp	diced peeled celery	25 mL
1 cup	grape tomatoes	250 mL
1 cup	dry white Italian wine	250 mL
1½ cups	cooked borlotti beans, drained and rinsed (see Tips, left)	375 mL
1 tbsp	salt	15 mL
1 lb	dried spaghetti	500 g
6 tbsp	grated Parmigiano-Reggiano, divided	90 mL

1. In a covered pasta pot over high heat, bring water to a rapid boil.

2. Meanwhile, in a large sauté pan, heat oil over medium heat. Add garlic and salt and pepper to taste and cook, stirring, until garlic is translucent but not browned, 2 to 3 minutes. Using a slotted spoon, remove garlic and discard. Add onion, celery and tomatoes, raise heat to high, and cook, stirring, until vegetables are tender, about 5 minutes. Add wine and cook, stirring, until reduced by half. Add borlotti beans, reduce heat to very low and simmer until thickened, 5 to 10 minutes. Remove from heat and set aside, if necessary.

3. While sauce is simmering, add salt and spaghetti to the boiling water and cook, uncovered, over high heat until pasta is al dente. Scoop out about 1 cup (250 mL) of the pasta water and set aside. Drain pasta.

4. Return sauté pan to element, add 2 tbsp (25 mL) of the reserved pasta water and raise heat to high. Add spaghetti and, using pasta tongs, toss to coat evenly, adding more pasta water if necessary. Add half of the Parmigiano-Reggiano and toss well.

5. Transfer to a large serving platter and sprinkle with remaining cheese. Serve immediately.

Variations

Substitute canned, rinsed cannellini beans, chickpeas or your favorite white beans for the borlotti beans.

Spaghetti with Pecorino Romano and Black Pepper

This is a typical dish from Rome. The ancient Romans were famous for their love of black pepper. Because there are only three ingredients in this dish — pasta, pepper and cheese — it is important to use peppercorns that are not stale. Sniff before you buy; they should be fragrant and fresh-smelling.

Serves 4 to 6

Tips

Italian chefs use pasta water the way French chefs use stock. In this recipe the pasta water is an important liquid-providing ingredient.

Instead of Parmigiano-Reggiano, for this Roman dish I chose Pecorino Romano, a sheep's-milk cheese with a piquant flavor. It is produced in the region of Lazio, where Rome is the capital city.

If you have leftovers, use them to make Soufflé of Spaghetti with Pecorino Romano and Black Pepper (see recipe, page 171).

1 tbsp	salt	15 mL
1 lb	dried spaghetti	500 mL
½ cup	grated Pecorino Romano, divided (see page 67)	125 mL
1 tsp	freshly ground black pepper	5 mL

1. In a covered pasta pot over high heat, bring water to a rapid boil. Add salt and spaghetti and cook, uncovered, until pasta is al dente. Scoop out about 1 cup (250 mL) of the pasta water and set aside. Drain pasta.

2. In a large sauté pan, bring ½ cup (125 mL) of the reserved pasta water to a boil over medium heat. Add spaghetti and, using pasta tongs, toss to coat evenly, adding more pasta water if necessary. Add half of the Pecorino Romano and the black pepper and toss well.

3. Transfer to a large serving platter and sprinkle with remaining cheese. Serve immediately.

Freshly Ground Pepper

Although for the sake of cooking quickly I bend my own rules when it comes to using already grated cheese, I am inflexible about pepper. There is a slight flavor and texture difference between freshly grated and pre-grated cheese, but there is an unbridgeable gap between already ground pepper that has been sitting in containers on the store shelf and freshly ground pepper from a mill. Pepper mills are inexpensive and durable. I recommend having two, one for white and one for black peppercorns. And freshness makes a difference in dried peppercorns too, so seek out those that are fresh and fragrant.

Penne con olive e funghi

Penne with Olives and Mushrooms

This is a simple pasta with mushrooms and olives. The green olives add color and flavor. If you use pitted olives, the preparation time is very fast.

Serves 4 to 6

Tips

To prepare the mushrooms for this recipe, slice off any woody stem ends and discard. Cut each mushroom in half vertically, then in half again.

It's always best to stay within the Italian market basket, and Italian olives will give you the most authentic flavor. Pitted green Italian olives marinated with garlic and/or red pepper, often sold in the deli section of supermarkets, will also work in this recipe. If Italian olives are completely unavailable, then substitute with green olives from the European market basket, such as from France or Greece. Spanish green olives are too acidic and salty for this dish.

If you have leftovers, use them to make Baked Penne with Olives and Mushrooms (see recipe, page 168).

3 tbsp	extra-virgin olive oil	45 mL
3	garlic cloves, quartered	3
	Salt and freshly ground black pepper	
2 cups	quartered white mushrooms (see Tips, left)	500 mL
1 cup	dry white Italian wine	250 mL
½ cup	chopped pitted green Italian olives (see Tips, left)	125 mL
1 tbsp	salt	15 mL
1 lb	dried penne	500 g
6 tbsp	grated Parmigiano-Reggiano, divided	90 mL

1. In a covered pasta pot over high heat, bring water to a rapid boil.

2. Meanwhile, in a large sauté pan, heat oil over high heat. Add garlic and salt and pepper to taste. Cook, stirring, until garlic is translucent but not browned, 2 to 3 minutes. Using a slotted spoon, remove garlic and discard. Add mushrooms. Reduce heat to medium and cook, stirring, for 5 minutes. Add wine and cook, stirring, for 5 minutes. Stir in olives, reduce heat to low and let simmer until sauce is thickened but not dry, about 5 minutes. Remove from heat and set aside, if necessary.

3. While sauce is simmering, add salt and penne to the boiling water and cook, uncovered, until pasta is al dente. Scoop out about 1 cup (250 mL) of the pasta water and set aside. Drain pasta.

4. Return sauté pan to element. Add 2 tbsp (25 mL) of the reserved pasta water and raise the heat to high. Add penne and, using a wooden spoon, toss to coat evenly, adding more pasta water if necessary. Add half of the Parmigiano-Reggiano and toss well.

5. Transfer to a large serving platter and sprinkle with remaining cheese. Serve immediately.

Variation

Substitute chopped pitted oil-cured black Italian olives for the green.

Penne con zucchine e pomodorini

Penne with Zucchini and Cherry Tomatoes

This pasta is best served in the summer, when zucchini are at their peak and tomatoes are ripe and sweet. Fresh basil leaves torn into small pieces by hand look better and taste better to me than basil that has been sliced with a knife.

Serves 4 to 6

Tips

Because this is a short, sturdy pasta, it is easier to toss using a wooden spoon rather than pasta tongs, which work best for longer pastas.

Use finely grated, not shredded, Parmigiano-Reggiano cheese. The fine teeth on a standard box grater produce nicely grated cheese for cooking. In the interests of time, particularly when making recipes from this chapter, purchase good-quality pre-grated cheese.

3 tbsp	extra-virgin olive oil	45 mL
3	garlic cloves, quartered	3
	Salt and freshly ground black pepper	
1¼ cups	diced unpeeled zucchini	300 mL
¾ cup	halved cherry tomatoes	175 mL
3 tbsp	hand-torn fresh basil leaves	45 mL
1 tbsp	salt	15 mL
1 lb	dried penne (see Variation, below)	500 g
6 tbsp	grated Parmigiano-Reggiano, divided	90 mL

1. In a covered pasta pot over high heat, bring water to a rapid boil.

2. Meanwhile, in a large sauté pan, heat oil over medium heat. Add garlic and salt and pepper to taste and cook, stirring, until garlic is translucent but not browned, 2 to 3 minutes. Using a slotted spoon, remove and discard garlic. Add zucchini, tomatoes and basil and reduce heat to low. Cover and let simmer until pasta is cooked.

3. While sauce is simmering, add salt and penne to the boiling water and cook, uncovered, over high heat until pasta is al dente. Scoop out about 1 cup (250 mL) of the pasta water and set aside. Drain pasta.

4. Add 2 tbsp (25 mL) of the reserved pasta water to zucchini mixture and raise heat to medium. Add penne and, using a wooden spoon, toss to coat evenly, adding more pasta water if necessary. Add half of the Parmigiano-Reggiano and toss well.

5. Transfer to a large serving platter and sprinkle with remaining cheese. Serve immediately.

Variation

Substitute fusilli for the penne.

Fusilli con mortadella e pistacchio

Fusilli with Mortadella and Pistachios

The combination of mortadella — Bologna's famous cooked pork sausage — and pistachios provides nice flavor and textural contrast in this dish. I prefer skinless pistachios, but I realize that the home cook would not take kindly to blanching and peeling the small nuts as we do at the restaurant. So I will settle for shelled pistachios, which will also give you a delicious result.

Serves 4 to 6

Tips

Mortadella comes in a plastic casing that is often left on for slicing. Be sure to remove the casing before layering the slices on the platter.

I like to use unsalted butter in my recipes because it contributes fresh flavor without adding extra salt.

12	paper-thin slices mortadella (about 4 oz/125 g)	12
1 tbsp	salt	15 mL
1 lb	dried fusilli (see Variations, below)	500 g
¼ cup	unsalted butter	50 mL
¾ cup	grated Parmigiano-Reggiano, divided	175 mL
¼ cup	chopped shelled pistachios	50 mL
	Salt and freshly ground black pepper	

1. In a covered pasta pot over high heat, bring water to a boil.

2. Line a large platter, including the rim, with mortadella slices. Set aside.

3. Add salt and fusilli to the boiling water and cook, uncovered, over high heat until pasta is al dente. Scoop out about 1 cup (250 mL) of the pasta water and set aside. Drain pasta.

4. In a large sauté pan over medium heat, combine ½ cup (125 mL) of the reserved pasta water, the butter, half of the Parmigiano-Reggiano and the fusilli. Using a wooden spoon, toss to coat evenly, adding more pasta water if necessary. Add pistachios and season to taste with salt and pepper. Toss well.

5. Transfer to the mortadella-lined platter and sprinkle with remaining cheese. Serve immediately.

Variations

Fusilli is a corkscrew-shaped pasta that catches sauce and holds it well. Substitute penne or rotini for the fusilli.

Substitute mortadella with pistachios for the plain mortadella.

> ### Mortadella
>
> If mortadella looks like American bologna, there's a good reason: it comes from Bologna, Italy — hence the slang name "baloney." The North American version is very different from the air-dried Italian original. American-style garlic-flavored mortadella is closer to baloney with added cubes of pork fat and black peppercorns. There are also excellent German mortadellas that contain pistachios.

Spaghetti cremose al formaggio

Spaghetti with Parmigiano-Reggiano Sauce

Not only does this pasta use some very basic ingredients that need no chopping or slicing, it is also an appealing combination of flavors: rich cream; fruity wine that adds a hint of acidity; sharp, salty cheese; mellow pasta. This is good for everyday as well as for company. Just add a green salad and you have dinner. If you want to serve wine, I suggest an Italian Pinot Bianco, which you can also use in the sauce.

Serves 4 to 6

Tip

When you combine the pasta with the sauce, be sure to toss well and long enough to coat the pasta evenly with the sauce. Don't be afraid to add more pasta water if you feel the results are too dry.

1 cup	dry white Italian wine	250 mL
½ cup	heavy or whipping (35%) cream	125 mL
⅔ cup	grated Parmigiano-Reggiano, divided	150 mL
	Salt and freshly ground white pepper	
1 tbsp	salt	15 mL
1 lb	dried spaghetti	500 g

1. In a covered pasta pot over high heat, bring water to a rapid boil.

2. Meanwhile, in a large sauté pan over high heat, bring wine to a boil and cook until slightly reduced, 5 to 6 minutes. Stir in cream, bring to a simmer, then stir in ¼ cup (50 mL) of the Parmigiano-Reggiano. Season to taste with salt and pepper. Cover, remove pan from heat and set aside.

3. While wine is reducing, add salt and spaghetti to the boiling water and cook, uncovered, until pasta is al dente. Scoop out about 1 cup (250 mL) of the pasta water and set aside. Drain pasta.

4. Return sauté pan to medium heat. Add ¼ cup (50 mL) of the reserved pasta water and cook until heated through. Add spaghetti and, using pasta tongs, toss to coat evenly, adding more pasta water if necessary. Add 3 tbsp (45 mL) of the Parmigiano-Reggiano and toss well.

5. Transfer to a large serving platter and sprinkle with remaining cheese. Serve immediately.

Parmigiano-Reggiano

This hard Italian cow's-milk cheese, one of two commonly used for grating (the other being Pecorino), is produced in Italy in Parma and Reggio-Emilia, in the region of Emilia-Romagna. Known for its rich, sharp flavor and used primarily for grating, it is aged for a minimum of 12 months (usually for export) and more typically for two years. Those cheeses labeled *stravecchio* have been aged for three years. The name Parmigiano-Reggiano is protected by the Italian DOP (*Denominazione di origine protetta*), which regulates the region, quality and production of this cheese.

Vermicelli con verza e pancetta

Vermicelli with Savoy Cabbage and Pancetta

This is an Italian version of bacon and cabbage, but the bacon is pancetta and the cabbage is the curly Savoy variety. This hearty pasta makes a great dish for fall and winter. Vermicelli is a little thinner than spaghettini and it cooks very fast. Be sure not to confuse this with the Asian product often sold under the same name, which is a thin rice noodle that is soaked rather than cooked.

Serves 4 to 6

Tips

Pancetta comes thinly sliced or in a chunk. To dice thinly sliced pancetta, first stack the slices, next cut them into thin julienne strips and last, dice the strips. To dice thick (chunk) pancetta, slice it ¼ inch (0.5 cm) thick. Julienne slices, then cut into ¼-inch (0.5 cm) dice. Pancetta is also sold in small packages already diced.

Removing the thick ribs of the Savoy cabbage before you dice the leaves improves the texture of this dish. Core the cabbage and separate the leaves, then fold each cabbage leaf in half and cut out and discard the rib.

3 tbsp	extra-virgin olive oil	45 mL
¾ cup	diced pancetta (see Tips, left)	175 mL
¼ cup	diced onion	50 mL
	Salt and freshly ground black pepper	
1 cup	dry white Italian wine	250 mL
1½ cups	diced deribbed Savoy cabbage (see Tips, left)	375 mL
1 tbsp	salt	15 mL
1 lb	dried Italian vermicelli (see Variations, below)	500 g
6 tbsp	grated Parmigiano-Reggiano, divided	90 mL

1. In a covered pasta pot over high heat, bring water to a rapid boil.

2. Meanwhile, in a large sauté pan, heat olive oil, pancetta and onion over high heat. Cook, stirring, until the onion is translucent, about 5 minutes. Season to taste with salt and pepper. Add wine and cook, stirring, until reduced by half. Stir in cabbage. Reduce heat to the lowest possible setting and simmer until pasta is cooked.

3. While the sauce is simmering, add salt and vermicelli to the boiling water and cook, uncovered, until pasta is al dente. Scoop out about 1 cup (250 mL) of the pasta water and set aside. Drain pasta.

4. Add 2 tbsp (25 mL) of the reserved pasta water to cabbage mixture and raise heat to high. Add vermicelli and, using pasta tongs, toss to coat evenly, adding more pasta water if necessary. Add half the Parmigiano-Reggiano and toss well.

5. Transfer to a large serving platter and sprinkle with remaining cheese. Serve immediately.

Variations

Substitute spaghettini or spaghetti for the vermicelli. Spaghettini will take slightly longer to cook, and spaghetti 1 or 2 minutes longer.

Savoy Cabbage

Most chefs prefer this variety of cabbage, which is called *cavolo verza* or *cavolo di Milano* in Italian. It is a head cabbage with loose, crinkled leaves that range in color from dark green on the outside to pale green inside. Its flavor is sweet and mild and it contributes an entirely different texture to a dish than its smooth-leafed relative. All cabbages are low in calories and provide fiber, folic acid and vitamins B, C and E, as well as calcium.

Linguine with Peas and Sage

Fresh peas and sage are a traditional Italian combination. Made with freshly shelled peas, this is a spring and summer pasta. Because this is the Pasta Express chapter and time is at a premium, frozen peas are an acceptable alternative. As always, please get the best-quality peas you can find — preferably organic, and definitely without butter sauce.

Serves 4 to 6

Tips

Never rinse pasta after draining it. The surface starch helps the sauce to cling and is important to producing the best-quality dish.

Any dry white Italian wine will work fine in this recipe. Here I'd probably use Pinot Bianco, which is a good basic dry white wine for use in Italian cooking.

If you have leftovers, use them to make Bell Peppers Filled with Pennette, Cherry Tomatoes and Butter (see recipe, page 170).

3 tbsp	extra-virgin olive oil	45 mL
3	garlic cloves, quartered	3
	Salt and freshly ground black pepper	
½ cup	chopped onion	125 mL
1½ cups	frozen green peas, defrosted (preferably small and organic)	375 mL
8 to 10	fresh sage leaves	8 to 10
1 cup	dry white Italian wine (see Tips, left)	250 mL
1 tbsp	salt	15 mL
1 lb	dried linguine (see Variation, below)	500 g
6 tbsp	grated Parmigiano-Reggiano, divided	90 mL

1. In a covered pasta pot over high heat, bring water to a boil.

2. Meanwhile, in a large sauté pan, heat oil over medium heat. Add garlic and salt and pepper to taste, and cook, stirring, until garlic is translucent but not browned, 2 to 3 minutes. Using a slotted spoon, remove and discard garlic. Add onion and cook, stirring, until soft and tender, about 5 minutes. Add peas, sage and wine. Bring to a boil, reduce heat and simmer until wine is reduced by half. Cover, remove from heat and set aside.

3. While the sauce is simmering, add salt and linguine to the boiling water. Cook, uncovered, over high heat until pasta is al dente. Scoop out about 1 cup (250 mL) of the pasta water and set aside. Drain pasta.

4. Add 2 tbsp (25 mL) of the reserved pasta water to pea mixture, return to element and raise the heat to high, adding more pasta water if necessary. Add linguine and, using pasta tongs, toss to coat evenly. Add half of the Parmigiano-Reggiano and toss well.

5. Transfer to a large serving platter and sprinkle with remaining cheese. Serve immediately.

Variation

Substitute spaghetti for the linguine.

Spaghetti con panna e noci

Spaghetti with Walnut Cream

This pasta is typical of the Veneto and Liguria regions of Italy, where nuts are a favorite ingredient. Nutritionists tell us that nuts in moderation are very good for us and that we probably don't eat enough of them. At the restaurant I chop them into two sizes: very fine — about the size of a peppercorn — for the sauce, and larger and rougher — from lentil to green pea size — for the topping. But this pasta will taste and look good no matter how they are chopped.

Serves 4 to 6

Tips

To chop the walnuts for this recipe, place in a food processor fitted with the steel blade and pulse until finely chopped.

A little dash of cinnamon adds a lot of interest to this sauce because it is fragrant and provides an unexpected flavor.

3 tbsp	extra-virgin olive oil	45 mL
¾ cup	finely chopped walnuts, divided (see Tips, left)	175 mL
⅛ tsp	ground cinnamon	0.5 mL
½ cup	heavy or whipping (35%) cream	125 mL
	Salt and freshly ground white pepper	
1 tbsp	salt	15 mL
1 lb	dried spaghetti	500 g
6 tbsp	grated Parmigiano-Reggiano, divided	90 mL

1. In a covered pasta pot over high heat, bring water to a rapid boil.

2. Meanwhile, in a large sauté pan, heat olive oil over medium heat. Add ½ cup (125 mL) of the walnuts and the cinnamon and cook, stirring, until walnuts begin to brown, about 5 minutes. Add cream, season to taste with salt and pepper and stir once (sauce will be very thick). Cover, remove pan from heat and set aside.

3. Add salt and spaghetti to the boiling water and cook, uncovered, until pasta is al dente. Scoop out about 1 cup (250 mL) of the pasta water and set aside. Drain pasta.

4. Add ¼ cup (50 mL) of the reserved pasta water to walnut mixture and raise heat to high. Add spaghetti and, using pasta tongs, toss to coat evenly, adding more pasta water if necessary. Add half of the Parmigiano-Reggiano and toss well.

5. Transfer to a large serving platter and sprinkle with remaining cheese and walnuts. Serve immediately.

Walnuts

Walnuts grow in many parts of Italy and are popular in savory as well as sweet dishes. Because of their high oil content, unshelled nutmeats can become rancid quickly. Due to their high omega-3 fatty acid content, walnuts are particularly vulnerable to rancidity. Always buy fresh nutmeats in small amounts and store any unused portions in tightly sealed containers in the freezer. Although high in calories (about 180 per ounce/30 g), walnuts are rich in protein, minerals, B vitamins, antioxidants and, as noted, healthy omega-3 fatty acids.

Penne con radicchio e pancetta

Penne with Radicchio and Pancetta

Red radicchio (the variety known as Chioggia) is widely available in the produce sections of supermarkets. Most is grown in California, Florida and Arizona from Italian seeds. The combination of radicchio and pancetta is an Italian classic.

Serves 4 to 6

Tips

To dice thinly sliced pancetta, first stack the slices, next cut into thin julienne strips, and last, dice the julienne strips. Pancetta also comes in a chunk, which is equally easy to dice. Just cut into ¼-inch (0.5 cm) slices, julienne the slices, and then dice the strips. You can also purchase pancetta already diced.

Always use a large pot and plenty of water when cooking pasta. To properly cook 1 pound (500 g) of pasta, you'll need a pot with a volume of at least 8 quarts (8 L) so that you can use 6 quarts (6 L) of water.

3 tbsp	extra-virgin olive oil	45 mL
¾ cup	diced pancetta (see Tips, left)	175 mL
1 cup	diced onion	250 mL
	Salt and freshly ground black pepper	
1½ cups	diced fresh radicchio	375 mL
1 cup	dry white Italian wine	250 mL
1 tbsp	salt	15 mL
1 lb	penne (see Variation, below)	500 g
6 tbsp	grated Parmigiano-Reggiano, divided	90 mL

1. In a covered pasta pot over high heat, bring water to a rapid boil.

2. Meanwhile, in a large sauté pan, heat oil over medium heat. Add pancetta, onion and salt and pepper to taste. Cook, stirring, until onion is translucent, about 3 minutes. Add radicchio and wine and stir well. Reduce heat to low and simmer until pasta is cooked.

3. While sauce is simmering, add salt and penne to the boiling water and cook, uncovered, over high heat until pasta is al dente. Scoop out about 1 cup (250 mL) of the pasta water and set aside. Drain pasta.

4. Add 2 tbsp (25 mL) of the reserved pasta water to radicchio mixture and raise the heat to high. Add penne and, using a wooden spoon, toss to coat evenly, adding more pasta water if necessary. Add half of the Parmigiano-Reggiano and toss well.

5. Transfer to a large serving platter and sprinkle with remaining cheese. Serve immediately.

Variation

Substitute fusilli for the penne.

Radicchio

Radicchio has become fashionable in the past couple of decades but this vegetable has been eaten since ancient Egyptian times. Pliny the Elder, a Roman statesman, praised its medicinal benefits in the first century A.D., and modern nutritional science has proved him right. Radicchio contains a substance called intybin, a digestive. There are several varieties of radicchio named for the regions in Italy where they are grown. The kind most available outside Italy is Chioggia, which is shaped like head lettuce. It is round, red-maroon in color with white-veined leaves and the size of a small grapefruit. The peak season is midwinter to spring. Store radicchio, wrapped in plastic, in the refrigerator for up to one week.

Spaghetti alla Vesuviana

This pasta is a good choice for people who don't like anchovies but may like the idea of caper-olive sauce. It's similar to Spaghetti alla Puttanesca (see recipe, page 93) but it lacks the saltiness of anchovies and the intensity of black olives. By the way, this dish has no relationship to the potato and chicken "vesuvio" dishes that were created in the city of Chicago and are famous there.

Serves 4 to 6

Tips

Remember, when your pasta has finished cooking, you want it to be firm and supple, not soft and mushy. It will cook a bit more after it is drained, from the residual heat, and also when you add it to the sauce.

Never rinse pasta after draining it. The surface starch helps the sauce to cling and is important to producing the best-quality dish.

3 tbsp	extra-virgin olive oil	45 mL
2	cloves garlic, thinly sliced	2
7	ripe tomatoes, chopped	7
3 tbsp	tiny (nonpareil) capers	45 mL
1/3 cup	chopped pitted Italian green olives	75 mL
1 tsp	minced fresh red finger chile (see Tips, page 55)	5 mL
1 tbsp	salt	15 mL
1 lb	dried spaghetti	500 g
2 tbsp	chopped Italian parsley leaves	25 mL
3 tbsp	grated Parmigiano-Reggiano	45 mL

1. In a covered pasta pot over high heat, bring water to a rapid boil.

2. Meanwhile, in a large sauté pan, heat oil over high heat. Add garlic and cook, stirring, until translucent but not browned, 2 to 3 minutes. Add tomatoes, capers, olives and chile and reduce heat to medium. Let simmer until pasta is cooked.

3. While sauce is simmering, add salt and spaghetti to the boiling water and cook, uncovered, over high heat until pasta is al dente. Scoop out about 1 cup (250 mL) of the pasta water and set aside. Drain pasta.

4. Add 2 tbsp (25 mL) of the pasta water to tomato mixture. Raise heat to high. Add spaghetti and, using pasta tongs, toss to coat evenly, adding more pasta water if necessary. Add parsley and Parmigiano-Reggiano and toss well.

5. Transfer to a large platter and serve immediately.

Italian Parsley

Also called flat-leaf parsley, this is the parsley used in Italian cooking. It is not the curly-leaf variety often used in restaurants as a plate garnish. Italian parsley is more fragrant and less bitter-tasting than curly-leaf parsley, and it has much more flavor. A biennial herb, parsley originated in the Mediterranean and has been cultivated for more than 2,000 years. It was first used medicinally. Parsley was sacred to the ancient Greeks, who adorned athletes and decorated tombs with it. The ancient Romans also used it as a garnish.

Ziti con pomodorini e ricotta fresca

Ziti with Cherry Tomatoes and Fresh Ricotta

Cut ziti (as opposed to long ziti) are thin and tubular and about 2 inches (5 cm) long. This is a great pasta to make in summer, when tomatoes are ripe and full of flavor.

Serves 4 to 6

Tips

Work like a chef. Have all your ingredients ready to go before you actually start to cook (see *Mise en Place*, page 15).

When you combine the pasta and sauce, be sure to toss well and for as long as it takes to coat the pasta evenly with the sauce.

Any dry white Italian wine will work fine in this recipe. Here I'd probably use Pinot Bianco, which is a good basic dry white wine for use in Italian cooking.

3 tbsp	extra-virgin olive oil	45 mL
1 tsp	thinly sliced garlic	5 mL
2½ cups	halved cherry tomatoes	625 mL
	Salt and freshly ground white pepper	
2 tbsp	hand-torn fresh basil leaves	25 mL
1½ cups	dry white Italian wine	375 mL
1 tbsp	salt	15 mL
1 lb	dried cut ziti (see Variation, below)	500 g
6 tbsp	grated Parmigiano-Reggiano, divided	90 mL
½ cup	fresh whole-milk ricotta	125 mL

1. In a covered pasta pot over high heat, bring water to a rapid boil.
2. Meanwhile, in a large sauté pan, heat oil over medium heat. Add garlic and cook, stirring with a wooden spoon, until lightly browned, about 3 minutes. Using a slotted spoon, remove and discard garlic. Add tomatoes and season to taste with salt and pepper. Stir. Add basil and wine and cook until the wine is reduced by half. Remove pan from heat and set aside.
3. While sauce is simmering, add salt and ziti to the boiling water and cook, uncovered, until pasta is al dente. Scoop out about 1 cup (250 mL) of the pasta water and set aside. Drain pasta.
4. Return tomato mixture to high heat. Add 2 tbsp (25 mL) of the reserved pasta water and bring to a simmer. Add ziti and, using a wooden spoon, toss to coat evenly, adding more pasta water if necessary. Add half of the Parmigiano-Reggiano and toss well.
5. Transfer to a large serving platter and spoon ricotta in 1 tsp (5 mL) dollops over top. Sprinkle with remaining cheese and serve immediately.

Variation

Dried cut ziti are short tubular pasta familiar in southern Italy, where tomatoes, basil and ricotta are in abundance. You can substitute penne, if you prefer.

Farfalle con Gorgonzola e fagiolini verdi

Farfalle with Gorgonzola and Green Beans

This dish uses very few ingredients — a bit of onion, fresh green beans and Gorgonzola cheese — but it has wonderful color and flavor. When the Gorgonzola melts over the cooked pasta and beans, it's magic.

Serves 4 to 6

Tip

I prefer the harder, sharper Gorgonzola piccante in this recipe. Gorgonzola piccante is available at specialty cheese shops and Italian markets; it comes in a wedge. But if you can't find it, use soft Gorgonzola, which is more widely available. But please use Italian cheese, not just any blue cheese, because the flavor will not be in keeping with the Italian market basket, and your pasta will lack authenticity.

3 tbsp	extra-virgin olive oil	45 mL
¼ cup	finely diced onion	50 mL
1½ cups	bias-cut (1 inch/2.5 cm) green beans	375 mL
	Salt and freshly ground white pepper	
2 cups	water	500 mL
1 tbsp	salt	15 mL
1 lb	dried farfalle (see Variation, below)	500 g
3 tbsp	grated Parmigiano-Reggiano	45 mL
1 cup	diced Gorgonzola (see Tip, left)	250 mL

1. In a covered pasta pot over high heat, bring water to a boil.

2. Meanwhile, in a large sauté pan, heat oil over medium heat. Add onion, green beans and salt and pepper to taste, and stir. Add water and cook until beans are tender, about 10 minutes. Remove from heat and set aside.

3. While beans are cooking, add salt and farfalle to the boiling water and cook, uncovered, until pasta is al dente. Scoop out about 1 cup (250 mL) of the pasta water and set aside. Drain pasta.

4. Return bean mixture to high heat. Add 2 tbsp (25 mL) of the reserved pasta water and farfalle. Using a wooden spoon, toss to coat evenly, adding more pasta water if necessary. Add Parmigiano-Reggiano and toss well.

5. Transfer to a large serving bowl and sprinkle with Gorgonzola. Using a large serving spoon, mix well until the cheese melts, creating a creamy sauce. Serve immediately.

Variation

Farfalle is a dried butterfly-shaped pasta (*farfalle* is butterfly in Italian) also known as bow-tie pasta. You can substitute penne in this recipe.

Meatless Pasta: Rich Flavors from Poor Kitchens

In Italy there are hundreds of ways to sauce pasta without using meat or fish. There are also many reasons why Italian people make meatless pasta. *La cucina povera* — the cooking of the poor — has existed in all regions of Italy, side by side with *la cucina ricca* — the cooking of the rich.

Certainly many people didn't have the means to purchase prime or even secondary cuts of meat. On a good day they might acquire the so-called "variety" meats, the animal's innards and extremities that were not considered desirable enough for the tables of the well-to-do. But much of the time they simply could not get meat, which meant they had to figure out how to cook without it. Vegetables, legumes, oil, olives and even cheese were much more accessible, and a little went a long way, especially when combined with pasta.

Another reason why so many meatless pasta sauces developed in Italy is religion. Italy is a Catholic country, and Catholics traditionally abstain from eating meat during the 40 days of Lent, as well as on Fridays. While fish and seafood were acceptable alternatives, they were not always an option for people of limited means.

Seasonality also played a role in this development. Unlike most meats, produce has seasons. Within the Italian market basket this means spring for peas, artichokes, asparagus and fava beans; summer for tomatoes, strawberries, basil and melons; fall for squash, endive, cauliflower, grapes, pears and pumpkins; and winter for citrus, radishes, turnips, radicchio, leeks and kale. Before airplanes and freezers, which provide us with an abundance of fresh produce year-round, fruits and vegetables were cooked and eaten at their peak, which meant that people had to invent ways of using them up.

Nowadays, for various reasons, the locavore movement is encouraging us to eat this way again. It's a direction I thoroughly support, because the taste of produce relates directly to its freshness. That's why I encourage you to make an effort to select ingredients that are in season and locally grown. The most complex part of cooking pasta is acquiring the freshest and best-quality ingredients and using superior pasta. Everything else is simple.

Spaghettini all'aglio, olio e peperoncini

Spaghettini with Garlic, Olive Oil and Chile Peppers

This simple southern Italian pasta is a restaurant staple often made with cheap dried red pepper flakes and mediocre olive oil. Trust me, made with those ingredients, that dish doesn't taste anything like the real thing. Even my recipe is a compromise, because the real Italian fresh red chile isn't available in North America, but it looks and tastes much more like the version you would find in Italy.

Serves 4 to 6

Tips

The Italian red chile, which is medium hot and slightly sweet, is not available here, but a good substitute is the California-grown red finger chile (also called Dutch or Holland chile) or the red Fresno chile. In a pinch you can use a ripe red jalapeño or cayenne chile, both of which are much hotter. If you're using these, mince them and reduce the quantity to about ¼ tsp (1 mL).

For best results grate the cheese yourself, but if time is at a premium, use already grated cheese. Whichever form you choose, just be sure to buy the very best Italian Parmigiano-Reggiano you can find and grate it finely to ensure you have the quantity called for in the recipe.

6 tbsp	extra-virgin olive oil	90 mL
1 tbsp	thinly sliced garlic	15 mL
1 tbsp	minced fresh red finger chile (see Tips, left)	15 mL
	Salt and freshly ground black pepper	
1 tbsp	salt	15 mL
1 lb	dried spaghettini (see Variation, below)	500 g
6 tbsp	grated Parmigiano-Reggiano (see Tips, left)	90 mL

1. In a covered pasta pot over high heat, bring water to a rapid boil.

2. Meanwhile, in a large sauté pan, heat oil over medium heat. Add garlic, chile and salt and pepper to taste. Cook, stirring, until garlic is lightly browned and chile is tender, 2 to 3 minutes. Remove from heat and set aside.

3. Add salt and spaghettini to the boiling water and cook, uncovered, over high heat until pasta is al dente. Scoop out about 1 cup (250 mL) of the pasta water and set aside. Drain pasta.

4. Return garlic-chile mixture to high heat. Add 2 tbsp (25 mL) of the reserved pasta water and raise heat to high. Add spaghettini and, using pasta tongs, toss to coat evenly, adding more pasta water if necessary.

5. Transfer to a large serving platter. Serve immediately and pass the Parmigiano-Reggiano in a dish on the side.

Variation

Substitute spaghetti for the spaghettini.

Extra-Virgin Olive Oil

Olive oil is extracted from the ripe fruit of the olive tree, and there is simply no substitution for the best quality (for more on extra-virgin olive oil, see page 19). The best Italian oils are labeled "first cold-pressed extra-virgin," meaning no heat has been used to extract the oil, resulting in a fresher taste. Olive oils can vary in color — from pale gold to green — depending on the time of year and the type of olives. They can also vary in flavor, from mild and fruity to pleasantly bitter. I suggest purchasing the oil in small bottles and tasting until you find your favorites. And I definitely recommend using extra-virgin olive oil for cooking because of the flavor it adds to any dish.

Penne rigate ai quattro formaggi

Penne Rigate with Four Cheeses

In restaurants outside Italy, four-cheese sauces are often thick Mornay sauces that blanket the pasta and become gummy when they cool. Here the cheese creates the sauce. It produces a different texture and flavor — in fact, a different pasta. The ridges in the penne rigate (rigate *is Italian for ridges*) help the sauce to cling.

Serves 4 to 6

3 tbsp	extra-virgin olive oil	45 mL
2 cups	dry white Italian wine	500 mL
1 tsp	finely minced garlic	5 mL
1 cup	heavy or whipping (35%) cream	250 mL
1/3 cup	shredded provolone	75 mL
1/3 cup	shredded scamorza	75 mL
1/3 cup	grated Pecorino Romano	75 mL
	Salt and freshly ground white pepper	
1 tbsp	salt	15 mL
1 lb	dried penne rigate (see Variations, below)	500 g
2 tbsp	unsalted butter	25 mL
6 tbsp	grated Parmigiano-Reggiano, divided	90 mL

1. In a covered pasta pot over high heat, bring water to a rapid boil.

2. Meanwhile, in a large sauté pan, heat oil over medium heat. Add wine and garlic. Cook, stirring, until reduced by half. Add cream and reduce heat to low. Simmer until slightly thickened, about 3 minutes. Add provolone, scamorza and Pecorino Romano. Cook, stirring, until cheese has melted, about 7 minutes. Season to taste with salt and pepper. Remove pan from heat and set aside. (The cheese will bind when the hot pasta is added.)

3. While sauce is simmering, add salt and penne rigate to the boiling water and cook, uncovered, over high heat until pasta is al dente. Scoop out about 1 cup (250 mL) of the pasta water and set aside. Drain pasta.

4. Return cheese mixture to medium heat. Add 2 tbsp (25 mL) of the reserved pasta water and the butter and heat through. Add penne and, using a wooden spoon, cook for 5 minutes while tossing to coat evenly, adding more pasta water if necessary. Add half of the Parmigiano-Reggiano and toss well.

5. Transfer to a large serving platter and sprinkle with remaining cheese. Serve immediately.

Variations

If you can't find penne rigate, substitute smooth penne (penne lisce) or pennette (small penne).

Provolone

Provolone, a semi-hard cow's-milk cheese, originated in southern Italy, but today it is produced all over Italy. However, the DOP ("protected designation of origin") seal is given only to Provolone Val Padana, which is produced in northern Italy: in Lombardy, Veneto, Trentino–Alto Adige and Emilia-Romagna. It is made in different shapes — a salami, a melon, a cone or a pear with a knob on top — but the most common is the pear shape. The flavor varies from sweet and mild to sharp, depending not only on aging but also on the type of rennet used in making the cheese. Rennet from calves produces a mild flavor (provolone dolce) and rennet from lambs or kids results in a sharper taste (provolone piccante). Dolce is aged for one to three months and piccante for three months to more than a year. Piccante is often used for grating. Both dolce and piccante can be smoked.

Scamorza

Scamorza cheese is a relative of mozzarella and was originally made in southern Italy, mostly from cow's milk, but sheep and water buffalo milk are also used occasionally. Today most scamorza is factory-made on a large scale in northern Italy, although there are still some artisanal producers. Like provolone, scamorza is made in shapes, mostly pear shapes. In cooking it melts as well as, if not better than, mozzarella. It is sometimes smoked, which increases its flavor.

Spaghetti alla napoletana

Spaghetti Napoletana

In Naples they use oregano, olives, tomatoes and buffalo mozzarella indiscriminately. The oregano is fresh and fragrant, the olives are cured in oil, not brine, and the intensely flavored tomatoes benefit from the volcanic soil. The mozzarella is made from the milk of water buffaloes and is soft and moist, with a unique and delicious flavor. This dish is one of Naples' truest preparations. Outside Naples, some compromises allow us to enjoy it: cherry tomatoes, oil-packed black olives and soft mozzarella made from cow's milk (see Tips, below).

Serves 4 to 6

Tips

Because oregano leaves are tiny, I like to use them whole in this recipe, just for something different.

In this recipe please do not use the commercially produced part-skim, low-moisture mozzarella intended for pizzas. When melted, it has a thick, plastic texture and a bland but often salty taste.

If you have leftovers, use them to make Frittata of Spaghetti Napoletana (see Variations, page 169).

5 tbsp	extra-virgin olive oil	75 mL
1½ cups	halved cherry tomatoes	375 mL
	Salt and freshly ground black pepper	
¼ cup	chopped pitted oil-cured black olives	50 mL
2 tbsp	fresh oregano leaves	25 mL
1 tbsp	salt	15 mL
1 lb	dried spaghetti	500 g
1 cup	diced fresh cow's-milk mozzarella or mozzarella di bufala (see page 242)	250 mL
6 tbsp	grated Parmigiano-Reggiano, divided	90 mL

1. In a covered pasta pot over high heat, bring water to a rapid boil.

2. Meanwhile, in a large sauté pan, heat oil over low heat. Add tomatoes and salt and pepper to taste and stir well. Cover and simmer for 5 minutes, until tomatoes are soft. Uncover and stir in olives and oregano. Cover and cook for 5 more minutes. Remove pan from heat and set aside.

3. While sauce is simmering, add salt and spaghetti to the boiling water and cook, uncovered, over high heat until pasta is al dente. Scoop out about 1 cup (250 mL) of the pasta water and set aside. Drain pasta.

4. Return tomato mixture to high heat. Add 2 tbsp (25 mL) of the reserved pasta water and heat through. Add spaghetti and, using pasta tongs, toss to coat evenly, adding more pasta water if necessary. Add mozzarella and half of the Parmigiano-Reggiano and toss well.

5. Transfer to a large serving platter and sprinkle with remaining cheese. Serve at once.

Variation

Substitute grape tomatoes for the cherry tomatoes.

Farfalle con porcini

Farfalle with Porcini Mushrooms

Unlike other recipes in which pasta is the star, here boldly flavored mushrooms take center stage. In Italy fresh porcinis are prized and eaten in autumn. When dried, their flavor becomes very concentrated. The farfalle shape (like a butterfly or bow tie) looks particularly appealing with sliced mushrooms.

Serves 4 to 6

Tips

To soften dried porcinis, place in a deep bowl and cover with hot water and a small plate to prevent them from floating. Let cool to room temperature. Remove plate and drain in a colander. (Reserve the soaking water, strain through a paper coffee filter — dried mushrooms are often very sandy — and refrigerate. It's great for adding flavor to soups and to add to water for cooking rice and vegetables.) Use your fingers to check for sand. If the mushrooms feel sandy, especially around the gills, rinse them well under cold running water.

If you have leftovers, use them to make Oven-Browned Farfalle with Porcini Mushrooms (see Variations, page 172).

3 tbsp	extra-virgin olive oil	45 mL
2 rounded cups	thinly sliced dried porcini mushrooms, loosely packed, rehydrated (see Tips, left)	525 mL
	Salt and freshly ground white pepper	
1 cup	water	250 mL
1½ cups	dry white Italian wine	375 mL
1 tbsp	salt	15 mL
1 lb	dried farfalle (see Variation, below)	500 g
¼ cup	unsalted butter (see Tips, page 60)	50 mL
¾ cup	grated Pecorino Romano, divided	175 mL

1. In a covered pasta pot over high heat, bring water to a rapid boil.

2. Meanwhile, in a large sauté pan, heat oil over medium heat. Add rehydrated mushrooms and salt and pepper to taste and stir well. Add water and cook until reduced by half. Add wine and cook until reduced by half, about 7 minutes. Remove from heat and set aside.

3. While sauce is simmering, add salt and farfalle to the boiling water and cook, uncovered, over high heat until pasta is al dente. Scoop out about 1 cup (250 mL) of the pasta water and set aside. Drain pasta.

4. Return mushroom mixture to high heat. Add 2 tbsp (25 mL) of the reserved pasta water and the butter. Add farfalle and, using a wooden spoon, toss to coat evenly, adding more pasta water if necessary. Add half of the Pecorino Romano and toss well.

5. Transfer to a large serving bowl and sprinkle with remaining cheese. Serve immediately.

Variation

Substitute penne for the farfalle.

The King of Mushrooms

Porcini mushrooms (*Boletus edulis*) are found in North America, Europe and Asia. In Italy they are considered the king of mushrooms — despite their name (*porcini* means "piglets"). Fresh porcini, which grow in a symbiotic relationship with pine and chestnut trees, are foraged in autumn. Those found in chestnut woods are considered the best.

Porcinis have a big, round fleshy cap and a short, thick stem. The cap, when sliced, reveals meaty white flesh that does not change color. The flavor is intense: earthy, nutty and aromatic. Dried porcini have a concentrated flavor and aroma, and they need to be rehydrated before use. Look for dried porcini that are firm, not dry and crumbling or powdery. They should have a strong mushroom smell; no smell means no flavor. Because they keep well tightly wrapped in a cool, dark place, it is a good idea to purchase in bulk from an Italian deli or online.

Fusilli con patate e piselli

Fusilli with Potatoes and Peas

For the ultimate experience in terms of taste and texture, use fresh green peas in season. When time is of the essence, the best-quality frozen peas, preferably petite and organic, make an acceptable substitute.

Serves 4 to 6

Tips

In summer, when fresh peas are available at farmers' markets, it's worth the time and effort to shell them for this dish.

To blanch peas for this recipe, cook shelled peas in lightly salted boiling water for 3 minutes. Drain in a colander and rinse under cold running water.

I like to use unsalted butter in my recipes because it contributes fresh flavor without adding extra salt.

3 tbsp	extra-virgin olive oil	45 mL
2 cups	diced unpeeled Yukon Gold potatoes	500 mL
	Salt and freshly ground white pepper	
¼ cup	finely diced onion	50 mL
1 cup	frozen green peas, defrosted (see Variations, below)	250 mL
2 tbsp	roughly chopped fresh oregano leaves	25 mL
½ cup	water	125 mL
1 cup	dry white Italian wine	250 mL
1 tbsp	salt	15 mL
1 lb	dried fusilli (see Variations, below)	500 g
¼ cup	unsalted butter (see Tips, left)	50 mL
¾ cup	grated Parmigiano-Reggiano, divided	175 mL

1. In a covered pasta pot over high heat, bring water to a rapid boil.

2. Meanwhile, in a large sauté pan, heat oil over medium heat. Add potatoes and salt and pepper to taste. Cook, stirring, until potatoes are firm to the bite and lightly browned, about 6 minutes. Add onion, peas and oregano and cook, stirring, until onion is soft, about 5 minutes. Add water and cook about 1 minute. Add wine and cook until reduced by half. Remove from heat and set aside.

3. While sauce is simmering, add salt and fusilli to boiling water and cook, uncovered, over high heat until pasta is al dente. Scoop out about 1 cup (250 mL) of the pasta water and set aside. Drain pasta.

4. Return potato mixture to high heat. Add 2 tbsp (25 mL) of the reserved pasta water and the butter and heat through. Add fusilli and, using a wooden spoon, toss to coat evenly, adding more pasta water if necessary. Add half of the Parmigiano-Reggiano and toss well.

5. Transfer to a large serving bowl and sprinkle with remaining cheese. Serve immediately.

Variations

Substitute 1 cup (250 mL) green beans, blanched and cut into 1-inch (2.5 cm) lengths, for the peas.

Substitute penne for the fusilli.

Cavatappi with Spinach and Poached Eggs

In this recipe the pasta with spinach and cheese is good just by itself, so you could omit the eggs. However, the poached eggs add another layer of flavor and texture, especially when the yolk is pierced and the rich yellow liquid melts into the hot pasta.

Serves 4 to 6

Tips

Substitute ready-to-use baby spinach for the leaf spinach. It's more convenient because it doesn't need to be stemmed.

Serve one egg with each portion of pasta.

For best results grate the cheese yourself, but if time is at a premium, use already grated cheese. Whichever form you choose, just be sure to buy the very best Italian Pecorino Romano you can find and grate it finely to ensure you have the quantity called for in the recipe.

6 tbsp	extra-virgin olive oil, divided	90 mL
1 tbsp	thinly sliced garlic	15 mL
	Salt and freshly ground white pepper	
3 cups	fresh stemmed spinach, packed	750 mL
1 cup	dry white Italian wine	250 mL
2 tbsp	salt, divided	25 mL
1 lb	dried cavatappi (see Variations, below)	500 g
3 tbsp	red wine vinegar	45 mL
4 to 6	eggs	4 to 6
¾ cup	grated Pecorino Romano, divided (see Tips, left)	175 mL

1. In a covered pasta pot over high heat, bring water to a rapid boil.

2. Meanwhile, in a large sauté pan, heat 3 tbsp (45 mL) of the oil over medium heat. Add garlic and salt and pepper to taste and cook, stirring, until the garlic is lightly browned, about 3 minutes. Add spinach and, using tongs, toss until spinach wilts. Add wine and cook until reduced by half. Add the remaining 3 tbsp (45 mL) olive oil and cook for 1 to 2 minutes, until most of the liquid released by the spinach evaporates. Remove from heat and set aside.

3. While sauce is cooking, add 1 tbsp (15 mL) of the salt and cavatappi to the boiling water and cook, uncovered, over high heat until pasta is al dente. Scoop out about 1 cup (250 mL) of the pasta water and set aside. Drain pasta.

4. Meanwhile, in a large pot of boiling water, combine vinegar and remaining 1 tbsp (15 mL) of salt. Reduce heat to medium. Crack eggs one at a time into a bowl and slide them into the simmering water. Cook until softly poached, 2 to 3 minutes. Using a slotted spoon, transfer eggs to a plate and set aside.

5. Return spinach mixture to high heat. Add 2 tbsp (25 mL) of the reserved pasta water and heat through. Add cavatappi and, using a wooden spoon, toss to coat evenly, adding more pasta water if necessary. Add half of the Pecorino Romano and toss well.

6. Transfer to a large platter and place poached eggs on top of the cavatappi. Sprinkle with remaining cheese and serve immediately.

Variations

Substitute penne or fusilli for the cavatappi.

Cavatappi con salsa di finocchio, caperi e pinoli

Cavatappi with Fennel Sauce, Capers and Pine Nuts

The ingredients in this dish come from southern Italy, where the capers would most likely be salt-cured and need rinsing before using. Ordinary brine-cured capers from a jar are just fine, but if you have the salt-cured version, by all means use them (see Tips, below). The combination of crunchy pine nuts, bitter capers and sweet fennel is particularly appealing.

Serves 4 to 6

Tips

In my opinion the capers and cheese provide enough salt. However, if you wish to add salt, please do so very sparingly. If you can find salt-cured capers from Sicily, soak them in cold water to cover, rinse under cold running water, spread on paper toweling and pat dry. Then use according to the recipe directions.

To toast pine nuts, spread in one layer on a baking sheet. Bake in a 350°F (180°C) oven for 7 to10 minutes. Check at 7 minutes, because the nuts can burn quickly.

3 tbsp	extra-virgin olive oil	45 mL
½ cup	diced onion	125 mL
1 tbsp	thinly sliced garlic	15 mL
1¾ cup	diced trimmed fennel bulb (see Tips, page 145)	425 mL
	Freshly ground white pepper	
1 cup	water	125 mL
1½ cups	dry white Italian wine	375 mL
3 tbsp	tiny (nonpareil) capers, drained	45 mL
1 tbsp	salt	15 mL
1 lb	dried cavatappi (see Variations, below)	500 g
¾ cup	grated Pecorino Romano, divided	175 mL
4 tbsp	toasted pine nuts (see Tips, left)	60 mL

1. In a covered pasta pot over high heat, bring water to a rapid boil.

2. Meanwhile, in a large sauté pan, heat oil over medium heat. Add onion, garlic, fennel and pepper to taste. Cook, stirring, until garlic is translucent but not browned, 2 to 3 minutes. Add water and continue to cook until vegetables are soft and tender, about 6 minutes. Add wine and cook until reduced by half. Add capers and simmer until sauce is slightly reduced, about 3 minutes. Remove from heat and set aside.

3. While sauce is cooking, add salt and cavatappi to the boiling water and cook, uncovered, over high heat until pasta is al dente. Scoop out about 1 cup (250 mL) of the pasta water and set aside. Drain pasta.

4. Return fennel mixture to high heat. Add 2 tbsp (25 mL) of the reserved pasta water and the cavatappi and, using pasta tongs, toss to coat evenly, adding more pasta water if necessary. Add half of the Pecorino Romano and toss well.

5. Transfer to a large serving bowl and sprinkle with pine nuts and remaining cheese. Serve immediately.

Variations

Substitute penne or fusilli for the cavatappi.

Orecchiette al sugo di melanzane

Orecchiette with Eggplant Sauce

The combination of eggplant, tomatoes and pasta is a natural marriage of flavors.

Serves 4 to 6

Tips

I like to peel eggplant because the skin can be bitter and tough — you can't tell just by looking at it.

Any dry white Italian table wine will work well in this recipe. Here I'd probably use Pinot Bianco, which is a good basic dry white wine for use in Italian cooking.

If you have leftovers, use them to make Oven-Browned Orecchiette with Eggplant Sauce (see Variations, page 172).

6 tbsp	extra-virgin olive oil	90 mL
1 tbsp	thinly sliced garlic	15 mL
¼ cup	finely diced onion	50 mL
2 cups	diced peeled eggplant (see Tips, left)	500 mL
	Salt and freshly ground white pepper	
1 cup	dry white Italian wine (see Tips, left)	250 mL
2 tbsp	hand-torn fresh basil leaves	25 mL
2½ cups	canned crushed Italian tomatoes	625 mL
1 tbsp	salt	15 mL
1 lb	dried orecchiette (see Variations, below)	500 g
2 tbsp	butter	25 mL
¾ cup	grated Parmigiano-Reggiano, divided	175 mL

1. In a covered pasta pot over high heat, bring water to a rapid boil.
2. Meanwhile, in a large sauté pan, heat oil over medium heat. Add garlic, onion, eggplant and salt and pepper to taste, and cook, stirring, until vegetables are soft, about 10 minutes. Add wine and basil and cook until wine is reduced by half. Stir in tomatoes and reduce heat to low. Simmer until sauce thickens slightly, about 5 minutes. Remove from heat and set aside.
3. While sauce is simmering, add salt and orecchiette to the boiling water and cook, uncovered, over high heat until pasta is al dente. Scoop out about 1 cup (250 mL) of the pasta water and set aside. Drain pasta.
4. Return eggplant mixture to high heat. Add 2 tbsp (25 mL) of the reserved pasta water and the butter and heat until butter melts. Add orecchiette and, using a wooden spoon, toss to coat evenly, adding more pasta water if necessary. Add half of the Parmigiano-Reggiano and toss well.
5. Transfer to a large serving platter and sprinkle with remaining cheese. Serve immediately.

Variations

Substitute penne or fusilli for the orecchiette.

Orecchiette con le cime di rapa

Orecchiette with Broccoli Rabe

Broccoli rabe is indigenous to the south of Italy. Orecchiette, the ear-shaped pasta, originated in the south as well, specifically in the region of Puglia. The flavors in this dish are simple and bold. The broccoli rabe florets are cut from the stems, which makes for an interesting contrast in shape and texture.

Serves 4 to 6

Tips

The Italian red chile, which is medium hot and slightly sweet, is not available here, but a good substitute is the California-grown red finger chile (also called Dutch or Holland chile) or the red Fresno chile. In a pinch you can use a ripe red jalapeño or cayenne chile, both of which are much hotter. If you're using these, mince them and reduce the quantity to about ¼ tsp (1 mL).

To blanch broccoli rabe, place in a large, long-handled sieve. Dip sieve into a pot of boiling, lightly salted water for 1 to 2 minutes. Remove and rinse well under cold running water. Drain well.

The robust Pecorino Romano complements the southern Italian ingredients and flavors in this recipe.

6 tbsp	extra-virgin olive oil, divided	90 mL
1 tbsp	thinly sliced garlic	15 mL
¼ cup	diced onion	50 mL
	Salt and freshly ground white pepper	
1 tsp	thinly sliced fresh red finger chile	5 mL
2 cups	1-inch (2.5 cm) pieces broccoli rabe florets and stems, blanched (see Tips, left)	500 mL
1 cup	dry white Italian wine	250 mL
1 tbsp	salt	15 mL
1 lb	dried orecchiette (see Variation, below)	500 g
9 tbsp	freshly grated Pecorino Romano, divided	135 mL

1. In a covered pasta pot over high heat, bring water to a rapid boil.

2. Meanwhile, in a large sauté pan, heat 3 tbsp (45 mL) of the oil over low heat. Add garlic, onion and salt and pepper to taste. Cook, stirring, until onion is soft, about 3 minutes. Stir in chile, broccoli rabe and wine. Raise heat to medium and simmer until wine is reduced by half and broccoli rabe is tender, about 5 minutes. Remove from heat and set aside.

3. While sauce is cooking, add salt and orecchiette to the boiling water and cook, uncovered, over high heat until pasta is al dente. Scoop out about 1 cup (250 mL) of the pasta water and set aside. Drain pasta.

4. Return broccoli rabe mixture to high heat. Add 2 tbsp (25 mL) of the reserved pasta water and heat through. Using a wooden spoon, toss to coat evenly, adding more pasta water if necessary. Add 3 tbsp (45 mL) of the Pecorino Romano and toss well.

5. Transfer to a serving platter and drizzle remaining olive oil over orecchiette. Sprinkle with remaining cheese and serve immediately.

Variation
Substitute penne for the orecchiette.

Broccoli Rabe
Also called rapini, broccoli rabe is a popular vegetable in Italy and the Mediterranean. Although its name is "broccoli" and it is a member of the Brassica family, it is more closely related to the turnip. Broccoli rabe has stems that are uniform in size leading up to a cluster of spiky leaves; the leaves surround a green bud that looks like a very small head of broccoli. Sometimes edible yellow flowers sprout from the head. Broccoli rabe has a nutty, pleasantly bitter flavor. It is available year-round but the peak seasons are from fall to spring.

Fusilli con salsa di sedano e ricotta salata

Fusilli with Celery Sauce and Ricotta Salata

Celery is healthful, refreshing and abundant, so why don't we use it more often? Celery plays a starring role in this recipe and gives the dish excellent flavor, especially in combination with the ricotta salata cheese, which is aged hard ricotta with a sharper flavor.

Serves 4 to 6

Tips

Celery has tough, fibrous strings that make it hard to chew. Peeling removes these strings.

If you have leftovers, use them to make Oven-Browned Fusilli with Celery Sauce and Ricotta Salata (see Variations, page 172).

3 tbsp	extra-virgin olive oil	45 mL
1 tbsp	thinly sliced garlic	15 mL
¼ cup	finely diced onion	50 mL
1½ cups	finely diced peeled celery	375 mL
	Salt and freshly ground white pepper	
1½ cups	water	375 mL
1 cup	dry white Italian wine	250 mL
1 tbsp	salt	15 mL
1 lb	dried fusilli (see Variations, below)	500 g
¼ cup	unsalted butter	50 mL
3 tbsp	grated Parmigiano-Reggiano	45 mL
½ cup	shredded ricotta salata (see Variations, below)	125 mL

1. In a covered pasta pot over high heat, bring water to a rapid boil.

2. Meanwhile, in a large sauté pan, heat oil over medium heat. Add garlic, onion, celery and salt and pepper to taste. Cook, stirring, until garlic is translucent but not brown, about 3 minutes. Add water and cook until vegetables are tender, about 8 minutes. Add wine and cook until reduced by half. Remove pan from heat and set aside.

3. While sauce is simmering, add salt and fusilli to the boiling water and cook, uncovered, over high heat until pasta is al dente. Scoop out about 1 cup (250 mL) of the pasta water and set aside. Drain pasta.

4. Return celery mixture to high heat. Add 2 tbsp (25 mL) of the reserved pasta water and the butter and cook until butter melts. Add fusilli and, using a wooden spoon, toss to coat evenly, adding more pasta water if necessary. Add Parmigiano-Reggiano and toss well.

5. Transfer to a large serving bowl and sprinkle with ricotta salata. Serve immediately.

Variations

Substitute fresh ricotta (ricotta fresca) for the ricotta salata.

Substitute penne or cavatappi for the fusilli.

Ricotta Salata

Ricotta salata is a pressed, salted and dried version of ricotta fresca, a whey cheese with a texture similar to cottage cheese but lighter. It is imported in very limited quantities from Italy. Whereas the flavor and texture of fresh ricotta are mild and creamy, ricotta salata is sharp and firm and can be shredded.

Conchiglie con olive nere e pistacchi

Conchiglie with Oil-Cured Olives and Pistachios

In this recipe the black oil-cured olives have a rich, mellow flavor that complements the color and flavor of the pistachios. When I cook this dish, I blanch, then halve, then peel the pistachios. Am I asking you to do this? I'd be happy if you would roughly chop or smash them with a rolling pin or heavy pot bottom. But please use salt sparingly, because unblanched salted pistachios are quite salty and some salt remains after blanching.

Serves 4 to 6

Tips

To blanch pistachios, place the shelled nutmeats in a long-handled sieve. Place in boiling unsalted water for 5 minutes. Remove and rinse under cold running water. Drain well, spread out on paper toweling and pat dry.

For best results grate the cheese yourself, but if time is at a premium, use already grated cheese. Whichever form you choose, just be sure to buy the very best Italian Pecorino Romano you can find and grate it finely to ensure you have the quantity called for in the recipe.

3 tbsp	extra-virgin olive oil	45 mL
¾ cup	quartered pitted oil-cured black olives	175 mL
½ cup	shelled salted pistachio nuts, blanched and drained (see Tips, left)	125 mL
	Salt and freshly ground white pepper	
1 cup	dry white Italian wine	250 mL
1 tbsp	salt	15 mL
1 lb	dried conchiglie (see Variations, below)	500 g
¾ cup	grated Pecorino Romano, divided	175 mL

1. In a covered pasta pot over high heat, bring water to a rapid boil.

2. Meanwhile, in a large sauté pan, heat oil over medium heat. Add olives, pistachios and salt and pepper to taste. Cook, stirring, for 2 minutes. Add wine and cook until reduced by half. Remove from heat and set aside.

3. While sauce is cooking, add salt and conchiglie to the boiling water and cook, uncovered, over high heat until pasta is al dente. Scoop out about 1 cup (250 mL) of the pasta water and set aside. Drain pasta.

4. Return olive mixture to high heat. Add 2 tbsp (25 mL) of the reserved pasta water and the conchiglie. Using a wooden spoon, toss to coat evenly, adding more pasta water if necessary. Add half of the Pecorino Romano and toss well.

5. Transfer to a large serving bowl and sprinkle with remaining cheese. Serve immediately.

Variations

If conchiglie, which are shaped like shells, are not available, substitute penne or fusilli.

> ### Pecorino Romano
> Pecorino Romano is a hard pressed sheep's-milk cheese with a sharp, salty and distinctive flavor. It is a DOC (*Denominazione di origine controllata*) cheese from Lazio, Sardinia and Tuscany that is made both artisanally and in factories. An ancient style of cheese, it has been made for 2,000 years and is believed to have been a staple ration for the armies of Rome.

Penne con verdure e erbe aromatiche

Penne with Vegetables and Aromatic Herbs

I like to think of this pasta as a hot vegetable salad. You would find these vegetables in a mature summer garden. In spring, substitute equal amounts of spring vegetables (see Variations, below).

Serves 4 to 6

Tips

I like to peel celery because the celery strings are very fibrous and often don't soften during cooking, resulting in a tough texture.

Because this is a short, sturdy pasta, it is easier to toss using a wooden spoon rather than pasta tongs, which work best for longer pastas.

Removing the thick ribs of the Savoy cabbage before you dice the leaves improves the texture of this dish. Core the cabbage and separate the leaves, then fold each cabbage leaf in half and cut out and discard the rib.

If you have leftovers, use them to make Bell Peppers Filled with Conchiglie with Vegetables and Aromatic Herbs (see Variations, page 170).

3 tbsp	extra-virgin olive oil	45 mL
¼ cup	diced onion	50 mL
¼ cup	diced peeled celery (see Tips, left)	50 mL
¼ cup	diced leek	50 mL
¼ cup	diced deribbed Savoy cabbage	50 mL
¼ cup	diced zucchini	50 mL
¼ cup	diced ripe plum or Roma tomato	50 mL
	Salt and freshly ground white pepper	
1 cup	water	250 mL
1½ cups	dry white Italian wine	375 mL
1 tbsp	chopped fresh Italian parsley leaves	15 mL
1 tbsp	chopped fresh basil leaves	15 mL
1 tbsp	chopped fresh sage leaves	15 mL
1 tbsp	chopped fresh oregano leaves	15 mL
1 tbsp	salt	15 mL
1 lb	dried penne (see Variations, below)	500 g
¾ cup	grated Pecorino Romano, divided	175 mL

1. In a covered pasta pot over high heat, bring water to a rapid boil.

2. Meanwhile, in a large sauté pan, heat oil over medium heat. Add onion, celery, leek, cabbage, zucchini, tomato and salt and pepper to taste and cook, stirring, for 2 minutes. Add water and cook until vegetables are tender, about 10 minutes. Add wine and cook until reduced by half. Add parsley, basil, sage and oregano and stir well. Remove from heat and set aside.

3. While sauce is cooking, add salt and penne to boiling water and cook, uncovered, over high heat until pasta is al dente. Scoop out about 1 cup (250 mL) of the pasta water and set aside. Drain pasta.

4. Return vegetable mixture to high heat. Add 2 tbsp (25 mL) of the reserved pasta water and the penne. Using a wooden spoon, toss to coat evenly, adding more pasta water if necessary. Add half of the Pecorino Romano and toss well.

5. Transfer to a large serving bowl and sprinkle with remaining cheese. Serve immediately.

Variations

In spring, substitute an equal amount of seasonal vegetables such as asparagus, carrots, fava beans, fennel or new potatoes for the leeks, cabbage and zucchini.

Substitute conchiglie or fusilli for the penne.

Maccheroni con piselli e cipolla

Maccheroni with Peas and Onions

Although the names are similar, maccheroni does not have the same shape as elbow macaroni. Rather it is a tubular pasta shaped like rigatoni and about 1¼ to 1½ inches (3 to 4 cm) long. It can have a smooth or ridged surface. This recipe, like the pasta, comes from southern Italy and is very much in the cucina povera ("cooking of the poor") style. In other words, it produces great flavors and colors from a few ordinary ingredients. Onions, peas and sage are a natural combination.

Serves 4 to 6

Tips

If you are using thawed frozen peas, reduce the cooking time to 3 minutes.

Pecorino Romano, a sheep's-milk cheese, complements the southern Italian flavors and ingredients in this pasta.

Work like a chef. Have all your ingredients ready to go before you actually start to cook (see *Mise en Place*, page 15).

3 tbsp	extra-virgin olive oil	45 mL
¾ cup	diced onion	175 mL
	Salt and freshly ground white pepper	
1 cup	dry white Italian wine	250 mL
2 tbsp	hand-torn fresh sage leaves	25 mL
1½ cups	fresh peas or thawed, if frozen	375 mL
1 tbsp	salt	15 mL
1 lb	dried maccheroni (see Variations, below)	500 g
¾ cup	grated Pecorino Romano, divided	175 mL

1. In a covered pasta pot over high heat, bring water to a rapid boil.

2. Meanwhile, in a large sauté pan, heat oil over medium heat. Add onion and salt and pepper to taste. Cook, stirring, until onion is soft, about 3 minutes. Add wine and sage, stir, and increase heat to medium. Cook until wine is reduced by half. Reduce heat to low, add peas and simmer just until tender, 5 to 8 minutes for fresh peas, less for frozen (see Tips, left).

3. While sauce is simmering, add salt and maccheroni to the boiling water and cook, uncovered, over high heat until al dente. Scoop out about 1 cup (250 mL) of the pasta water and set aside. Drain pasta.

4. Add 2 tbsp (25 mL) of the reserved pasta water to pea mixture. Increase heat to high. Add maccheroni and, using a wooden spoon, toss to coat evenly, adding more pasta water if necessary. Add half of the Pecorino Romano and toss well.

5. Transfer to a large serving bowl and sprinkle with remaining cheese. Serve immediately.

Variations

Substitute penne or cut ziti for the maccheroni.

Maccheroni dolci ai broccoletti

Maccheroni with Sweetened Broccoli

Here's an interesting piece of culinary lore: broccoli is an Italian vegetable brought to North America by Italians, who planted it and made it popular in the 1920s. In this recipe it is cooked with golden raisins and freshly made green grape purée. This results in a sweet — but not too sweet — flavor, which is balanced by the slightly acidic white wine. Add toasted pine nuts and what's not to like?

Serves 4 to 6

Tips

One well-rounded cup (275 mL) of seedless green grapes puréed in a food processor yields about 1 cup (250 mL) grape purée.

To toast pine nuts, spread them in one layer on a baking sheet. Bake in a 350°F (180°C) oven for 7 to 10 minutes. Check at 7 minutes, because the nuts can burn quickly.

If you have leftovers, use them to make Baked Maccheroni with Sweetened Broccoli (see Variations, page 168).

3 tbsp	extra-virgin olive oil	45 mL
½ cup	finely diced onion	125 mL
	Salt and freshly ground white pepper	
¼ cup	golden raisins	50 mL
2 cups	quartered broccoli florets	500 mL
1 cup	seedless green grape purée (see Tips, left)	250 mL
1 cup	dry white Italian wine	250 mL
1 tbsp	salt	15 mL
1 lb	dried maccheroni (see Variations, below)	500 g
2 tbsp	toasted pine nuts	25 mL
¾ cup	grated Pecorino Romano, divided	175 mL

1. In a covered pasta pot over high heat, bring water to a rapid boil.

2. Meanwhile, in a large sauté pan, heat oil over low heat. Add onion and salt and pepper to taste. Cook, stirring, until onion is tender and soft, about 3 minutes. Add raisins, broccoli and grape purée and increase heat to medium. Stir, and simmer until broccoli is firm to the bite, about 5 minutes. Add wine and cook until reduced by half. Remove from heat and set aside.

3. While sauce is simmering, add salt and maccheroni to the boiling water and cook, uncovered, over high heat until pasta is al dente. Scoop out about 1 cup (250 mL) of the pasta water and set aside. Drain pasta.

4. Return broccoli mixture to high heat. Add pine nuts and 2 tbsp (25 mL) of the reserved pasta water. Add maccheroni and, using a wooden spoon, toss to coat evenly, adding more pasta water if necessary. Add half of the Pecorino Romano and toss well.

5. Transfer to a large serving platter and sprinkle with remaining cheese. Serve immediately.

Variations

Substitute penne, fusilli or orecchiette for the maccheroni.

Pine Nuts

Pine nuts are, as the name implies, the edible seeds of pine trees. Most pine nuts come from four tree varieties: Mexican piñon (*Pinus cembroides*), Colorado pinyon (*P. edulis*), Italian stone pine (*P. pinea*) and Chinese nut pine (*P. koralensis*). The pine nuts of Italian trees have a mild flavor compared to Chinese pine nuts, which are strongly flavored. Pine nuts may be eaten raw but are usually toasted. Because of their high oil content, they turn rancid quickly. Fresh pine nuts should smell sweet, not stale or rancid. Store them refrigerated in an airtight container for up to a month or frozen for up to three months.

Penne rigate alla vodka

Penne Rigate with Vodka

Believe it or not, this vodka sauce is an authentic Italian preparation. You see vodka sauces in Italy all the time, but where they came from is a mystery, because Italians don't drink much vodka. Still, it makes a very good pasta sauce.

Serves 4 to 6

Tips

Work like a chef. Have all your ingredients ready to go before you actually start to cook (see *Mise en Place*, page 15.)

Always use a large pot and plenty of water when cooking pasta. To properly cook 1 pound (500 g) of pasta, you'll need a pot with a volume of at least 8 quarts (8 L) so that you can use 6 quarts (6 L) of water.

If you have leftovers, use them to make Oven-Browned Penne Rigate with Vodka (see Variations, page 172).

3 tbsp	extra-virgin olive oil	45 mL
1 tsp	thinly sliced garlic	5 mL
3	fresh Roma tomatoes, diced	3
	Salt and freshly ground white pepper	
¼ cup	vodka	50 mL
2 cups	canned crushed Italian tomatoes	500 mL
1 tbsp	hand-torn fresh basil leaves	15 mL
2 tbsp	heavy or whipping (35%) cream	25 mL
1 tbsp	salt	15 mL
1 lb	dried penne rigate (see Variation, below)	500 g
6 tbsp	grated Parmigiano-Reggiano, divided	90 mL

1. In a covered pasta pot over high heat, bring water to a rapid boil.
2. Meanwhile, in a large sauté pan, heat oil over medium heat. Add garlic, fresh tomatoes and salt and pepper to taste. Cook, stirring, until garlic is translucent but not browned and tomatoes are soft and tender, about 6 minutes. Add vodka and cook until reduced by half. Add canned tomatoes and reduce heat to low. Add basil and simmer slowly until sauce thickens, about 5 minutes. Add cream, stir to mix, and simmer for 1 minute. Remove from heat and set aside.
3. While sauce is simmering, add salt and penne rigate to the boiling water and cook, uncovered, over high heat until pasta is al dente. Scoop out about 1 cup (250 mL) of the pasta water and set aside. Drain pasta.
4. Return pan to high heat, add 2 tbsp (25 mL) of the reserved pasta water and heat through. Add penne rigate and, using a wooden spoon, toss to coat evenly, adding more pasta water if necessary. Add half of the Parmigiano-Reggiano and toss well.
5. Transfer to a large serving platter and sprinkle with remaining cheese. Serve immediately.

Variation

Substitute penne lisce (smooth penne) for the penne rigate.

Pennette al burro e pomodorini

Pennette with Cherry Tomatoes and Butter

Cherry tomatoes, butter, basil and pasta — how simple can you get? Hopefully the cherry tomatoes will be perfectly ripe and full of flavor.

Serves 4 to 6

Tips

I like to slice the tomatoes horizontally in relation to the stem end to make small circles.

For best results grate the cheese yourself, but if time is at a premium, use already grated cheese. Whichever form you choose, just be sure to buy the very best Italian Parmigiano-Reggiano you can find and grate it finely to ensure you have the quantity called for in the recipe.

3 tbsp	extra-virgin olive oil	45 mL
1½ cups	sliced cherry tomatoes (see Tips, left)	375 mL
	Salt and freshly ground white pepper	
½ cup	dry white Italian wine	125 mL
3 tbsp	hand-torn fresh basil leaves	45 mL
1 tbsp	salt	15 mL
1 lb	dried pennette (see Variations, below)	500 g
⅔ cup	unsalted butter	150 mL
⅔ cup	grated Parmigiano-Reggiano, divided	150 mL

1. In a covered pasta pot over high heat, bring water to a rapid boil.

2. Meanwhile, in a large sauté pan, heat oil over medium heat. Add tomatoes and salt and pepper to taste and cook, stirring, until tomatoes are heated through (they should remain semi-firm). Add wine and basil and cook until wine is reduced slightly but tomatoes still have some shape, about 6 minutes. Remove pan from heat and set aside.

3. While wine is reducing, add salt and pennette to the boiling water and cook, uncovered, over high heat until pasta is al dente. Scoop out about 1 cup (250 mL) of the pasta water and set aside. Drain pasta.

4. Return tomato mixture to high heat. Add 2 tbsp (25 mL) of the reserved pasta water and the butter and heat until butter melts. Add pennette and, using a wooden spoon, toss to coat evenly, adding more pasta water if necessary. Add 3 tbsp (45 mL) of the Parmigiano-Reggiano and toss well.

5. Transfer to a large serving platter and sprinkle with remaining cheese. Serve immediately.

Variations

Substitute grape tomatoes for the cherry tomatoes.

Substitute penne for the pennette.

Tortiglioni addolciti con cavolfiore

Tortiglioni with Sweet Cauliflower

In this dish the sweetness of cauliflower is accentuated by two varieties of raisins. The addition of white wine cuts the sweetness and the fresh red chile adds a pleasant kick. I think it makes an interesting and tasty combination.

Serves 4 to 6

Tips

The Italian red chile, which is medium hot and slightly sweet, is not available here, but a good substitute is the California-grown red finger chile (also called Dutch or Holland chile) or the red Fresno chile. In a pinch you can use a ripe red jalapeño or cayenne chile, both of which are much hotter. If you're using these, mince them and reduce the quantity to about ¼ tsp (1 mL).

I like to use Pecorino Romano in this dish because the sharp flavor of the sheep's-milk cheese is a nice contrast to the sweet raisins.

3 tbsp	extra-virgin olive oil	45 mL
2 cups	quartered cauliflower florets	500 mL
	Salt and freshly ground white pepper	
½ cup	finely diced onion	125 mL
3 tbsp	pine nuts	45 mL
2 tbsp	golden raisins	25 mL
2 tbsp	dark raisins	25 mL
1 tbsp	thinly sliced red finger chile (see Tips, left)	15 mL
2 cups	dry white Italian wine	500 mL
1 tbsp	salt	15 mL
1 lb	dried tortiglioni (see Variations, below)	500 g
6 tbsp	grated Pecorino Romano, divided	90 mL

1. In a covered pasta pot over high heat, bring water to a rapid boil.

2. Meanwhile, in a large sauté pan, heat oil over medium-high heat. Add cauliflower and cook, stirring constantly, until browned in spots, about 10 minutes. Season to taste with salt and pepper. Add onion, pine nuts, raisins, chile and wine. Cover, reduce heat to low and simmer until wine is reduced and vegetables are tender, 10 to 12 minutes. Remove pan from heat and set aside.

3. While sauce is simmering, add salt and tortiglioni to the boiling water and cook, uncovered, over high heat until pasta is al dente. Scoop out about 1 cup (250 mL) of the pasta water and set aside. Drain pasta.

4. Return cauliflower mixture to high heat. Add 2 tbsp (25 mL) of the reserved pasta water and heat through. Add tortiglioni and, using a wooden spoon, toss to coat evenly, adding more pasta water if necessary. Add half of the Pecorino Romano and toss well.

5. Transfer to a large serving platter and sprinkle with remaining cheese. Serve immediately.

Variations

Tortiglioni is a hollow pasta that is wider than penne but narrower than rigatoni and cut straight across the ends. It also goes by another name, succhiette, meaning "drill bit." Substitute penne, maccheroni or rigatoni for the tortiglioni.

Tortiglioni with Corn and Leeks

I have specified sweet corn in this recipe because traditionally the corn grown in Italy and the rest of Europe was field corn, which was dried and fed to animals. The sweet corn in this pasta goes well with the delicate onion flavor of the leeks, a vegetable that is often neglected even by chefs, who usually put it in the stock or soup pot.

Serves 4 to 6

Tips

Always use a large pot and plenty of water when cooking pasta. To properly cook 1 pound (500 g) of pasta, you'll need a pot with a volume of at least 8 quarts (8 L) so that you can use 6 quarts (6 L) of water.

Never rinse pasta after draining it. The surface starch helps the sauce to cling and is important to producing the best-quality dish.

If you have leftovers, use them to make Bell Peppers Filled with Tortiglioni with Corn and Leeks (see Variations, page 170).

3 tbsp	extra-virgin olive oil	45 mL
¼ cup	finely diced onion	50 mL
1 cup	fresh sweet corn kernels	250 mL
	Salt and freshly ground white pepper	
1 cup	diced leeks	250 mL
1 cup	dry white Italian wine	250 mL
¼ cup	unsalted butter	50 mL
1 tbsp	salt	15 mL
1 lb	dried tortiglioni (see Variations, below)	500 g
6 tbsp	grated Parmigiano-Reggiano, divided	90 mL

1. In a covered pasta pot over high heat, bring water to a rapid boil.

2. Meanwhile, in a large sauté pan, heat oil over low heat. Add onion, corn and salt and pepper to taste and cook, stirring, for 1 minute. Cover and cook until corn is tender, about 4 minutes. Add leeks, wine and butter, stir well and cover. Simmer until leeks are tender, about 10 minutes. Remove pan from heat and set aside.

3. While leeks are simmering, add salt and tortiglioni to the boiling water and cook, uncovered, until pasta is al dente. Scoop out about 1 cup (250 mL) of the pasta water and set aside. Drain pasta.

4. Return corn mixture to high heat, add 2 tbsp (25 mL) of the pasta water and heat through. Add tortiglioni and, using a wooden spoon, toss to coat evenly, adding more pasta water if necessary. Add half of the Parmigiano-Reggiano and toss well.

5. Transfer to a large serving bowl and sprinkle with remaining cheese. Serve immediately.

Variations

Substitute penne or rigatoni for the tortiglioni.

Sweet Corn

Sweet corn is a naturally occurring spontaneous genetic mutation of field corn. It is sweet rather than starchy. Although sweet corn varieties were developed and widely produced commercially in the 20th century, Native Americans actually discovered the mutation and began growing it. The Iroquois gave a variety called papoon to European colonists in 1779, and by 1921 sweet corn was listed in a Connecticut seed catalog. There are currently hundreds of sweet corn varieties, and plant breeders are developing even more. Sweet corn is not only delicious but also nutritious. While it loses some vitamin C in cooking, the process actually increases its antioxidant levels.

Perciatelli con cime di rapa e fagioli

Perciatelli with Broccoli Rabe and Cannellini Beans

Pasta, broccoli rabe and beans make a classic combination from central through to southern Italy. Thick pasta rods such as perciatelli are traditional, but in Puglia they toss orecchiette with this sauce.

Serves 4 to 6

Tips

The Italian red chile, which is medium hot and slightly sweet, is not available here, but a good substitute is the California-grown red finger chile (also called Dutch or Holland chile) or the red Fresno chile. In a pinch you can use a ripe red jalapeño or cayenne chile, both of which are much hotter. If you're using these, mince them and reduce the quantity to about ¼ tsp (1 mL).

I prefer to use Italian cannellini beans because they come from the Italian market basket, but domestic ones work well too.

6 tbsp	extra-virgin olive oil, divided	90 mL
1 tbsp	thinly sliced garlic	15 mL
¼ cup	diced onion	50 mL
	Salt and freshly ground white pepper	
1 tsp	thinly sliced fresh red finger chile (see Tips, left)	5 mL
1½ cups	1-inch (2.5 cm) slices of broccoli rabe, blanched	375 mL
1 cup	dry white Italian wine	250 mL
¾ cup	rinsed, drained canned cannellini beans	175 mL
1 tbsp	salt	15 mL
1 lb	dried perciatelli (see Variations, below)	500 g
⅔ cup	grated Pecorino Romano, divided	150 mL

1. In a covered pasta pot over high heat, bring water to a rapid boil.

2. Meanwhile, in a large sauté pan, heat 3 tbsp (45 mL) of the olive oil over low heat. Add garlic, onion and salt and pepper to taste. Cook, stirring, until onion is tender, about 3 minutes. Add chile, broccoli rabe and wine. Increase heat to medium and cook until broccoli rabe is tender and wine is reduced by half. Add beans, reduce heat to low and cook, stirring, until slightly thickened, about 6 minutes. Remove from heat and set aside.

3. While sauce is cooking, add salt and perciatelli to the boiling water and cook, uncovered, over high heat until pasta is al dente. Scoop out about 1 cup (250 mL) of the pasta water and set aside. Drain pasta.

4. Return broccoli rabe mixture to high heat and add 2 tbsp (25 mL) of the reserved pasta water. Add perciatelli and, using pasta tongs, toss to coat evenly, adding more pasta water if necessary. Add 3 tbsp (45 mL) of the Pecorino Romano and toss well.

5. Transfer to a large serving platter. Drizzle with remaining olive oil and sprinkle with remaining cheese. Serve immediately.

Variations

Perciatelli is dried long, thick bucatini-like tubular pasta from southern Italy. Substitute thick spaghetti or bucatini.

Substitute chickpeas or great Northern beans for the cannellini beans.

Perciatelli con i peperoni

Perciatelli with Bell Peppers

This is a dish for summer, when sweet bell peppers are abundant and at their best. It is typical of pasta you would eat in Rome and in parts of Italy that are further south.

Serves 4 to 6

Tips

Work like a chef. Have all your ingredients ready to go before you actually start to cook (see *Mise en Place*, page 15.)

When you combine the pasta and sauce, be sure to toss well and for as long as it takes to coat the pasta evenly with the sauce.

For best results grate the cheese yourself, but if time is at a premium, use already grated cheese. Whichever form you choose, just be sure to buy the very best Italian Pecorino Romano you can find and grate it finely to ensure you have the quantity called for in the recipe.

If you have leftovers, use them to make Frittata of Perciatelli with Bell Peppers (see Variations, page 169).

6 tbsp	extra-virgin olive oil, divided	90 mL
1 tbsp	thinly sliced garlic	15 mL
¼ cup	diced onion	50 mL
½ cup	diced green bell pepper	125 mL
½ cup	diced yellow bell pepper	125 mL
½ cup	diced red bell pepper	125 mL
¼ cup	white wine vinegar	50 mL
	Salt and freshly ground white pepper	
1 cup	dry white Italian wine	250 mL
1 tbsp	fresh oregano leaves	15 mL
1 tbsp	salt	15 mL
1 lb	dried perciatelli (see Variations, below)	500 g
⅔ cup	grated Pecorino Romano, divided	150 mL

1. In a covered pasta pot over high heat, bring water to a rapid boil.

2. Meanwhile, in a large sauté pan, heat 3 tbsp (45 mL) of the olive oil over low heat. Add garlic, onion, bell peppers, vinegar and salt and pepper to taste. Cook, stirring, until vegetables are well coated with oil and heated through, about 3 minutes. Cover and simmer until vegetables are soft and tender, about 5 minutes. Add wine and oregano and raise heat to medium. Cook until wine is reduced by half. Remove from heat and set aside.

3. While sauce is simmering, add salt and perciatelli to the boiling water and cook, uncovered, over high heat until pasta is al dente. Scoop out about 1 cup (250 mL) of the pasta water and set aside. Drain pasta.

4. Return pepper mixture to high heat. Add 2 tbsp (25 mL) of the reserved pasta water. Add perciatelli and, using pasta tongs, toss to coat evenly, adding more pasta water if necessary. Add 3 tbsp (45 mL) of the Pecorino Romano and toss well.

5. Transfer to a large serving bowl and drizzle with remaining olive oil. Sprinkle with remaining cheese and serve immediately.

Variations

Substitute thick spaghetti or bucatini for the perciatelli.

Linguine al limone e menta

Linguine with Lemon and Mint

The combination of lemon and mint is common in southern Italy, a legacy of the Moorish occupation. Today mint is not widely used in cooking, but it's a shame to waste it on garnishing drinks and desserts. It has a fragrant, distinctive flavor and a cool aftertaste that works well in savory dishes such as this pasta sauce.

Serves 4 to 6

Tips

Peel the lemon very thinly using a vegetable peeler, being careful not to include any of the bitter white pith; then julienne the peel. Use the zest of 4 large or 6 small lemons.

I like to tear the basil leaves by hand rather than slicing them, because I think they look and taste better.

If you have leftovers, use them to make leftover Frittata of Linguine with Lemon and Mint (see recipes, page 169).

1 tbsp	granulated sugar	15 mL
	Zest of 4 to 6 fresh lemons (see Tips, left)	
3 tbsp	extra-virgin olive oil	45 mL
	Salt and freshly ground white pepper	
1 cup	dry white Italian wine	250 mL
6 tbsp	hand-torn fresh mint leaves	90 mL
1 tbsp	salt	15 mL
1 lb	dried linguine (see Variation, below)	500 g
¼ cup	unsalted butter	50 mL
¾ cup	grated Parmigiano-Reggiano, divided	175 mL

1. In a covered pasta pot over high heat, bring water to a rapid boil.

2. Meanwhile, in a saucepan over high heat, bring 1 quart (1 L) of water to a boil. Add sugar, return to a boil and cook until sugar dissolves. Add strips of lemon zest and cook for 4 minutes. Drain, place lemon strips on a plate and set aside.

3. In a large sauté pan, heat oil over medium heat. Add lemon strips and salt and pepper to taste and cook, stirring, for 2 minutes. Add wine and cook until reduced by half. Stir in mint and remove pan from heat. Set aside.

4. While sauce is simmering, add salt and linguine to the boiling water and cook, uncovered, over high heat until pasta is al dente. Scoop out about 1 cup (250 mL) of the pasta water and set aside. Drain pasta.

5. Return lemon-mint mixture to high heat. Add 2 tbsp (25 mL) of the reserved pasta water and the butter and heat through. Add linguine and, using pasta tongs, toss to coat evenly, adding more pasta water if necessary. Add half of the Parmigiano-Reggiano and toss well.

6. Transfer to a large serving platter and sprinkle with remaining cheese. Serve immediately.

Variation

Substitute spaghetti for the linguine.

Mint

There are hundreds of varieties of mint. Those most often used in cooking are peppermint and spearmint. Their flavors differ slightly because menthol, a volatile oil, gives peppermint its characteristic flavor and aroma, and R-carvone is the chemical compound that predominates in spearmint. This being Italian cooking, there is a Corsican mint that is native to mainland Italy, Corsica, Sardinia and France, which derives its flavor from a chemical compound called pulegone.

Linguine con pomodori secchi

Linguine with Sun-Dried Tomatoes

* * *

This is a good dish for when tomatoes are not in season. It is colorful and easy to prepare and has bold flavors. I use the dry-packed, not oil-packed, sun-dried tomatoes. Because they will be cooked, they don't need to be fully rehydrated, just blanched in boiling water and drained.

Serves 4 to 6

Tips

Always use a large pot and plenty of water when cooking pasta. To properly cook 1 pound (500 g) of pasta, you'll need a pot with a volume of at least 8 quarts (8 L) so that you can use 6 quarts (6 L) of water.

I always use unsalted butter in my recipes because it adds fresh flavor without adding extra salt.

3 tbsp	extra-virgin olive oil	45 mL
1 tbsp	thinly sliced garlic	15 mL
1 cup	thinly sliced blanched sun-dried tomatoes, packed (see Sun-Dried Tomatoes, below)	250 mL
	Salt and freshly ground white pepper	
1½ cups	dry white Italian wine	375 mL
1 tbsp	salt	15 mL
1 lb	dried linguine (see Variation, below)	500 g
¼ cup	unsalted butter	50 mL
9 tbsp	grated Pecorino Romano, divided	135 mL

1. In a covered pasta pot over high heat, bring water to a rapid boil.

2. Meanwhile, in a large sauté pan, heat oil over medium heat. Add garlic and cook, stirring, until very lightly browned, about 3 minutes. Add sun-dried tomatoes and salt and pepper to taste and cook, stirring constantly, until mixture thickens, about 3 minutes. Do not let tomatoes burn. Add wine and cook until reduced by half. Remove from heat and set aside.

3. While sauce is simmering, add salt and linguine to the boiling water and cook, uncovered, over high heat, until pasta is al dente. Scoop out about 1 cup (250 mL) of the pasta water and set aside. Drain pasta.

4. Return tomato mixture to high heat. Add 2 tbsp (25 mL) of the reserved pasta cooking water and the butter. Add linguine and, using pasta tongs, toss to coat evenly, adding more pasta water if necessary. Add 3 tbsp (45 mL) of the Pecorino Romano and toss well.

5. Transfer to a large serving bowl and sprinkle with remaining cheese. Serve immediately.

Variation

Substitute spaghetti for the linguine.

Sun-Dried Tomatoes

Sun-dried tomatoes originated in Italy as a way to preserve fresh tomatoes for the winter. Ripe red plum tomatoes were dried in the hot sun on tile rooftops. Today they are available in two forms: packaged dry or preserved in oil. I prefer imported Italian dry-packed sun-dried tomatoes because they don't add extra oil. To cook them in a pasta sauce or use them in soups or stews, blanch them in boiling water for 4 minutes and drain. To use in dishes that do not involve additional cooking, such as salads or antipasto, cover with boiling water and let stand for 1 to 2 hours. If you prefer not to wait after adding the boiling water, cover and refrigerate overnight. Save the soaking liquid for use in recipes calling for water or stock.

Linguine alla cipolla

Linguine with Caramelized Onions

This is my pasta version of an onion tart. The combination of caramelized onions and rich cheese is synergistic, creating a lot of flavor while using very few ingredients. It's easy to make, and the linguine cooks while the onions are caramelizing.

Serves 4 to 6

Tips

For the best results grate the cheese yourself, but if time is at a premium, use already grated cheese. Whichever form you choose, just be sure to buy the very best Italian Parmigiano-Reggiano you can find and grate it finely to ensure you have the quantity called for in the recipe.

Remember, when your pasta has finished cooking, you want it to be firm and supple, not soft and mushy. It will cook a bit more from the residual heat after it is drained, and also when you add it to the sauce.

If you have leftovers, use them to make Frittata of Linguine with Caramelized Onions (see Variations, page 169).

3 tbsp	extra-virgin olive oil	45 mL
3	garlic cloves, sliced paper thin	3
	Salt and freshly ground black pepper	
1¾ cups	diced onions	425 mL
½ cup	dry white Italian wine	125 mL
1 tbsp	salt	15 mL
1 lb	dried linguine (see Variation, below)	500 g
2 tbsp	chopped Italian parsley leaves	25 mL
6 tbsp	grated Parmigiano-Reggiano, divided	90 mL

1. In a covered pasta pot over high heat, bring water to a rapid boil.

2. Meanwhile, in a large sauté pan, heat olive oil over medium heat. Add garlic and salt and pepper to taste and cook, stirring, until garlic is lightly browned, about 3 minutes. Using a slotted spoon, remove garlic and discard. Add onions and cook, stirring, until lightly browned, 10 to 15 minutes. Add wine, reduce heat to low and simmer for 1 minute to thicken slightly. Remove from heat and set aside.

3. While onions are caramelizing, add salt and linguine to the boiling water and cook, uncovered, over high heat, until pasta is al dente. Scoop out about 1 cup (250 mL) of the pasta water and set aside. Drain pasta.

4. Add ½ cup (125 mL) of the reserved pasta water to caramelized onions and raise heat to high. Add linguine and parsley and, using pasta tongs, toss to coat evenly, adding more pasta water if necessary. Add half of the Parmigiano-Reggiano and toss well.

5. Transfer to a large serving platter and sprinkle with remaining cheese and freshly ground black pepper to taste. Serve immediately.

Variation

If you don't have linguine, substitute spaghetti.

Ruote di Carro with Zucchini and Bell Peppers

This is a summertime pasta — fresh, colorful and simple. Zucchini and bell peppers go very well together, and the ruote have a fun shape.

Serves 4 to 6

Tips

Because this is a short, sturdy pasta, it is easier to toss using a wooden spoon rather than pasta tongs, which work best for longer pastas.

When you combine the pasta and sauce, be sure to toss well and for as long as it takes to coat the pasta evenly with the sauce.

3 tbsp	extra-virgin olive oil	45 mL
1 tsp	thinly sliced garlic	5 mL
¼ cup	finely diced red bell pepper	50 mL
¼ cup	finely diced yellow bell pepper	50 mL
¼ cup	finely diced green bell pepper	50 mL
½ cup	diced unpeeled zucchini	125 mL
	Salt and freshly ground black pepper	
1 cup	dry white Italian wine	250 mL
2 tbsp	hand-torn fresh basil leaves	25 mL
1 tbsp	salt	15 mL
1 lb	dried ruote di carro (see Variations, below)	500 g
2 tbsp	unsalted butter, softened	25 mL
6 tbsp	grated Parmigiano-Reggiano, divided	90 mL

1. In a covered pasta pot over high heat, bring water to a rapid boil.

2. Meanwhile, in a large sauté pan, heat oil over medium heat. Add garlic, bell peppers, zucchini and salt and pepper to taste. Cook, stirring, until vegetables are tender, about 5 minutes. Add wine and cook until reduced by half. Reduce heat, add basil and simmer slowly until slightly thickened. Remove from heat and set aside.

3. While sauce is simmering, add salt and ruote di carro to the boiling water and cook, uncovered, over high heat, until pasta is al dente. Scoop out about 1 cup (250 mL) of the pasta water and set aside. Drain pasta.

4. Return pepper mixture to high heat. Add 2 tbsp (25 mL) of the reserved pasta water and the butter and heat through. Add ruote and, using a wooden spoon, toss to coat evenly, adding more pasta water if necessary. Add half of the Parmigiano-Reggiano and toss well.

5. Transfer to a large serving platter and sprinkle with remaining cheese. Serve immediately.

Variations

Ruote di carro — literally, "cart wheels" — are also known as wagon wheels. Substitute rotelle or penne for the ruote.

Ruote di carro con cavolo verza e pomodorini

Ruote di Carro with Cabbage and Cherry Tomatoes

There are many varieties of head cabbage, but chefs favor the Savoy type for its tender texture and sweet flavor. The outside leaves are deep green, but closer to the center they become yellow and white. Using both outer and inner leaves provides a variety of colors and flavors from one vegetable.

Serves 4 to 6

Tip

Cabbage leaves have a tough vein running through the center that needs to be removed by folding each leaf in half lengthwise, then cutting out the vein.

3 tbsp	extra-virgin olive oil	45 mL
1 tsp	thinly sliced garlic	5 mL
¼ cup	diced onion	50 mL
2 cups	diced deveined inner and outer Savoy cabbage leaves (see Tip, left)	500 mL
1 cup	halved cherry tomatoes	250 mL
	Salt and freshly ground white pepper	
1½ cups	dry white Italian wine	375 mL
1 tbsp	salt	15 mL
1 lb	dried ruote di carro (see Variations, below)	500 g
6 tbsp	grated Parmigiano-Reggiano, divided	90 mL

1. In a covered pasta pot over high heat, bring water to a rapid boil.

2. Meanwhile, in a large sauté pan, heat oil over medium heat. Add garlic, onion, cabbage, tomatoes and salt and pepper to taste. Stir well. Cover and cook until vegetables are soft and tender, about 5 minutes. Uncover, add wine and cook until reduced by half. Remove from heat and set aside.

3. While sauce is simmering, add salt and ruote di carro to the boiling water and cook, uncovered, over high heat, until pasta is al dente. Scoop out about 1 cup (250 mL) of the pasta water and set aside. Drain pasta.

4. Return pan to element. Add 2 tbsp (25 mL) of the reserved pasta water to cabbage mixture and raise heat to high. Add ruote and, using a wooden spoon, toss to coat evenly, adding more pasta water if necessary. Add half of the Parmigiano-Reggiano and toss well.

5. Transfer to a large serving platter and sprinkle with remaining cheese. Serve immediately.

Variations

Ruote di carro — literally, "cart wheels" — are also known as wagon wheels. Substitute rotelle or penne for the ruote.

Ziti con porri e cipolle

Ziti with Leeks and Onions

Leeks and onions echo each other's flavors, but they are different in that leeks are sweeter and milder, and onions are sharper and stronger. In combination they complement one another. This recipe is a nice combination of contrasting flavors and it's very simple.

Serves 4 to 6

Tips

Any dry white Italian table wine will work well in this recipe. Here I'd probably use Pinot Bianco, which is a good basic dry white wine for use in Italian cooking.

Because this is a short, sturdy pasta, it is easier to toss using a wooden spoon rather than pasta tongs, which work best for longer pastas.

If you have leftovers, use them to make Oven-Browned Ziti with Leeks and Onions (see Variations, page 172).

5 tbsp	extra-virgin olive oil	75 mL
1 tsp	thinly sliced garlic	5 mL
1½ cups	diced onion	375 mL
	Salt and freshly ground white pepper	
1½ cups	diced leeks	375 mL
1 cup	dry white Italian wine (see Tips, left)	250 mL
1 tbsp	salt	15 mL
1 lb	dried cut ziti (see Variations, below)	500 g
6 tbsp	grated Parmigiano-Reggiano, divided	90 mL

1. In a covered pasta pot over high heat, bring water to a rapid boil.

2. Meanwhile, in a large sauté pan, heat oil over medium heat. Add garlic and cook, stirring, until lightly browned, 3 to 4 minutes. Using a slotted spoon, remove garlic and discard. Add onion and season to taste with salt and pepper. Cook, stirring, until tender, about 3 minutes. Add leeks and wine and cook until leeks are tender and wine is reduced by half. Remove pan from heat and set aside.

3. While sauce is cooking, add salt and ziti to the boiling water and cook, uncovered, over high heat, until pasta is al dente. Scoop out about 1 cup (250 mL) of the pasta water and set aside. Drain pasta.

4. Return pan to high heat. Add 2 tbsp (25 mL) of the reserved pasta water and heat through. Add ziti and, using a wooden spoon, toss to coat evenly, adding more pasta water if necessary. Add half of the Parmigiano-Reggiano and toss well.

5. Transfer to a large serving platter and sprinkle with remaining cheese. Serve immediately.

Variations

Cut ziti is a short tubular pasta that is very popular in southern Italy. Substitute penne or rigatoni for the ziti.

Trofie al pesto di rucola
Trofie with Arugula Pesto

Trofie come from Liguria, a region in northern Italy located on the Mediterranean Sea. This interesting shape is made by rolling short lengths of strand pasta on a flat surface until they are twisted. Trofie are 1 to 2 inches (2.5 to 5 cm) long and in North America can be found in shops specializing in pasta imported from Italy. Their shape adds interest to this recipe and helps hold the pesto sauce, but if you can't find trofie, other pastas work well too (see Variations, below). The pesto in this sauce is made from arugula rather than basil, which gives it a very different but equally delicious flavor.

Serves 4 to 6

Tips

Store any unused pesto in a covered glass jar and refrigerate for up to four days. Use as a simple sauce in which to toss hot pasta, to top Polenta Crostini (see recipe, page 353) or in other recipes calling for pesto.

If you have leftovers, use them to make Timbale of Trofie with Arugula Pesto (see Variations, page 175).

3 cups	arugula, divided	750 mL
2	garlic cloves, peeled	2
3 tbsp	pine nuts	45 mL
1 cup + 2 tbsp	grated Parmigiano-Reggiano, divided	275 mL
3/4 cup	grated Pecorino Sardo (see Variations, below)	175 mL
2/3 cup	extra-virgin olive oil	150 mL
	Salt	
1 tbsp	salt	15 mL
1 lb	dried trofie (see Variations, below)	500 g

1. In a covered pasta pot over high heat, bring water to a rapid boil.

2. In a large pot of boiling salted water, place 2½ cups (625 mL) of the arugula. Cook for 10 seconds. Drain and immediately immerse in a basin of ice water. Let cool for 3 minutes, drain and squeeze dry.

3. In a food processor fitted with a metal blade, combine blanched arugula, garlic, pine nuts, ¾ cup (175 mL) of the Parmigiano-Reggiano and the Pecorino Sardo. Pulse for 3 seconds. Add oil in a steady stream and pulse until arugula is roughly puréed (do not overprocess). Add salt to taste and pulse again. Set aside.

4. Add 1 tbsp (15 mL) salt and trofie to the boiling water and cook, uncovered, until pasta is al dente. Scoop out about 1 cup (250 mL) of the pasta water and set aside. Drain pasta.

5. Add 2 tbsp (25 mL) of the reserved pasta water to a large sauté pan over medium heat. Add 1 cup (250 mL) of the arugula pesto and simmer for 2 minutes. Add trofie and, using a wooden spoon, toss to coat evenly, adding more pasta water if necessary. Add remaining ½ cup (125 mL) fresh arugula and 3 tbsp (45 mL) of the remaining cheese. Toss well. Transfer to a large serving platter and sprinkle with remaining cheese. Serve immediately.

Variations

If Pecorino Sardo is not available, substitute Pecorino Romano. Substitute strozzapretti or penne for the trofie.

> ### Pecorino Sardo
> Pecorino Sardo is a sheep's-milk cheese made in Sardinia. It can be soft or hard, depending upon how long it is aged. There are basically two types of Pecorino Sardo: dolce (mild), which is aged for 20 to 60 days, and maturo (mature or aged), which is aged for 4 to 12 months and is sharp and tangy. The longer-aged cheeses become hard and granular and are similar in flavor to Pecorino Romano.

Trofie alle olive nere e verdi

Trofie with Oil-Cured Black and Green Olives

Because trofie come from Liguria, you'll achieve the best results by using oil-cured black and green olives from the same region. When the ingredients come from a particular region, they give a dish its own identity. That said, you will also achieve good results using other top-quality olives. Try to stay within the Italian market basket — green Cerignola olives from Puglia and black olives from Tuscany or Sicily are also good choices.

Serves 4 to 6

Tips

Don't scrimp on ingredients. Always buy the best quality you can find and afford. It will make a big difference to the results you produce.

If you have leftovers, use them to make Timbale of Trofie with Oil-Cured Black and Green Olives (see recipe, page 175).

3 tbsp	extra-virgin olive oil	45 mL
1 tsp	thinly sliced garlic	5 mL
¾ cup	halved cherry tomatoes	175 mL
	Salt and freshly ground white pepper	
½ cup	chopped pitted oil-cured green olives	125 mL
½ cup	chopped pitted oil-cured black olives	125 mL
1 cup	dry white Italian wine	250 mL
1 tbsp	salt	15 mL
1 lb	dried trofie (see Variations, below)	500 g
6 tbsp	grated Parmigiano-Reggiano, divided	90 mL

1. In a covered pasta pot over high heat, bring water to a rapid boil.

2. Meanwhile, in a large sauté pan, heat olive oil over medium heat. Add garlic and cook, stirring, until lightly browned, about 3 minutes. Using a slotted spoon, remove garlic and discard. Add tomatoes and season to taste with salt and pepper. Reduce heat to low, add olives and wine and stir. Cover and simmer until tomatoes are tender and wine is reduced by half, about 5 minutes. Remove from heat and set aside.

3. While sauce is simmering, add salt and trofie to the boiling water and cook, uncovered, over high heat until pasta is al dente. Scoop out about 1 cup (250 mL) of the pasta water and set aside. Drain pasta.

4. Return sauté pan to element and increase heat to high. Add 2 tbsp (25 mL) of the reserved pasta water and the trofie and, using a wooden spoon, toss to coat evenly, adding more pasta water if necessary. Add half of the Parmigiano-Reggiano and toss well.

5. Transfer to a large serving platter and sprinkle with remaining cheese. Serve immediately.

Variations

Trofie are a thin, tightly rolled pasta. Substitute strozzapretti or penne for the trofie.

Trofie with Spicy Fava Beans

Fresh fava beans are often hard to find, even in season, so I asked myself one day, "What would Italians living in South America use to recreate recipes from home if there were no fava beans available?" I suspect they would use fresh lima beans, which are native to South and Meso-America. So if you can't find fresh favas, use fresh lima beans instead.

Serves 4 to 6

Tip

The Italian red chile, which is medium hot and slightly sweet, is not available here, but a good substitute is the California-grown red finger chile (also called Dutch or Holland chile) or the red Fresno chile. In a pinch you can use a ripe red jalapeño or cayenne chile, both of which are much hotter. If you're using these, mince them and reduce the quantity to about ¼ tsp (1 mL).

5 tbsp	extra-virgin olive oil	75 mL
1 tsp	thinly sliced garlic	5 mL
1 tbsp	thinly sliced fresh red finger chile (see Tip, left)	15 mL
1 cup	halved cherry tomatoes	250 mL
1½ cups	blanched peeled fresh fava beans (see Variations, below)	375 mL
	Salt and freshly ground white pepper	
1 cup	dry white Italian wine	250 mL
1 tbsp	salt	15 mL
1 lb	dried trofie (see Variations, below)	500 g
6 tbsp	grated Parmigiano-Reggiano, divided	90 mL

1. In a covered pasta pot over high heat, bring water to a rapid boil.

2. Meanwhile, in a large sauté pan, heat oil over medium heat. Add garlic and cook, stirring, until lightly browned, about 3 minutes. Using a slotted spoon, remove garlic and discard. Add chile, tomatoes and fava beans and stir. Season to taste with salt and pepper. Add wine and cover. Reduce heat to low and simmer until tomatoes are soft and wine is somewhat reduced, about 5 minutes. Remove from heat and set aside.

3. While sauce is simmering, add salt and trofie to the boiling water and cook, uncovered, over high heat until pasta is al dente. Scoop out about 1 cup (250 mL) of the pasta water and set aside. Drain pasta.

4. Return tomato-bean mixture to high heat, add 2 tbsp (25 mL) of the reserved pasta water and heat through. Add trofie and, using a wooden spoon, toss to coat evenly, adding more pasta water if necessary. Add half of the Parmigiano-Reggiano and toss well.

5. Transfer to a large serving platter and sprinkle with remaining cheese. Serve immediately.

Variations

If fresh fava beans are not available, substitute fresh lima beans but do not peel.

Substitute penne or strozzapretti for the trofie.

Orecchiette con rucola e pomodoro

Orecchiette with Arugula and Tomatoes

This dish is also known as tricolor recchie (recchie al tre colori) because it contains white orecchiette, green arugula and red tomatoes — the colors of the Italian flag.

Serves 4 to 6

3 tbsp	extra-virgin olive oil	45 mL
1 tbsp	thinly sliced garlic	15 mL
1½ cups	canned diced Italian tomatoes, drained	375 mL
	Salt and freshly ground white pepper	
1 tbsp	salt	15 mL
1 lb	dried orecchiette (see Variation, below)	500 g
1½ cups	sliced (2 inches/5 cm) arugula, packed (see Tips, left)	375 mL
½ cup	grated Pecorino Romano, divided	125 mL

Tips

If you can find it, purchase wild arugula from a farmers' market. It has a particularly bold flavor that works well in this recipe. But if domestic arugula is the only kind available, by all means use it — you'll still produce a delicious pasta.

Remember, when your pasta has finished cooking, you want it to be firm and supple, not soft and mushy. It will cook a bit more from the residual heat after it is drained and also when you add it to the sauce.

If you have leftovers, use them to make Bell Peppers Filled with Orecchiette with Arugula and Tomatoes (see Variations, page 170).

1. In a covered pasta pot over high heat, bring water to a rapid boil.

2. Meanwhile, in a large sauté pan, heat oil over medium heat. Add garlic and cook, stirring, until translucent but not browned, 2 to 3 minutes. Add tomatoes and salt and pepper to taste. Reduce heat to low and simmer until sauce thickens slightly, about 10 minutes. Remove from heat and set aside.

3. While sauce is simmering, add salt and orecchiette to the boiling water and cook, uncovered, over high heat until pasta is al dente. Scoop out about 1 cup (250 mL) of the pasta water and set aside. Drain pasta.

4. Return tomato mixture to high heat. Add 2 tbsp (25 mL) of the reserved pasta water and heat through. Add orecchiette and, using a wooden spoon, toss to coat evenly, adding more pasta water if necessary. Add arugula and cook just until it wilts, about 30 seconds. Taste for seasoning, adding salt and pepper if necessary. Add half of the Pecorino Romano and toss well.

5. Transfer to a large serving bowl and sprinkle with remaining cheese. Serve immediately.

Variation

Apulia (Puglia, in Italian) in southeastern Italy lays claim to being the origin of orecchiette, a rustic ear-shaped pasta. Substitute penne for the orecchiette.

Arugula

Arugula (*rucola* in Italian) is native to the Mediterranean, where it has been grown since Roman times; the Romans considered it an aphrodisiac and its seeds were used for flavoring oils. Before the 1990s it was usually harvested in the wild, but now it is widely cultivated. Unlike lettuce, arugula has a strong, peppery taste, which is more pronounced in wild varieties. It is used in salads, with pasta, on pizzas and to make pesto. In Italy a digestive alcohol called rucolino is made from arugula and consumed in small quantities after meals.

Strozzapretti with Tuscan Kale

Kale and pasta is a common combination in Italy but relatively unusual elsewhere. Tuscan kale, or black kale, has a deep, earthy flavor that is very comforting. It is also loaded with nutrients. Italians call it black cabbage (cavalo), *although its crinkled leaves are deep blue-green, not black, and it does not develop a head like cabbage.*

Serves 4 to 6

Tips

To remove the tough ribs from the kale, fold each leaf in half lengthwise and slice off the rib with a sharp knife.

Strozzapretti, meaning "priest strangler," is a hand-rolled tubular pasta about 4 inches (10 cm) long that originated in Emilia-Romagna, Tuscany and Umbria. It comes both fresh and dried, but fresh strozzapretti is rarely available outside Italy. The name implies a couple of possibilities: that the pasta was so delicious some gluttonous priest choked on it, or that the housewife making it was so angry she could choke a priest in the same way she "choked" or shaped the pasta.

3 tbsp	extra-virgin olive oil	45 mL
1 tsp	thinly sliced garlic	5 mL
½ cup	halved cherry tomatoes	125 mL
1½ cups	diced deribbed Tuscan kale (see Tips, left)	375 mL
	Salt and freshly ground white pepper	
1 tbsp	salt	15 mL
1 lb	dried strozzapretti (see Variations, below)	500 g
6 tbsp	grated Parmigiano-Reggiano, divided	90 mL

1. In a covered pasta pot over high heat, bring water to a rapid boil.

2. Meanwhile, in a large sauté pan, heat oil over medium heat. Add garlic and cook, stirring, until lightly browned, 3 to 4 minutes. Remove garlic and discard. Add tomatoes, kale, and salt and pepper to taste. Reduce heat to low, cover and cook until kale is soft and tender, about 10 minutes.

3. While kale is cooking, add salt and strozzapretti to the boiling water and cook, uncovered, over high heat, until pasta is al dente. Scoop out about 1 cup (250 mL) of the pasta water and set aside. Drain.

4. Add ¼ cup (50 mL) of the pasta water to kale and raise heat to high. Add strozzapretti and, using a wooden spoon, toss to coat evenly, adding more pasta water if necessary. Add half of the Parmigiano-Reggiano and toss well.

5. Transfer to a large serving platter and sprinkle with remaining cheese. Serve immediately.

Variations

Substitute penne for the strozzapretti.

Substitute Swiss chard for the Tuscan kale.

Tuscan Kale

Also known as *cavalo nero* (black cabbage), *lacinato* (crinkly), dinosaur or dino kale and black palm, this member of the cabbage family (*Brassica oleracea*) has ancient roots. Curly and flat-leafed cabbage varieties existed in the fourth century B.C. in Greece and are considered the ancestors of today's cabbages and kale. Tuscan kale was developed in Tuscany in the 18th century. It has crinkled deep blue-green leaves and grows 3 to 4 feet tall at maturity. The leaves have a tough central rib that should be cut out and discarded. The flavor has been described as sweet and meaty. Tuscan kale provides vitamins A and C, calcium, iron and alpha-linolenic acid, as well as antioxidants.

Spaghettini al pomodoro e basilico

Spaghettini with Tomatoes and Basil

This is a simple pasta that is easy to make and very quick. The thin spaghettini cooks quickly and the results are very tasty. This recipe is another example of how Italians use the same ingredients over and over but combine them in different ways for different end results.

Serves 4 to 6

Tips

For best results grate the cheese yourself, but if time is at a premium, use already grated cheese. Whichever form you choose, just be sure to buy the very best Italian Parmigiano-Reggiano you can find and grate it finely to ensure you have the quantity called for in the recipe.

If you have leftovers, use them to make Soufflé of Spaghettini with Tomatoes and Basil (see Variations, page 171).

6 tbsp	extra-virgin olive oil	90 mL
1 tsp	thinly sliced garlic	5 mL
2 cups	canned diced Italian tomatoes, drained	500 mL
	Salt and freshly ground white pepper	
¼ cup	hand-torn fresh basil leaves	50 mL
1 tbsp	salt	15 mL
1 lb	dried spaghettini (see Variation, below)	500 g
3 tbsp	grated Parmigiano-Reggiano	45 mL
	plus additional for passing at the table	

1. In a covered pasta pot over high heat, bring water to a rapid boil.

2. Meanwhile, in a large sauté pan, heat oil over medium heat. Add garlic and cook, stirring, until translucent but not browned, about 3 minutes. Using a slotted spoon, remove garlic and discard. Add tomatoes, salt and pepper to taste, and basil. Stir well. Simmer until tomatoes are cooked through, about 5 minutes. Remove from heat and set aside.

3. While sauce is simmering, add salt and spaghettini to the boiling water and cook, uncovered, over high heat until pasta is al dente. Scoop out about 1 cup (250 mL) of the pasta water and set aside. Drain pasta.

4. Return tomato mixture to high heat. Add ¼ cup (50 mL) of the reserved pasta water. Add spaghettini and, using pasta tongs, toss to coat evenly, adding more pasta water if necessary. Add Parmigiano-Reggiano and toss well.

5. Transfer to a large serving platter and serve immediately. Accompany with a dish of Parmigiano-Reggiano.

Variation

Substitute spaghetti for the spaghettini.

Spaghetti ai capperi e limone

Spaghetti with Capers and Lemon

If you like the zing of salt, this dish is for you. The capers and the cheese are both salty, while the lemon zest, white wine and fresh tomato add acid, which balances the flavors.

Serves 4 to 6

Tips

To zest the lemons for this recipe you can peel the thin outer rind with a vegetable peeler and mince. Or you can use a sharp-toothed hand-held grater to remove the skin, being careful not to capture any of the white pith, which is bitter.

If you have leftovers, use them to make Soufflé of Spaghetti with Capers and Lemon (see recipe, page 171).

3 tbsp	extra-virgin olive oil	45 mL
3	cloves garlic, sliced paper thin	3
	Salt and freshly ground black pepper	
	Zest of 6 lemons (see Tips, left)	
2 tbsp	tiny (nonpareil) capers, drained	25 mL
2	medium unpeeled ripe tomatoes, diced	2
1 cup	dry white Italian wine	250 mL
1 tbsp	salt	15 mL
1 lb	dried spaghetti	500 g
6 tbsp	grated Parmigiano-Reggiano, divided	90 mL

1. In a covered pasta pot over high heat, bring water to a rapid boil.

2. Meanwhile, in a large sauté pan, heat oil over medium heat. Add garlic and salt and pepper to taste. Cook, stirring, until garlic is lightly browned, about 3 minutes. Using a slotted spoon, remove garlic and discard. Add lemon zest, capers and tomatoes and stir well. Reduce heat to low, cover and simmer until vegetables are tender and soft, about 5 minutes. Uncover and add wine. Cook, uncovered, until reduced by half. Remove from heat and set aside.

3. While sauce is simmering, add salt and spaghetti to the boiling water. Cook, uncovered, over high heat until pasta is al dente. Scoop out about 1 cup (250 mL) of the pasta water and set aside. Drain pasta.

4. Return sauté pan to element. Add 2 tbsp (25 mL) of the reserved pasta water and raise heat to high. Add spaghetti and, using pasta tongs, toss to coat evenly, adding more pasta water if necessary. Add half of the Parmigiano-Reggiano and toss well.

5. Transfer to a large serving platter and sprinkle with remaining cheese. Serve immediately.

Variation

Add 2 tbsp (25 mL) finely chopped pitted black or green Italian olives when adding the capers.

Capers

Capers, which have been used in cooking for millennia, are the immature flower buds of a spiny perennial shrub native to the Mediterranean, *Capparis spinosa*. Today they are readily available pickled in vinegar or preserved in granular salt. Like olives, capers need curing to develop their characteristic strong, sharp flavor, which comes from mustard oil present in the plant tissues. Generally, the smaller the caper, the more valuable it is; nonpareil (about $1/4$ inch or 0.5 cm) is the smallest grade. In addition to caper buds, caper fruits (also known as caper berries), which are the size of small olives, are also eaten pickled.

Spaghetti alla Puttanesca

What a rude name for a delicious pasta! In Italian, puttana means "prostitute." As if that were not controversial enough, in Italy there is endless argument on exactly how to properly prepare this well-known dish. This much is certain: it originated either in Rome or further south; it uses ingredients native to the region; and it is spicy, salty and bold. It is not strictly meatless, but it would be silly to put Spaghetti alla Puttancesca in the seafood chapter, because it contains such a small amount of anchovies.

Serves 4 to 6

Tips

To remove excess salt from canned anchovies, place them in a fine-mesh sieve and rinse them briefly under gently running cold water. Drain and pat dry with paper toweling.

Always use a large pot and plenty of water when cooking pasta. To properly cook 1 pound (500 g) of pasta, you'll need a pot with a volume of at least 8 quarts (8 L) so that you can use 6 quarts (6 L) of water.

3 tbsp	extra-virgin olive oil	45 mL
2	garlic cloves, sliced paper thin	2
Pinch	finely chopped red finger chile	Pinch
2 tbsp	finely minced rinsed anchovies (see Tips, left)	10 mL
5	ripe unpeeled tomatoes, diced	5
3 tbsp	minced pitted oil-cured black olives	45 mL
1½ tbsp	minced tiny (nonpareil) capers	22 mL
1 tbsp	salt	45 mL
1 lb	dried spaghetti	500 g
1 tbsp	roughly chopped Italian parsley leaves	15 mL
6 tbsp	grated Parmigiano-Reggiano, divided	90 mL

1. In a covered pasta pot over high heat, bring water to a rapid boil.

2. Meanwhile, in a large sauté pan, heat oil over medium heat. Add garlic and cook, stirring, until lightly browned, about 3 minutes. Add chile, anchovies, tomatoes, olives and capers. Simmer until vegetables are soft and tender, about 10 minutes. Remove from heat.

3. While sauce is simmering, add salt and spaghetti to boiling water and cook, uncovered, over high heat until pasta is al dente. Scoop out about 1 cup (250 mL) of the pasta water and set aside. Drain pasta.

4. Return sauté pan to element. Add 2 tbsp (25 mL) of the reserved pasta water and raise heat to high. Add spaghetti and, using pasta tongs, toss to coat evenly, adding more pasta water if necessary. Add parsley and half of the Parmigiano-Reggiano. Toss well.

5. Transfer to a large serving platter and sprinkle with remaining cheese. Serve immediately.

Vermicelli alla melanzane e mozzarella

Vermicelli with Eggplant and Mozzarella

Vermicelli is thinner than spaghettini, which is thinner than spaghetti — a good example of how Italians change the width of pasta by a fraction of a centimeter and then give it a different name. That being said, vermicelli cooks very fast, and its delicacy lends itself to the fresh flavors in this recipe.

Serves 4 to 6

Tips

Buffalo mozzarella is imported from Italy and is relatively expensive, but it is worth experiencing once in a while. You can always substitute the readily available fresh cow's-milk mozzarella (fior di latte).

Vermicelli is thin Italian strand pasta, thinner than spaghettini. Be sure not to confuse it with thin Asian rice noodles, which often use the same name.

If you have leftovers, use them to make Soufflé of Vermicelli with Eggplant and Mozzarella (see Variations, page 171).

3 tbsp	extra-virgin olive oil	45 mL
3	cloves garlic, sliced paper thin	3
	Salt and freshly ground white pepper	
2 cups	diced peeled eggplant	500 mL
4	ripe unpeeled tomatoes, diced	4
3	hand-torn fresh basil leaves	3
1 cup	dry white Italian wine	250 mL
1 tbsp	salt	15 mL
1 lb	dried Italian vermicelli (see Variations, below)	500 g
3 tbsp	grated Parmigiano-Reggiano	45 mL
¾ cup	diced mozzarella di bufala (see Tips, left)	175 mL

1. In a covered pasta pot over high heat, bring water to a rapid boil.

2. Meanwhile, in a large sauté pan, heat oil over medium heat. Add garlic and salt and pepper to taste and cook, stirring, until garlic is lightly browned, about 3 minutes. Using a slotted spoon, remove garlic and discard. Add eggplant, tomatoes and basil. Cover and simmer until sauce thickens, about 10 minutes. Uncover, add wine and simmer until wine is reduced by half.

3. While sauce is simmering, add salt and vermicelli to the boiling water and cook, uncovered, over high heat until pasta is al dente. Scoop out about 1 cup (250 mL) of the pasta water and set aside. Drain pasta.

4. Add 2 tbsp (25 mL) of the reserved pasta water to sauté pan and raise heat to high. Add vermicelli and, using pasta tongs, toss to coat evenly, adding more pasta water if necessary. Add Parmigiano-Reggiano and toss well.

5. Transfer to a large serving platter and sprinkle with mozzarella di bufala. Serve immediately.

Variations

Substitute spaghettini or angel hair for the vermicelli.

Vermicelli alla marinara

Vermicelli alla Marinara

This is a clean, simple, fresh-tasting and colorful pasta with tomato sauce. Most of the preparation time is devoted to cooking the sauce.

Serves 4 to 6

Tips

Always use a large pot and plenty of water when cooking pasta. To properly cook 1 pound (500 g) of pasta, you'll need a pot with a volume of at least 8 quarts (8 L) so that you can use 6 quarts (6 L) of water.

If you have leftovers, use them to make Soufflé of Vermicelli alla Marinara (see Variations, page 171).

3 tbsp	extra-virgin olive oil	45 mL
2	cloves garlic, thinly sliced	2
2 cups	ripe tomatoes, diced	500 mL
	Salt and freshly ground white pepper	
1 tbsp	salt	15 mL
1 lb	dried Italian vermicelli (see Variation, below)	500 g
3 tbsp	chopped Italian parsley	45 mL

1. In a covered pasta pot over high heat, bring water to a rapid boil.

2. Meanwhile, in a large sauté pan, heat oil over medium heat. Add garlic and cook, stirring, until translucent but not browned, about 3 minutes. Add tomatoes, season to taste with salt and pepper and stir. Cook, stirring occasionally, until thickened and sauce coats the back of a spoon, 5 to 6 minutes.

3. While sauce is simmering, add salt and vermicelli to the boiling water and cook, uncovered, over high heat until pasta is al dente. Scoop out about 1 cup (250 mL) of the pasta water and set aside. Drain pasta.

4. Add 2 tbsp (25 mL) of the reserved pasta water to tomato mixture and raise heat to high. Add vermicelli and, using pasta tongs, toss to coat evenly, adding more pasta water if necessary. Add parsley and toss well.

5. Transfer to a large serving platter and serve immediately.

Variation

Vermicelli is thin Italian strand pasta, thinner than spaghettini. Be sure not to confuse it with thin Asian rice noodles, which often use the same name. Instead of the vermicelli, substitute spaghettini.

Pasta with Poultry and Meat: Sauces with Substance

Almost Al Dente

All the pasta in this chapter is cooked a bit less than usual — to almost al dente — because it is simmered for about 3 minutes with the sauce while being tossed with the pasta. During this time it cooks further and the more intense meaty flavors meld with the pasta.

Italian pasta cuisine has just a handful of sauces made with meat, sausage and cured meats that are familiar outside Italy. These include amatriciana (see recipe, page 126), bolognese (see recipe, page 248) and carbonara (see recipe, page 125). Poultry sauces are even less familiar because there are fewer of them in the traditional repertory. In Italy chickens, turkey, duck and game birds were rarely used to make pasta sauces. These meats, along with game, were considered important main courses. However, a couple of my poultry sauces are traditional: Bigoli with Venetian Duck Ragù (page 106) and Pappardelle with Chicken Livers (page 103), while others are my concession to the 21st century. Chicken is extremely popular; in my restaurant, if I didn't offer pasta sauces made with chicken, I can't imagine what would happen.

Less Becomes More

Historically, what was true of Italy's cuisine was once true for the Western world. The aristocrats — kings, noblemen, clergy — had wealth and households with cooks, so their food was always more refined and costly. On the other hand, people of lesser means had to find ways to eat meat in the quantities they could afford. A little bit of meat with pasta as the primary plate was an ideal solution. Many of the recipes in this chapter use small amounts of highly flavorful cured meats such as sausage, guanciale, mortadella, pancetta, prosciutto and speck. In some recipes the serving platter is lined with thinly sliced cured meats such as prosciutto and mortadella. This adds a new and different dimension of flavor to a dish because something special happens when you pile hot sauced pasta onto room-temperature prosciutto. The prosciutto (or other cured meat) releases its flavor and aroma quite differently than it does when it is cooked in the dish. Just remember, whether you're making a sauce using poultry, meat or sausage, as always, the pasta is still the star and the sauce takes second billing.

The Short and the Long of Sauces

The recipes in this chapter are arranged as follows: poultry sauces (chicken, duck and turkey), then meat sauces (beef, lamb, veal, pork and pork sausage and cured pork in several varieties). In most cases they take 30 to 45 minutes to prepare from start to finish.

The ragùs and sugos are special. A few take about three hours, but for most of that time the sauce cooks unattended in a slow oven or is barely simmering on the range top. Trust me, the resulting intensely flavorful, very authentic ragù is worth the wait. Be aware that you can double the recipes for ragù and sugo and freeze them for up to a month. My suggestion is to save the long-cooking sauces for the weekend, when you have time, and double the recipe so you can freeze half for another day. These sauces are also suited to being cooked one day and served the next. The flavor deepens during the period in the refrigerator. In addition, the fat rises to the surface, where it solidifies and can be easily removed and discarded.

Fettuccine con sugo di pollo e fave

Fettuccine with Chicken-Tomato Sauce and Fava Beans

This is a recipe I created because everyone loves fettuccine and chicken, and I love fava beans.

Serves 4 to 6

Tips

To prepare fennel for this recipe, cut off the feathery fronds and save for garnish; cut off the stems and save for flavoring soup or stock. Trim the root end off the bulb and discard. Trim and discard any stems remaining on the bulb. Cut the bulb in half and remove the tough core. Rinse bulb halves under running water. The fennel is now ready to dice.

To blanch the fava beans for use in this recipe, bring a large pot of lightly salted water to a boil. Cook peeled fava beans for 1 minute, then drain and rinse under cold running water. This sets the color of the beans and preserves it during cooking.

If you have leftovers, use them to make Timbale of Fettuccine with Chicken-Tomato Sauce and Fava Beans (see Variations, page 175).

3 tbsp	extra-virgin olive oil	45 mL
¼ cup	each finely diced onion, peeled celery and trimmed fennel bulb (see Tips, left)	50 mL
1 tsp	paper-thin garlic slices	5 mL
1 cup	diced skinless, boneless chicken thigh meat (about 6 oz/175 g)	250 mL
¼ cup	dry white Italian wine	50 mL
3 cups	canned crushed Italian tomatoes	500 mL
	Salt and freshly ground black pepper	
1 tbsp	salt	15 mL
1 lb	dried fettuccine (see Variations, below)	500 g
¾ cup	peeled fava beans, blanched (see Tips, left)	175 mL
¾ cup	grated Parmigiano-Reggiano, divided	175 mL

1. In a covered pasta pot over high heat, bring water to a rapid boil.

2. Meanwhile, in a large sauté pan, heat oil over high heat until hot but not smoking. Add onion, celery, fennel and garlic and cook, stirring, until golden, about 5 minutes. Stir in chicken and wine. Reduce heat to medium and simmer until wine has reduced by half. Add tomatoes, reduce heat to low and simmer until thickened, about 20 minutes. Season to taste with salt and pepper. Remove from heat and set aside.

3. While sauce is simmering, add salt and fettuccine to boiling water and cook, uncovered, over high heat, until pasta is almost al dente. Scoop out about 1 cup (250 mL) of the pasta water and set aside. Drain pasta.

4. Return sauté pan to medium heat. Add 2 tbsp (25 mL) of the reserved pasta water and fava beans and simmer until heated through, about 3 minutes. Add fettuccine and cook for about 3 minutes, until pasta is al dente, using pasta tongs to toss and coat evenly, adding more pasta water if necessary. Add half of the Parmigiano-Reggiano and toss. Transfer to a serving bowl and sprinkle with remaining cheese. Serve immediately.

Variations

If fresh fava beans are unavailable, substitute fresh blanched green beans cut in 1-inch (2.5 cm) lengths, or fresh young lima beans (no need to peel).

Substitute spaghetti or linguine for the fettuccine.

Radiatori al petto di pollo e broccoli

Radiatori with Chicken Breast and Broccoli

This dish is not traditionally Italian, but I developed the recipe because most people enjoy eating chicken breast. The sauce doesn't contain cream, so it is quite light and, when combined with broccoli, very nutritious. Radiatori (the plural of radiatore, or radiator) are short, chunky pasta with rippled ridges that resemble radiator grills.

Serves 4 to 6

Tips

Three medium-large boneless, skinless chicken breasts will yield about 1½ cups (375 mL) of diced chicken.

Work like a chef. Have all your ingredients ready to go before you actually start to cook (see *Mise en Place*, page 15).

3 tbsp	extra-virgin olive oil	45 mL
¼ cup	finely diced prosciutto	50 mL
¼ cup	finely diced onion	50 mL
1½ cups	quartered broccoli florets	375 mL
1½ cups	diced skinless, boneless chicken breast	375 mL
	Salt and freshly ground black pepper	
1 cup	dry white Italian wine	250 mL
1 tbsp	salt	15 mL
1 lb	dried radiatori (see Variations, below)	500 g
¾ cup	grated Parmigiano-Reggiano, divided	175 mL

1. In a covered pasta pot over high heat, bring water to a rapid boil.

2. Meanwhile, in a large sauté pan, heat oil over medium heat. Add prosciutto and onion and, cook, stirring, until prosciutto is cooked through and onion is soft and tender, about 5 minutes. Stir in broccoli and chicken and season to taste with salt and pepper. Cook, stirring, until broccoli is tender and chicken is cooked through, about 10 minutes. Add wine and cook until reduced by half. Remove from heat and set aside.

3. While sauce is simmering, add salt and radiatori to boiling water and cook, uncovered, over high heat, until pasta is almost al dente. Scoop out about 1 cup (250 mL) of the pasta water and set aside. Drain pasta.

4. Return sauté pan to medium heat. Add 2 tbsp (25 mL) of the pasta cooking water and heat through. Add radiatori and continue to cook for about 3 minutes, until pasta is al dente, using a wooden spoon to toss and coat evenly, adding more pasta water if necessary. Add half of the Parmigiano-Reggiano and toss well.

5. Transfer to a large serving bowl and sprinkle with remaining cheese. Serve immediately.

Variations

Substitute penne, conchiglie or ruote for the radiatori.

Orecchiette al petto di pollo e funghi

Orecchiette with Chicken Breast and Mushrooms

The traditional shape of orecchiette ("little ears") is attributed to Puglia; it is made both fresh and dried. In this recipe I have combined a traditional pasta with flavors and ingredients that are popular today.

Serves 4 to 6

Tips

To dice thinly sliced pancetta, stack the slices on top of each other and cut them in half lengthwise, then in half again. Slice the pieces horizontally into ¼-inch (0.5 cm) pieces. You can also purchase pancetta in a chunk, cut it into ¼-inch (0.5 cm) slices, julienne those slices, then dice them ¼ inch (0.5 cm) thick or buy it already diced.

Cremini mushrooms are sometimes labeled "baby bella." To cut them attractively into eight equal pieces, cut each mushroom in half lengthwise, cut each half in half, then cut each quarter in half.

If you have leftovers, use them to make Baked Orecchiette with Chicken Breast and Mushrooms (see Variations, page 168).

3 tbsp	extra-virgin olive oil	45 mL
¼ cup	finely diced pancetta (see Tips, left)	50 mL
¼ cup	finely diced onion	50 mL
2½ cups	fresh cremini mushrooms, cut into 8 equal pieces (see Tips, left)	625 mL
	Salt and freshly ground white pepper	
1½ cups	diced skinless chicken breast	375 mL
1 cup	dry red Italian wine	250 mL
1 tbsp	salt	15 mL
1 lb	dried orecchiette (see Variation, below)	500 g
¾ cup	grated Parmigiano-Reggiano, divided	175 mL

1. In a covered pasta pot over high heat, bring water to a rapid boil.

2. Meanwhile, in a large sauté pan, heat oil over medium heat. Add pancetta and onion. Cook, stirring, until onion is translucent, about 3 minutes. Add mushrooms and cook, stirring, until tender, about 7 minutes. Season to taste with salt and pepper. Stir in chicken and increase heat to high. Add wine and cook until reduced by three-quarters. Reduce heat to low and simmer until chicken is cooked through. Remove from heat and set aside.

3. While sauce is simmering, add salt and orecchiette to the boiling water and cook, uncovered, over high heat until pasta is almost al dente. Scoop out about 1 cup (250 mL) of the pasta water and set aside. Drain pasta.

4. Return sauté pan to medium heat. Add 2 tbsp (25 mL) of the reserved pasta water and heat through. Add orecchiette and continue to cook for about 3 minutes, until pasta is al dente, using a wooden spoon to toss and coat evenly, adding more pasta water if necessary. Add half of the Parmigiano-Reggiano and toss well.

5. Transfer to a serving bowl. Sprinkle with remaining cheese and serve immediately.

Variation

Substitute penne for the orecchiette.

Pappardelle al fegatini di pollo

Pappardelle with Chicken Livers

This is an authentic sauce that is typical of Tuscan cooking — simple peasant food. Pappardelle is a Tuscan ribbon pasta that comes in both fresh and dry versions. The fresh version usually has fluted edges and the dried version has straight edges. The name comes from the Italian verb *pappare*, "to gobble up." It's easy to imagine that good but thrifty cooks created this dish; it's a way to use the liver after the chicken has been roasted for the main course.

Serves 4 to 6

Tips

Be sure to use canned Italian tomatoes, not those grown domestically, in this recipe — for their deep flavor as well as their authenticity.

For best results grate the cheese yourself, but if time is at a premium, use already grated cheese. Whichever form you choose, just be sure to buy the very best Italian Parmigiano-Reggiano you can find and grate it finely to ensure you have the quantity called for in the recipe.

3 tbsp	extra-virgin olive oil	45 mL
¼ cup	finely diced pancetta	50 mL
¼ cup	finely diced onion	50 mL
¼ cup	finely diced peeled celery	50 mL
⅔ cup	chopped trimmed chicken livers (about 6 oz/175 g)	150 mL
½ cup	dry red Italian wine	125 mL
2 cups	canned crushed Italian tomatoes (see Tips, left)	500 mL
2 tbsp	hand-torn fresh sage leaves	25 mL
	Salt and freshly ground black pepper	
1 tbsp	salt	15 mL
1 lb	dried pappardelle (see Variations, below)	500 g
¾ cup	grated Parmigiano-Reggiano, divided	175 mL

1. In a covered pasta pot over high heat, bring water to a rapid boil.

2. Meanwhile, in a large sauté pan, heat oil over medium heat. Add pancetta, onion and celery and cook, stirring, until vegetables are soft and tender, about 5 minutes. Add chicken livers and cook, stirring, until cooked through and no pink remains, about 10 minutes. Add wine and cook until reduced by half. Stir in tomatoes and sage and reduce heat to low. Season to taste with salt and pepper. Simmer, uncovered, until sauce thickens, about 10 minutes. Remove from heat and set aside.

3. While sauce is simmering, add salt and pappardelle to the boiling water and cook, uncovered, over high heat until pasta is almost al dente. Scoop out about 1 cup (250 mL) of the pasta water and set aside. Drain pasta.

4. Return sauté pan to medium heat. Add 2 tbsp (25 mL) of the reserved pasta water and heat through. Add pappardelle and continue to cook for about 3 minutes, until pasta is al dente, using pasta tongs to toss and coat evenly, adding more pasta water if necessary. Add half of the Parmigiano-Reggiano and toss well.

5. Transfer to a large serving bowl and sprinkle with remaining cheese. Serve immediately.

Variations

Substitute fettuccine or linguine for the pappardelle.

Substitute fresh pappardelle (see recipes, pages 222 and 227) for the dried. Cook it to the al dente stage and toss it gently in the sauce until coated, without further cooking.

Farfalle alla ragù salsiccia d'anatra

Farfalle with Duck Sausage Ragù

In central Italy — Emilia-Romagna, Tuscany and Umbria — duck and game birds are familiar fare. In this recipe you make your own duck sausage in less than two minutes, with duck meat ground by the butcher. Professional grinding equipment makes for a better texture than a food processor (see Tip, page 105). I consider this comfort food.

Serves 4 to 6

Tip

To dice thinly sliced pancetta, stack the slices on top of each other and cut them in half lengthwise, then in half again. Then slice the pieces horizontally into 1/4-inch (0.5 cm) pieces. You can also purchase pancetta in a chunk, cut it into 1/4-inch (0.5 cm) slices, julienne those slices, then dice them 1/4 inch (0.5 cm) thick. You can also buy it already diced.

Duck Sausage

8 oz	ground duck breast, leg or thigh meat (see Tip, right)	250 g
1/8 tsp	ground coriander	0.5 mL
1/8 tsp	ground cinnamon	0.5 mL
1/8 tsp	ground mace	0.5 mL
1/8 tsp	cracked fennel seeds	0.5 mL
1/8 tsp	coarsely ground black pepper	0.5 mL
1/8 tsp	salt	0.5 mL
1/2 tsp	red wine vinegar	2 mL
1 tbsp	extra-virgin olive oil	15 mL

Sauce and Pasta

3 tbsp	extra-virgin olive oil	45 mL
1/4 cup	finely diced pancetta	50 mL
1/4 cup	finely diced onion	50 mL
1/4 cup	finely diced peeled carrot	50 mL
1/4 cup	finely diced peeled celery	50 mL
	Salt and freshly ground black pepper	
1/4 cup	dry red Italian wine	50 mL
1 1/4 cups	canned crushed Italian tomatoes	300 mL
2 tbsp	heavy or whipping (35%) cream	25 mL
	Salt and freshly ground black pepper	
1 tbsp	salt	15 mL
1 lb	dried farfalle (see Variations, page 105)	500 g
3/4 cup	grated Parmigiano-Reggiano, divided	75 mL

1. *Sausage:* In a non-reactive bowl combine duck, coriander, cinnamon, mace, fennel seeds, pepper, salt and vinegar. Mix well.

2. In a large sauté pan, heat oil over medium-high heat. Add duck mixture and cook, stirring, until meat is cooked through and no pink remains, using the edge of a spatula to break mixture into small pieces. Remove from heat and set aside.

3. *Pasta and Sauce:* In a covered pasta pot over high heat, bring water to a rapid boil.

4. Meanwhile, in a large sauté pan, heat oil over medium heat. Add pancetta, onion, carrot, celery and salt and pepper to taste. Cook, stirring, until vegetables are soft and translucent, about 10 minutes. Add wine and reserved sausage meat. Cook, stirring, until wine is reduced by half. Add tomatoes and cream and season to taste with salt and pepper. Reduce heat to low and simmer until sauce thickens, about 10 minutes. Remove from heat and set aside.

5. While sauce is simmering, add salt and farfalle to the boiling water and cook, uncovered, over high heat until pasta is almost al dente. Scoop out about 1 cup (250 mL) of the pasta water and set aside. Drain pasta.

6. Return sauté pan to medium heat. Add 2 tbsp (25 mL) of the reserved pasta water and heat through. Add farfalle and continue to cook for about 3 minutes, until pasta is al dente, using a wooden spoon to toss and coat evenly, adding more pasta water if necessary. Add half of the Parmigiano-Reggiano and toss well.

7. Transfer to a large serving bowl and sprinkle with remaining cheese. Serve immediately.

Variations

Substitute penne or fusilli for the farfalle.

Ragù or Sugo?

Sometimes long-cooking Italian sauces are called ragù and sometimes sugo. The distinction (as with most Italian cooking) can be confusing. *Ragù* comes from the French *ragoût* (which means "stew") and dates to the period in history when French cuisine was widely admired and emulated by the Italian upper classes. Basically, a ragù is a long-cooking sauce that has a main ingredient, usually meat. *Sugo* technically means "juice." However, it can also refer to a long-cooking sauce that contains meat or even fish, but neither of which is the main ingredient. That ingredient may be removed after cooking and served as a separate course, leaving its flavor in the sugo, which then becomes a pasta sauce, or it may act as a secondary ingredient.

Bigoli con ragù d'anatra veneziana

Bigoli with Venetian Duck Ragù

This is a classic recipe from Venice, where ducks are a favorite bird. The sauce is not quick but it's simple to prepare, because once all the ingredients are added it cooks slowly by itself in the oven. And it has the depth of flavor that comes only from long, slow cooking.

Serves 4 to 6

Tips

Be sure to use tomato purée, not paste, which is much thicker and too dense for this recipe.

All ragùs are better the day after being cooked. You can cook the ragù through step 2, then bring it to room temperature quickly by using a cold-water bath. (Set the pot in a large, shallow bowl, then fill bowl with cold water and ice cubes to reach halfway up the pot; stir ragù to speed cooling.) Cover and refrigerate overnight or for up to 2 days. When ready to use, discard surface fat, transfer ragù to a sauté pan and reheat slowly over low heat, stirring occasionally with a wooden spoon, while the pasta is cooking. When the pasta is cooked, ladle out 1 cup (250 mL) of the cooking water and reserve. Finish the recipe according to the directions.

• Preheat oven to 250°F (120°C)

3 tbsp	extra-virgin olive oil	45 mL
¼ cup	finely diced pancetta	50 mL
¼ cup	finely diced onion	50 mL
¼ cup	finely diced carrot	50 mL
¼ cup	finely diced peeled celery	50 mL
8 oz	diced boneless duck meat	250 g
	Salt and freshly ground black pepper	
½ cup	dry red Italian wine	125 mL
1 cup	canned Italian tomato purée (see Tips, left)	250 mL
3 cups	water	750 mL
1 tbsp	salt	15 mL
1 lb	dried bigoli or thick spaghetti	500 g
¾ cup	grated Parmigiano-Reggiano, divided	175 mL

1. In a heavy ovenproof 3-quart (3 L) saucepan or Dutch oven with a tight-fitting lid, heat oil over high heat. Add pancetta, onion, carrot and celery and cook, stirring occasionally, until vegetables are soft, about 7 minutes. Stir in duck and season to taste with salt and pepper. Add wine and cook until reduced by half. Add tomato purée and water and bring to a boil.

2. Cover and bake in preheated oven until ragù reduces slightly, 1½ to 2 hours. Remove from oven, uncover, place on very low heat and continue to simmer, stirring occasionally from the bottom, until ragù is thick and rich, about 30 minutes.

3. Meanwhile, in a covered pasta pot over high heat, bring water to a rapid boil. Add salt and bigoli and cook, uncovered, over high heat until pasta is almost al dente. Scoop out about 1 cup (250 mL) of the pasta water and set aside. Drain pasta.

4. In a large sauté pan, heat 2 tbsp (25 mL) of the reserved pasta water over medium heat. Add duck ragù and simmer, mashing with a potato masher or fork until meat is shredded. Add bigoli and continue to cook for about 3 minutes, until pasta is al dente, using pasta tongs to toss and coat evenly, adding more pasta water if necessary. Add half of the Parmigiano-Reggiano and toss well.

5. Transfer to a large serving bowl and sprinkle with remaining cheese. Serve immediately.

Fusilli al tacchino e fave

Fusilli with Turkey and Fava Beans

Years ago if you wanted turkey, that meant buying the whole bird, but today fresh turkey parts are widely available, which makes it easy to use this tasty bird in a variety of dishes. This contemporary recipe is colorful, flavorful and quick.

Serves 4 to 6

Tips

To blanch the fava beans for use in this recipe, bring a large pot of lightly salted water to a boil. Cook peeled fava beans for 1 minute, then drain and rinse under cold running water. This sets the color of the beans and preserves it during cooking.

Of course, any dry white Italian table wine will work well in this recipe, but my choice would be Pinot Bianco, which is a good basic dry white wine for use in Italian cooking.

If you have leftovers, use them to make Baked Fusilli with Turkey and Fava Beans (see recipe, page 168).

3 tbsp	extra-virgin olive oil	45 mL
¼ cup	diced pancetta	50 mL
¼ cup	diced onion	50 mL
¼ cup	quartered cherry tomatoes	50 mL
1 cup	diced skinless, boneless turkey breast	250 mL
½ cup	blanched, peeled fava beans (see Tips, left)	125 mL
1 cup	dry white Italian wine (see Tips, left)	250 mL
	Salt and freshly ground black pepper	
1 tbsp	salt	15 mL
1 lb	dried fusilli (see Variations, below)	500 g
¾ cup	grated Parmigiano-Reggiano, divided	175 mL

1. In a covered pasta pot over high heat, bring water to a rapid boil.

2. Meanwhile, in a large sauté pan, heat oil over medium heat. Add pancetta and onion and cook, stirring, until onion is soft, about 3 minutes. Stir in tomatoes, turkey and fava beans. Cover, reduce heat to low, and simmer until heated through, 2 to 3 minutes. Uncover, raise the heat to medium, add wine and cook until reduced by half. Season to taste with salt and pepper. Remove pan from heat and set aside.

3. While sauce is simmering, add salt and fusilli to the boiling water and cook, uncovered, over high heat until pasta is almost al dente. Scoop out about 1 cup (250 mL) of the pasta water and set aside. Drain pasta.

4. Return turkey mixture to medium heat. Add 2 tbsp (25 mL) of the reserved pasta water and heat through. Add fusilli and continue to cook for about 3 minutes, until pasta is al dente, using a wooden spoon to toss and coat evenly, adding more pasta water if necessary. Add half of the Parmigiano-Reggiano and toss well.

5. Transfer to a large serving bowl. Sprinkle with remaining cheese and serve immediately.

Variations

Substitute 1 cup (250 mL) of ½-inch (1 cm) pieces peeled celery or blanched green beans for the fava beans. You can also substitute 1 cup (250 mL) fresh lima beans for the fava beans.

Fusilli pasta, which is shaped like a corkscrew, is named for the tool used to clean the insides of gun barrels (*fusilli* means "rifles" in Italian). Substitute rotini for the fusilli.

Radiatori con ragù al salsiccia di tacchino

Radiatori with Turkey Sausage Ragù

The rich, aromatic taste of this ragù depends on the fresh homemade turkey sausage that you put into it. The sausage takes less than two minutes to mix, and it is lower in fat — but not in flavor — than most prepared sausages.

Serves 4 to 6

Tips

Any dry white Italian table wine will work fine in this recipe. Here I'd probably use Pinot Bianco, which is a good basic dry white wine for use in Italian cooking.

Work like a chef. Have all your ingredients ready to go before you actually start to cook (see *Mise en Place*, page 15).

Sausage

1/8 tsp	ground cloves	0.5 mL
1/8 tsp	ground cinnamon	0.5 mL
1/8 tsp	ground nutmeg	0.5 mL
1/8 tsp	ground cayenne	0.5 mL
1/8 tsp	fine freshly ground black pepper	0.5 mL
1/8 tsp	salt	0.5 mL
2 tbsp	dry white Italian wine	25 mL
8 oz	ground turkey	250 g

Pasta and Sauce

3 tbsp	extra-virgin olive oil	45 mL
1/4 cup	diced pancetta	50 mL
1/4 cup	diced onion	50 mL
1/4 cup	diced carrot	50 mL
1/4 cup	diced peeled celery	50 mL
	Salt and freshly ground black pepper	
1/2 cup	dry white Italian wine	125 mL
1 1/4 cups	canned crushed Italian tomatoes	300 mL
2 tbsp	heavy or whipping (35%) cream	25 mL
1 tbsp	salt	15 mL
1 lb	dried radiatori (see Variations, page 109)	500 g
3/4 cup	grated Parmigiano-Reggiano, divided	175 mL

1. *Sausage:* In a stainless steel bowl, combine cloves, cinnamon, nutmeg, cayenne, pepper, salt, wine and turkey. Mix well and set aside (see Tips, page 109).

2. *Pasta and Sauce:* In a covered pasta pot over high heat, bring water to a rapid boil.

3. Meanwhile, in a large sauté pan, heat oil over medium heat. Add pancetta, onion, carrot and celery and stir. Season to taste with salt and pepper. Cook, stirring, until pancetta is lightly browned and vegetables are soft and tender, about 5 minutes. Add wine and cook until reduced by half. Add reserved turkey sausage and cook, stirring and breaking up with a spatula, until meat is fully cooked and no pink remains, about 10 minutes. Add tomatoes, reduce heat to low and simmer, uncovered, until sauce reduces, about 20 minutes. Add cream, stir, and simmer for 3 minutes to thicken sauce and meld flavors. Remove from heat and set aside.

These days ground turkey is available at supermarkets in either white or dark meat.

The turkey sausage can be made up to 2 days in advance, in which case, cover and refrigerate immediately after mixing.

4. While sauce is simmering, add salt and radiatori to the boiling water and cook, uncovered, over high heat until pasta is almost al dente. Scoop out about 1 cup (250 mL) of the pasta water and set aside. Drain pasta.

5. Return the sauté pan to medium heat. Add 2 tbsp (25 mL) of the reserved pasta water and heat through. Add radiatori and continue to cook for about 3 minutes, until pasta is al dente, using a wooden spoon to toss and coat evenly, adding more pasta water if necessary. Add half of the Parmigiano-Reggiano and toss well.

6. Transfer to a large serving bowl and sprinkle with remaining cheese. Serve immediately.

Variations

Radiatori is short, chunky pasta shaped to look like the grills of a radiator. It emerged around 1945 and is a fun shape, especially for kids. If radiatori are unavailable, substitute rotini or fusilli.

Pancetta

Pancetta is pork belly that has been spiced — fennel seed, garlic, nutmeg, black pepper and garlic are common, and sometimes hot red pepper is added — and salt cured. It is sometimes, but not usually, smoked. There are many regional versions of pancetta in Italy. Outside Italy, pancetta is often sold rolled and is used thinly sliced to flavor dishes. Pancetta can be refrigerated, tightly wrapped, for up to 3 weeks or frozen for up to 6 months.

Linguine con sugo di tacchino

Linguine with Turkey-Tomato Sauce

Turkey is a fabulous bird! Its meat is very versatile, and speaking as a chef, I'm glad we are finally moving beyond eating it primarily at Thanksgiving and in turkey sandwiches. Fresh turkey parts are so widely available these days there is no reason not to enjoy it often. This sugo is cooked like a ragù, for 3 hours. Because it is so long-cooking I recommend doubling the recipe and freezing half for up to a month.

Serves 4 to 6

Tips

I prefer the richer flavor and moist texture of dark turkey meat rather than the white breast meat for this long-cooking sugo.

This sauce is even better the day after being cooked. Follow the instructions for cooling, storing and reheating ragùs (see Tips, page 106).

If you have leftovers, use them to make Frittata of Linguine with Turkey-Tomato Sauce (see Variations, page 169).

• Preheat oven to 250°F (120°C)

3 tbsp	extra-virgin olive oil	45 mL
¼ cup	diced pancetta	50 mL
¼ cup	diced onion	50 mL
¼ cup	diced carrot	50 mL
¼ cup	diced peeled celery	50 mL
1½ cups	diced skinless, boneless turkey meat, preferably dark (about 8 oz/250 g; see Tips, left)	375 mL
	Salt and freshly ground black pepper	
½ cup	dry red Italian wine	125 mL
3 cups	canned crushed Italian tomatoes	750 mL
1 cup	water	250 mL
1 tbsp	salt	15 mL
1 lb	dried linguine (see Variations, below)	500 g
¾ cup	grated Parmigiano-Reggiano, divided	175 mL

1. In a heavy ovenproof 3-quart (3 L) saucepan or Dutch oven with a tight-fitting lid, heat olive oil over high heat. Add pancetta, onion, carrot and celery and cook, stirring, until vegetables are soft and golden, about 5 minutes. Stir in turkey, season to taste with salt and pepper and cook, stirring, until turkey is cooked and no pink remains, about 8 minutes. Add wine and cook until reduced by half. Add tomatoes and water and bring to a boil.

2. Cover, transfer to preheated oven and bake until sugo reduces slightly, 1½ to 2 hours. Remove from oven, uncover, place on very low heat and continue to simmer, stirring occasionally from the bottom, until sugo is thick and rich, about 30 minutes.

3. Meanwhile, in a covered pasta pot over high heat, bring water to a rapid boil. Add salt and linguine and cook, uncovered, over high heat until pasta is almost al dente. Scoop out about 1 cup (250 mL) of the pasta water and set aside. Drain pasta.

4. In a large sauté pan, heat 2 tbsp (25 mL) of the reserved pasta water over medium heat. Add turkey sauce and heat through. Add linguine and continue to cook for about 3 minutes, until pasta is al dente, using pasta tongs to coat evenly, adding more pasta water if necessary. Add half of the Parmigiano-Reggiano and toss well.

5. Transfer to a large serving bowl and sprinkle with remaining cheese. Serve immediately.

Variations

Substitute spaghetti or fettuccine for the linguine.

Rigatoni con tacchino, zucchine e pomodori

Rigatoni with Turkey, Zucchini and Tomatoes

This simple and nutritious recipe offers another opportunity to enjoy delicious turkey. Rigatoni is popular in southern and central Italy. It is short, fat tubular pasta, usually with ridges and cut straight at both ends. The combination of ridges and the relatively large hole is ideal for catching and holding sauce.

Serves 4 to 6

Tips

Although you will be able to produce a delicious result using white meat, I prefer dark in this dish because the meat remains moist during cooking and the flavor is more pronounced.

For convenience, purchase pancetta that is already diced.

Always use a large pot and plenty of water when cooking pasta. To properly cook 1 pound (500 g) of pasta, you'll need a pot with a volume of at least 8 quarts (8 L) so that you can use 6 quarts (6 L) of water.

Never rinse pasta after draining it. The surface starch helps the sauce to cling and is important to producing the best-quality dish.

3 tbsp	extra-virgin olive oil	45 mL
¼ cup	diced pancetta	50 mL
¼ cup	diced onion	50 mL
1½ cups	cubed (⅔ inch/1.5 cm) boneless, skinless turkey meat, preferably dark (about 12 oz/375 g; see Tips, left)	375 mL
	Salt and freshly ground black pepper	
½ cup	dry white Italian wine	125 mL
¾ cup	diced skin-on zucchini	175 mL
¾ cup	quartered cherry tomatoes	175 mL
1 tsp	hand-torn fresh basil leaves	5 mL
1 tbsp	salt	15 mL
1 lb	dried rigatoni (see Variation, below)	500 g
¾ cup	grated Parmigiano-Reggiano, divided	175 mL

1. In a covered pasta pot over high heat, bring water to a rapid boil.

2. Meanwhile, in a large sauté pan, heat oil over medium heat. Add pancetta and onion and cook, stirring, until pancetta is cooked through and onion is soft and tender, about 5 minutes. Add turkey and season to taste with salt and pepper. Cook until turkey is cooked through and no pink remains, about 10 minutes. Add wine, zucchini, tomatoes and basil and cook until vegetables are soft and wine is reduced by half. Remove from heat and set aside.

3. While sauce is simmering, add salt and rigatoni to the boiling water and cook, uncovered, over high heat until almost al dente. Scoop out about 1 cup (250 mL) of the pasta water and set aside. Drain pasta.

4. Return sauté pan to medium heat. Add 2 tbsp (25 mL) of the reserved pasta water and heat through. Add rigatoni and continue to cook for about 3 minutes, until pasta is al dente, using a wooden spoon to toss and coat evenly, adding more pasta water if necessary. Add half of the Parmigiano-Reggiano and toss well.

5. Transfer to a large serving bowl and sprinkle with remaining cheese. Serve immediately.

Variation

Substitute penne for the rigatoni.

Cavatappi al sugo di manzo

Cavatappi with Beef-Tomato Sauce

Cavatappi are slender corkscrew-shaped pasta about 1 inch (2.5 cm) long. They are also known as cellentani or "double elbows." The surface is usually ridged, which helps to catch and hold the sauce. Several Italian mass producers of pasta manufacture dried cavatappi or cellentani; it is available in well-stocked supermarkets.

Serves 4 to 6

Tips

Any dry red Italian table wine will work well in this recipe, but my wine of choice would be Primitivo because it comes from southern Italy, where you would be likely to find this sauce. It would also be a good wine to drink with this pasta.

The beef sauce is easy to make but takes a while to cook. For convenience, double the recipe and freeze half in a resealable plastic bag for up to 1 month. Like a ragù, it will improve in flavor if it is allowed to rest for a day or two after being cooked. For detailed instructions on reheating ragùs, see Tips, page 106.

• Preheat oven to 250°F (120°C)

3 tbsp	extra-virgin olive oil	45 mL
¼ cup	diced onion	50 mL
1 tsp	thinly sliced garlic	5 mL
1¼ cups	cubed (½ inch/1cm) boneless beef shoulder (about 6 oz/175 g)	300 mL
1 cup	dry red Italian wine (see Tips, left)	250 mL
2 cups	canned crushed Italian tomatoes	500 mL
1 cup	water	250 mL
	Salt and freshly ground black pepper	
1 tbsp	salt	15 mL
1 lb	dried cavatappi (see Variations, below)	500 g
¾ cup	grated Parmigiano-Reggiano, divided	175 mL

1. In a heavy ovenproof 3-quart (3 L) saucepan or Dutch oven with a tight-fitting lid, heat oil over medium heat. Add onion and garlic and cook, stirring, until vegetables are soft and translucent, about 3 minutes. Add beef and wine and cook, stirring, until wine is reduced by half. Add tomatoes and water and bring to a boil. Season to taste with salt and pepper.

2. Cover and bake in preheated oven until beef is tender, about 2½ hours. Remove from oven, uncover, place on very low heat and simmer, stirring occasionally from the bottom, until sauce is thick and rich, about 30 minutes.

3. While sauce is simmering, in a covered pasta pot over high heat, bring water to a rapid boil. Add salt and cavatappi and cook, uncovered, over high heat until pasta is almost al dente. Scoop out about 1 cup (250 mL) of the pasta water and set aside. Drain pasta.

4. Transfer sugo to a large sauté pan. Add 2 tbsp (25 mL) of the reserved pasta water to beef mixture and raise heat to medium. Bring to a simmer, add cavatappi and continue to cook for about 3 minutes, until pasta is al dente, using a wooden spoon to toss and coat evenly, adding more pasta water if necessary. Add half of the Parmigiano-Reggiano and toss well.

5. Transfer to a large serving bowl and sprinkle with remaining cheese. Serve immediately.

Variations

If cavatappi, also known as cellentani, is not available, substitute fusilli or penne.

Spaghetti con le polpettine di vitello

Spaghetti with Veal Meatballs

Spaghetti and meatballs is the favorite pasta of many non-Italian people I know. However, many Italians insist that there is no such dish in Italy. In some ways they are right: the baseball-sized meatballs served in American restaurants are certainly not Italian. But meatballs appear in many festive southern Italian dishes, and southern Italians do eat spaghetti and meatballs, which are usually made from a combination of meats — pork, beef or veal and lamb. This recipe uses veal alone for a more delicate taste. Since the meatballs are small, you get more meatballs as you eat your spaghetti.

Serves 4 to 6

Tip

Work like a chef. Have all your ingredients ready to go before you actually start to cook (see *Mise en Place*, page 15).

- Preheat oven to 350°F (180°C)
- Rimmed baking sheet, lightly greased

Meatballs

8 oz	medium ground veal shoulder, divided (see Variations, right)	250 g
1	egg, lightly beaten	1
¼ cup	fine dry white breadcrumbs	50 mL
1 tsp	minced garlic	5 mL
1 tbsp	finely chopped Italian parsley leaves	15 mL
¼ cup	grated Parmigiano-Reggiano	50 mL
⅛ tsp	freshly grated nutmeg	0.5 mL
½ tsp	salt	2 mL
¼ tsp	freshly ground black pepper	1 mL

Tomato Sauce

3 tbsp	extra-virgin olive oil	45 mL
1 tbsp	thinly sliced garlic	15 mL
4 cups	canned crushed Italian tomatoes	1 L
1 tbsp	hand-torn fresh basil leaves	15 mL
1 tsp	granulated sugar	5 mL
	Salt and freshly ground black pepper	
1 tbsp	salt	15 mL
1 lb	dried spaghetti	500 g
¾ cup	grated Parmigiano-Reggiano, divided	175 mL

1. *Meatballs:* In a food processor combine half of the veal, egg, breadcrumbs, garlic, parsley, Parmigiano-Reggiano, nutmeg, salt and pepper. Process until puréed, stopping machine to scrape down sides if necessary. This should take about 20 seconds. Do not overprocess or the veal will overheat and the texture will be ruined. Transfer to a mixing bowl. Add remaining veal and mix well.

2. Shape into meatballs about 1 inch (2.5 cm) in diameter and place on prepared baking sheet. Bake in preheated oven until cooked through, about 15 minutes. Set aside.

3. *Tomato Sauce:* In a large sauté pan, heat oil over medium heat. Add garlic and cook, stirring, until translucent but not browned, 2 to 3 minutes. Add tomatoes, basil and sugar and season to taste with salt and pepper. Reduce heat to low. Add reserved meatballs and simmer, uncovered, occasionally stirring carefully from the bottom, until sauce is thick and rich, about 1 hour.

Ideally the breadcrumbs for this recipe should be all white, from the interior of a loaf of Italian bread, finely ground and dried. Italian bakeries are a good source for breadcrumbs. Some of my non-Italian friends use panko crumbs, which are outside the Italian market basket, but they tell me they are just fine for this recipe.

The tomato sauce in this recipe can be used all by itself with pasta, or in recipes such as Caponata (see page 181).

4. Meanwhile, in a covered pasta pot over high heat, bring water to a rapid boil. Add salt and spaghetti and cook, uncovered, over high heat until pasta is almost al dente. Scoop out about 1 cup (250 mL) of the pasta water and set aside. Drain pasta.

5. Add 2 tbsp (25 mL) of the reserved pasta water to sauté pan. Add spaghetti and continue to cook for about 3 minutes, until pasta is al dente, using pasta tongs to toss and coat evenly, adding more pasta water if necessary. Add half of the Parmigiano-Reggiano and toss well.

6. Transfer to a large serving platter. Sprinkle with remaining cheese and serve immediately.

Variations

Substitute ground chicken or turkey thigh for the veal in the meatballs.

Substitute equal parts of ground pork, beef and lamb for the veal in the meatballs.

Pappardelle al ragù misto

Pappardelle with a Mixed Meat Ragù

●●●

When you want deep, rich flavor in a meat sauce, ground meat is not the answer. Ground meat is good for sausage and meatballs, but to produce real flavor in a ragù you need to use chunks of meat. In this recipe, pieces of beef, veal and pork shoulder are cooked to shreds, producing an intensely flavored sauce with appealing texture. When I prepare this at home I always double the recipe and freeze half.

Serves 4 to 6

Tip

To dice thinly sliced pancetta, stack the slices on top of each other and cut them in half lengthwise, then in half again. Then slice the pieces horizontally into ¼-inch (0.5 cm) pieces. You can also purchase pancetta in a chunk, cut it into ¼-inch (0.5 cm) slices, julienne those slices, then dice them ¼ inch (0.5 cm) thick. You can also buy it already diced.

• Preheat oven to 250°F (120°C)

3 tbsp	extra-virgin olive oil	45 mL
¼ cup	diced pancetta (see Tip, left)	50 mL
¼ cup	diced onion	50 mL
¼ cup	diced carrot	50 mL
¼ cup	diced peeled celery	50 mL
	Salt and freshly ground black pepper	
⅓ cup	cubed (1 inch/2.5 cm) boneless beef shoulder, trimmed of visible fat, very firmly packed (about 2½ oz/75 g)	75 mL
⅓ cup	cubed (1 inch/2.5 cm) boneless veal shoulder, trimmed of visible fat, very firmly packed (about 2½ oz/75 g)	75 mL
⅓ cup	cubed (1 inch/2.5 cm) boneless pork shoulder, trimmed of visible fat, very firmly packed (about 2½ oz/75 g)	75 mL
1 cup	dry red Italian wine (see Tips, right)	250 mL
1 cup	canned crushed Italian tomatoes	250 mL
3 cups	water	750 mL
1 tbsp	salt	15 mL
1 lb	dried pappardelle (see Variations, page 117)	500 g
¾ cup	grated Parmigiano-Reggiano	175 mL

1. In a heavy ovenproof 3-quart (3 L) saucepan or Dutch oven with a tight-fitting lid, heat oil over medium heat. Add pancetta, onion, carrot and celery and stir. Season to taste with salt and pepper. Cook, stirring, until vegetables are lightly golden, about 5 minutes. Add beef, veal and pork and stir, cooking until meat is cooked and no pink remains, about 10 minutes. Add wine, stir, and cook, stirring, until reduced by half. Add tomatoes and water and bring to a boil. Lower the heat.

2. Cover and bake in preheated oven until ragù reduces slightly, 1½ to 2 hours. Remove from oven, uncover, place on very low heat and continue to simmer, stirring occasionally from the bottom, until ragù is thick and rich, about 30 minutes.

3. Meanwhile, in a covered pasta pot over high heat, bring water to a rapid boil. Add salt and pappardelle and cook, uncovered, until pasta is almost al dente. Scoop out about 1 cup (250 mL) of the pasta water and set aside. Drain pasta.

Tips

Any dry red Italian table wine will work well in this recipe. My wine of choice would be Chianti because it comes from Tuscany, where you would be likely to find this sauce.

All ragùs improve in flavor if they rest for a day or two. Complete steps 1 and 2, then cover and refrigerate for up to 2 days. When ready to use, discard surface fat, transfer ragù to a sauté pan and reheat slowly over low heat, stirring. Continue with steps 3 through 5.

4. In a large sauté pan over medium heat, combine ragù and 2 tbsp (25 mL) of the reserved pasta water. Bring to a simmer and, using a fork or potato masher, shred the chunks of meat. Add pappardelle and continue to cook for about 3 minutes, until pasta is al dente, using pasta tongs to toss and coat evenly, adding more pasta water if necessary. Add half of the Parmigiano-Reggiano and toss well.

5. Transfer to a large serving bowl and sprinkle with remaining cheese. Serve immediately.

Variations

This sauce also goes well with fresh pappardelle (see recipes, pages 222 and 227). If using fresh pappardelle, cook it to the al dente stage and, using a wooden spoon, toss it gently in the sauce until coated, without further cooking.

Substitute dried fettuccine if you can't find pappardelle.

Fettuccine with Lamb-Tomato Sauce

Lamb is a favorite meat in Italy (especially at Easter), so much so that they have different names for lambs of different maturity, not just spring lamb. Agnello de latte or abbacchio is 4 weeks old, agnello is 9 to 12 weeks old, and agnellone is 6 months old. But because this sauce calls for lamb shoulder, any type will be fine as long as it's lamb and not mutton. This is a long-cooking ragù typical of the city of Rome and the Lazio region in general.

Serves 4 to 6

Tips

For best results grate the cheese yourself, but if time is at a premium, use already grated cheese. Whichever form you choose, just be sure to buy the very best Italian Parmigiano-Reggiano you can find and grate it finely to ensure you have the quantity called for in the recipe.

All ragùs are better the day after being cooked. For detailed instructions on reheating ragùs, see Tips, page 106.

• Preheat oven to 250°F (120°C)

3 tbsp	extra-virgin olive oil	45 mL
¼ cup	diced onion	50 mL
2 tbsp	thinly sliced garlic	25 mL
1¼ cups	trimmed cubed (½ inch/1 cm) lamb shoulder (about 6 oz/175 g)	300 mL
	Salt and freshly ground black pepper	
½ cup	dry red Italian wine	125 mL
3 cups	canned crushed Italian tomatoes	750 mL
1 cup	water	250 mL
1 tbsp	salt	15 mL
1 lb	dried fettuccine (see Variations, below)	500 g
¾ cup	grated Parmigiano-Reggiano (see Tips, left)	175 mL

1. In a heavy ovenproof 3-quart (3 L) saucepan or Dutch oven with a tight-fitting lid, heat oil over medium heat. Add onion and garlic and cook, stirring, until soft and lightly browned, about 5 minutes. Add lamb and stir. Season to taste with salt and pepper. Cook until meat is cooked and no pink remains, about 10 minutes. Add wine and cook, stirring, until reduced by half. Add tomatoes and water, stir, and bring to a boil.

2. Cover and bake in preheated oven until sugo reduces slightly, 1½ to 2 hours. Remove from oven, uncover, place on very low heat and continue to simmer, stirring occasionally from the bottom, until sugo is thick and rich, about 30 minutes.

3. Meanwhile, in a covered pasta pot over high heat, bring water to a rapid boil. Add salt and fettuccine and cook, uncovered, until pasta is almost al dente. Scoop out about 1 cup (250 mL) of the pasta water and set aside. Drain pasta.

4. Meanwhile, transfer sugo to a large sauté pan. Add 2 tbsp (25 mL) of the reserved pasta water and bring to a simmer over medium heat. Add fettuccine and continue to cook for about 3 minutes, until pasta is al dente, using pasta tongs to toss and coat evenly, adding more pasta water if necessary. Add half of the Parmigiano-Reggiano and toss well.

5. Transfer to a large serving bowl and sprinkle with remaining cheese. Serve immediately.

Variations

The lamb-tomato sauce also goes well with fresh fettuccine (see recipes, pages 222 and 226). Cook it to the al dente stage and toss it gently in the sauce until coated, without further cooking.

If you can't find fettuccine, substitute linguine.

Cavatappi al sugo di maiale

Cavatappi with Pork-Tomato Sauce

Cavatappi is a ridged, hollow, corkscrew-shaped pasta (also called cellentani or "double elbows") that is well suited to catch and hold this thick, rich, slow-cooking sugo. The little bit of pancetta, which complements the pork, really enhances the flavor profile of the sauce.

Serves 4 to 6

Tips

Any dry red Italian table wine will work well in this recipe. My wine of choice would be Primitivo because it is produced in southern Italy, where you would also be likely to find this sauce.

You can cook the sugo through step 2, then cover and refrigerate it overnight or for up to 2 days. When ready to use, discard surface fat, transfer to a sauté pan and reheat slowly, stirring while the pasta is cooking. When the pasta is cooked, ladle out 1 cup (250 mL) pasta cooking water and reserve. Finish the recipe according to the directions.

- Preheat oven to 250°F (120°C)

3 tbsp	extra-virgin olive oil	45 mL
¼ cup	diced pancetta	50 mL
¼ cup	diced onion	175 mL
1 tsp	thinly sliced garlic	5 mL
	Salt and freshly ground black pepper	
¾ cup	cubed (½ inch/1 cm) trimmed boneless pork shoulder, packed (about 6 oz/175 g)	175 mL
1 cup	dry red Italian wine	250 mL
3 cups	canned crushed Italian tomatoes	750 mL
1 cup	water	250 mL
1 tbsp	salt	15 mL
1 lb	dried cavatappi (see Variation, below)	500 g
¾ cup	grated Parmigiano-Reggiano, divided	175 mL

1. In a heavy ovenproof 3-quart (3 L) saucepan or a Dutch oven with a tight-fitting lid, heat oil over medium heat. Add pancetta, onion and garlic and salt and pepper to taste. Cook, stirring. until vegetables are soft and translucent but not browned, about 5 minutes. Add pork and wine and stir. Simmer until wine is reduced by half. Add tomatoes and water and bring to a boil.

2. Cover, transfer to preheated oven and bake until sugo reduces slightly, 1½ to 2 hours. Remove from oven, uncover, place on very low heat and continue to simmer, stirring occasionally from the bottom, until sugo is thick and rich, about 30 minutes.

3. Meanwhile, in a covered pasta pot over high heat, bring water to a rapid boil. Add salt and cavatappi and cook, uncovered, over high heat until pasta is almost al dente. Scoop out about 1 cup (250 mL) of the pasta water and set aside. Drain pasta.

4. Transfer pork mixture to a large sauté pan. Add 2 tbsp (25 mL) of the reserved pasta water and the cavatappi. Continue to cook for about 3 minutes, until pasta is al dente, using pasta tongs to toss and coat evenly, adding more pasta water if necessary. Add half of the Parmigiano-Reggiano and toss well.

5. Transfer to a serving platter and sprinkle with remaining cheese. Serve immediately.

Variation

Cavatappi, also called cellentani, is dried short double-spiral tube-shaped pasta. If you can't find it, substitute fusilli.

Orecchiette con ragù di salsiccia

Orecchiette with Pork Sausage Ragù

This is a simple, traditional sauce you might find in south-central Italy. The ear-shaped orecchiette are attributed to Puglia (Apulia), where they were first made fresh and by hand.

Serves 4 to 6

Tips

You'll need about one 8- to 9-inch link (20 to 25 cm) of Italian sausage, 1 inch (2.5 cm) in diameter, for this recipe. To cook, remove sausage from casing and discard casing. Place sausage in skillet and cook over medium heat until no pink remains, chopping with a wooden spoon or spatula to break it into smaller pieces.

If you have leftovers, use them to make Baked Orecchiette with Pork Sausage Ragù (see Variations, page 168).

3 tbsp	extra-virgin olive oil	45 mL
¼ cup	diced pancetta	50 mL
¼ cup	diced onion	50 mL
	Salt and freshly ground black pepper	
¾ cup	chopped cooked sweet or hot Italian sausage (about 6 oz/175 g; see Tips, left)	175 mL
1 cup	dry red Italian wine	250 mL
3 cups	canned crushed Italian tomatoes	750 mL
½ cup	heavy or whipping (35%) cream	125 mL
1 tbsp	salt	15 mL
1 lb	dried orecchiette (see Variation, below)	500 g
¾ cup	grated Parmigiano-Reggiano, divided	175 mL

1. In a covered pasta pot over high heat, bring water to a rapid boil.

2. Meanwhile, in a large sauté pan, heat oil over medium heat. Add pancetta and onion and season to taste with salt and pepper. Cook, stirring, until pancetta is lightly browned and onion is soft and tender, about 5 minutes. Add sausage and cook until heated through. Add wine and reduce by half. Add tomatoes, reduce heat to low and cook, stirring, until sauce is thick enough to coat the back of a spoon, 10 to 15 minutes. Add cream and cook for 5 minutes to meld flavors. Remove pan from heat and set aside.

3. While sauce is simmering, add salt and orecchiette to boiling water and cook, uncovered, over high heat, until pasta is almost al dente. Scoop out about 1 cup (250 mL) of the pasta water and set aside. Drain pasta.

4. Return sauté pan to medium heat. Add 2 tbsp (25 mL) of the pasta water and bring to a simmer. Add orecchiette and continue to cook until pasta is al dente, using a wooden spoon to toss and coat evenly, adding more pasta water if necessary. Add half of the Parmigiano-Reggiano and toss well.

5. Transfer to a large serving bowl and sprinkle with remaining cheese. Serve immediately.

Variation

If orecchiette is not available, substitute penne.

Maccheroni alla salsiccia e ricotta fresca

Maccheroni with Pork Sausage and Fresh Ricotta

Maccheroni does not have the same shape as elbow macaroni, although, just to confuse non-Italians, Italians often use maccheroni *as a generic term for all pasta. That being said,* maccheroni *is a tubular pasta shaped like rigatoni. It is hollow, about 1¼ to 1½ inches (3 to 4 cm) long, and can have either a smooth or ridged surface. After all that, this is very tasty sauce that is easy to make.*

Serves 4 to 6

Tips

I usually season my sauces in the initial stages of cooking so the flavors have time to bloom. I always taste the final product and, if necessary, add more salt and pepper just before serving.

You'll need about one 8- to 9-inch link (20 to 25 cm) of Italian sausage, 1 inch (2.5 cm) in diameter, for this recipe. To cook, remove sausage from casing and discard casing. Place sausage in skillet and cook over medium heat until no pink remains, chopping with a wooden spoon or spatula to break it into smaller pieces.

3 tbsp	extra-virgin olive oil	45 mL
1 tbsp	thinly sliced garlic	15 mL
	Salt and freshly ground black pepper	
¾ cup	chopped cooked sweet or hot Italian pork sausage (about 6 oz/175 g; see Tips, left)	175 mL
½ cup	dry red Italian wine	125 mL
2 cups	canned crushed Italian tomatoes	500 mL
⅓ cup	heavy or whipping (35%) cream	75 mL
1 tbsp	salt	15 mL
1 lb	dried maccheroni (see Variations, below)	500 g
5 tbsp	grated Parmigiano-Reggiano, divided	75 mL
5 tbsp	fresh ricotta	75 mL

1. In a covered pasta pot over high heat, bring water to a rapid boil.

2. Meanwhile, in a large sauté pan, heat oil over medium heat. Add garlic, season to taste with salt and pepper, and cook, stirring, until garlic is translucent, about 3 minutes. Add sausage and cook, stirring, just until heated through. Add wine and reduce by half. Add tomatoes and cook, stirring, for 5 minutes, until heated through. Add cream, reduce heat to low and simmer until sauce is thick enough to coat the back of a spoon, about 2 minutes. Taste and adjust seasoning. Remove pan from heat and set aside.

3. While sauce is simmering, add salt and maccheroni to the boiling water and cook, uncovered, over high heat until pasta is almost al dente. Scoop out about 1 cup (250 mL) of the pasta water and set aside. Drain pasta.

4. Return sauté pan to element. Add 2 tbsp (25 mL) of the reserved pasta water and bring to a simmer over low heat. Add maccheroni and continue to cook for about 3 minutes, until pasta is al dente, using a wooden spoon to toss and coat evenly, adding more pasta water if necessary. Add 3 tablespoons (45 mL) of the Parmigiano-Reggiano and toss well.

5. Transfer to a large serving bowl and sprinkle with remaining cheese. Drop fresh ricotta in dollops evenly over top. Serve immediately.

Variations

Substitute rigatoni or penne for the maccheroni.

Pennette una tira l'altra

Pennette with Pork Sausage and Mixed Vegetables

The Italian name for this recipe, *una tira l'altra*, literally means "one who pulls the other one." It's idiomatic, and nobody knows which pulls what — the pork sausage or the vegetables. At any rate, this is a very traditional Tuscan sauce, full-flavored and very satisfying.

Serves 4 to 6

Tips

To trim fennel, cut off the root end and discard. Cut off the stems and fronds and save them for flavoring soups or for garnish. Cut any outer stems off the bulb and discard. Cut the bulb in half vertically. Using a sharp knife, cut out the wedge-shaped core and discard. Rinse under cold running water. The fennel is now ready to dice.

One 8- to 9-inch (20 to 25 cm) sausage, 1 inch (2.5 cm) in diameter, yields about 6 ounces (175 g).

3 tbsp	extra-virgin olive oil	45 mL
¼ cup	diced pancetta	50 mL
¼ cup	diced onion	50 mL
¼ cup	diced carrot	50 mL
¼ cup	diced peeled celery	50 mL
¼ cup	diced trimmed fennel bulb (see Tips, left)	50 mL
	Salt and freshly ground black pepper	
6 oz	uncooked sweet or hot Italian sausage, casing removed (see Tips, left)	175 g
1 cup	dry red Italian wine	250 mL
1 cup	canned crushed Italian tomatoes	250 mL
4	fresh hand-torn basil leaves	4
1 tbsp	salt	15 mL
1 lb	dried pennette (see Variations, below)	500 g
6 tbsp	grated Parmigiano-Reggiano, divided	90 mL

1. In a covered pasta pot over high heat, bring water to a rapid boil.
2. Meanwhile, in a large sauté pan, heat oil over medium heat. Add pancetta, onion, carrot, celery and fennel and stir. Season to taste with salt and pepper. Cook, stirring, until vegetables are soft and lightly browned, about 10 minutes. Add sausage and cook, stirring and chopping into small pieces with a spoon, until cooked through and no pink remains. Add wine and cook until reduced by half. Add tomatoes and basil, reduce heat to low, and simmer for 20 minutes, stirring occasionally. Remove from heat and set aside.
3. While sauce is simmering, add salt and pennette to the boiling water and cook, uncovered, over high heat until pasta is almost al dente. Scoop out about 1 cup (250 mL) of the pasta water and set aside. Drain pasta.
4. Return sauté pan to medium heat. Add 2 tbsp (25 mL) of the reserved pasta water and bring to a simmer. Add pennette and continue to cook for about 3 minutes, until pasta is al dente, using a wooden spoon to toss and coat evenly, adding more pasta water if necessary. Add half of the Parmigiano-Reggiano and toss well.
5. Transfer to a large serving bowl. Sprinkle with remaining cheese and serve immediately.

Variations

If pennette is not available, substitute penne or rigatoni.

Ruote with Pork Sausage and Arugula

Ruote di carro is a contemporary pasta shape — flat, round and hollow, with spokes radiating from the center. These "cart wheels" are visually suited to this quick, easy recipe that uses sausage rounds.

Serves 4 to 6

Tips

To cook sausage, heat 1 tbsp (15 mL) extra-virgin olive oil in a medium skillet over medium heat. Add the sausage and turn frequently until browned on all sides and cooked through. When cool enough to handle, cut into ¼-inch (0.5 cm) slices.

3 tbsp	extra-virgin olive oil	45 mL
½ cup	diced pancetta	125 mL
½ cup	diced onion	125 mL
6 oz	cooked sweet or hot Italian sausage, sliced into thin rounds (about 1 standard Italian sausage; see Tips, left)	175 g
	Salt and freshly ground black pepper	
½ cup	dry white Italian wine	125 mL
1 tbsp	salt	15 mL
1 lb	dried ruote di carro (see Variations, below)	500 g
1 cup	fresh arugula, packed	250 mL
¾ cup	grated Parmigiano-Reggiano, divided	175 mL

1. In a covered pasta pot over high heat, bring water to a rapid boil.

2. Meanwhile, in a large sauté pan, heat oil over medium heat. Add pancetta and onion and cook, stirring, until pancetta is cooked through and onion is soft, about 5 minutes. Add sausage and season to taste with salt and pepper. Cook until sausage is heated through. Add wine and cook until reduced by half. Remove pan from heat and set aside.

3. While wine is reducing, add salt and ruote to the boiling water and cook, uncovered, over high heat until pasta is almost al dente. Scoop out about 1 cup (250 mL) of the pasta water and set aside. Drain pasta.

4. Return sauté pan to medium heat. Add 2 tbsp (25 mL) of the reserved pasta water and bring to a simmer. Add ruote and continue to cook for about 3 minutes, until pasta is al dente, using a wooden spoon to toss and coat evenly, adding more pasta water if necessary. Add arugula and half of the Parmigiano-Reggiano and toss well to ensure arugula is evenly distributed.

5. Transfer to a large serving platter. Sprinkle with remaining cheese and serve immediately.

Variations

If ruote is unavailable, use rotelle or fusilli.

Spaghetti alla carbonara

Spaghetti with Guanciale, Eggs and Pecorino Romano

People outside of Italy think of carbonara as a cream and bacon sauce — definitely incorrect. The name of this dish comes from carbone, *meaning "coal." Some say it was the coal miners' favorite dish and that the black pepper resembles coal dust. Others say it is made with ingredients — eggs and bacon — that could be bought from the same vendors who delivered coal to your home. Yet another claims it was created by an Italian secret society, the Carbonari. All these tales aside, it is a very tasty dish, one that has been made for centuries in Rome. It is based on preserved meat (I believe guanciale to be the best and most authentic) and contains no cream.*

Serves 4 to 6

Tips

Although it won't be authentic, if you can't find guanciale, substitute pancetta instead.

It is fine to use eggs that haven't been pasteurized in this recipe, because they coagulate in cooking, which means they have reached the "safe zone" (160°F/71°C) where any salmonella that might be present will be killed.

3 tbsp	extra-virgin olive oil	45 mL
⅓ cup	diced paper-thin guanciale (see Tips, left)	75 mL
	Salt and freshly ground black pepper	
1 tbsp	salt	15 mL
1 lb	dried spaghetti	500 g
1	egg yolk (see Tips, left)	1
3	large eggs	3
½ cup	grated Pecorino Romano, divided	125 mL

1. In a covered pasta pot over high heat, bring water to a rapid boil.

2. Meanwhile, in a large sauté pan, heat oil over medium heat. Add guanciale and season to taste with salt and pepper. Cook, stirring, until guanciale becomes golden brown, about 10 minutes. Remove from heat and set aside.

3. Add salt and spaghetti to the boiling water and cook, uncovered, over high heat until pasta is almost al dente. Scoop out about 1 cup (250 mL) of the pasta water and set aside. Drain pasta.

4. Return sauté pan to medium heat. Add 2 tbsp (25 mL) of the pasta water and heat through. Add spaghetti and continue to cook for about 3 minutes, until pasta is al dente, using pasta tongs to toss and coat evenly, adding more pasta water if necessary. Remove from heat and set aside.

5. In a small bowl, combine egg yolk, eggs and 2 tbsp (25 mL) of the Pecorino Romano and whisk until mixture forms a ribbon when whisk is lifted from the bowl. Add to sauté pan (do not return pan to heat or you will scramble the eggs). Using pasta tongs, toss to coat evenly while eggs cook in the residual heat and sauce coats the pasta thickly, adding more pasta water if necessary.

6. Transfer to a large serving platter. Sprinkle with remaining cheese and add a few turns of black pepper straight from the pepper mill. Serve immediately.

Bucatini all'Amatriciana

The origins of this dish are contentious. It is claimed by Rome, the capital city of the Lazio region, and also by the town of Amatrice, about 60 miles away. There is even a dispute about the pasta used. Romans use bucatini (like thick spaghetti with a hole in the middle) and elsewhere it's often made with spaghetti or a short pasta. In Amatrice it has no onions; in Rome the chefs add onions. Although the dish is well-known outside Italy, it is often poorly prepared. For authenticity, guanciale, or salt-cured pork jowl (see below) is essential, — not pancetta or bacon, which are usually substituted outside Italy.

Serves 4 to 6

Tips

While completing the cooking process in the pan, toss the pasta continuously to ensure that the liquid is evenly distributed throughout and that it doesn't stick.

If you have leftovers, use them to make Timbale of Bucatini all'Amatriciana (see Variations, page 175).

3 tbsp	extra-virgin olive oil	45 mL
½ cup	finely diced guanciale (see Variations, below)	125 mL
¾ cup	dry white Italian wine	175 mL
¼ tsp	very thinly sliced red finger chile, packed (see Tips, page 76)	1 mL
3 cups	canned crushed Italian tomatoes	750 mL
	Salt and freshly ground black pepper	
1 tbsp	salt	15 mL
1 lb	dried bucatini (see Variations, below)	500 g
¾ cup	grated Pecorino Romano, divided	175 mL

1. In a covered pasta pot over high heat, bring water to a rapid boil.

2. Meanwhile, in a large sauté pan, heat oil over medium heat. Add guanciale and cook, stirring, until lightly browned, about 5 minutes. Add wine and chile and cook until wine is reduced by half. Add tomatoes and reduce heat to low. Season to taste with salt and pepper. Simmer very slowly for 30 minutes, until sauce thickens.

3. While sauce is simmering, add salt and bucatini to the boiling water and cook, uncovered, over high heat until pasta is almost al dente. Scoop out about 1 cup (250 mL) of the pasta water and set aside. Drain pasta.

4. When sauce has finished cooking, add 2 tbsp (25 mL) of the reserved pasta water and, if necessary, return to a simmer. Add bucatini and continue to cook for about 3 minutes, until pasta is al dente, using pasta tongs to toss and coat evenly, adding more pasta water if necessary. Add half of the Pecorino Romano and toss well.

5. Transfer to a large serving bowl and sprinkle with remaining cheese. Serve immediately.

Variations

If you can't find guanciale, substitute pancetta.

Bucatini is thick strand pasta that is hollow in the center. If it isn't available use thick spaghetti.

> ### Guanciale
> Guanciale is bacon from the pork cheek or jowl (*guancia* means "cheek") that is cured but not smoked. It is rubbed in salt, black and red pepper and sometimes sugar, then hung and aged. Roman in origin, it is an essential ingredient in Bucatini all'Amatriciana. Because it is often hard to find in North America, this dish is frequently made with pancetta.

Garganelli con sugo di mortadella

Garganelli with Mortadella Sauce

Garganelli is short tubular pasta with angled ends that looks as if a square of pasta has been rolled up diagonally. It's a nice shape, and several manufacturers make it for distribution outside Italy. This is an authentic sauce from Emilia-Romagna, a region of Italy that is rich in butter, cream, cheese and eggs.

Serves 4 to 6

Tips

When using mortadella, be sure to remove the plastic casing, which is often left on when it is sliced.

Never rinse pasta after draining it. The surface starch helps the sauce to cling and is important to producing the best-quality dish.

3 tbsp	extra-virgin olive oil	45 mL
¼ cup	diced pancetta	50 mL
¼ cup	diced onion	50 mL
½ cup	dry white Italian wine	125 mL
¼ cup	heavy or whipping (35%) cream	50 mL
½ cup	diced mortadella	125 mL
1 tbsp	salt	15 mL
1 lb	dried garganelli (see Variations, below)	500 g
¾ cup	grated Parmigiano-Reggiano, divided	175 mL
	Salt and freshly ground black pepper	

1. In a covered pasta pot over high heat, bring water to a rapid boil.
2. Meanwhile, in a large sauté pan, heat oil over medium heat. Add pancetta and onion and cook, stirring, until pancetta is cooked through and onion is translucent, about 5 minutes. Add wine and cook until reduced by half. Add cream and mortadella and reduce heat to low. Simmer for 2 minutes. Remove from heat and set aside.
3. While sauce is simmering, add salt and garganelli to the boiling water and cook, uncovered, until pasta is almost al dente. Scoop out about 1 cup (250 mL) of the pasta water and set aside. Drain pasta.
4. Return sauté pan to low heat and add 2 tbsp (25 mL) of the reserved pasta water. Return to a simmer. Add garganelli and continue to cook for about 3 minutes, until pasta is al dente, using a wooden spoon to toss and coat evenly, adding more pasta water if necessary. Add half of the Parmigiano-Reggiano and season to taste with salt and pepper. Toss well.
5. Transfer to a large serving platter and sprinkle with remaining cheese. Serve immediately.

Variations

Substitute penne or cut ziti for the garganelli.

Maccheroni con mortadella, panna e uove

Maccheroni with Mortadella, Cream and Eggs

This is a very mellow, satisfying sauce from the region of Emilia-Romagna, where dairy products are bountiful. It's rich but simple to prepare. Maccheroni is not elbow macaroni but a short tubular pasta, about as long as a little finger, with straight-cut ends. In this recipe the egg yolks are tossed with the finished sauced pasta to enrich and thicken it. They should not be scrambled, which can happen over direct heat.

Serves 4 to 6

Tips

Be sure to remove the plastic casing from the mortadella slices in case the deli or meat market left it on before slicing.

It is fine to use eggs that haven't been pasteurized in this recipe, because they coagulate while being tossed with the hot pasta, which means they have reached the "safe zone" (160°F/71°C) where any salmonella that might be present will be killed.

If you have leftovers, use them to make Tart of Maccheroni with Mortadella, Cream and Eggs (see Variations, page 174).

12	paper-thin mortadella slices	12
3 tbsp	extra-virgin olive oil	45 mL
¼ cup	diced onion	50 mL
	Salt and freshly ground black pepper	
½ cup	dry white Italian wine	125 mL
2 cups	heavy or whipping (35%) cream	500 mL
1 tbsp	salt	15 mL
1 lb	dried maccheroni (see Variation, below)	500 g
6 tbsp	grated Parmigiano-Reggiano, divided	90 mL
6	egg yolks, well beaten	6

1. In a covered pasta pot over high heat, bring water to a rapid boil.

2. Cover the well and rim of a large serving platter with mortadella slices. Set aside.

3. Meanwhile, in a large sauté pan, heat oil over medium heat. Add onion, season to taste with salt and pepper, and cook, stirring, until onion is soft and translucent, about 3 minutes. Add wine, reduce the heat to low and cook until reduced by half. Add cream and cook, stirring, for 1 minute. Remove from heat and set aside.

4. Add salt and maccheroni to the boiling water and cook, uncovered, until pasta is almost al dente. Scoop out about 1 cup (250 mL) of the pasta water and set aside. Drain pasta.

5. Return sauté pan to medium heat. Add 2 tbsp (25 mL) of the reserved pasta water, stir, and return to a simmer. Add maccheroni and continue to cook for about 3 minutes, until pasta is al dente, using a wooden spoon to toss and coat evenly, and adding more pasta water if necessary. Remove from heat and add half of the Parmigiano-Reggiano. Toss well. Add egg yolks and toss well to coat evenly.

6. Spoon onto the mortadella-lined serving platter. Sprinkle with remaining cheese and serve immediately.

Variation
Substitute penne for the maccheroni.

Fusilli alla pancetta e olive verdi

Fusilli with Pancetta and Green Olives

Green Italian olives have a different flavor profile from the more common Spanish ones. They are piquant, but not as pungent or acidic. I particularly like green Cerignola olives (they also come in black), which are large and sweet. Cerignolas contribute a lot to this recipe, so they're worth looking for at Italian grocers, gourmet shops and online, where they are readily available.

Serves 4 to 6

Tips

Although this dish has a lot of flavor, the pasta has very little sauce, so the pasta is cooked to the al dente stage and then very quickly finished in the pan.

Always use a large pot and plenty of water when cooking pasta. To properly cook 1 pound (500 g) of pasta, you'll need a pot with a volume of at least 8 quarts (8 L) so that you can use 6 quarts (6 L) of water.

1 tbsp	salt	15 mL
1 lb	dried fusilli (see Variations, below)	500 g
3 tbsp	extra-virgin olive oil	45 mL
¾ cup	diced pancetta	175 mL
½ cup	sliced pitted green Cerignola olives (see Variations, below)	125 mL
	Salt and freshly ground black pepper	
¾ cup	grated Parmigiano-Reggiano, divided	175 mL

1. In a covered pasta pot over high heat, bring water to a rapid boil. Add salt and fusilli and cook, uncovered, until pasta is al dente. Scoop out about 1 cup (250 mL) of the pasta water and set aside. Drain pasta.

2. In a large sauté pan, heat oil over medium heat. Add pancetta and cook, stirring, until cooked through, about 5 minutes. Add 2 tbsp (25 mL) of the reserved pasta water. Add olives and cook 2 to 3 minutes.

3. Add fusilli, remove from heat and toss well with a wooden spoon to coat evenly, adding more pasta water if necessary. Season to taste with salt and pepper. Sprinkle with half of the Parmigiano-Reggiano and toss well.

4. Transfer to a large serving bowl and sprinkle with remaining cheese. Serve immediately.

Variations

Substitute any green Italian olive for the Cerignolas. You may use the pitted green Italian olives that are often marinated in oil with garlic and sometimes red chile flakes, which are widely available.

Substitute penne or rotini for the fusilli.

> ### Cerignola Olives
> Cerignolas are large oval olives produced in southern Italy that can be green or black, depending on maturity. The best are handpicked and brine-cured with just enough vinegar to preserve a sweet, mellow flavor. The green olives are firmer in texture; the black are softer and more flavorful. They add a wonderfully authentic touch to these recipes, although you can obviously substitute other Italian olives.

Pennette con pancetta e asparagi

Pennette with Pancetta and Asparagus

Pennette are smaller, thinner penne about the same length and width as the asparagus pieces in this recipe. This is a simple pasta that is very easy to make and looks quite pretty.

Serves 4 to 6

Tips

Many shops stock pancetta that is already diced.

I usually season my sauces in the initial stages of cooking so the flavors have time to bloom. I always taste the final product and, if necessary, add more salt and pepper just before serving.

Never rinse pasta after draining it. The surface starch helps the sauce to cling and is important to producing the best-quality dish.

Because this is a short, sturdy pasta, it is easier to toss using a wooden spoon rather than pasta tongs, which work best for longer pastas.

3 tbsp	extra-virgin olive oil	45 mL
¾ cup	diced pancetta	175 mL
¼ cup	diced onion	50 mL
1 cup	sliced (2 inches/5 cm) pencil-thin asparagus	250 mL
	Salt and freshly ground black pepper	
1 cup	dry white Italian wine	250 mL
1 tbsp	salt	15 mL
1 lb	dried pennette (see Variations, below)	500 g
¾ cup	grated Parmigiano-Reggiano, divided	175 mL

1. In a covered pasta pot over high heat, bring water to a rapid boil.

2. Meanwhile, in a large sauté pan, heat oil over medium heat. Add pancetta and onion and cook, stirring, until pancetta is cooked through and onion is tender, about 5 minutes. Add asparagus, season to taste with salt and pepper and cook, stirring, until asparagus is tender, about 5 minutes. Add wine and cook until reduced by half. Remove from heat and set aside.

3. While sauce is simmering, add salt and pennette to the boiling water and cook, uncovered, over high heat until pasta is almost al dente. Scoop out about 1 cup (250 mL) of the pasta water and set aside. Drain pasta.

4. Return sauté pan to medium heat. Add 2 tbsp (25 mL) of the reserved pasta water and return to a simmer. Add pennette and continue to cook for about 3 minutes, until pasta is al dente, using a wooden spoon to toss and coat evenly, and adding more pasta water if necessary. Add half of the Parmigiano-Reggiano and toss well.

5. Transfer to a large serving bowl and sprinkle with remaining cheese. Serve at once.

Variations

If pennette is not available, substitute penne or cut ziti.

Penne with Pancetta and Gorgonzola Cheese

In this recipe the Gorgonzola and cream are smooth and rich. Topping the pasta with chopped walnuts adds contrast in both texture and flavor.

Serves 4 to 6

Tips

For 1 cup (250 mL) Gorgonzola, packed, you'll need about 6 oz (175 g).

Don't scrimp on ingredients. Always buy the best quality you can find and afford. It will make a big difference to the results you produce.

If you have leftovers, use them to make Tart of Penne with Pancetta and Gorgonzola Cheese (see Variations, page 174).

3 tbsp	extra-virgin olive oil	45 mL
¾ cup	diced pancetta	175 mL
¼ cup	diced onion	50 mL
	Salt and freshly ground black pepper	
½ cup	dry white Italian wine	125 mL
¼ cup	heavy or whipping (35%) cream	50 mL
1 cup	Gorgonzola piccante at room temperature, packed (see Tips, left)	250 mL
1 tbsp	salt	15 mL
1 lb	dried penne (see Variations, below)	500 mL
3 tbsp	grated Parmigiano-Reggiano	45 mL
6 tbsp	roughly chopped walnuts	90 mL

1. In a covered pasta pot over high heat, bring water to a rapid boil.

2. Meanwhile, in a large sauté pan over medium heat, combine oil, pancetta and onion. Season to taste with salt and pepper. Cook, stirring, until pancetta is cooked through, about 5 minutes. Add wine and reduce by half. Add cream, reduce heat to low and simmer for 2 to 3 minutes to thicken and meld. Add Gorgonzola in 4 batches, stirring after each addition. Stir until sauce is smooth. Remove from heat.

3. Meanwhile, add salt and penne to the boiling water and cook, uncovered, over high heat until pasta is almost al dente. Scoop out about 1 cup (250 mL) of the pasta water and set aside. Drain pasta.

4. Return sauté pan to medium heat. Add 2 tbsp (25 mL) of the reserved pasta water and simmer for 2 to 3 minutes. Add penne and continue to cook for about 3 minutes, until pasta is al dente, using a wooden spoon to toss and coat evenly, and adding more pasta water if necessary. Add Parmigiano-Reggiano and toss well.

5. Transfer to a large serving platter and sprinkle with walnuts. Serve immediately.

Variations

If Gorgonzola piccante is not available, use Gorgonzola dolce. Substitute fusilli for the penne.

Gorgonzola Cheese: Dolce and Piccante

Gorgonzola is a blue-veined cheese made from cow's milk. The DOC (*Denominazione di origine controllata*) restricts its production to Lombardy and Piedmont. Young cheeses (aged two to six months) are soft and called Gorgonzola dolce. The longer-aged cheeses (Gorgonzola piccante) are firmer.

Rigatoni alla molisana

Rigatoni with Pancetta, Peperoncini and Pecorino Romano

As the Italian name suggests, this recipe is typical of the Molise region in central Italy. It is simple, colorful and fun. The dish bears some resemblance to carbonara (see recipe, page 125) except that it does not contain eggs, which makes it easier to prepare because there is no danger of scrambling them. Please use a particularly fragrant extra-virgin olive oil, because it will be drizzled over the finished pasta. I have friends who keep Italian bread handy when they make this dish, for soaking up the oil. Pasta plus bread seems like overkill but — maybe not?

Serves 4 to 6

Tips

For convenience, use pancetta that is already diced.

If you have leftovers, use them to make Tart of Rigatoni with Pancetta, Peperoncini and Pecorino Romano (see Variations, page 174).

5 tbsp	extra-virgin olive oil, divided	75 mL
¾ cup	diced pancetta	175 mL
¼ cup	diced onion	50 mL
1½ tsp	thinly sliced garlic, packed	7 mL
⅛ tsp	thinly sliced red finger chile, packed (see Tips, page 74)	0.5 mL
	Salt and freshly ground black pepper	
½ cup	dry white Italian wine	125 mL
1 tbsp	salt	15 mL
1 lb	dried rigatoni (see Variations, below)	500 g
9 tbsp	grated Pecorino Romano, divided	135 mL
1 tbsp	hand-torn fresh basil leaves	15 mL
1 tbsp	roughly chopped fresh Italian parsley leaves	15 mL

1. In a covered pasta pot over high heat, bring water to a rapid boil.

2. Meanwhile, in a large sauté pan, heat 3 tbsp (45 mL) of the oil over medium heat. Add pancetta, onion, garlic and chile and stir. Season to taste with salt and pepper. Cook, stirring, until pancetta is browned and vegetables are tender, about 10 minutes. Add wine and cook until reduced by half. Remove from heat and set aside.

3. While sauce is simmering, add salt and rigatoni to the boiling water and cook, uncovered, over high heat until pasta is almost al dente. Scoop out about 1 cup (250 mL) of the pasta water and set aside. Drain pasta.

4. Return pan to medium heat. Add 2 tbsp (25 mL) of the reserved pasta water and return to a simmer. Heat through. Add rigatoni and continue to cook for about 3 minutes, until pasta is al dente, using a wooden spoon to toss and coat evenly, and adding more pasta water if necessary. Add 6 tbsp (90 mL) of the Pecorino Romano and the basil and parsley; toss well.

5. Transfer to a large serving platter. Drizzle with remaining olive oil and sprinkle with remaining cheese. Serve immediately.

Variations

Substitute penne or maccheroni for the rigatoni.

Farfalle al prosciutto e pesto

Farfalle with Prosciutto and Pesto

Prosciutto goes very well with the fresh herb flavors of pesto. I recommend that you make the pesto a day or two ahead and refrigerate it. Then when you're ready to prepare this pasta, it's a snap to make. It's worth looking for the Pecorino Sardo used in the pesto. This is a hard, or grana, sheep's-milk cheese from Sardinia that is smoother and has a richer flavor than the more widely available Pecorino Romano.

Serves 4 to 6

Tips

When making pesto, do not run the blender continuously, because that will heat the pesto and damage its color and flavor. The secret is to pulse so you produce an uneven purée. Store finished pesto in a jar with a tight-fitting lid in the refrigerator for up to four days.

Pecorino Sardo is available at gourmet cheese markets and some Italian grocers. If you can't find it, substitute an equal quantity of Pecorino Romano.

Pesto Genovese

30	fresh basil leaves, stems removed	30
2	peeled garlic cloves	2
3 tbsp	pine nuts	45 mL
½ cup	freshly grated Parmigiano-Reggiano	125 mL
½ cup	freshly grated Pecorino Sardo (see Tips, left)	125 mL
¾ cup	extra-virgin olive oil	175 mL
	Salt	

Pasta

14 to 16	paper-thin slices prosciutto (about 6 oz/175 g)	14 to 16
1 tbsp	salt	15 mL
1 lb	dried farfalle (see Variations, below)	500 g
⅔ cup	Pesto Genovese (see recipe above)	150 mL
¾ cup	grated Parmigiano-Reggiano, divided	175 mL
	Salt and freshly ground black pepper	

1. *Pesto Genovese:* In a food processor fitted with a metal blade, combine basil, garlic, pine nuts, Parmigiano-Reggiano and Pecorino Sardo. Pulse for 3 seconds. Add olive oil and continue to pulse until mixture has been roughly puréed, scraping down sides as necessary. Add salt and pulse again (see Tips, left).

2. *Pasta:* Cover the well and rim of a large serving platter with prosciutto slices. Set aside.

3. In a covered pasta pot over high heat, bring water to a rapid boil. Add salt and farfalle and cook, uncovered, until pasta is almost al dente. Scoop out about 1 cup (250 mL) of the pasta water and set aside. Drain pasta.

4. Meanwhile, in a large sauté pan over medium heat, combine 2 tbsp (25 mL) of the pasta water and pesto. Stir well. Add farfalle and cook for about 3 minutes, until pasta is al dente, using a wooden spoon to toss and coat evenly, and adding more pasta water if necessary. Add half of the Parmigiano-Reggiano and toss well. Season to taste with salt and pepper and toss.

5. Transfer to the prosciutto-lined platter and sprinkle with remaining cheese. Serve immediately.

Variations

Substitute penne, pennette or cut ziti for the farfalle.

Penne al prosciutto e funghi

Penne with Prosciutto and Mushrooms

When a platter is lined
with paper-thin prosciutto
and hot pasta is piled on
top, something wonderful
happens: as the pasta heats
the prosciutto, the meat
releases its flavor. When you
serve the pasta with a little
bit of the prosciutto in each
portion, it is very fragrant in
a way that is different from
cooked prosciutto.

Serves 4 to 6

Tips
Prosciutto is best eaten at
room temperature, at which
point the flavor blooms nicely.
If you are leaving it out for
longer than 30 minutes, be
sure to cover it with plastic
wrap to prevent oxidation.

To prepare the mushrooms
for this recipe, trim ends
and slice each mushroom
vertically into eight pieces
as follows: in half, then
each half in half, then each
quarter in half.

14 to 16	paper-thin slices prosciutto	14 to 16
3 tbsp	extra-virgin olive oil	45 mL
¼ cup	diced pancetta	50 mL
¼ cup	diced onion	50 mL
	Salt and freshly ground black pepper	
1 rounded cup	sliced cremini mushrooms (see Tips, left)	275 mL
½ cup	dry red Italian wine	125 mL
1 tbsp	salt	15 mL
1 lb	dried penne (see Variations, below)	500 g
¾ cup	grated Parmigiano-Reggiano, divided	175 mL

1. In a covered pasta pot over high heat, bring water to a rapid boil.

2. Line the rim and well of a large serving platter with prosciutto slices. Set aside.

3. Meanwhile, in a large sauté pan, heat oil over medium heat. Add pancetta and onion and stir. Season to taste with salt and pepper. Add mushrooms and cook, stirring, until vegetables are soft and tender, about 10 minutes. Add wine and cook until reduced by half. Remove from heat and set aside.

4. Add salt and penne to the boiling water and cook until pasta is almost al dente. Scoop out about 1 cup (250 mL) of the pasta water and set aside. Drain pasta.

5. Return sauté pan to medium heat. Add 2 tbsp (25 mL) of the reserved pasta water and heat through. Add penne and continue to cook for about 3 minutes, until pasta is al dente, using a wooden spoon to toss and coat evenly, and adding more pasta water if necessary. Add half of the Parmigiano-Reggiano and toss well.

6. Transfer to prosciutto-lined platter. Sprinkle with remaining cheese and serve immediately.

Variations
Substitute pennette or cut ziti for the penne.

> ### Prosciutto
> Prosciutto is Italian ham that has been seasoned and salt-cured (but not smoked), then air-dried. There are two kinds: prosciutto cotto (cooked) and prosciutto crudo (uncooked but cured and ready to eat). Prosciutto crudo is the kind used in these recipes and is usually sold, sliced paper-thin, in gourmet markets and Italian delis. Proscuitto is a DOP (*Denominazione di origine protetta*) product labeled by city or region of origin. The two most familiar exports are prosciutto di Parma, from Parma, and prosciutto di San Daniele, from Friuli–Venezia Giulia.

Bigoli allo speck e broccoli

Bigoli with Speck and Broccoli

Speck is a very special cold-smoked, dry-cured prosciutto-like ham indigenous to the Alto Adige region of northern Italy. It is less pungent than pancetta and more flavorful than prosciutto. In this recipe it combines well with broccoli and the thick bigoli.

Serves 4 to 6

Tips

You'll need to stir the broccoli constantly to ensure it doesn't burn.

I usually season my sauces in the initial stages of cooking so the flavors have time to bloom. I always taste the final product and, if necessary, add more salt and pepper just before serving.

Any dry white Italian table wine will work well in this recipe. Here I'd probably use Pinot Bianco, which is a good basic dry white wine for use in Italian cooking.

14 to 16	paper-thin slices speck (about 6 oz/175 g; see Variations, below)	14 to 16
3 tbsp	extra-virgin olive oil	45 mL
2 cups	quartered broccoli florets	500 mL
	Salt and freshly ground black pepper	
½ cup	dry white Italian wine (see Tips, left)	125 mL
1 cup	water	250 mL
1 tbsp	salt	15 mL
1 lb	dried bigoli (see Variations, below)	500 g
¾ cup	grated Parmigiano-Reggiano, divided	175 mL

1. In a covered pasta pot over high heat, bring water to a rapid boil.

2. Line the rim and well of a large serving platter with speck. Set aside.

3. Meanwhile, in a large sauté pan, heat oil over medium heat. Add broccoli and salt and pepper to taste and cook until broccoli turns dark green, about 5 minutes, stirring constantly so broccoli does not burn. Add wine and cook until reduced by half. Add water and simmer until broccoli is tender, about 5 minutes. Remove from heat.

4. While sauce is simmering, add salt and bigoli to the boiling water and cook, uncovered, over high heat until pasta is almost al dente. Scoop out about 1 cup (250 mL) of the pasta water and set aside. Drain pasta.

5. Return sauté pan to medium heat and add 2 tbsp (25 mL) of the reserved pasta water. Cook for 3 minutes to heat through. Add bigoli and continue to cook for about 3 minutes, until pasta is al dente, using pasta tongs to toss and coat evenly, and adding more pasta water if necessary. Add half of the Parmigiano-Reggiano and toss.

6. Transfer to the speck-lined platter. Sprinkle with remaining cheese and serve immediately.

Variations

If speck is not available, substitute prosciutto.

If bigoli is not available, substitute thick spaghetti.

> **Speck**
>
> Speck is a type of bacon that is popular in Italy and Germany. It is made from hog legs rather than the belly, cured with salt and spices (often juniper berries and garlic) and cold-smoked. In Italy it originated in the northern Alto Adige region. If you can't find Italian speck, a good substitute is Austrian speck, available at German delicatessens.

Ruote di carro con speck e mascarpone

Ruote with Speck and Mascarpone

This is a fun recipe because it is easy to make, it produces a lusciously creamy sauce and the wheel-shaped pasta is very festive. The crisp oven-baked speck is so tempting you might want to make extra for pre-dinner snacking. If you start nibbling it's hard to stop, though, and you may not have enough for the pasta.

Serves 4 to 6

Tips

If speck is not available, substitute prosciutto.

If you have leftovers, use them to make Timbale of Ruote with Speck and Mascarpone (see Variations, page 175).

- Preheat oven to 400°F (200°C)
- Rimmed baking sheet

6	paper-thin slices speck (about 3 oz/90 g)	6
3 tbsp	extra-virgin olive oil	45 mL
1/4 cup	diced pancetta	50 mL
1/4 cup	diced onion	50 mL
	Salt and freshly ground black pepper	
1/2 cup	dry white Italian wine	125 mL
3/4 cup	mascarpone	175 mL
1 tbsp	salt	15 mL
1 lb	dried ruote di carro (see Variations, below)	500 g
3/4 cup	grated Parmigiano-Reggiano, divided	175 mL

1. In a covered pasta pot over high heat, bring water to a rapid boil.

2. Line a baking sheet with parchment paper. Lay speck slices on the paper, ensuring edges don't touch. Bake in preheated oven until speck is crisp but not burned, about 10 to 12 minutes. Remove from oven and let cool to room temperature.

3. Meanwhile, in a large sauté pan, heat oil over medium heat. Add pancetta and onion and stir well. Season to taste with salt and pepper. Cook, stirring until pancetta is cooked through and onion is soft and tender, about 5 minutes. Add wine and cook until reduced by half. Add mascarpone, reduce heat to low and stir well. Simmer for 2 minutes. Remove pan from heat and set aside.

4. While sauce is simmering, add salt and ruote to the boiling water and cook, uncovered, over high heat until pasta is almost al dente. Scoop out about 1 cup (250 mL) of the pasta water and set aside. Drain pasta.

5. Return sauté pan to low heat. Add 2 tbsp (25 mL) of the reserved pasta water and bring to a simmer. Add ruote and continue to cook for about 3 minutes, until pasta is al dente, using a wooden spoon to toss and coat evenly, and adding more pasta water if necessary. Add half of the Parmigiano-Reggiano and toss well.

6. Transfer to a large serving platter and sprinkle with remaining cheese. Crumble half of the reserved crisped speck and sprinkle it over the ruote. Scatter remaining whole slices of speck at random over the pasta. Serve immediately.

Variations

Substitute rotelle or penne for the ruote.

Pasta with Seafood: Something Special

Italy's mainland is wrapped in one long seacoast. Only its northern and part of its eastern borders are on land. And then there are the islands — Sardinia, Sicily, Elba and many small ones — which are completely surrounded by sea. Except for some parts of the Italian Alps, no place in Italy is more than 75 miles from the sea, which is why fresh seafood has always been plentiful. Even so, it has always been considered a delicacy and a celebratory food in and of itself.

When I was growing up in New York, we ate fish at home on special occasions such as Christmas. And we ate the fish after the pasta, which is a very traditional Italian practice. Outside Italy, however, people who like pasta, especially restaurant diners, really want pasta *with* seafood. I believe we eat pasta that way more often than Italians.

I still feel that pasta with seafood is special, and with a few exceptions such as calamari and shrimp, not for every day. For most home cooks, getting fresh seafood is a challenge. And if fresh ingredients are of the utmost importance to the success of my recipes, fresh seafood is doubly so. Make sure you have an excellent fishmonger who sells only the freshest products. And don't overlook the option of ordering fresh seafood online. Several purveyors will deliver fresh seafood to your door — at a premium, of course.

If you don't have good fish markets, I recommend using certain frozen products. For instance, some frozen calamari and shrimp may be better than the "fresh" versions that are readily available. But I'm very particular about others — for instance, scallops. If you can't find fresh scallops, skip that recipe or substitute shrimp rather than using the frozen version.

Many of the fish of Italy are impossible to find outside the country, so I have substituted some readily available flavor-cousins in these recipes. That being said, Italians until recently seldom, if ever, ate salmon. But they do today. So although it isn't "authentic" in the traditional sense, I have included a salmon and pasta recipe. And for a festive occasion, there is a recipe for fresh lobster and pasta — very extravagant.

The recipes in this chapter call for dried pasta because the flavors need to be transferred from the sauce to the pasta. Dried pasta can stand up to slightly longer cooking in the sauce than fresh pasta, which is often too delicate. However, this being Italian cooking, there are seafood recipes especially for fresh pasta in the chapter Simple Luxury: Fresh Pasta Tossed in Sauce: Pappardelle with Shrimp and Peas (page 258), Stracci with Clams (page 265), Quadrati with Calamari Ragù (page 267) and Quadrati with Mussels (page 271). These recipes all use fresh pasta, although dried pasta can be substituted.

Please, No Cheese

One American preference — sprinkling grated cheese on seafood pasta — is definitely not Italian. In Italy it is considered almost sacrilegious, although it is really a matter of preference and cultural conformity. For instance, we always finish a risotto — even a seafood risotto — with cheese. Go figure. But to be authentically Italian, you should never serve cheese with seafood pasta.

Bucatini ai calamari
Bucatini with Calamari

Bucatini are like thick, hollow spaghetti tubes. After they are cooked and drained, some water remains inside the tubes. And when they are tossed in sauce, some of the sauce finds its way into the tubes as well, adding to the overall flavor.

Serves 4 to 6

Tips

Frozen squid (calamari) rings — or a combination of rings and tentacles — are fine for this dish. You can defrost them under cold running water and drain, or you can add the frozen calamari directly to the pan and cook until defrosted.

Any dry white Italian table wine will work well in this recipe. Here I'd probably use a Pinot Bianco, which is a good basic dry white wine for use in Italian cooking.

3 tbsp	extra-virgin olive oil	45 mL
1 tsp	thinly sliced garlic	5 mL
1/8 tsp	dried red pepper flakes	0.5 mL
10 oz	cleaned calamari in 1/2-inch (1 cm) rings, plus tentacles, or all rings	300 g
1 cup	dry white Italian wine (see Tips, left)	250 mL
1 cup	drained canned diced Italian tomatoes	250 mL
1 cup	canned crushed Italian tomatoes	250 mL
1 tbsp	salt	15 mL
1 lb	dried bucatini (see Variations, below)	500 g
	Salt and freshly ground black pepper	
1 tbsp	chopped Italian parsley leaves	15 mL

1. In a covered pasta pot over high heat, bring water to a rapid boil.

2. Meanwhile, in a large sauté pan, heat oil over medium heat. Add garlic and pepper flakes and cook, stirring, until garlic is translucent but not brown, about 3 minutes. Add calamari and wine and bring to a boil. Reduce heat and simmer, stirring, for 1 minute, then add diced and crushed tomatoes and simmer until mixture is thick enough to lightly coat the back of a spoon, about 10 minutes.

3. While sauce is simmering, add salt and bucatini to the boiling water and cook, uncovered, over high heat until pasta is al dente. Scoop out about 1 cup (250 mL) of the pasta water and set aside. Drain pasta.

4. Add 1/2 cup (125 ml) of the reserved pasta water to tomato mixture. Add bucatini and continue to cook for 2 to 3 minutes to meld flavors, using pasta tongs to toss and coat evenly, and adding more pasta water if necessary. Season to taste with salt and pepper.

5. Transfer to a large serving bowl and sprinkle with parsley. Serve immediately.

Variations
Substitute thick spaghetti or linguine for the bucatini.

Calamari
Squid are often called by their Italian name in English-speaking countries, perhaps because *calamari* sounds more appetizing. Squid are very versatile for cooking. The body can be stuffed, cut into flat fillets or sliced into rings. The tentacles and even the ink from the ink sac are edible. The only inedible parts of the squid are its beak and its gladius, or pen, a hard, feather-shaped internal support structure. Most calamari sold at fish markets are so-called "fresh frozen," defrosted.

Bucatini al sugo di cozze

Bucatini with Mussel Sauce

In this dish the pasta and the mussel sauce simmer together, melding the flavors. If bucatini is not available, substitute thick spaghetti or linguine.

Serves 4 to 6

Tips

I usually season my sauces in the initial stages of cooking so the flavors have time to bloom. I always taste the final product and, if necessary, add salt and pepper just before serving.

I like to tear basil leaves by hand rather than slicing them, because I think they look and taste better.

Live mussels will close their shells when moved or tapped. Discard any uncooked mussels with open shells, and any fully cooked mussels with shells that fail to open.

1 tbsp	salt	15 mL
1 lb	dried bucatini (see Variations, below)	500 g
3 tbsp	extra-virgin olive oil	45 mL
1 tsp	thinly sliced garlic	5 mL
⅛ tsp	salt	0.5 mL
12 oz	fresh mussels, cleaned (see box below)	375 g
1 cup	dry white Italian wine	250 mL
½ cup	canned crushed Italian tomatoes	125 mL
2 tbsp	hand-torn basil leaves	25 mL
	Salt and freshly ground black pepper	
1 tbsp	finely chopped Italian parsley leaves	15 mL

1. In a covered pasta pot over high heat, bring water to a rapid boil. Add salt and bucatini and cook, uncovered, over high heat until pasta is al dente. Scoop out about 1 cup (250 mL) of the pasta water and set aside. Drain pasta.

2. In a large sauté pan, heat oil over medium heat. Add garlic and salt and cook, stirring, until garlic is translucent but not browned, 2 to 3 minutes. Add mussels and wine. Cover and simmer for 2 minutes to develop flavors. Add tomatoes, ½ cup (125 mL) of the reserved pasta water and the basil. Simmer, covered, until mussels have fully opened, liquid is reduced by half and sauce is thick enough to lightly coat the back of a spoon. Discard any mussels that have not opened.

3. Add bucatini to mussel mixture and continue to cook for 2 to 3 minutes, using pasta tongs to toss and coat evenly, and adding more pasta water if necessary. Season to taste with salt and pepper.

4. Transfer to a large serving bowl, arranging mussels on top of pasta. Sprinkle with parsley and serve immediately.

Variations

Substitute thick spaghetti or linguine for the bucatini.

Mussels

Purchase mussels with unbroken, unchipped shells that are tightly closed. Store them in the refrigerator, uncovered so they can breathe. Most of the mussels we use today are farmed and don't require aggressive cleaning but some have threads attached to the shell. To remove this "beard," grasp it with a dry towel and pull sharply toward the hinge side of the mussel (pulling toward the opening side might tear and kill the mussel inside the shell). After de-bearding, brush any sand, barnacles, etc., from the shells with a stiff brush. Rinse well.

Bucatini con la razza e patate

Bucatini with Skate and Potatoes

Skate or skate wing is a sweet-tasting ray fish found throughout the world and available in large markets. The mint in this recipe is a legacy of the Moorish occupation of southern Italy, and a refreshing flavor note.

Serves 4 to 6

Tips

Depending upon the time of year, skate may have an ammonia odor. If this is the case, soak it in acidulated water (water with lemon juice) before cooking. If you can't find skate, substitute an equal quantity of fresh sea scallops.

I usually season my sauces in the initial stages of cooking so the flavors have time to bloom. I always taste the final product and, if necessary, add more salt and pepper just before serving.

3 tbsp	extra-virgin olive oil	45 mL
¼ cup	diced onion	50 mL
¼ cup	diced pancetta	50 mL
1 cup	diced unpeeled Yukon Gold potatoes	250 mL
1 cup	diced skate wing (see Tips, left)	250 mL
	Salt and freshly ground white pepper	
1 cup	dry white Italian wine	250 mL
1 tbsp	salt	15 mL
1 lb	dried bucatini (see Variations, below)	500 g
2 tbsp	hand-torn mint leaves	25 mL

1. In a covered pasta pot over high heat, bring water to a rapid boil.

2. Meanwhile, in a large sauté pan, heat oil over medium heat. Add onion and pancetta. Cook, stirring, until onion is translucent but not brown, about 5 minutes. Add potatoes and skate and cook, stirring, for 5 minutes to meld flavors. Season with salt and pepper to taste. Add wine and cook until reduced by half and potatoes are nearly cooked through, about 8 minutes. Remove from heat and set aside.

3. While sauce is simmering, add salt and bucatini to the boiling water and cook, uncovered, over high heat until pasta is al dente. Scoop out about 1½ cups (375 mL) of the pasta water and set aside. Drain pasta.

4. Return sauté pan to medium heat and add 1 cup (250 L) of the reserved pasta water. Add bucatini and continue to cook for 2 to 3 minutes, using pasta tongs to toss and coat evenly, until potatoes are tender and skate separates into shreds, adding more pasta water if necessary. Season to taste with salt and pepper.

5. Transfer to a large serving bowl and sprinkle with mint. Toss to distribute mint and serve immediately.

Variations

Substitute thick spaghetti or linguine for the bucatini.

> ### Skate
> The skate is a ray fish related to sharks. Its flesh is white and sweet and tastes somewhat like scallops. The only edible parts are two wing fillets. These are sold with the skin removed, but any remaining membrane must be removed with a flexible boning knife before cooking.

Cavatappi con tonno e capperi

Cavatappi with Tuna and Capers

Although meaty, tuna is a delicate fish, and the piquant capers provide a nice flavor contrast. Please purchase the best and freshest tuna you can buy, or use top-quality frozen tuna that has been defrosted. I prefer belly meat, but the loin is good as well.

Serves 4 to 6

Tips

In this recipe you can substitute defrosted frozen tuna for the fresh.

Before cooking tuna, always remove and discard the mid-lateral strip of dark meat, which is easy to see. It has a strong, bitter flavor.

Work like a chef. Have all your ingredients ready to go before you actually start to cook (see *Mise en Place*, page 15).

7 tbsp	extra-virgin olive oil, divided	105 mL
2 tbsp	diced onion	25 mL
2 tbsp	diced peeled celery	25 mL
1 rounded cup	diced boneless, skinless fresh tuna (see Tips, left)	275 mL
1 cup	dry white Italian wine	250 mL
2 tbsp	tiny (nonpareil) capers, drained	25 mL
1 tbsp	salt	15 mL
1 lb	dried cavatappi (see Variations, below)	500 g
	Salt and freshly ground black pepper	

1. In a covered pasta pot over high heat, bring water to a rapid boil.

2. Meanwhile, in a large sauté pan, heat 5 tbsp (75 mL) of the oil over medium heat. Add onion and celery and cook, stirring, until vegetables are soft but not brown, about 3 minutes. Add tuna, wine and capers and cook, stirring, until tuna is cooked through, about 5 minutes. Using a fork, mash into flakes. Remove from heat and set aside.

3. Add salt and cavatappi to the boiling water and cook, uncovered, over high heat until pasta is al dente. Scoop out about 1 cup (250 mL) of the pasta water and set aside. Drain pasta.

4. Return sauté pan to high heat. Add ½ cup (125 mL) of the reserved pasta water and cavatappi. Using a wooden spoon, toss to coat evenly. Cook, tossing, until liquid reduces by half, about 3 minutes. Add remaining olive oil and toss well. Season to taste with salt and pepper.

5. Transfer to a large serving bowl and serve immediately.

Variations

Cavatappi pasta comes from southern Italy. It is a tubular corkscrew pasta about 1 inch (2.5 cm) long and usually has a ridged surface. It's sometimes called cellentani or "double elbows." Substitute fusilli or penne for the cavatappi.

Cavatappi al ragù di merluzzo

Cavatappi with Cod Ragù

This dish reminds me of the Veneto region of Italy, where fish are plentiful and they often cook with bacala, or dried salt cod that has been reconstituted. I have used fresh cod in this recipe because it is usually easy to get from a good fish purveyor (see Tips, page 149).

Serves 4 to 6

Tips

If fresh cod is unavailable, use defrosted frozen cod fillets.

To prepare fennel, cut off the feathery fronds and save them for garnish; cut off the stems and save them for flavoring soup or stock. Trim the root end off the bulb and discard. Trim and discard any stems remaining on the bulb. Cut the bulb in half and remove the tough core. Rinse bulb halves under running water. It is now ready to dice.

5 tbsp	extra-virgin olive oil, divided	75 mL
2 tbsp	diced onion	25 mL
2 tbsp	diced peeled celery	25 mL
2 tbsp	diced trimmed fennel bulb	25 mL
1 rounded cup	diced fresh boneless, skinless cod (see Tips, left)	275 mL
1 cup	dry white Italian wine	250 mL
1 tbsp	salt	15 mL
1 lb	dried cavatappi (see Variations, below)	500 g
	Salt and freshly ground white pepper	

1. In a covered pasta pot over high heat, bring water to a rapid boil.

2. Meanwhile, in a large sauté pan, heat 3 tbsp (45 mL) of the olive oil over medium heat. Add onion, celery and fennel and cook, stirring, until vegetables are soft but not browned, about 5 minutes. Add cod and wine, bring to a boil, then reduce heat and simmer for 5 minutes. Using a fork, mash cod into flakes. Remove from heat and set aside.

3. While sauce is simmering, add salt and cavatappi to the boiling water and cook, uncovered, over high heat until pasta is al dente. Scoop out about 1 cup (250 mL) of the pasta water and set aside. Drain pasta.

4. Return sauté pan to high heat. Add ½ cup (125 mL) of the reserved pasta water and cavatappi. Using a wooden spoon, toss to coat evenly and cook until liquid is reduced by half, about 3 minutes. Drizzle with remaining olive oil, toss to coat and season to taste with salt and pepper.

5. Transfer to a large serving bowl and serve immediately.

Variations

Substitute penne or fusilli for the cavatappi.

Fennel

Indigenous to the Mediterranean and known since antiquity, fennel is a large perennial herb with feathery fronds, small yellow flowers and a bulb-like base. The bulb and the seeds are prized in Italian cooking for their anise-like flavor. The bulb and often the fronds are used both raw and cooked in sides, salads, pastas and risottos. The seeds are a distinctive ingredient in Italian sausages. Fennel is widely cultivated in North America, where it is often incorrectly called anise.

Conchiglie con gamberi, zucchine e pomodori secchi

Conchiglie with Shrimp, Zucchini and Sun-Dried Tomatoes

The flavor of dried tomatoes is deeper and richer than that of canned tomatoes and more intense and concentrated than for fresh tomatoes.

Serves 4 to 6

Tips

Use dry-packed, not oil-packed, sun-dried tomatoes, preferably imported from Italy. I prefer Italian dry-packed sun-dried tomatoes because they don't add any extra oil to a sauce. For use in this recipe, blanch them in boiling water for 4 minutes and drain.

Most of the shrimp you can buy has been previously frozen and defrosted. Shrimp that are frozen in blocks or individually quick-frozen (IQF) are the best form for the home cook.

For flavor, my favorite shrimp is the Texas brown. My second-favorite is the black tiger. White shrimp, the most popular, are an acceptable option. Cutting the shrimp in half lengthwise allows them to cook more evenly while making for an interesting appearance and texture.

6 tbsp	extra-virgin olive oil, divided	90 mL
½ cup	diced skin-on zucchini	125 mL
2 tbsp	sun-dried tomato strips, rehydrated, lightly packed (see Tips, left)	25 mL
½ cup	dry white Italian wine	125 mL
1 cup	halved (lengthwise) peeled, deveined shrimp (see Tips, left)	250 mL
2 tbsp	hand-torn fresh basil leaves, lightly packed	25 mL
1 tbsp	salt	15 mL
1 lb	dried conchiglie (see Variations, below)	500 g
	Salt and freshly ground white pepper	

1. In a covered pasta pot over high heat, bring water to a rapid boil.

2. In a large sauté pan, heat 3 tbsp (45 mL) of the olive oil over medium heat. Add zucchini and stir. Add sun-dried tomatoes and wine and bring to a boil, then reduce heat and simmer until wine is reduced by half. Add shrimp and basil and stir. Cover pan and remove from heat. Set aside.

3. Add salt and conchiglie to the boiling water and cook, uncovered, over high heat until pasta is al dente. Scoop out about 1 cup (250 mL) of the pasta water and set aside. Drain pasta.

4. Return sauté pan to high heat. Add ½ cup (125 mL) of the reserved pasta water and conchiglie and, using a wooden spoon, toss to coat evenly. Continue to cook until liquid is reduced by half and shrimp are cooked through but not rubbery, about 3 minutes. Drizzle with remaining oil and season to taste with salt and pepper. Toss well.

5. Transfer to a large serving bowl and serve immediately.

Variations

Substitute penne or fusilli for the conchiglie.

Farfalle alle cappesante e asparagi

Farfalle with Sea Scallops and Asparagus

The combination of fresh sweet scallops and fresh asparagus makes this a very special dish. It is also easy to cook.

Serves 4 to 6

Tips

Fresh scallops are very perishable. You can find them at good fish markets or online in a size range from jumbo to average. You will need about ¾ lb (375 g) of scallops for this recipe.

Substitute an equal quantity of peeled, deveined shrimp if you can't get fresh scallops. Frozen scallops will not produce a successful dish.

3 tbsp	extra-virgin olive oil	45 mL
1 cup	fresh jumbo sea scallops, quartered (see Tips, left)	250 mL
1 cup	sliced (1½ inches/4 cm) pencil-thin asparagus	250 mL
	Salt and freshly ground white pepper	
1 cup	dry white Italian wine	250 mL
1 tbsp	salt	15 mL
1 lb	dried farfalle (see Variation, below)	500 g
¼ cup	unsalted butter	50 mL

1. In a covered pasta pot over high heat, bring water to a rapid boil.

2. Meanwhile, in a large sauté pan, heat oil over high heat. Add scallops and asparagus. Cook, stirring, until scallops are just opaque, being careful not to overcook (do not brown). Season to taste with salt and pepper. Add wine, cover pan and remove from heat. Set aside.

3. Add salt and farfalle to the boiling water and cook, uncovered, over high heat until pasta is al dente. Scoop out about 1 cup (250 mL) of the pasta water and set aside. Drain pasta.

4. Return sauté pan to high heat and add ¼ cup (50 mL) of the pasta water and farfalle and continue to cook for 3 minutes, using a wooden spoon to toss and coat evenly. Add butter and season to taste with salt and pepper. Toss well.

5. Transfer to a large serving bowl and serve immediately.

Variation

Substitute penne for the farfalle.

Scallops

Scallops are bivalve mollusks, that is, they have two hinged shells. The edible part of the scallop is the adductor muscle, used to open and shut the shell. Sea scallops are the largest and most common species available in North America. They come from the coastal waters off the mid-Atlantic and northeastern states and average 20 to 30 per pound. Jumbo scallops from Alaska average 6 to 8 per pound. Bay scallops, also called Nantucket scallops, are the smallest of all and not as plentiful as some other varieties. They are harvested from the coast of North Carolina up to Maine and average 90 per pound. Because of the limited supply, they are the most expensive.

Farfalle con ragù di baccala

Farfalle with Dried Cod Ragù

Farfalle, *also called bow-tie pasta, comes from the Italian word* farfalla — *"butterfly." This shape is generally thought to have originated in Lombardia and Emilia-Romagna in northern Italy. Dried cod is a staple in Veneto. Cod is a sweet-tasting fish that becomes even sweeter when dried, although the salt used to preserve it intensifies its flavor. The potatoes absorb and diffuse the saltiness.*

Serves 4 to 6

Tip

One 7-ounce (210 g) fillet of salt cod, fully soaked, yields about 1 cup (250 mL) diced. Buy boneless, skinless salt cod fillets from a fish market or order them online; Canadian salt cod from Labrador is good. To soak the cod, rinse off excess surface salt with cold running water, then place the fillet in a glass dish, adding milk to cover by 2 inches (5 cm). Cover and refrigerate overnight. When you're ready to cook, drain the fish, rinse again, pat dry and dice.

3 tbsp	extra-virgin olive oil	45 mL
1 tbsp	thinly sliced garlic	15 mL
2 tbsp	diced onion	25 mL
2 tbsp	diced peeled Yukon Gold potato	25 mL
1 cup	diced soaked boneless salt cod (see Tip, left)	250 mL
1 cup	canned crushed Italian tomatoes	250 mL
1 tsp	fresh oregano leaves, packed	5 mL
1 tbsp	salt	15 mL
1 lb	dried farfalle (see Variation, below)	500 g
	Freshly ground black pepper	

1. In a covered pasta pot over high heat, bring water to a rapid boil.

2. Meanwhile, in a large sauté pan, heat oil over medium heat. Add garlic and onion and cook, stirring, until soft but not browned, about 3 minutes. Add potato and cook, stirring, for 1 minute. Add cod, tomatoes and oregano and reduce heat to low. Simmer, uncovered, until cod plumps and sauce thickens, about 10 minutes. Remove from heat and set aside.

3. While sauce is simmering, add salt and farfalle to the boiling water and cook, uncovered, over high heat until pasta is al dente. Scoop out about 1 cup (250 mL) of the pasta water and set aside. Drain pasta.

4. Return sauté pan to medium heat. Add ½ cup (125 mL) of the reserved pasta water and continue to cook for 2 to 3 minutes, using a wooden spoon to toss and coat evenly, and adding more pasta water if necessary. Season to taste with pepper and toss well.

5. Transfer to a large serving bowl and serve immediately.

Variation

Substitute penne for the farfalle.

Baccala

The Italian word for salt cod is *baccala*, and although not an indigenous Mediterranean ingredient, dried salt cod from North America became a traditional part of the cuisines of Italy, France, Spain and Greece because it could be preserved and easily transported between the New World and the Old. There are two forms of dried cod: *baccala*, which is salted and dried, and *stoccofisso* ("stockfish"), which is air-dried without salt. Salt cod is used in cooking because it imparts a unique flavor to any dish.

Fusilli al ragù di calamari e zafferano

Fusilli with Calamari-Saffron Ragù

This combination is from the south of Italy, where calamari are plentiful, along with fresh hot red chile peppers and saffron, both souvenirs of the Moors. Because of the addition of fresh chile, basil and saffron, this dish has more sweetness and contrast than Bucatini with Calamari (page 141).

Serves 4 to 6

Tip

The Italian red chile, which is medium hot and slightly sweet, is not available here, but a good substitute is the California-grown red finger chile (also called Dutch or Holland chile) or the red Fresno chile. In a pinch you can use a long red or cayenne chile, both of which are much hotter. If you're using these, mince them and reduce the quantity to about 1/4 tsp (1 mL).

3 tbsp	extra-virgin olive oil	45 mL
1 tsp	thinly sliced garlic	5 mL
1 tsp	thinly sliced red finger chile (see Tip, left)	5 mL
1 cup	calamari rings and tentacles (about 8 oz/250 g)	250 mL
1/2 cup	dry white Italian wine	125 mL
Pinch	saffron threads	Pinch
1/2 cup	canned crushed Italian tomatoes	125 mL
1/2 cup	drained canned diced Italian tomatoes	125 mL
1 tbsp	hand-torn fresh basil leaves	15 mL
1 tbsp	salt	15 mL
1 lb	dried fusilli (see Variations, below)	500 g
	Salt and freshly ground black pepper	

1. In a covered pasta pot over high heat, bring water to a rapid boil.

2. Meanwhile, in a large sauté pan, heat oil over medium heat. Add garlic and cook, stirring, until translucent but not browned, 2 to 3 minutes. Add chile and calamari and cook, stirring, until chile softens, about 5 minutes. Add wine and saffron and increase heat to high. Stir in tomatoes and basil. When mixture comes to a boil, reduce heat to low and simmer until thickened. Remove pan from heat and set aside.

3. While sauce is simmering, add salt and fusilli to the boiling water and cook, uncovered, over high heat until pasta is al dente. Scoop out about 1 cup (250 mL) of the pasta water and set aside. Drain pasta.

4. Return sauté pan to high heat. Add 1/4 cup (50 mL) of the reserved pasta water and heat through. Reduce heat to low, add fusilli and continue to cook for 2 to 3 minutes, using a wooden spoon to toss and coat evenly, and adding more pasta water if necessary. Season to taste with salt and pepper. Transfer to a serving bowl and serve immediately.

Variations

Substitute defrosted frozen calamari rings, or rings and tentacles, for the fresh.

Substitute penne for the fusilli.

Saffron

Golden orange in color and bitter tasting, saffron is the stigmas of a purple crocus. It is the world's most expensive spice by weight. Saffron is sold as either powder or threads. Powder loses flavor more quickly; threads are more durable and can be stored in an airtight container in a cool, dark place for up to 6 months.

Fusilli con gamberi e fave

Fusilli with Shrimp and Fava Beans

This dish has the flavors of Italy south of Rome. Shrimp are plentiful in the coastal waters and fava beans and basil are abundant on land. Fusilli is a corkscrew pasta similar in shape to rotini, which is slightly larger, thicker and curlier. In Italian fusilli *means "rifle" — the pasta is named for the corkscrew-shaped tool used for cleaning gun barrels. The shape is excellent for catching and holding sauce.*

Serves 4 to 6

Tip

I prefer to make this recipe using colossal (fewer than 15 shrimp per pound/500 g) brown shrimp, which are available at some fish markets. Top-quality defrosted frozen pink or white shrimp make acceptable substitutes, as do the smaller extra-jumbo (16 to 20 per pound/500g) or jumbo (21 to 25 per pound/500 g) shrimp.

5 tbsp	extra-virgin olive oil, divided	75 mL
1 cup	peeled, deveined shrimp, halved lengthwise (see Tips, left)	250 mL
½ cup	peeled blanched fava beans	125 mL
½ cup	canned diced Italian tomatoes	125 mL
½ cup	dry white Italian wine	125 mL
1 tbsp	hand-torn fresh basil leaves	15 mL
	Salt and freshly ground black pepper	
1 tbsp	salt	15 mL
1 lb	dried fusilli (see Variations, below)	500 g

1. In a covered pasta pot over high heat, bring water to a rapid boil.

2. Meanwhile, in a large sauté pan, heat 3 tbsp (45 mL) of the oil over medium heat. Add shrimp and fava beans and cook, stirring, until shrimp begin to turn opaque, about 2 minutes. Add tomatoes, wine, basil and salt and pepper to taste and simmer, stirring occasionally, until thickened, about 5 minutes. Remove pan from heat and set aside.

3. While sauce is simmering, add salt and fusilli to the boiling water and cook, uncovered, over high heat until pasta is al dente. Scoop out about 1 cup (250 mL) of the pasta water and set aside. Drain pasta.

4. Return sauté pan to high heat. Add ½ cup (125 mL) of the reserved pasta water and heat through. Add fusilli and continue to cook for 3 minutes, using a wooden spoon to toss and coat evenly, and adding more pasta water if necessary. Drizzle with remaining oil, season to taste with salt and pepper and toss well.

5. Transfer to a large serving bowl and serve immediately.

Variations

Substitute fresh lima beans for the fava beans.

Substitute penne for the fusilli.

Fava Beans

Also known as broad beans, fava beans occupy a place of honor in Italian cooking. In North America they are available from April through June. Young, tender beans can be cooked and eaten without peeling, but more mature beans develop a tough membrane that needs to be removed (it is easily pulled off when the beans are cooked). To shell favas, split the pods open and push the beans out. One pound (500 g) of pods yields about 1 cup (250 mL) of shelled beans. Some people have a hereditary disorder called favism that produces a severe allergic reaction to the bean and its pollen, so make guests aware that you are serving favas.

Pasta mischiata con fagioli e cozze alle napoletana

Pennette with Cannellini Beans and Mussels Neapolitan Style

This recipe was originally pasta mischiata, which means "mixed pasta." The flavors are very Neapolitan. Traditionally it was made with three kinds of pasta that were cooked, then cut into short pieces: penne, fusilli and spaghetti. How did it originate? My best guess is that every household had leftover cooked pasta or partial packages of uncooked pasta, plus leftover cooked cannellini beans. I have changed the pasta to pennette, which are roughly the same size as cannellini beans; you could also use maccheroni. But if you want to be authentic, use the mixed pasta described in the Variations, right.

Serves 4 to 6

Tips

You can use canned cannellini beans or cook dried ones yourself.

Greco or Fiano are white wines produced in southern Italy, where this dish originates. If you can't find them, substitute Pinot Bianco or Pinot Grigio.

2 tbsp	extra-virgin olive oil	25 mL
1 tbsp	thinly sliced garlic	15 mL
1 tsp	thinly sliced fresh red finger chile (see Tips, page 74)	5 mL
24	cleaned fresh mussels	24
1 cup	dry white Italian wine such as Greco or Fiano (see Tips, left)	250 mL
1 cup	rinsed drained cooked cannellini beans (see Tips, left)	250 mL
½ cup	drained canned Italian tomatoes, coarsely chopped	125 mL
½ cup	organic vegetable broth, divided	125 mL
3 cups	cooked pennette (see Variations, below)	750 mL
	Salt and freshly ground white pepper	

1. In a large sauté pan, heat oil over medium heat. Add garlic and chile and cook, stirring, until garlic is translucent but not browned, 2 to 3 minutes. Add mussels and wine. Cover and cook until mussels open, 3 to 5 minutes. (discard any that do not open). Add beans, tomatoes and ¼ cup (50 mL) of the broth and simmer for 3 minutes. Add cooked pasta and remaining broth and simmer, stirring, until liquid has been reduced by half. Season to taste with salt and pepper.

2. Serve immediately in warmed individual bowls.

Variations

Substitute 1½ cups (375 mL) cooked pennette with ½ cup (125 mL) each of cooked fusilli, penne and spaghetti, all cut into short pieces. You may also use the same amounts of any leftover dried pasta, just making sure to break the long pasta into short pieces.

Substitute penne for the pennette.

Pennette con gamberetti e asparagi

Pennette with Shrimp and Asparagus

Pennette are smaller, thinner penne, and the surface is usually ridged (rigate), making it easy for sauce to cling. The name comes from penne, or "pen" in Italian — the hollow pasta is cut diagonally at each end to resemble old-fashioned nibs or the points on feather pens. Shrimp and asparagus make a fresh, colorful, flavorful combination.

Serves 4 to 6

Tips

I prefer to use fresh brown U-15 (colossal) shrimp (fewer than 15 shrimp per pound/500g) in this recipe, but top-quality frozen pink or white shrimp are acceptable substitutes, as are smaller extra-jumbo (16 to 20 per pound/500g) or jumbo (21 to 25 per pound/500g) shrimp.

Always use a large pot and plenty of water when cooking pasta. To properly cook 1 pound (500 g) of pasta, you'll need a pot with a volume of at least 8 quarts (8 L) so that you can use 6 quarts (6 L) of water.

Never rinse pasta after draining it. The surface starch helps the sauce to cling and is important to producing the best-quality dish.

3 tbsp	extra-virgin olive oil	45 mL
1 cup	sliced (2 inches/5 cm) pencil-thin asparagus	250 mL
1 cup	peeled, deveined colossal shrimp, halved lengthwise (see Tips, left)	250 mL
½ cup	dry white Italian wine	125 mL
1 tbsp	salt	15 mL
1 lb	dried pennette (see Variation, below)	500 g
¼ cup	unsalted butter	50 mL
	Salt and freshly ground white pepper	

1. In a covered pasta pot over high heat, bring water to a rapid boil.
2. Meanwhile, in a large sauté pan, heat oil over medium heat. Add asparagus and cook, stirring, for 1 minute. Add shrimp and continue to cook until they just begin to lose their transparency, about 30 seconds. Add wine, cover and remove pan from heat. Set aside.
3. Add salt and pennette to the boiling water and cook, uncovered, over high heat until pasta is al dente. Scoop out about 1 cup (250 mL) of the pasta water and set aside. Drain pasta.
4. Return sauté pan to medium heat. Add pennette and, using a wooden spoon, toss to coat evenly. Add ¼ cup (50 mL) of the reserved pasta water and continue to cook until liquid is reduced by half, 3 to 5 minutes. Add butter and season to taste with salt and pepper.
5. Transfer to a large serving bowl and serve immediately.

Variation
If you can't find pennette, substitute penne.

Pennette al tonno e olive

Pennette with Tuna and Oil-Cured Olives

The combination of tuna, olive oil and black olives is very Sicilian. Pennette has a nice shape to complement the flaked tuna.

Serves 4 to 6

Tips

Before cooking tuna, always remove and discard the mid-lateral strip of dark meat, which is easy to see. It has a strong, bitter flavor.

I usually season my sauces in the initial stages of cooking so the flavors have time to bloom. I always taste the final product and, if necessary, add more salt and pepper just before serving.

True oil-cured olives, which are cured in oil not brine, are expensive and hard to find. If you can't find real oil-cured olives, substitute oil-packed olives.

5 tbsp	extra-virgin olive oil, divided	75 mL
¼ cup	minced onion	50 mL
1 cup	diced skinless, boneless fresh tuna (see Tips, left)	250 mL
	Salt and freshly ground white pepper	
¾ cup	dry white Italian wine	175 mL
2 tbsp	finely chopped pitted oil-cured black olives (see Tips, left)	25 mL
1 tbsp	salt	15 mL
1 lb	dried pennette (see Variation, below)	500 g

1. In a covered pasta pot over high heat, bring water to a rapid boil.

2. Meanwhile, in a large sauté pan, heat 3 tbsp (45 mL) of the oil over medium heat. Add onion and cook, stirring, until translucent but not brown, 2 to 3 minutes. Add tuna and cook until opaque, about 5 minutes. Season to taste with salt and pepper. Add wine and olives and simmer for 5 minutes, mashing tuna with a fork to flake. Remove from heat and set aside.

3. Add salt and pennette to the boiling water and cook, uncovered, over high heat until pasta is al dente. Scoop out about 1 cup (250 mL) of the pasta water and set aside. Drain pasta.

4. Return sauté pan to medium heat. Add ½ cup (125 mL) of the reserved pasta water and heat through. Add pennette and continue to cook for 2 to 4 minutes, using a wooden spoon to toss and coat evenly, adding more pasta water if necessary. Drizzle with remaining olive oil and season to taste with salt and pepper.

5. Transfer to a large serving bowl and serve immediately.

Variation

If you can't find pennette, substitute penne.

Linguine al salmone e salsa di pomodoro

Linguine with Salmon and Tomato Sauce

Although salmon is not indigenous to Italy, it has become a popular food there. This is a simple, contemporary sauce. Pasta, as always, is the star, salmon is a co-star and the tomato sauce is a supporting actor. I prefer wild rather than farmed salmon, but whichever one you use, the important thing is that it be fresh.

Serves 4 to 6

Tip

I like to tear the basil leaves by hand rather than slicing them because I think they look and taste better.

3 tbsp	extra-virgin olive oil	45 mL
1 tsp	thinly sliced garlic	5 mL
1 cup	diced boneless, skinless salmon	250 mL
1 cup	dry white Italian wine	250 mL
2 cups	canned crushed Italian tomatoes	500 mL
2 tbsp	hand-torn fresh basil leaves	25 mL
½ tsp	granulated sugar	2 mL
1 tbsp	salt	15 mL
1 lb	dried linguine (see Variation, below)	500 g
	Salt and freshly ground black pepper	

1. In a covered pasta pot over high heat, bring water to a rapid boil.

2. Meanwhile, in a large sauté pan, heat oil over medium heat. Add garlic and cook, stirring, until translucent but not browned, 2 to 3 minutes. Add salmon and wine and simmer until wine is reduced by half. Add tomatoes, basil and sugar. Reduce heat to low and simmer, stirring occasionally, until sauce thickens, about 6 minutes. Remove from heat and set aside.

3. While sauce is simmering, add salt and linguine to the boiling water and cook, uncovered, over high heat until pasta is al dente. Drain.

4. Return sauté pan to medium heat. Add linguine and, using pasta tongs, toss to coat evenly. Season to taste with salt and pepper.

5. Transfer to a large serving bowl and serve immediately.

Variation

Substitute spaghetti for the linguine.

Linguine con le vongole

Linguine with Clams

Linguine with clams is another regional favorite. The clams I find in Italy are small and the meat is very tender. Clams from the North American market suitable for this dish are usually called littlenecks and are no more than 2 inches (5 cm) in diameter. The simple addition of sautéed breadcrumbs adds another level of texture and flavor to this dish.

Serves 4 to 6

Tips

I prefer the texture, taste and appearance of dried breadcrumbs made from the inside of a loaf of Italian bread. An Italian bakery is the best source for these, or you can make them yourself from Italian bread by pulsing it in a food processor. Friends of mine who don't have access to an Italian bakery substitute panko crumbs. Although they are outside the Italian market basket, they make a better substitute than the dried breadcrumbs sold in cardboard containers at the supermarket.

7 tbsp	extra-virgin olive oil, divided	105 mL
4 tbsp	white Italian breadcrumbs (see Tips, left)	60 mL
1 tbsp	thinly sliced garlic	15 mL
1 tsp	thinly sliced fresh red finger chile (see Tips, page 74)	5 mL
30	fresh small clams such as littlenecks, scrubbed clean (see Tips, page 265)	30
1 cup	dry white Italian wine	250 mL
1 cup	bottled clam juice, preferably low-sodium	250 mL
1 tbsp	salt	15 mL
1 lb	dried linguine (see Variation, below)	500 g
	Salt and freshly ground white pepper	
2 tbsp	chopped Italian parsley leaves	25 mL

1. In a covered pasta pot over high heat, bring water to a rapid boil.

2. In a small sauté pan over medium heat, heat 2 tbsp (25 mL) of the oil. Add breadcrumbs and cook, stirring, until golden but not dark brown, about 3 minutes. Remove pan from heat and set aside.

3. Meanwhile, in a large sauté pan, heat 3 tbsp (45 mL) of the oil over medium heat. Add garlic and stir. Add chile and cook, stirring, until garlic is translucent but not browned, 2 to 3 minutes. Add clams, wine and clam juice. Cover and simmer slowly until all clams have opened, about 8 minutes. Remove pan from heat and set aside, keeping covered. Discard any clams that have not opened.

4. While sauce is simmering, add salt and linguine to the boiling water and cook, uncovered, over high heat until pasta is al dente. Scoop out about 1½ cups (375 mL) of the pasta water and set aside. Drain pasta.

5. Return large sauté pan to high heat. Add 1 cup (250 mL) of the reserved pasta water and heat through. Add linguine and continue to cook until the flavors meld and liquid is well reduced, about 6 minutes, using pasta tongs to toss and coat evenly. Drizzle with remaining oil and season to taste with salt and pepper. Add parsley and toss well.

6. Transfer to a large serving bowl and sprinkle with reserved breadcrumbs. Serve immediately.

Variation

Substitute spaghetti for the linguine.

Linguine all'aragosta

Linguine with Lobster

This recipe is for the adventuresome cook who is feeling extravagant. It's a celebratory dish — every so often this is one great pasta to make! Prepare this in summer, when lobster is more plentiful. Fresh northern lobster from Maine or eastern Canada is absolutely necessary; frozen lobster meat or lobster tail won't cut it. Many fishmongers will cook the lobster for you and some will even crack it and extract the meat, which is a great way to go if you don't want to deal with cooking it yourself.

Serves 4 to 6

Tips

I like to tear the basil leaves by hand rather than slicing them, because I think they look and taste better.

Plan to cook the lobster the same day you purchase it. Refrigerate it as soon as you reach home, remembering that lobsters need to breathe. If you prefer (it's more humane), 15 minutes before you intend to cook it, chill the lobster (with the rubber bands still binding the claws) in the freezer to slow down its metabolism.

5 tbsp	extra-virgin olive oil, divided	75 mL
3 tbsp	diced onion	45 mL
3 tbsp	diced peeled celery	45 mL
1 cup	dry white Italian wine	250 mL
1	northern lobster (3 lb/1.5 kg), cooked and shelled, meat cut into nuggets (1½ to 2 cups/375 to 500 mL)	1
3 tbsp	hand-torn basil leaves	45 mL
1 tbsp	salt	15 ml
1 lb	dried linguine	500 g
	Salt and freshly ground white pepper	

1. In a covered pasta pot over high heat, bring water to a rapid boil.

2. Meanwhile, in a large sauté pan, heat 3 tbsp (45 mL) of the oil over medium heat. Add onion and celery and cook, stirring, until vegetables are translucent but not brown, about 5 minutes. Add wine, lobster meat and basil and remove from heat. Set aside.

3. Add salt and linguine to the boiling water and cook, uncovered, over high heat until pasta is al dente. Drain.

4. Return sauté pan to high heat. Add linguine and, using pasta tongs, toss to coat evenly. Drizzle with remaining oil and toss well. Season to taste with salt and pepper.

5. Transfer to a large serving bowl and serve immediately.

Variations

If you can't find one 3-pound (1.5 kg) lobster, buy two smaller lobsters to equal 3 pounds. Some fish markets will cook and shell the lobster you choose.

Substitute spaghetti for the linguine.

Cooking Live Lobster

Place lobster on a cutting board horizontally on its back. Holding the tail firmly with a heavily gloved hand and cutting away from your hand, place the tip of a 10-inch (25 cm) chef's knife midway between the last pair of legs. Slice firmly toward the head, splitting the front of the lobster's body in half without cutting through the top shell. The lobster will be dead; however, its legs and tail may continue to twitch — a residual response. Meanwhile, in a large pasta pot, bring 6 quarts (6 L) of water to a boil. Add 2 tbsp (25 mL) salt. Immediately place the lobster head first into the boiling water. Lower heat so the water simmers and cook about 25 minutes, until shell is a vivid shade of red. Using tongs, transfer to a cutting board and let cool to room temperature before removing the meat.

Rigatoni al sugo di polpi

Rigatoni with Octopus Sauce

In recent years we have learned to appreciate and enjoy calamari (squid) — deep-fried, grilled or with pasta — but we haven't given octopus much of a chance. In Italy (where it is called polpo) as well as other Mediterranean countries, octopus is considered a delicacy. Baby octopus meat is particularly white, mild and sweet-tasting. You can buy fully cleaned baby octopus from a good fish market or from several online companies, but since you only need a small amount, it's more economical to purchase what you need from the fish market.

Serves 4 to 6

Tips

I like to tear basil leaves by hand rather than slicing them, because I think they look and taste better.

Any dry white table wine will work well in this recipe, but an Italian wine will help to create a more authentic flavor. In this recipe I'd probably use Pinot Bianco, which is a good basic dry white wine for use in Italian cooking.

3 tbsp	extra-virgin olive oil	45 mL
1 tsp	thinly sliced garlic	5 mL
2 tbsp	minced onion	25 mL
1 cup	sliced (½ inch/1 cm) cleaned baby octopus	250 mL
1 cup	dry white Italian wine (see Tips, left)	250 mL
1½ cups	canned crushed Italian tomatoes	375 mL
2 tbsp	hand-torn fresh basil leaves	25 mL
1 tbsp	salt	15 mL
1 lb	dried rigatoni (see Variations, below)	500 g
	Salt and freshly ground black pepper	

1. In a covered pasta pot over high heat, bring water to a rapid boil.

2. Meanwhile, in a large sauté pan, heat oil over medium heat. Add garlic and onion. Cook, stirring, until translucent but not browned, 2 to 3 minutes. Add octopus, wine, tomatoes and basil. Reduce heat to low and simmer, stirring occasionally, until octopus is tender and sauce is thick enough to coat the back of a spoon, 20 to 30 minutes.

3. While sauce is simmering, add salt and rigatoni to the boiling water and cook, uncovered, until pasta is al dente. Scoop out about 1 cup (250 mL) of the pasta water and set aside. Drain pasta.

4. Return sauté pan to medium heat. Add ½ cup (125 mL) of the reserved pasta water and heat through. Add rigatoni and continue to cook for 2 to 3 minutes, using a wooden spoon to toss and coat evenly, and adding more pasta water if necessary. Season to taste with salt and pepper. Toss well.

5. Transfer to a large serving bowl and serve immediately.

Variations
Substitute penne or cut ziti for the rigatoni.

> ### Octopus
> The octopus is a cephalopod ("head-footed" fish) related to squid and is found in temperate waters worldwide. It is marketed fresh, frozen or dried. Most octopus in fish markets has been cleaned before being packed and frozen. You can store fully frozen octopus in the freezer for up to one month. Defrost in cold running water for about 30 minutes per pound (500 g). Once it is thawed, cook within three days. Raw octopus meat is purplish but turns white when cooked.

Rigatoni con ragù di pesce spada

Rigatoni with Swordfish Ragù

Swordfish is very prevalent in the waters off Sicily, and the combination of firm, meaty swordfish, fennel, tomato and mint is quintessentially Sicilian. Rigatoni is a short tube pasta larger than penne but with straight-cut ends. It is very popular in central and southern Italy.

Serves 4 to 6

Tips

To trim fennel, cut off the root end and discard. Trim off the stems and feathery fronds and save for flavoring soups and to use as garnish. Trim off any stems from the bulb and slice bulb in half. Remove core and discard. The bulb is now ready to mince, dice or slice.

I usually season my sauces in the initial stages of cooking so the flavors have time to bloom. I always taste the final product and, if necessary, add more salt and pepper just before serving.

5 tbsp	extra-virgin olive oil, divided	75 mL
2 tbsp	minced onion	25 mL
2 tbsp	minced peeled celery	25 mL
2 tbsp	minced trimmed fennel bulb (see Tips, left)	25 mL
1½ cups	diced boneless, skinless swordfish	375 mL
	Salt and freshly ground black pepper	
1 cup	dry white Italian wine	250 mL
1 cup	canned crushed Italian tomatoes	250 mL
2 tbsp	hand-torn fresh mint leaves	25 mL
1 tbsp	salt	15 mL
1 lb	dried rigatoni (see Variations, below)	500 g

1. In a covered pasta pot over high heat, bring water to a rapid boil.

2. Meanwhile, in a large sauté pan, heat 3 tbsp (45 mL) of the oil over medium heat. Add onion, celery and fennel. Cook, stirring, until vegetables are soft but not browned, about 5 minutes. Add swordfish and stir. Season to taste with salt and pepper. Add wine, tomatoes and mint. Reduce heat to low and simmer for 20 minutes, until mixture is thick enough to coat the back of a spoon. Using a fork, mash swordfish until it flakes. Remove from heat and set aside.

3. While sauce is simmering, add salt and rigatoni to the boiling water and cook, uncovered, over high heat until pasta is al dente. Scoop out about 1 cup (250 mL) of the pasta water and set aside. Drain pasta.

4. Return sauté pan to medium heat. Add ½ cup (125 mL) of the reserved pasta water and heat through. Add rigatoni and continue to cook for about 3 minutes, using a wooden spoon to toss and evenly coat, adding more pasta water if necessary. Add remaining olive oil, season to taste with salt and pepper and toss well.

5. Transfer to a large serving bowl and serve immediately.

Variations

Substitute penne, cut ziti or maccheroni for the rigatoni.

Spaghetti al ragù coda di rospo

Spaghetti with Monkfish Ragù

Monkfish is often called "poor man's lobster" because it somewhat resembles northern lobster in flavor and texture. If it is well trimmed of membrane, it makes a flavorful pasta dish at a fraction of the cost and labor required for real lobster.

Serves 4 to 6

Tips

To trim fennel, cut off the root end and discard. Trim off the stems and feathery fronds and save for flavoring soups and to use as garnish. Trim off any stems from the bulb and slice bulb in half. Remove core and discard. The bulb is now ready to mince, dice or slice.

Even though monkfish is available skinless and boneless, some silver membrane usually remains. This should be removed by grasping the end of the membrane with a kitchen towel and pulling it while sliding a boning knife between the membrane and the flesh.

3 tbsp	extra-virgin olive oil	45 mL
2 tbsp	diced onion	25 mL
2 tbsp	diced peeled celery	25 mL
2 tbsp	diced trimmed fennel bulb	25 mL
	Salt and freshly ground white pepper	
1 cup	diced skinless, boneless monkfish	250 mL
1 cup	dry white Italian wine	250 mL
½ cup	canned crushed Italian tomatoes	125 mL
1 tbsp	salt	15 mL
1 lb	dried spaghetti	500 g

1. In a covered pasta pot over high heat, bring water to a rapid boil.

2. Meanwhile, in a large sauté pan, heat oil over medium heat. Add onion, celery and fennel and cook, stirring, until vegetables are tender but not browned, about 5 minutes. Season to taste with salt and pepper. Add monkfish, wine and tomatoes. Reduce heat to low and simmer for 20 minutes. Using a fork, mash monkfish until it flakes. Continue to cook until sauce thickens slightly, about 3 minutes. Cover and remove from heat. Set aside.

3. While sauce is simmering, add salt and spaghetti to the boiling water and cook, uncovered, over high heat until pasta is al dente. Scoop out about 1 cup (250 mL) of the pasta water and set aside. Drain pasta.

4. Return sauté pan to medium heat. Add ½ cup (125 mL) of the reserved pasta water and spaghetti and continue to cook for 2 to 3 minutes, using pasta tongs to toss and coat evenly, and adding more pasta water if necessary. Season to taste with salt and pepper. Toss well.

5. Transfer to a large serving bowl and serve immediately.

Monkfish

Monkfish, a particularly unattractive fish with a huge, ugly head and oversized mouth, is found in the northwest Atlantic (it is also known as goosefish, anglerfish, molligut, bellyfish, layerfish and fishing frog). Although very tasty, it has traditionally not been popular among home cooks because remnants of the tough membrane that clings to the flesh need to be removed before cooking. Monkfish is available year-round as whole tails, with skin removed, or as fillets. Purchase monkfish fillet that smells like the ocean, without any fishy odor, and looks moist and shiny. The fish should be dense and firm. To store monkfish, rinse under cold water, pat dry with paper towels and place in a glass baking dish on a rack set over, but not in, crushed ice. Cover the dish with plastic wrap and refrigerate until ready to use. Use within two days of purchase.

Spaghetti with Seafood

This is a classic and festive dish, but it may be difficult to bring together all this high-quality seafood on the same day. So use whatever you can find fresh and double the amount. For example, say you have mussels, calamari and shrimp but no octopus and clams. Just double the quantities of shrimp and mussels.

Serves 4 to 6

Tips

I usually season my sauces in the initial stages of cooking so the flavors have time to bloom. I always taste the final product and, if necessary, add salt and pepper just before serving.

I like to tear basil leaves by hand rather than slicing them, because I think they look and taste better.

5 tbsp	extra-virgin olive oil, divided	75 mL
1 tsp	thinly sliced garlic	5 mL
1 tsp	thinly sliced fresh red finger chile (see Tips, right)	5 mL
12	small clams, scrubbed free of grit (see Tips, page 265)	12
1½ cups	dry white Italian wine, divided	375 mL
½ cup	clam juice, preferably low-sodium	125 mL
12	mussels, debearded and scrubbed free of grit	12
¼ cup	calamari rings and tentacles	50 mL
¼ cup	1-inch (2.5 cm) pieces cleaned baby octopus	50 mL
¼ cup	halved (lengthwise) peeled, deveined shrimp	50 mL
1 cup	canned crushed Italian tomatoes	250 mL
2 tbsp	hand-torn fresh basil leaves	25 mL
	Salt and freshly ground black pepper	
1 tbsp	salt	15 mL
1 lb	dried spaghetti	500 g

1. In a covered pasta pot over high heat, bring water to a rapid boil.

2. Meanwhile, in a large sauté pan, heat 3 tbsp (45 mL) of the oil over medium heat. Add garlic and chile and cook, stirring, until garlic is translucent but not browned, 2 to 3 minutes. Add clams, 1 cup (250 mL) of the wine and the clam juice and cover. Simmer until all clams are open. Add mussels, calamari, octopus, shrimp, remaining wine, tomatoes and basil. Simmer over very low heat just until mixture thickens and lightly coats the back of a spoon, about 5 minutes (do not boil, or the seafood will overcook). Season to taste with salt and pepper. Remove pan from heat and set aside. Discard any clams or mussels that have not opened.

3. Add salt and spaghetti to the boiling water and cook, uncovered, over high heat until pasta is al dente. Scoop out about 1 cup (250 mL) of the pasta water and set aside. Drain pasta.

Tips

The Italian red chile, which is medium hot and slightly sweet, is not available here, but a good substitute is the California-grown red finger chile (also called Dutch or Holland chile) or the red Fresno chile. In a pinch you can use a ripe red jalapeño or cayenne chile, both of which are much hotter. If you're using these, mince them and reduce the quantity to about ¼ tsp (1 mL).

Always use a large pot and plenty of water when cooking pasta. To properly cook 1 pound (500 g) of pasta, you'll need a pot with a volume of at least 8 quarts (8 L) so that you can use 6 quarts (6 L) of water.

4. Return sauté pan to medium heat. Add ½ cup (125 mL) of the reserved pasta water and spaghetti. Continue to cook for 3 minutes, using pasta tongs to toss and coat evenly, adding more pasta water if necessary. Add remaining olive oil, season to taste with salt and pepper and toss well.

5. Transfer to a large serving bowl and serve immediately.

Variations

If available, use fresh brown U-15 (colossal) shrimp (fewer than 12 per pound/500 g). But top-quality frozen pink or white shrimp are acceptable substitutes, as are smaller extra-jumbo (16 to 20 per pound/500 g) or jumbo (21 to 25 per pound/500 g) shrimp.

Substitute equal amounts of available seafood for unavailable seafood, for example, 24 mussels for 12 clams and 12 mussels; ½ cup (125 mL) calamari rings for ¼ cup (50 mL) calamari rings and ¼ cup (50 mL) octopus.

Substitute ½ cup (125 mL) shrimp for the octopus.

Makeovers: Using Leftovers and Pasta

One day while I was working on this book, my wife asked if I would cook dinner for our children, as she had an unexpected meeting to attend. So there I was, a chef out of water, so to speak. I was home with no sous-chefs, no prep chefs, no well-stocked pantry and cooler, no menu for the evening — and two hungry children. I opened the refrigerator to see what I could find: some leftover grilled chicken, a small dish of cooked spinach and a hunk of cheese. I know what a French chef would have done with this: make an omelet. But I'm Italian, so I reached for a package of pasta. While the pasta was cooking, I made an impromptu sauce from those perfectly edible leftovers and served up the combination. The kids loved it.

That was when I realized that pasta is the perfect medium for leftovers. If you've been using this book already, you may have figured out that I'm inclined to pontificate about my favorite underutilized vegetables and herbs (celery, leeks, kale, cabbage, mint). Similarly I have come to the conclusion that leftovers are underutilized too, probably because they have a negative image. Wholesome cooked foods that are properly refrigerated for a short time do not decrease in flavor. In fact, when vegetables marinate in their cooking juices, their flavors are enhanced. The same is true of seafood, poultry and meat: they have a chance to absorb the seasonings they were cooked with. The only thing wrong with good leftovers is that they are cold and usually skimpy — there is rarely enough for a good second meal. Cooking them in a sauce and combining them with pasta solves both problems.

With this in mind I created a chart (see below) that will help you, the home cook, create appetizing pastas from bits of cooked fish, poultry, meats and vegetables left over from previous meals. All you need to transform these odds and ends into a delicious meal is a pound (500 g) of pasta, a little olive oil, onion and wine. If you are cooking for children you may want to substitute an equal quantity of organic chicken or vegetable broth for the wine.

Thinking about leftover food moved me along to leftover pasta. What would happen, I wondered, if you prepared a recipe from this cookbook and didn't eat it all? The easiest solution is to refrigerate it and reheat it in the microwave for lunch within a day or two of cooking. But what if you needed something for dinner and you wanted it to be a little more special? So I came up with ways to turn leftover pasta into appetizing second meals: casseroles, stuffed bell peppers, frittatas, oven-browned gratins, soufflés, timbales and even creamy savory tarts.

Because everyone who cooks always has leftovers, I hope this chapter will help you use them in dishes that you and your family will enjoy. *Buon appetito!*

Making Pasta from Leftovers

The following chart will help you transform leftovers that are likely to be in your refrigerator from time to time into a delicious pasta dish. Remember, your leftovers should never be more than three days old, not only because of food safety but also because foods start to lose their flavor and texture if stored too long. And, to work in these recipes, they should be fully cooked.

Note: The following quantities are appropriate for 1 lb (500 g) of pasta and will make 4 to 6 servings.

Fully Cooked Vegetables	*and*	Meat *or* Poultry *or* Seafood	
Choose 1 or 2 (total: 2 cups/500 mL)	Choose 1 (1 cup/250 mL)		
mushrooms, spinach, asparagus, green beans, peas, carrots, cabbage, tomatoes, escarole, kale, broccoli, fava beans, cauliflower, potatoes, corn, zucchini, lentils, white beans	veal, pork, lamb, sausage	chicken, turkey	salmon, shrimp, monkfish, swordfish, tuna

Pasta from Leftovers: Master Recipe

Tips

Use two vegetables, such as 1 cup (250 mL) mushrooms plus 1 cup (250 mL) green beans, to equal 2 cups (500 mL). Or just use a single vegetable, such as 2 cups (500 mL) mushrooms.

Chop cooked vegetables coarsely by hand or by pulsing briefly in a food processor.

To chop meat, poultry or fish, place in the bowl of a food processor fitted with the steel blade and pulse briefly into ¼-inch (0.5 cm) pieces.

Omit the cheese if your pasta includes fish or seafood.

3 tbsp	extra-virgin olive oil	45 mL
2 tbsp	diced onion	25 mL
2 cups	cooked vegetables, coarsely chopped, with any juices (see Tips, left)	500 mL
1 cup	cooked meat, poultry or fish, chopped (see Tips, left)	250 mL
½ cup	dry white Italian wine or chicken or vegetable broth	125 mL
1 tbsp	salt	15 mL
1 lb	dried pasta	500 g
3 tbsp	grated Parmigiano-Reggiano, optional (see Tips, left)	45 mL

1. In a covered pasta pot over high heat, bring water to a rapid boil.

2. Meanwhile, in a large sauté pan, heat oil over medium heat. Add onion and cook, stirring, until translucent, about 3 minutes. Add vegetables and cook, stirring, until heated through, about 4 minutes. Add meat, poultry or fish and cook, stirring, until heated through, about 2 minutes. Add wine and cook until reduced by half. Remove from heat and set aside.

3. While sauce is heating, add salt and pasta to the boiling water and cook, uncovered, over high heat until pasta is al dente. Scoop out about 1 cup (250 mL) of the pasta water and set aside. Drain pasta.

4. Return sauté pan to element, add 2 tbsp (25 mL) of the reserved pasta water to sauté pan and heat through. Add cooked pasta and, using pasta tongs or a wooden spoon, toss to coat evenly, adding more pasta water if necessary.

5. Transfer to a large serving bowl or platter. If pasta does not include fish or seafood, sprinkle with Parmigiano-Reggiano. Serve immediately.

Variations

Use 2½ cups (625 mL) vegetables and omit the meat, poultry or fish. Or combine ½ cup (125 mL) cooked sausage with ½ cup (125 mL) meat or poultry to equal 1 cup (250 mL) of meat.

Where's the Beef?

Most often, leftover beef is in the form of steak, hamburger, meat loaf or roast beef. When these forms of cooked beef are reheated, they become dry and tough, so I don't recommend using leftover beef in this recipe. If, however, you have some braised beef made from shoulder, chuck or shank, slowly cooked for hours, you can shred it and use it — provided the flavors used in the original recipe are not too far outside the European market basket (no soy sauce, ginger or lemongrass, please).

Remane di fusilli al tacchino e fave al forno

Baked Fusilli with Turkey and Fava Beans

Pasta al forno — al forno meaning "in the oven" — or baked pasta is famous throughout Italy. The most familiar example is lasagna. Baked pasta dishes can be very laborious, but if you already have the pasta and sauce left over, then all you need to do is warm up the pasta, add a little cheese and bake it. Pasta al forno, presto!

Serves 2 to 3

Tip

Instead of using a sauté pan, combine leftover pasta and water in a microwave-safe dish, cover and reheat in the microwave on High until hot, 2 to 3 minutes. Uncover and stir well before transferring to baking dish.

- Preheat oven to 350°F (180°C)
- 2-quart (2 L) baking dish, lightly greased

½ cup	water, divided	125 mL
½ recipe	Fusilli with Turkey and Fava Beans (see recipe, page 107)	½ recipe
¼ cup	shredded fresh mozzarella	50 mL
3 tbsp	grated Parmigiano-Reggiano	45 mL

1. In a large sauté pan, combine half of the water and the Fusilli with Turkey and Fava Beans. Warm over medium heat and, using a wooden spoon, stir to loosen pasta and coat with liquid. If pasta seems dry, add remaining water.

2. Transfer to prepared baking dish. Sprinkle with mozzarella and Parmigiano-Reggiano.

3. Bake in preheated oven until pasta is hot throughout and cheese is browned, about 30 minutes. Remove from oven and serve immediately.

Variations

Baked Maccheroni and Cheese: Substitute ½ recipe Maccheroni and Cheese (see recipe, page 203) for the Fusilli with Turkey and Fava Beans.

Baked Orecchiette with Pork Sausage Ragù: Substitute ½ recipe Orecchiette with Pork Sausage Ragù (see recipe, page 120) for the Fusilli with Turkey and Fava Beans.

Baked Orecchiette with Chicken Breast and Mushrooms: Substitute ½ recipe Orecchiette with Chicken Breast and Mushrooms (see recipe, page 102) for the Fusilli with Turkey and Fava Beans.

Baked Penne with Olives and Mushrooms: Substitute ½ recipe Penne with Olives and Mushrooms (see recipe, page 40) for the Fusilli with Turkey and Fava Beans.

Baked Maccheroni with Sweetened Broccoli: Substitute ½ recipe Maccheroni with Sweetened Broccoli (see recipe, page 71) for the Fusilli with Turkey and Fava Beans.

Remane di frittata di linguine al limone e menta

Leftover Frittata of Linguine with Lemon and Mint

Frittatas — flat baked omelets — are familiar throughout Italy. They are started in a sauté pan on top of the stove and finished in the oven (make sure the sauté pan has an ovenproof handle). You can serve frittata wedges hot from the oven, let them cool to room temperature or cover and refrigerate them, then reheat in a microwave (I call that leftover leftovers).

Serves 6 to 8

Tips

An electric knife slices frittata perfectly.

If you prefer, loosen the edges and bottom of the frittata with a spatula and slice and serve from the pan.

- Preheat oven to 350°F (180°C)
- Large ovenproof sauté pan

½ cup	water, divided	125 mL
½ recipe	Linguine with Lemon and Mint (see recipe, page 78)	½ recipe
8	large eggs, beaten	8
3 tbsp	grated Parmigiano-Reggiano	45 mL

1. In a large sauté pan, combine half of the water and the Linguine with Lemon and Mint. Warm over medium heat and, using a wooden spoon, stir to loosen pasta and coat well with liquid. If pasta seems dry, add remaining water. Cook until water is absorbed.

2. Add eggs and Parmigiano-Reggiano. Using a wooden spoon, stir to coat evenly.

3. Transfer to preheated oven and bake until firm to the touch, about 30 minutes.

4. Using a thin spatula, loosen edges and bottom of frittata. Place a 14-inch (35 cm) plate on top of sauté pan and flip frittata onto plate. Using a sharp serrated knife, slice frittata into 6 or 8 wedges. Serve immediately or at room temperature.

Variations

Frittata of Spaghetti Napoletana: Substitute ½ recipe Spaghetti Napoletana (see recipe, page 58) for the Linguine with Lemon and Mint.

Frittata of Perciatelli with Bell Peppers: Substitute ½ recipe Perciatelli with Bell Peppers (see recipe, page 77) for the Linguine with Lemon and Mint.

Frittata of Vermicelli with Eggplant and Mozzarella: Substitute ½ recipe Vermicelli with Eggplant and Mozzarella (see recipe, page 94) for the Linguine with Lemon and Mint.

Frittata of Linguine with Caramelized Onions: Substitute ½ recipe Linguine with Caramelized Onions (see recipe, page 81) for the Linguine with Lemon and Mint.

Fritatta of Linguine with Turkey-Tomato Sauce: Substitute ½ recipe Linguine with Turkey-Tomato Sauce (see recipe, page 110) for the Linguine with Lemon and Mint.

Remane di peperoni ripieni di pennette al burro e pomodorini

Bell Peppers Filled with Pennette, Cherry Tomatoes and Butter

Stuffed peppers filled with ground meat and rice, covered with tomato sauce and baked, is a very American dish, although the idea has resonance in other cuisines. Stuffing peppers with leftover pasta creates a good meatless dish that can serve as a main course or a side.

Serves 3

Tips

The pepper caps make a nice garnish but if you prefer you can serve this dish "topless."

Instead of using a sauté pan, combine leftover pasta and water in a microwave-safe dish, cover and reheat in the microwave on High until hot, 2 to 3 minutes. Uncover and stir to mix.

Cut a thin slice off the bottom of each pepper without cutting through to the cavity, to help the peppers stand level and upright in the baking dish.

If you prefer, before softening the peppers, cut them in half vertically. Arrange cut side up in the prepared baking dish, then fill halves and sprinkle with the cheese.

- Preheat oven to 350°F (180°C)
- 2-quart (2 L) baking dish, lightly greased

3	green bell peppers, ¼ inch (0.5 cm) of tops sliced off and set aside (see Tips, left), cored and seeded	3
½ cup (approx.)	water, divided	125 mL
½ recipe	Pennette with Cherry Tomatoes and Butter (see recipe, page 73)	½ recipe
2 tbsp	dry white Italian breadcrumbs	25 mL
¼ cup	shredded fresh mozzarella	50 mL

1. In a large microwave-safe dish, combine peppers without their caps with ¼ cup (50 mL) of the water. Loosely cover and microwave on High for 5 minutes. Remove and let cool to room temperature.

2. In a large sauté pan over medium heat, combine remaining water and Pennette. Using a wooden spoon, stir to coat well with liquid. If pasta seems dry, add remaining water. Cook until water evaporates.

3. Spoon into peppers. Sprinkle with breadcrumbs and mozzarella and place in prepared baking dish. Bake in preheated oven until cheese is browned, about 30 minutes.

4. Remove from oven, transfer to a serving platter and, if desired, top each pepper with a reserved pepper cap. Serve immediately.

Variations

Substitute red or yellow bell peppers for the green.

Bell Peppers Filled with Linguine, Peas and Sage: Substitute ½ recipe Linguine with Peas and Sage (see recipe, page 46) for the Pennette.

Bell Peppers Filled with Tortiglioni, Corn and Leeks: Substitute ½ recipe Tortiglioni with Corn and Leeks (see recipe, page 75) for the Pennette.

Bell Peppers Filled with Conchiglie with Vegetables and Aromatic Herbs: Substitute ½ recipe Conchiglie with Vegetables and Aromatic Herbs (see recipe, page 68) for the Pennette.

Bell Peppers Filled with Orecchiette, Arugula and Tomatoes: Substitute ½ recipe Orecchiette with Arugula and Tomatoes (see recipe, page 88) for the pennette.

Soufflet di penne rigate al quattro formaggi

Soufflé of Penne Rigate with Four Cheeses

If a pasta with four cheeses was good, then a pasta-and-four-cheese soufflé should be just as good. It is nice to have the proper size of soufflé dish so the soufflé puffs slightly over the top of the dish. Be sure to serve this immediately because, like all soufflés, it deflates quickly after being removed from the oven.

Serves 3

Tips

Instead of using a sauté pan, combine leftover pasta and water in a microwave-safe dish, cover and reheat in the microwave on High until hot, 2 to 3 minutes. Uncover and stir to mix pasta and liquid.

Fill the soufflé dish to within ½ inch (1 cm) of the top to allow the soufflé to rise above the rim.

- Preheat oven to 375°F (190°C)
- 1½-quart (1.5 L) soufflé dish

½ cup	water	125 mL
½ recipe	Penne Rigate with Four Cheeses (see recipe, page 56)	½ recipe
2 tbsp	extra-virgin olive oil	25 mL
¼ cup	dry white breadcrumbs	50 mL
6	egg whites, stiffly beaten	6

1. In a large sauté pan, combine water and Penne Rigate with Four Cheeses. Warm over medium heat and, using a wooden spoon, stir to loosen pasta and coat well with liquid. Cook until water is absorbed. Transfer to a large bowl and set aside.

2. Coat bottom and sides of soufflé dish with olive oil and cover evenly with breadcrumbs.

3. Using a rubber or silicone spatula, gently fold egg whites, in three batches, into reserved penne. Transfer to prepared soufflé dish.

4. Bake in preheated oven until soufflé is puffed and golden and a tester inserted in the center comes out clean. Serve immediately.

Variations

Soufflé of Vermicelli with Eggplant and Mozzarella: Substitute ½ recipe Vermicelli with Eggplant and Mozzarella (see recipe, page 94) for the Penne Rigate.

Soufflé of Spaghettini with Tomatoes and Basil: Substitute ½ recipe Spaghettini with Tomatoes and Basil (see recipe, page 91) for the Penne Rigate.

Soufflé of Vermicelli alla Marinara: Substitute ½ recipe Vermicelli alla Marinara (see recipe, page 95) for the Penne Rigate.

Soufflé of Spaghetti with Capers and Lemon: Substitute ½ recipe Spaghetti with Capers and Lemon (see recipe, page 92) for the Penne Rigate.

Soufflé of Spaghetti with Pecorino Romano and Black Pepper: Substitute ½ recipe Spaghetti with Pecorino Romano and Black Pepper (see recipe, page 39) for the Penne Rigate.

Remane di ruote di carro con zucchine e peperoni gratinate

Oven-Browned Ruote di Carro with Zucchini and Bell Peppers

An Italian gratinate is like a French gratin, a casserole baked until the top is crisp and browned.

Serves 2 to 3

Tip

Instead of using a sauté pan, combine leftover pasta and water in a microwave-safe dish, cover and reheat in the microwave on High until hot, 2 to 3 minutes. Uncover and stir to mix pasta and liquid.

- Preheat oven to 350°F (180°C)
- 2-quart (2 L) baking dish, lightly greased

½ cup	water	125 mL
½ recipe	Ruote di Carro with Zucchini and Bell Peppers (see recipe, page 82)	½ recipe
2 tbsp	dry white Italian breadcrumbs	25 mL
¼ cup	shredded fresh mozzarella	50 mL

1. In a large sauté pan, combine water and Ruote di Carro with Zucchini and Bell Peppers. Warm over medium heat and, using a wooden spoon, toss to loosen pasta and coat well with liquid. Cook until water is absorbed.

2. Transfer to prepared baking dish and sprinkle with breadcrumbs and mozzarella. Bake in preheated oven until pasta is hot and cheese is browned, about 30 minutes. Serve immediately.

Variations

Oven-Browned Ziti with Leeks and Onions: Substitute ½ recipe Ziti with Leeks and Onions (see recipe, page 84) for the Ruote di Carro with Zucchini and Bell Peppers.

Oven-Browned Penne Rigate with Vodka: Substitute ½ recipe Penne Rigate with Vodka (see recipe, page 72) for the Ruote di Carro with Zucchini and Bell Peppers.

Oven-Browned Farfalle with Porcini Mushrooms: Substitute ½ recipe Farfalle with Porcini Mushrooms (see recipe, page 59) for the Ruote di Carro with Zucchini and Bell Peppers.

Oven-Browned Fusilli with Celery Sauce and Ricotta Salata: Substitute ½ recipe Fusilli with Celery Sauce and Ricotta Salata (see recipe, page 66) for the Ruote di Carro with Zucchini and Bell Peppers.

Oven-Browned Orecchiette with Eggplant Sauce: Substitute ½ recipe Orecchiette with Eggplant Sauce (see recipe, page 64) for the Ruote di Carro with Zucchini and Bell Peppers.

Torta di remane di spaghetti con panna e noci

Tart of Spaghetti with Walnut Cream

This is somewhat like a pasta quiche: very tasty and satisfying. If you make the pastry dough the day before you cook, it is very quick to prepare the tart. This makes a good brunch, supper or buffet dish.

Serves 4 to 6

Tips

The tart dough may be mixed in a food processor fitted with a plastic dough blade. Pulse to combine the dry ingredients, then add the butter and pulse until pea-size nuggets form. Drizzle in water through the feed tube and pulse just until dough forms. Proceed with recipe.

"Scant" means about 1 tbsp (15 mL) less than a cup (250 mL).

To cut in butter, use two forks, a pastry blender or your fingers.

- 10-inch (25 cm) pie plate or quiche pan

Crust

1 scant cup	unbleached all-purpose flour	235 mL
5 tbsp	cold unsalted butter, cubed	70 mL
1/4 tsp	salt	1 mL
3 tbsp	cold water	45 mL

Filling

1/2 cup	water	125 mL
1/2 recipe	Spaghetti with Walnut Cream (see recipe, page 47)	1/2 recipe
2 tbsp	heavy or whipping (35%) cream	25 mL
2 tbsp	grated Parmigiano-Reggiano	25 mL
2 tbsp	finely chopped walnuts	25 mL

1. In a bowl, combine flour, butter and salt. Cut in butter until pea-size nuggets form. Add water in a steady stream, stirring until dough forms. Shape into a disk and wrap in plastic. Refrigerate for at least 3 hours or overnight.

2. Preheat oven to 400°F (200°C). In a large sauté pan over medium heat, add water, Spaghetti, cream and Parmigiano-Reggiano. Stir to loosen pasta and coat with liquid. Cook until water is absorbed and pasta is coated. Remove from heat and set aside.

3. On a floured surface, roll reserved dough to fit pan. Place in pan and trim sides. Fill with spaghetti mixture and spread evenly, using a plastic spatula. Sprinkle walnuts evenly over top. Cover top loosely with aluminum foil and bake until pastry is golden brown and spaghetti mixture is hot and thick, about 30 minutes. Remove from oven and let cool to room temperature. Cut into wedges and serve immediately.

Variations

Tart of Rigatoni with Pancetta, Peperoncini and Pecorino Romano: Substitute 1/2 recipe Rigatoni with Pancetta, Peperoncini and Pecorino Romano (see recipe, page 133) for the Spaghetti.

Tart of Maccheroni with Mortadella, Cream and Eggs: Substitute 1/2 recipe Maccheroni with Mortadella, Cream and Eggs (see recipe, page 128) for the Spaghetti with Walnut Cream.

Tart of Penne with Pancetta and Gorgonzola Cheese: Substitute 1/2 recipe Penne with Pancetta and Gorgonzola Cheese (see recipe, page 132) for the Spaghetti with Walnut Cream.

Timballo di remane di garganelli con sugo di mortadella

Timbale of Garganelli with Mortadella Sauce

The 1996 movie Big Night *made people outside Italy aware of the timbale, an elaborate drum-shaped mold of layered ingredients and pasta that, if prepared correctly, can be baked, then unmolded to reveal an unbroken pasta mound that serves quite a crowd. This is a very simple version of a timbale, using leftover pasta. You can use any shape of ovenproof dish, but a deep 1-quart (1 L) stainless steel bowl resembles the shape of a timbale. A 4-cup (1 L) straight-sided soufflé dish also works.*

Serves 3 to 4

- Preheat oven to 350°F (180°C)
- 4-cup (1 L) deep ovenproof bowl, lightly greased

½ cup	water	125 mL
½ recipe	Garganelli with Mortadella Sauce (see recipe, page 127)	½ recipe
¼ cup	freshly grated Parmigiano-Reggiano	50 mL
2	large eggs, beaten	2
2 tbsp	extra-virgin olive oil	25 mL

1. In a large sauté pan, over medium heat combine water and Garganelli with Mortadella Sauce. Using a wooden spoon, toss to coat well with liquid. Cook until water is absorbed. Transfer to a mixing bowl, add cheese and eggs and mix well.

2. Add garganelli mixture to prepared bowl and pack firmly, using a plastic spatula. Smooth top and cover tightly with aluminum foil. Place in a deep roasting pan and add boiling water to halfway up the bowl. Bake in preheated oven until a wooden skewer inserted in the center comes out clean, about 45 minutes.

3. Remove from roasting pan, uncover bowl and let rest for 10 minutes. Loosen edges and bottom with a thin metal spatula. Place a serving plate on top of the bowl, invert both together, and shake timbale to loosen and unmold. Slice into 3 to 4 wedges with a sharp serrated knife and serve immediately.

Variations

Timbale of Trofie with Arugula Pesto: Substitute ½ recipe Trofie with Arugula Pesto (see recipe, page 85) for the Garganelli.

Timbale of Trofie with Oil-Cured Black and Green Olives: Substitute ½ recipe Trofie with Oil-Cured Black and Green Olives (see recipe, page 86) for the Garganelli.

Timbale of Bucatini all'Amatriciana: Substitute ½ recipe Bucatini all'Amatriciana (see recipe, page 126) for the Garganelli.

Timbale of Ruote with Speck and Mascarpone: Substitute ½ recipe Ruote with Speck and Mascarpone (see recipe, page 137) for the Garganelli.

Timbale of Fettuccine with Chicken-Tomato Sauce and Fava Beans: Substitute ½ recipe Fettuccine with Chicken-Tomato Sauce and Fava Beans (see recipe, page 99) for the Garganelli.

BITTERS CAMPARI AMARO

LISTINO PREZZI
BIBITE

CAMPARI & SODA	8
APEROL SPRITZ	8
AMARETTO & O.J.	7.50

MARTINI

NEGRONI	8
RUBY RED	9
ESPRESSO	9
LIMONCELLO	9

Pasta Salads: Contemporary Concoctions

The concept of pasta salad belongs to non-Italian cooks. Sometime during the 1950s macaroni salads appeared in the United States, Australia, Hawaii and even the Philippines. The salads were based on elbow macaroni and mayonnaise; additional ingredients ranged from chopped onions and celery to ripe olives, chicken or ham, pineapple chunks, raisins, bacon, chopped hard-boiled eggs, sliced carrots, green peas, shredded Cheddar cheese — you name it. Macaroni salad was a specialty of home cooks and a staple at delicatessens, but it was certainly not Italian.

However, as the years went by, chefs created more interesting salads, using pasta shapes other than elbow macaroni, lighter dressings and more balanced ingredients. The pasta salad was here to stay, at least outside Italy.

Today people still want pasta salads with vegetables and often protein — poultry, meat or fish. And the preference is for lighter, oil-based dressings rather than mayonnaise. These contemporary pasta salads can be prepared and eaten the same day or prepared a day in advance and refrigerated, then allowed to stand at room temperature just long enough to take off the chill. If fresh vegetables, extra-virgin olive oil and flavorful meats are used in the preparation, a marinating period will result in a good-tasting dish.

Now, is that an Italian concept of pasta? No, of course not, but people's needs change over time. Pasta salads are a response to the demand for ready-to-eat foods prepared in advance — a description of delicatessen foods in general. Purists will still argue that pasta salads are not Italian. But if they taste good, the ingredients are within the Italian/European market basket (no soy sauce, lemongrass and ginger, please) and you enjoy eating them on a warm summer day — why not? Treat the ingredients for pasta salads with the same reverence that applies to all pasta dishes: excellent olive oil, quality meats and cheeses, and seasonal vegetables at their peak.

In the following recipes pasta co-stars with the other ingredients. As with sauces, keep salad dressings for pasta to a minimum.

Short and Dry

When making salads, I suggest using short-cut pasta and pasta shapes rather than long string or ribbon pasta. Dried pasta is better suited to pasta salads than fresh because it is sturdier and holds up to being thoroughly tossed. And when you cook the pasta, it's better to cook it a little past the al dente stage, because pasta tends to harden when refrigerated or standing at room temperature.

Not Too Cold

You may make pasta salads up to one day in advance. For optimum results make pasta salad the day it will be eaten. If you refrigerate it, before serving please let it stand outside the refrigerator long enough — about 20 minutes — to take off the chill. Cold tends to dampen flavors that will bloom at room temperature.

Cavatappi in insalata al salmone affumicato

Cavatappi Salad with Smoked Salmon

Salmon is definitely not in the Italian market basket and smoked salmon is not part of Italian culinary traditions. But today it's a very popular food: in Italy's major cities people can order salmon at restaurants. So here is a simple but tasty recipe for a pasta salad with smoked salmon that is very easy to make.

Serves 4 to 6

Tip

Pasta for salads should be cooked more than al dente but not so much that it becomes mushy. Pasta tends to harden at room temperature, and especially when refrigerated.

• Rimmed baking sheet

1 tbsp	salt	15 mL
1 lb	dried cavatappi (see Variations, below)	500 g
⅓ cup	extra-virgin olive oil	75 mL
1¼ cups	diced (½ inch/1 cm) smoked salmon	300 mL
2 tbsp	hand-torn fresh basil leaves	25 mL
	Freshly ground black pepper	
1 tbsp	tiny (nonpareil) capers, drained	15 mL
1 tsp	finely grated lemon zest, packed	5 mL

1. In a covered pasta pot over high heat, bring water to a rapid boil. Add salt and cavatappi and cook, uncovered, until pasta is slightly more than al dente. Drain, spread on baking sheet and let cool for 5 minutes.

2. Transfer to a large mixing bowl and add olive oil, smoked salmon and basil. Using a wooden spoon, toss to coat evenly. Season to taste with pepper.

3. Transfer to a serving platter. Serve immediately or refrigerate, covered. Let stand at room temperature for up to 20 minutes to take the chill off before serving.

Variations

Substitute penne or fusilli for the cavatappi.

Cavatappi in insalata al tacchino e caponata

Cavatappi Salad with Turkey and Caponata

Caponata is a traditional Sicilian eggplant relish that is popular throughout Italy and now the world. The sweet-sour flavor is Moorish, a legacy from Arabs who occupied southern Italy for centuries. Homemade caponata is a labor of love, as you will see from the recipe that I have included for the adventuresome cook. If you want to make this colorful, piquant salad quickly, use a jar of good imported Italian caponata.

Serves 4 to 6

Tips

Use a prepared Italian caponata or, if you're feeling ambitious, make your own (see recipe, page 181).

Any dry white Italian table wine will work well in this recipe, but I'd probably use Pinot Bianco, which is a good basic dry white wine for use in Italian cooking.

- Rimmed baking sheet

3 tbsp	extra-virgin olive oil	45 mL
3	garlic cloves, finely sliced	3
	Salt and freshly ground black pepper	
1 lb	skinless, boneless turkey breast, diced (½ inch/1 cm)	500 g
½ cup	dry white Italian wine (see Tips, left)	125 mL
1 tbsp	salt	15 mL
1 lb	dried cavatappi (see Variations, below)	500 g
1½ cups	caponata (see Tips, left)	375 mL

1. In a large sauté pan, heat olive oil over medium heat. Add garlic and salt and pepper to taste and cook, stirring, until garlic is lightly browned, about 3 minutes. Using a slotted spoon, remove and discard garlic. Add turkey and wine. Reduce heat to low, cover and cook until turkey is cooked through, about 10 minutes. Transfer to a large mixing bowl and let cool to room temperature.

2. In a covered pasta pot over high heat, bring water to a rapid boil. Add salt and cavatappi and cook, uncovered, until pasta is slightly more than al dente. Drain, spread on baking sheet and let cool for 5 minutes.

3. Add cooled cavatappi and caponata to turkey mixture. Using a wooden spoon, toss to coat evenly. Season to taste with salt and pepper and toss well.

4. Transfer to a large serving platter. Serve immediately or refrigerate, covered. Let stand at room temperature for up to 20 minutes to take the chill off before serving.

Variations

Substitute fusilli or penne for the cavatappi.

Caponata

Makes about 3 cups (750 mL)

Tip

Work like a chef. Have all your ingredients ready to go before you actually start to cook (see *Mise en Place*, page 15).

3 to 3½ cups	peeled eggplant, diced (½ inch/1 cm)	750 to 875 mL
1 tbsp	salt	15 mL
½ cup	extra-virgin olive oil, divided	125 mL
¾ cup	diced peeled celery	175 mL
½ cup	diced onion	125 mL
1 tsp	minced garlic	5 mL
3	garlic cloves, thinly sliced	3
½ cup	tomato sauce (see recipe, page 114)	125 mL
4 to 5	hand-torn fresh basil leaves	4 to 5
2 tbsp	halved pitted oil-cured black olives	25 mL
1 tsp	tiny (nonpareil) capers	5 mL
2 tbsp	red wine vinegar	25 mL
1 tbsp	granulated sugar	15 mL
	Salt and freshly ground black pepper	

1. Place eggplant in a colander and sprinkle with salt. Set aside for 30 minutes. Blot dry with paper towels.

2. In a saucepan, heat 5 tbsp (75 mL) of the oil over medium heat. Add eggplant and cook, stirring, until soft and tender, about 9 minutes. Transfer to a large plate and set aside.

3. In a pot of salted boiling water, cook celery until tender, about 5 minutes. Drain, transfer to a plate and let cool to room temperature.

4. In a saucepan, heat remaining oil over medium heat. Add onion and minced and sliced garlic and cook, stirring, until onion is soft and tender, about 3 minutes. Add tomato sauce, basil, celery, olives and capers and stir well. Stir in vinegar and sugar. Lower heat and simmer, stirring occasionally, until slightly thickened, about 10 minutes. Add reserved eggplant, stir well, and remove from heat. Season to taste with salt and pepper.

5. Transfer to a covered container and refrigerate for up to 4 days.

Conchiglie in insalata ai calamari e pomodori secchi

Conchiglie Salad with Calamari and Sun-Dried Tomatoes

Conchiglie are small seashell-shaped pasta, so they are visually appropriate for seafood. Typically calamari is served grilled, seasoned with salt, pepper, lemon juice and olive oil, or it is served hot, stuffed and baked or in a sauce for pasta (see recipes, pages 141 and 150). Eating it in a salad is different, interesting and, I believe, very refreshing.

Serves 4 to 6

Tip

In this recipe use dry-packed sun-dried tomatoes rather than those that are packed in olive oil, because you don't want to add any more oil to the salad. Put dry-packed sun-dried tomatoes in a bowl and pour in hot water to cover. Place a plate on top to keep the tomatoes submerged, and soak until tender and rehydrated, about 20 minutes. Drain and use in the recipe. Save the soaking liquid, covered and refrigerated, for use in recipes where liquid or broth is called for.

• Rimmed baking sheet

1 tbsp	salt	15 mL
1 lb	dried conchiglie (see Variations, below)	500 g
3 tbsp	extra-virgin olive oil	45 mL
3	garlic cloves, thinly sliced	3
	Salt and freshly ground black pepper	
1½ cups	calamari rings and tentacles	375 mL
½ cup	Italian sun-dried tomatoes, cut into thin strips (see Tip, left)	125 mL
½ cup	dry white Italian wine	125 mL
2 tbsp	fresh lemon juice	25 mL
2 tbsp	chopped Italian parsley leaves	25 mL

1. In a covered pasta pot over high heat, bring water to a rapid boil. Add salt and conchiglie and cook, uncovered, until pasta is slightly more than al dente. Drain, spread on baking sheet and let cool for 5 minutes.

2. Meanwhile, in a large sauté pan, heat olive oil over medium heat. Add garlic and salt and pepper to taste and cook, stirring, until garlic is lightly browned, about 3 minutes. Using a slotted spoon, remove and discard garlic. Add calamari, sun-dried tomatoes, wine and lemon juice. Reduce heat to low, cover and cook until calamari are cooked through, about 8 minutes. Transfer to a large mixing bowl and let cool to room temperature.

3. Add cooled conchiglie and parsley to calamari mixture. Using a wooden spoon, toss to coat evenly. Season to taste with pepper.

4. Transfer to a large serving platter. Serve immediately or refrigerate, covered. Let stand at room temperature for up to 20 minutes to take the chill off before serving.

Variations

Substitute penne or fusilli for the conchiglie.

Conchiglie in insalata con la polpa di granchio e fagiolini verdi

Conchiglie Salad with Crabmeat and Green Beans

Served hot, crabmeat with peas and pasta is a traditional combination. Here green beans cut in small pieces take the place of peas, and the pasta is served at room temperature. If possible, in season use perfectly fresh green beans from a farmers' market. I believe you will appreciate their outstanding flavor and texture.

Serves 4 to 6

Tips

Always use a large pot and plenty of water when cooking pasta. To properly cook 1 pound (500 g) of pasta, you'll need a pot with a volume of at least 8 quarts (8 L) so that you can use 6 quarts (6 L) of water.

Never rinse pasta after draining it. The surface starch helps the sauce to cling and is important to producing the best-quality dish.

• Rimmed baking sheet

1 tbsp	salt	15 mL
1 lb	dried conchiglie (see Variations, below)	500 g
½ cup	extra-virgin olive oil, divided	125 mL
3	garlic cloves, thinly sliced	3
	Salt and freshly ground black pepper	
1½ cups	sliced green beans (¼ inch/0.5 cm)	375 mL
½ cup	dry white Italian wine	125 mL
1½ cups	pasteurized jumbo lump crabmeat	375 mL
½ cup	fresh lemon juice	125 mL
	Salt and freshly ground black pepper	

1. In a covered pasta pot over high heat, bring water to a rapid boil. Add salt and conchiglie and cook, uncovered, until pasta is slightly more than al dente. Drain, spread on baking sheet and let cool for 5 minutes.

2. Meanwhile, in a large sauté pan, heat ¼ cup (50 mL) of the oil over medium heat. Add garlic and salt and pepper to taste and cook, stirring, until garlic is light brown, about 3 minutes. Using a slotted spoon, remove and discard garlic. Add beans and wine. Stir, reduce heat to low, cover and cook until beans are half-cooked, about 4 minutes. Transfer to a large mixing bowl and let cool to room temperature.

3. Add cooled conchiglie, remaining olive oil, crabmeat and lemon juice. Using a wooden spoon, toss to coat evenly. Season to taste with salt and pepper.

4. Transfer to a large platter. Serve immediately or refrigerate, covered. Let stand at room temperature for up to 20 minutes to take the chill off before serving.

Variations

Substitute penne or fusilli for the conchiglie.

Insalata di farfalline alla caprese

Farfalline Salad with Mozzarella, Tomatoes and Basil

This is like caprese salad (basil, tomatoes and fresh water-buffalo mozzarella) with pasta. Farfalline are small bow-tie (butterfly) pasta. Fresh cow's-milk mozzarella is readily available in supermarkets, but you can raise the bar on this recipe by using fresh mozzarella di bufala made from water-buffalo milk; it's available at cheese shops and gourmet Italian grocers.

Serves 4 to 6

Tip

I like to tear the basil leaves by hand rather than slicing them, because I think they look and taste better.

* Rimmed baking sheet

1 tbsp	salt	15 mL
1 lb	dried farfalline (see Variations, below)	500 g
¼ cup	extra-virgin olive oil	50 mL
1 cup	diced fresh cow's-milk mozzarella or mozzarella di bufala	250 mL
1 cup	halved cherry tomatoes	250 mL
½ cup	hand-torn fresh basil leaves	125 mL
	Salt and freshly ground black pepper	

1. In a covered pasta pot over high heat, bring water to a rapid boil. Add salt and farfalline and cook, uncovered, until pasta is slightly more than al dente. Drain, spread on baking sheet and let cool for 5 minutes.

2. Transfer to a large mixing bowl. Add olive oil, mozzarella, tomatoes and basil. Using a wooden spoon, toss to coat evenly. Season to taste with salt and pepper.

3. Transfer to a large serving platter. Serve immediately or refrigerate, covered. Let stand at room temperature for up to 20 minutes to take the chill off before serving.

Variations

Substitute penne, farfalle or fusilli for the farfalline.

Insalata di farfalline con le gamberetti e broccoli

Farfalline Salad with Shrimp and Broccoli

Shrimp and broccoli go well together in color, flavor and texture. This salad could be served either warm or at room temperature. Both the shrimp and the broccoli florets are cut vertically, which allows for more even distribution. In my opinion this is preferable to coming across whole shrimp and big clumps of broccoli.

Serves 4 to 6

Tip

I use medium-size shrimp in this recipe, about 41 to 50 per pound (500 g). Eight ounces (250 g) by weight yields about 1½ cups (375 mL) halved raw shrimp.

• Rimmed baking sheet

1 tbsp	salt	15 mL
1 lb	dried farfalline (see Variations, below)	500 g
7 tbsp	extra-virgin olive oil, divided	105 mL
3	garlic cloves, thinly sliced	3
	Salt and freshly ground black pepper	
1½ cups	very thinly vertically sliced broccoli florets	375 mL
½ cup	halved cherry tomatoes	125 mL
1½ cups	halved (lengthwise) peeled, deveined shrimp (see Tip, left)	375 mL
½ cup	dry white Italian wine	125 mL
2 tbsp	fresh lemon juice	25 mL
2 tbsp	hand-torn fresh basil leaves	25 mL

1. In a covered pasta pot over high heat, bring water to a rapid boil. Add salt and farfalline and cook, uncovered, until pasta is slightly more than al dente. Drain, spread on baking sheet and let cool for 5 minutes.

2. Meanwhile, in a large sauté pan, heat 3 tbsp (45 mL) of the olive oil over medium heat. Add garlic and salt and pepper to taste and cook, stirring, until garlic is lightly browned, about 3 minutes. Using a slotted spoon, remove garlic and discard. Add broccoli and tomatoes. Reduce heat to low, cover and cook until half-cooked, about 3 minutes. Uncover and add shrimp, wine and lemon juice. Raise heat to high, cover and cook until shrimp are cooked through but still tender, about 4 minutes. Transfer to a large mixing bowl and let cool to room temperature.

3. Add cooled pasta, remaining olive oil and basil to broccoli-shrimp mixture. Using a wooden spoon, toss to coat evenly. Season to taste with salt and pepper.

4. Transfer to a large serving platter. Serve immediately or refrigerate, covered. Let stand at room temperature for up to 20 minutes to take the chill off before serving.

Variations

Substitute penne, fusilli or farfalle for the farfalline.

Fusilli in insalata con olive nere e verdi

Fusilli Salad with Black and Green Olives

Because olives are the main ingredient, this salad is particularly nice for a buffet. Fusilli is indigenous to the Campagna region of south-central Italy. In the best of all possible worlds we would use olives and olive oil from that region, but other Italian olive oil and Italian olives work well too.

Serves 4 to 6

Tip

If you want to create an authentic-tasting pasta, be sure to use Italian olives. But even if your olives aren't Italian, so long as they are top quality and from the European market basket, you'll still produce a delicious result (the only exception is green Spanish olives, which are too acidic and salty for this dish). The olives are already salty, so no additional salt is needed.

• Rimmed baking sheet

1 tbsp	salt	15 mL
1 lb	dried fusilli (see Variations, below)	500 g
¼ cup	extra-virgin olive oil	50 mL
¾ cup	halved, pitted oil-cured Italian black olives	175 mL
¾ cup	halved, pitted brined Italian green olives	175 mL
2 tbsp	roughly chopped fresh Italian parsley leaves	25 mL
	Freshly ground black pepper	

1. In a covered pasta pot over high heat, bring water to a rapid boil. Add salt and fusilli and cook, uncovered, until pasta is slightly more than al dente. Drain, spread on baking sheet and let cool for 5 minutes.

2. Transfer fusilli to a large mixing bowl. Add olive oil, olives and parsley. Using a wooden spoon, toss to coat evenly. Season to taste with pepper.

3. Transfer to a large serving platter. Serve immediately or refrigerate, covered. Let stand at room temperature for up to 20 minutes to take the chill off before serving.

Variations
Substitute penne, garganelli or cut ziti for the fusilli.

Fusilli in insalata alle zucchine e ricotta fresca

Fusilli Salad with Zucchini and Fresh Ricotta

This salad is designed for summer, when zucchini is fresh and at its peak. Please use the very best, freshest ricotta you can find. Ricotta is frequently used as a filling for pasta and also in desserts such as cheesecake, but here you can really taste the flavor of a good ricotta.

Serves 4 to 6

Tips

Don't scrimp on ingredients. Always buy the best quality you can find and afford. It will make a big difference to the results you produce.

I like to tear basil leaves by hand rather than slicing them, because I think they look and taste better.

• Rimmed baking sheet

1 tbsp	salt	15 mL
1 lb	dried fusilli (see Variations, below)	500 g
½ cup	extra-virgin olive oil, divided	125 mL
3	cloves garlic, thinly sliced	3
	Salt and freshly ground black pepper	
1½ cups	diced unpeeled zucchini	375 mL
½ cup	dry white Italian wine	125 mL
¾ cup	fresh ricotta (see Variations, below)	175 mL
2 tbsp	hand-torn fresh basil leaves	25 mL
	Salt and freshly ground black pepper	

1. In a covered pasta pot over high heat, bring water to a rapid boil. Add salt and fusilli and cook, uncovered, until pasta is slightly more than al dente. Drain, spread on baking sheet and let cool for 5 minutes.

2. Meanwhile, in a large sauté pan, heat ¼ cup (50 mL) of the olive oil over medium heat. Add garlic and salt and pepper to taste. Cook, stirring, until garlic is lightly browned, about 3 minutes. Using a slotted spoon, remove and discard garlic. Add zucchini and wine. Reduce heat to low, cover and cook until zucchini is half-cooked, about 5 minutes. Transfer to a large mixing bowl and let cool to room temperature.

3. Add fusilli, remaining olive oil, ricotta and basil. Using a wooden spoon, toss to coat evenly. Season to taste with salt and pepper.

4. Transfer to a large serving platter. Serve immediately or refrigerate, covered. Let stand at room temperature for up to 20 minutes to take the chill off before serving.

Variations

Substitute ⅓ cup (75 mL) grated Pecorino Romano for the ricotta.

Substitute penne, cut ziti or cavatappi for the fusilli.

Insalata di maccheroni, pollo grigliate e radicchio

Maccheroni Salad with Grilled Chicken and Radicchio

This is a nontraditional combination that speaks to my non-Italian customers' preference for pasta and chicken. Grilling is a favorite way to cook in summer. I particularly enjoy the contrast between the cooked chicken and the fresh, crisp radicchio.

Serves 4 to 6

Tip

Always use a large pot and plenty of water when cooking pasta. To properly cook 1 pound (500 g) of pasta, you'll need a pot with a volume of at least 8 quarts (8 L) so that you can use 6 quarts (6 L) of water.

- Rimmed baking sheet

9 tbsp	extra-virgin olive oil, divided	135 mL
¼ cup	fresh lemon juice	50 mL
3	cloves garlic, thinly sliced	3
2	boneless, skinless chicken breasts, each 8 to 10 oz (250 to 300 g)	2
	Salt and freshly ground black pepper	
1 tbsp	salt	15 mL
1 lb	dried maccheroni (see Variations, below)	500 g
2 cups	diced radicchio	500 mL

1. In a mixing bowl combine 5 tbsp (75 mL) of the olive oil, lemon juice and garlic and stir well. Add chicken and turn to coat on all sides. Season to taste with salt and pepper. Cover with plastic wrap and refrigerate for 1 hour.

2. Preheat grill to medium. Remove chicken from marinade and grill, turning once, until cooked through (no hint of pink should remain in the chicken, but it should still be juicy). Remove from grill, transfer to a plate and let cool until cool enough to handle. Cutting against the grain, slice into ¼-inch (0.5 cm) strips. Set aside.

3. Meanwhile, in a covered pasta pot over high heat, bring water to a rapid boil. Add salt and maccheroni and cook, uncovered, until slightly more than al dente. Drain, spread on baking sheet and let cool for 5 minutes.

4. Transfer cooled maccheroni to a large mixing bowl. Add chicken, remaining olive oil and radicchio. Using a wooden spoon, toss to coat evenly. Season to taste with salt and pepper.

5. Transfer to a large serving platter. Serve immediately or refrigerate, covered. Let stand at room temperature for up to 20 minutes to take the chill off before serving.

Variations

Sauté the chicken breast with a little olive oil in a sauté pan on top of the range until cooked through.

Substitute penne, fusilli or cut ziti for the maccheroni.

Maccheroni Salad with Roasted Bell Peppers

Roasting or grilling bell peppers changes their flavor and texture completely. They become sweet, mellow and very tender — almost a different vegetable from crisp raw peppers. I like the three colors in this salad, but feel free to use one color or two, whatever looks best at the market.

Serves 4 to 6

Tips

Because bell peppers are among the vegetables with the highest pesticide residues, I recommend buying organic peppers if possible.

If you prefer, roast and dice the peppers the night before you intend to use them. Toss with $\frac{1}{4}$ cup (50 mL) of the olive oil and season to taste with salt and pepper. Cover and refrigerate until ready to use.

After removing the charred skin, do not rinse the roasted peppers; a few flecks of charred skin won't ruin the recipe.

• Preheat broiler
• Broiling pan or rimmed baking sheet

2	green bell peppers, cored and seeded (see Tips, left)	2
2	yellow bell peppers, cored and seeded	2
2	red bell peppers, cored and seeded	2
$\frac{1}{2}$ cup	extra-virgin olive oil, divided	125 mL
	Salt and freshly ground black pepper	
1 tbsp	salt	15 mL
1 lb	dried maccheroni (see Variations, below)	500 g
2 tbsp	hand-torn fresh basil leaves	25 mL

1. Cut tops and bottoms off peppers. Cut stems from tops and discard. Cut peppers in half. In a large mixing bowl combine tops, bottoms and halved peppers, $\frac{1}{4}$ cup (50 mL) of the olive oil and salt and pepper to taste. Using a wooden spoon, toss to coat evenly.

2. Transfer peppers to broiling pan and place under broiler. Broil at high heat until skin becomes charred and deep black. Transfer to clean lunch-size brown paper bags and close bags tightly by folding over the top. Allow to cool to room temperature. When peppers are cool, using plastic gloves, remove the charred skin and discard. Do not rinse peppers. On a cutting board, cut peppers into medium dice. Place in a large mixing bowl and set aside.

3. Meanwhile, in a covered pasta pot over high heat, bring water to a rapid boil. Add salt and maccheroni and cook, uncovered, until pasta is slightly more than al dente. Drain, spread on a baking sheet and let cool for 5 minutes.

4. Add maccheroni to diced peppers along with remaining olive oil and basil. Using a wooden spoon, toss to coat evenly. Season to taste with salt and pepper.

5. Transfer to a large serving platter. Serve immediately or refrigerate, covered. Let stand at room temperature for up to 20 minutes to take the chill off before serving.

Variations

Use 6 peppers of your choice, all one color or two colors.

Substitute penne, cut ziti or ruote di carro for the maccheroni.

Orecchiette in insalata al cavolfiore grigliate

Orecchiette Salad with Grilled Cauliflower

Grilled cauliflower turns out unevenly charred in spots. It's a good demonstration of Italian gastronomy — the moment you begin to cook Italian food evenly and perfectly, it stops being Italian. The imperfections create the synergy. If you cook it evenly it's like a song with one note. At the restaurant I grill the cauliflower, but for the home cook it is easier to roast it.

Serves 4 to 6

Tips

Cutting the florets vertically into 1/4-inch (0.5 cm) slices makes for good distribution throughout the salad.

The cauliflower should be so brown that it is almost charred in places.

- Preheat oven to 450°F (230°C)
- Rimmed baking sheet or broiling pan

3 rounded cups	fresh cauliflower florets	800 mL
6 tbsp	extra-virgin olive oil, divided	90 mL
	Salt and freshly ground black pepper	
1 tbsp	salt	15 mL
1 lb	dried orecchiette (see Variations, below)	500 g
2 tbsp	chopped fresh Italian parsley leaves	25 mL

1. In a mixing bowl combine cauliflower, 2 tbsp (25 mL) of the olive oil and salt and pepper to taste. Using a wooden spoon, toss to coat evenly. Transfer to baking sheet and bake in preheated oven until cauliflower is tender and deeply browned, 15 to 25 minutes. Remove from oven and let cool to room temperature.

2. Meanwhile, in a covered pasta pot over high heat, bring water to a rapid boil. Add salt and orecchiette and cook, uncovered, until pasta is slightly more than al dente. Drain, spread on a baking sheet and let cool for 5 minutes.

3. Slice cooked florets lengthwise into 1/4-inch (0.5 cm) slices. Transfer cooled orecchiette to a large mixing bowl. Add remaining olive oil, parsley and cauliflower with any juices. Using a wooden spoon, toss to coat evenly. Season to taste with salt and pepper.

4. Transfer to a large serving platter. Serve immediately or refrigerate, covered. Bring to room temperature before serving.

Variations

Instead of roasting the cauliflower, you can grill it on an outdoor grill, turning as necessary. Or you can broil it under the broiler, turning as necessary.

Substitute penne, ruote di carro or fusilli for the orecchiette.

Cauliflower

Closely related to broccoli and in the same family as cabbage, Brussels sprouts, kale and collard greens, cauliflower is a cool-weather vegetable available in early spring and late fall. It is very nutritious — high in fiber, vitamins B and C, and phytochemicals, which are thought to reduce the risk of certain cancers. In addition to the most common white form, cauliflower varieties include green (or broccoflower), orange (which has the most vitamin C) and purple (which turns green when cooked).

Paccheri in insalata al pomodorini e finocchio

Paccheri Salad with Cherry Tomatoes and Fresh Fennel

••

This is one pasta salad you should not refrigerate. Serve it immediately after it is made, because fennel doesn't respond well to refrigeration. At room temperature it is sweet and aromatic and the anise flavor is less prominent. When chilled, the anise flavor predominates and the sweetness diminishes.

Serves 4 to 6

Tip

To prepare the fennel for this recipe, cut off the root end and discard. Cut off the stems and feathery fronds and save for stock and garnishing. Trim any remaining stem ends from the bulb, slice the bulb in half and cut out the core. Rinse the bulb in cold water to remove any sand or grit. The fennel is now ready to dice.

• Rimmed baking sheet

1 tbsp	salt	15 mL
1 lb	dried paccheri (see Variations, below)	500 g
⅓ cup	extra-virgin olive oil	75 mL
½ cup	halved yellow cherry tomatoes (see Variations, below)	125 mL
½ cup	halved red cherry tomatoes	125 mL
¾ cup	diced trimmed fresh fennel bulb (see Tip, left)	175 mL
2 tbsp	hand-torn fresh basil leaves	25 mL
	Salt and freshly ground black pepper	

1. In a covered pasta pot over high heat, bring water to a rapid boil. Add salt and paccheri and cook, uncovered, over high heat until pasta is slightly more than al dente. Drain, spread on baking sheet and let cool for 5 minutes.

2. Transfer cooled paccheri to a large mixing bowl. Add olive oil, tomatoes, fennel and basil. Using a wooden spoon, toss to coat evenly. Season to taste with salt and pepper.

3. Transfer to a large serving platter and serve immediately.

Variations

Use all red or all yellow cherry tomatoes instead of mixed red and yellow.

Substitute penne or rigatoni for the paccheri.

Paccheri in insalata gran misto primavera

Paccheri Salad with Spring Vegetables

Spring vegetables star in this salad. They are briefly blanched to set their color and to bring out their full flavor. But don't limit yourself to spring vegetables — in summer or fall, substitute an equal amount of vegetables that are in season then.

Serves 4 to 6

Tip

To blanch vegetables, bring 2½ quarts (2.5 L) water and 2 tsp (10 mL) salt to a rolling boil. Cook vegetables for 3 minutes. Drain, immerse in a bowl of icewater until cold, then drain. Or drain under cold running water until cooled to room temperature.

- Rimmed baking sheet

1 tbsp	salt	15 mL
1 lb	dried paccheri (see Variations, below)	500 g
⅓ cup	extra-virgin olive oil	75 mL
½ cup	sliced (1 inch/2.5 cm) pencil-thin asparagus tips, blanched	125 mL
½ cup	fresh peeled fava beans, blanched	125 mL
½ cup	diced carrots, blanched	125 mL
½ cup	green peas, blanched	125 mL
½ cup	sliced (¼ inch/0.5 cm) green beans, blanched	125 mL
2 tbsp	hand-torn fresh basil leaves	25 mL
	Salt and freshly ground black pepper	

1. In a covered pasta pot over high heat, bring water to a rapid boil. Add salt and paccheri and cook, uncovered, until pasta is slightly more than al dente. Drain, spread on baking sheet and let cool for 5 minutes.

2. Transfer pasta to a large mixing bowl. Add olive oil, asparagus, fava beans, carrots, peas, green beans and basil. Using a wooden spoon, toss to coat evenly. Season to taste with salt and pepper.

3. Transfer to a large serving platter. Serve immediately or refrigerate, covered. Let stand at room temperature for up to 20 minutes to take the chill off before serving.

Variations

Substitute fresh lima beans for the fava beans.

Substitute 1¼ cups (300 mL) of your choice of blanched seasonal vegetables for the vegetables listed, for instance, sliced broccoli and cauliflower florets, diced unpeeled Yukon Gold potatoes, diced zucchini or sliced yellow beans.

Substitute penne, fusilli or rigatoni for the paccheri.

Insalata di pennette e asparagi grigliate

Pennette Salad with Grilled Asparagus

For many people summertime and grilling are synonymous. Grilled asparagus takes on a delicious smoky flavor and an appealing appearance from the grill marks. Of course you can simply blanch or sauté the asparagus, or even oven-bake it until it browns. The pennette, which are small, look very attractive with the thin asparagus.

Serves 4 to 6

Tip

If you prefer, after tossing the asparagus in the olive oil, bake it in a preheated oven at 450°F (230°C), on a rimmed baking sheet lined with parchment paper, until well browned, turning once, about 30 minutes. You can also sauté it in the olive oil in a large sauté pan over high heat, turning once, until well browned.

- Preheat grill
- Rimmed baking sheet

1 lb	pencil-thin asparagus, ends trimmed	500 g
6 tbsp	extra-virgin olive oil, divided	90 mL
	Salt and freshly ground black pepper	
1 tbsp	salt	15 mL
1 lb	dried pennette (see Variations, below)	500 g
2 tbsp	hand-torn fresh basil leaves	25 mL

1. Place asparagus in a rectangular dish with 2 tbsp (25 mL) of the olive oil and, using tongs, toss to coat completely (see Tip, left). Place crosswise on a preheated grill, season to taste with salt and pepper and grill, turning once, until cooked through and scored deeply with grill marks. Return to dish and let cool to room temperature. Slice horizontally into 2-inch (5 cm) pieces, beginning with the tips.

2. Meanwhile, in a covered pasta pot over high heat, bring water to a rapid boil. Add salt and pennette and cook, uncovered, until pasta is slightly more than al dente. Drain, spread on baking sheet and let cool for 5 minutes.

3. Transfer cooled pennette to a large mixing bowl. Add asparagus, including any accumulated liquid, remaining olive oil and basil. Using a wooden spoon, toss to coat evenly. Season to taste with salt and pepper.

4. Transfer to a large serving platter. Serve immediately or refrigerate, covered. Let stand at room temperature for up to 20 minutes to take the chill off before serving.

Variations

Substitute penne or cut ziti for the pennette.

Insalata di pennette al tonno e fagiolini

Pennette Salad with Tuna and Green and Yellow Beans

Tuna and fresh green and yellow beans are familiar ingredients. However, if you buy fresh beans from the farmers' market and use olive oil–packed canned tuna imported from Italy, I believe you will be rewarded with excellent flavor.

Serves 4 to 6

Tip

Available in some supermarkets and most gourmet food stores, Italian tuna packed in olive oil is worth looking for, particularly if it is from Sicily. The main ingredients are tuna and olive oil, and the moist, sweet-tasting meat adds intense flavor to a salad. It is slightly more expensive than domestic canned tuna, but not prohibitively so.

• Rimmed baking sheet

½ cup	extra-virgin olive oil, divided	125 mL
3	garlic cloves, thinly sliced	3
	Salt and freshly ground pepper	
¾ cup	bias-cut sliced (1 inch/2.5 cm) green beans	175 mL
¾ cup	bias-cut sliced (1 inch/2.5 cm) yellow beans	175 mL
½ cup	dry white Italian wine	125 mL
¼ cup	water	50 mL
1 tbsp	salt	15 mL
1 lb	dried pennette (see Variations, below)	500 g
1 cup	drained canned white Italian tuna in olive oil, packed (see Tip, left)	250 mL
2 tbsp	hand-torn fresh basil leaves	25 mL

1. In a large sauté pan, heat ¼ cup (50 mL) of the oil over medium heat. Add garlic and salt and pepper to taste and cook, stirring with a wooden spoon, until garlic is lightly browned, about 3 minutes. Using a slotted spoon, remove garlic and discard. Add beans, wine and water. Reduce heat to low. Cover and cook until beans are half-cooked, about 3 minutes. Transfer to a large mixing bowl and let cool to room temperature.

2. Meanwhile, in a covered pasta pot over high heat, bring water to a rapid boil. Add salt and pennette and cook, uncovered, until pasta is slightly more than al dente. Drain, spread on baking sheet and let cool for 5 minutes.

3. Add cooled pennette to bean mixture, including accumulated liquid. Add remaining olive oil, tuna and basil. Using a wooden spoon, toss to break up tuna and coat evenly. Season to taste with salt and pepper.

4. Transfer to a large serving platter. Serve immediately or refrigerate, covered. Let stand at room temperature for up to 20 minutes to take the chill off before serving.

Variations

Use all green or all yellow beans.

Substitute penne or cut ziti for the pennette.

Radiatori in insalata con carote alla menta

Radiatori Salad with Carrots and Mint

Carrots and mint are a familiar flavor combination, usually served as a vegetable. Here is a simple way to enjoy these complementary flavors with pasta.

Serves 4 to 6

Tip

Always use a large pot and plenty of water when cooking pasta. To properly cook 1 pound (500 g) of pasta, you'll need a pot with a volume of at least 8 quarts (8 L) so that you can use 6 quarts (6 L) of water.

• Rimmed baking sheet

½ cup	extra-virgin olive oil, divided	125 mL
3	garlic cloves, thinly sliced	3
	Salt and freshly ground black pepper	
1½ cups	diced carrots	375 mL
2 tbsp	fresh whole mint leaves	25 mL
½ cup	water	125 mL
1 tbsp	salt	15 mL
1 lb	dried radiatori (see Variations, below)	500 g

1. In a large sauté pan, heat ¼ cup (50 mL) of the olive oil over medium heat. Add garlic and salt and pepper to taste and cook, stirring, until garlic is lightly browned, about 3 minutes. Using a slotted spoon, remove and discard garlic. Add carrots, mint and water. Reduce the heat to low, cover and cook until carrots are soft and tender, about 5 minutes. Transfer to a large mixing bowl and let cool to room temperature.

2. Meanwhile, in a covered pasta pot over high heat, bring water to a rapid boil. Add salt and radiatori and cook, uncovered, until pasta is slightly more than al dente. Drain, spread on baking sheet and let cool for 5 minutes.

3. Add cooled radiatori and remaining olive oil to carrot mixture. Using a wooden spoon, toss to coat evenly. Season to taste with salt and pepper.

4. Transfer to a large serving platter. Serve immediately or refrigerate, covered. Let stand at room temperature for up to 20 minutes to take the chill off before serving.

Variations

Substitute penne or fusilli for the radiatori.

Radiatori in insalata con lenticchie e avocado

Radiatori Salad with Lentils and Avocado

Here I have combined healthy lentils with pancetta and avocado, a very nontraditional ingredient that has become popular in urban Italy. This salad is hearty because of the protein-packed lentils, and could easily serve as a main course.

Serves 4 to 6

Tips

If at all possible, make an effort to use Italian lentils from Castelluccio, Umbria, in this recipe — they are very special. They carry their own European PGI (protected geographic indication) status and are available in gourmet Italian markets. Compared to other lentils, they are very small and brownish green and hold their shape during cooking. Always pick out and discard any debris and rinse lentils thoroughly before using.

Don't cut or dice the avocado until you are ready to use it, because it turns brown very quickly. This doesn't affect the flavor but does diminish its visual appeal.

• Rimmed baking sheet

7 tbsp	extra-virgin olive oil, divided	105 mL
2 tbsp	finely diced pancetta	25 mL
¼ cup	diced onion	50 mL
¼ cup	diced peeled celery	50 mL
½ cup	dry red Italian wine	125 mL
1 cup	brown or green lentils (see Tips, left)	250 mL
¼ tsp	chopped fresh rosemary leaves	1 mL
1 tbsp	tomato paste	15 mL
3 cups	water	750 mL
1 tbsp	salt	15 mL
1 lb	dried radiatori (see Variations, below)	500 g
2	avocados, peeled, pitted and diced	2
2 tbsp	hand-torn fresh basil leaves	25 mL
	Salt and freshly ground black pepper	

1. In a large sauté pan, heat 3 tbsp (45 mL) of the olive oil over medium heat. Add pancetta, onion and celery. Cook, stirring, until onion and celery are soft and translucent, 4 to 5 minutes. Add wine and cook until reduced by half. Add lentils, rosemary, tomato paste and water and stir. Reduce heat to medium-low and simmer, stirring occasionally, until lentils are soft and tender, about 25 minutes. Transfer to a large mixing bowl and let cool to room temperature.

2. Meanwhile, in a covered pasta pot over high heat, bring water to a rapid boil. Add salt and radiatori and cook, uncovered, until pasta is slightly more than al dente. Drain, spread on baking sheet and let cool for 5 minutes.

3. Add cooled radiatori, remaining olive oil, avocado and basil to lentil mixture and, using a wooden spoon, toss to coat evenly. Season to taste with salt and pepper.

4. Transfer to a large serving platter and serve immediately or refrigerate, covered. Let stand at room temperature for up to 20 minutes to take the chill off before serving.

Variations

Substitute penne, fusilli or ruote di carro for the radiatori.

Ruote di carro in insalata con pancetta e piselli

Ruote di Carro Salad with Fresh Peas and Pancetta

This is simply peas and pancetta with cart wheel pasta and a hint of sage. What's not to like?

Serves 4 to 6

Tips

As always, when fresh peas are in season I recommend using them instead of those that have been frozen. Blanch them in boiling, lightly salted water for 4 minutes, drain and proceed with the recipe.

Because pancetta is quite salty, I like to use only pepper in the final seasoning.

• Rimmed baking sheet

½ cup	extra-virgin olive oil, divided	125 mL
3	garlic cloves, thinly sliced	3
	Salt and freshly ground black pepper	
½ cup	diced onion	125 mL
1 cup	diced pancetta	250 mL
1½ cups	frozen green peas, defrosted (see Tips, left)	375 mL
10 to 12	fresh sage leaves	10 to 12
¾ cup	water	175 mL
1 tbsp	salt	15 mL
1 lb	ruote di carro (see Variations, below)	500 g

1. In a large sauté pan, heat ¼ cup (50 mL) of the olive oil over medium heat. Add garlic and salt and pepper to taste and cook, stirring, until garlic is lightly browned, about 3 minutes. Using a slotted spoon, remove and discard garlic. Add onion, pancetta, peas, sage and water. Reduce heat to low. Cover and cook until peas are soft and tender, about 5 minutes. Transfer to a large mixing bowl and let cool to room temperature.

2. Meanwhile, in a covered pasta pot over high heat, bring water to a rapid boil. Add salt and ruote di carro and cook, uncovered, until pasta is slightly more than al dente. Drain, spread on baking sheet and let cool for 5 minutes.

3. Add cooled ruote di carro and remaining olive oil to the pea mixture and, using a wooden spoon, toss to coat evenly. Season to taste with additional pepper.

4. Transfer to a large serving platter and serve immediately or refrigerate, covered. Let stand at room temperature for up to 20 minutes to take the chill off before serving.

Variations

Substitute penne, radiatori or fusilli for the ruote di carro.

Ruote di carro in insalata con prosciutto e melone

Ruote di Carro Salad with Prosciutto and Melon

This could be served as either a salad or a first course. It makes a perfect dish for a brunch buffet. Serve it with a spoon and fork so that people can help themselves to a little prosciutto with the pasta and melon.

Serves 4 to 6

Tip

Don't scrimp on ingredients. Always buy the best quality you can find and afford. It will make a big difference to the results you produce.

- Rimmed baking sheet

16	paper-thin slices prosciutto	16
1 tbsp	salt	15 mL
1 lb	dried ruote di carro (see Variations, below)	500 g
¼ cup	extra-virgin olive oil	50 mL
1½ cups	diced ripe cantaloupe	375 mL
	Salt and freshly ground white pepper	

1. Line rim and well of a large serving platter with prosciutto. Set aside.

2. In a covered pasta pot over high heat, bring water to a rapid boil. Add salt and ruote di carro and cook, uncovered, until pasta is slightly more than al dente. Drain, spread on baking sheet and let cool for 5 minutes.

3. Transfer to a large mixing bowl and add olive oil and cantaloupe. Using a wooden spoon, toss to coat evenly. Season to taste with salt and pepper.

4. Spoon mixture onto prosciutto-lined platter. Serve immediately or refrigerate, covered. Let stand at room temperature for up to 20 minutes to take the chill off before serving.

Variations

Substitute penne, radiatori or fusilli for the ruote di carro.

Pasta for Kids: Cooking for Conservative Palates

Other people's children may be adventuresome eaters who relish every new food put before them, but my wife, Jenifer, and I have children with conservative palates. When I was growing up, my palate was not very receptive to new tastes either. My mother often used to cook spinach, and my reaction was, "How awful!" But she didn't provide much opportunity for discussion, so I ate it, and as an adult I have come to appreciate a dish of fresh spinach quickly sautéed in olive oil and garlic and seasoned with salt and freshly ground pepper. My palate has matured, as we hope our children's will too.

Strategic Cooking

No one wants to force their children to eat foods they don't enjoy. But at the same time we don't want to bring them up on a bland diet that lacks variety and as a result isn't likely to provide the full range of nutrients they need. While my kids won't eat spinach in olive oil or a plate of broccoli, they will eat spinach and broccoli cleverly disguised in a pasta sauce.

In our home the strategy is to cook foods that are fairly familiar and nutritious. Chicken and turkey are proteins that children usually like, and as parents we like them too. They are tender, nutritious and not loaded with fat. Children love apples, celery, walnuts and grapes, foods that combine well with pasta. Of course, we also treat them to pasta and cheese, a gooey experience that is completely satisfying.

If you're cooking for very young children, short pasta they can eat with a fork or spoon is the best choice, for obvious reasons. You don't have to be a rocket scientist to recognize that spaghetti and meatballs is a challenge for kids under the age of 10. Twirling long strands of pasta into a neat package that goes from bowl to mouth without mishap requires a level of skill and coordination that is lacking even in some adults. And when it comes to the vegetables, you need to cut them, so why not cut them in interesting ways? For example, dice carrots and celery to resemble building blocks, shapes familiar to every child. Halve grapes or tomatoes horizontally to make circles. And there are several fun pasta shapes that will interest kids: farfalle (butterflies), conchiglie (seashells), orecchiette (little ears) and ruote di carro (cart wheels).

Few things are more gratifying to a parent than seeing a child finish his or her dinner. Using pasta as a base and adding healthy vegetables in the sauce is one technique for reducing the number of times you need to have the "Eat your vegetables" conversation. Pasta is a great way to cook balanced meals for your kids that will help keep them not only healthy but happy.

Maccheroni ai formaggi

Maccheroni and Cheese

Say "strawberries and cream" in England or "ham and eggs" in America, and everybody knows what you mean: a delicious common denominator. In Italy it's "come il cacio su'maccheroni" — like cheese on macaroni. Everybody loves macaroni and cheese, but Italian macaroni and cheese is nothing like what you find elsewhere. Italians vary the cheeses to suit local tastes, sometimes combining fontina, caciotta, Taleggio and Gorgonzola. For this recipe I picked cheeses that are widely available in North America. If you think even the small amount of Gorgonzola is too much of a stretch for your children's palates, simply leave it out (see Variations, right). And if ground pepper arouses their suspicions, omit it too.

Serves 4 to 6

Tip

If you have leftovers, use them to make Baked Maccheroni and Cheese (see recipe, page 168).

½ cup	fresh ricotta	125 mL
½ cup	mascarpone	125 mL
¼ cup	Gorgonzola dolce	50 mL
¼ cup	grated Parmigiano-Reggiano	50 mL
1 tbsp	salt	15 mL
1 lb	dried maccheroni (see Variations, below)	500 g
	Freshly ground black pepper	

1. In a large mixing bowl combine ricotta, mascarpone, Gorgonzola and Parmigiano-Reggiano. Using an electric mixer on low speed, beat until smooth and creamy. Let rest for 15 minutes.

2. Meanwhile, in a covered pasta pot over high heat, bring water to a rapid boil. Add salt and maccheroni and cook, uncovered, until pasta is al dente. Drain.

3. Add maccheroni to cheese mixture and, using a large wooden spoon, toss to coat evenly.

4. Transfer to a large serving platter and top with freshly ground black pepper to taste. Serve immediately.

Variations

Substitute penne, cut ziti or ruote di carro for the maccheroni.

Omit the Gorgonzola entirely and increase the Parmigiano-Reggiano to ½ cup (125 mL).

Omit the pepper.

Orecchiette al petto di pollo e rosmarino

Orecchiette with Chicken Breast and Rosemary

Most children like the white meat of chicken. Here it is lightly flavored with sautéed garlic, a subtle hint of rosemary and salty Parmigiano-Reggiano cheese. You may want to tell your kids that orecchiette *means "little ears" in Italian, hence the shape. I believe you will enjoy eating this pasta as well.*

Serves 4 to 6

Tips

For best results grate the cheese yourself, but if time is at a premium, use already grated cheese. Whichever form you choose, just be sure to buy the very best Italian Parmigiano-Reggiano you can find and grate it finely to ensure you have the quantity called for in the recipe.

Remember, when your pasta has finished cooking, you want it to be firm and supple, not soft and mushy. It will cook a bit more from the residual heat after it is drained, and also when you add it to the sauce.

3 tbsp	extra-virgin olive oil	45 mL
1 tsp	thinly sliced garlic	5 mL
	Salt and freshly ground black pepper	
½ cup	diced onion	125 mL
1½ cups	diced skinless, boneless chicken breast	375 mL
15	fresh rosemary leaves, minced	15
2 cups	vegetable broth	500 mL
1 tbsp	salt	15 mL
1 lb	dried orecchiette (see Variations, below)	500 g
6 tbsp	grated Parmigiano-Reggiano, divided	90 mL

1. In a covered pasta pot over high heat, bring water to a rapid boil.

2. Meanwhile, in a large sauté pan, heat oil over medium heat. Add garlic and salt and pepper to taste. Cook, stirring, until garlic is lightly browned, about 3 minutes. Using a slotted spoon, remove garlic and discard. Add onion, chicken, rosemary and vegetable broth and stir. Reduce heat to low, cover and simmer until onion is tender and chicken is cooked through. Remove from heat and set aside.

3. While sauce is simmering, add salt and orecchiette to the boiling water and cook, uncovered, over high heat until pasta is al dente. Scoop out about 1 cup (250 mL) of the pasta cooking water and set aside. Drain pasta.

4. Return sauté pan to high heat and add 2 tbsp (25 mL) of the reserved pasta water. Stir and heat through. Add orecchiette and, using a wooden spoon, toss to coat evenly, adding more pasta water if necessary. Add half of the Parmigiano-Reggiano and toss well.

5. Transfer to a large serving platter and sprinkle with remaining cheese. Serve immediately.

Variations

Substitute ruote di carro or penne for the orecchiette.

Orecchiette con spinaci e ricotta salata

Orecchiette with Spinach and Ricotta Salata

Ricotta salata is the hard aged version of soft fresh ricotta cheese. It is available at cheese shops and Italian markets. In this recipe the shaved cheese offers an interesting texture. I use regular rather than baby spinach, because it has a better flavor and texture when cooked.

Serves 4 to 6

Tips

Don't scrimp on ingredients. Always buy the best quality you can find and afford. It will make a big difference to the results you produce.

Never rinse pasta after draining it. The surface starch helps the sauce to cling and is important to producing the best-quality dish.

6 tbsp	extra-virgin olive oil	90 mL
1 tbsp	thinly sliced garlic	15 mL
3 cups	diced stemmed curly spinach	750 mL
	Salt and freshly ground pepper	
1 tbsp	salt	15 mL
1 lb	dried orecchiette (see Variations, below)	500 g
3 tbsp	grated Parmigiano-Reggiano	45 mL
6 tbsp	shaved ricotta salata (see Variations, below)	90 mL

1. In a covered pasta pot over high heat, bring water to a rapid boil.

2. Meanwhile, in a large sauté pan over medium heat, heat olive oil. Add garlic and cook, stirring with a wooden spoon, until lightly browned, about 3 minutes. Using a slotted spoon, remove garlic and discard. Add spinach and salt and pepper to taste, stir and reduce heat to low. Cover and simmer until spinach is soft and tender, about 2 minutes. Remove from heat and set aside.

3. Add salt and orecchiette to the boiling water and cook, uncovered, over high heat until pasta is al dente. Scoop out about 1 cup (250 mL) of the pasta cooking water and set aside. Drain pasta.

4. Return sauté pan to high heat, uncover and add 2 tbsp (25 mL) of the reserved pasta water. Stir and heat through. Add orecchiette and, using a wooden spoon, toss to coat evenly, adding more pasta water if necessary. Add Parmigiano-Reggiano and toss well.

5. Transfer to a large serving platter and sprinkle with ricotta salata. Serve immediately.

Variations

Substitute shaved Parmigiano-Reggiano for the ricotta salata.

Substitute ruote di carro or penne for the orecchiette.

Penne con pomodorini

Penne with Tomatoes

●●

Penne resemble the quill end of the feather pen (penna in Italian) that people used to write with before the invention of fountain and ballpoint pens. The shape is easy for children to eat with a fork. This recipe resembles Pennette with Cherry Tomatoes and Butter (see recipe, page 73). However, because it is meant for children I have omitted the wine and substituted olive oil for the butter.

Serves 4 to 6

Tips

Cut tomatoes in half horizontally so they look like circles. It's a fun shape for children.

Always use a large pot and plenty of water when cooking pasta. To properly cook 1 pound (500 g) of pasta, you'll need a pot with a volume of at least 8 quarts (8 L) so that you can use 6 quarts (6 L) of water.

3 tbsp	extra-virgin olive oil	45 mL
1 tsp	thinly sliced garlic	5 mL
	Salt and freshly ground black pepper	
1½ cups	halved cherry tomatoes (see Tips, left)	375 mL
6	hand-torn fresh basil leaves	6
1 tbsp	salt	15 mL
1 lb	dried penne (see Variations, below)	500 g
6 tbsp	grated Parmigiano-Reggiano, divided	90 mL

1. In a covered pasta pot over high heat, bring water to a rapid boil.

2. Meanwhile, in a large sauté pan, heat oil over medium heat. Add garlic and salt and pepper to taste. Cook, stirring, until garlic is lightly browned, about 3 minutes. Using a slotted spoon, remove garlic and discard. Add tomatoes and basil. Stir, reduce heat to low, cover and simmer until tomatoes are soft and tender, about 5 minutes. Remove from heat and set aside.

3. While sauce is simmering, add salt and penne to the boiling water and cook, uncovered, over high heat until pasta is al dente. Scoop out about 1 cup (250 mL) of the pasta cooking water and set aside. Drain pasta.

4. Return sauté pan to high heat and add 2 tbsp (25 mL) of the reserved pasta water. Stir and heat through. Add penne and, using a wooden spoon, toss to coat evenly, adding more pasta water if necessary. Add half of the Parmigiano-Reggiano and toss well.

5. Transfer to a large serving platter and sprinkle with remaining cheese. Serve immediately.

Variations

Substitute ruote di carro or orecchiette for the penne.

Rigatoni con tacchino e finocchio

Rigatoni with Turkey and Fennel

Turkey is very flavorful and children usually like it as much as, if not more than, chicken. Fennel is very sweet and goes well with the other flavors in this recipe. Rigatoni — short tube pasta with ridged sides, cut straight at both ends — is easy for children to eat.

Serves 4 to 6

Tip

To trim fennel, cut off the root end and discard. Cut off the stems and fronds and save them for stock and garnishing. Cut any stems off the bulb and discard. Cut bulb in half and remove the core. Place in a bowl of cold water and rinse well. The bulb is now ready to dice.

3 tbsp	extra-virgin olive oil	45 mL
1 tsp	thinly sliced garlic	5 mL
	Salt and freshly ground black pepper	
1 cup	diced trimmed fennel bulb (see Tip, left)	250 mL
1 cup	diced boneless, skinless turkey breast	250 mL
1 cup	halved cherry tomatoes	250 mL
6	hand-torn fresh basil leaves	6
1 tbsp	salt	15 mL
1 lb	dried rigatoni (see Variations, below)	500 g
6 tbsp	grated Parmigiano-Reggiano, divided	90 mL

1. In a covered pasta pot over high heat, bring water to a rapid boil.

2. In a large sauté pan, heat oil over medium heat. Add garlic and salt and pepper to taste and cook, stirring, until garlic is lightly browned, about 3 minutes. Using a slotted spoon, remove garlic and discard. Add fennel, turkey, cherry tomatoes and basil. Reduce heat to low, cover and simmer until vegetables are tender and turkey is cooked through, about 7 minutes. Remove from heat and set aside.

3. While sauce is simmering, add salt and rigatoni to the boiling water. Cook, uncovered, over high heat until pasta is al dente. Scoop out about 1 cup (250 mL) of the pasta cooking water and set aside. Drain pasta.

4. Return sauté pan to high heat and add 2 tbsp (25 mL) of the reserved pasta water. Heat through. Add rigatoni and, using a wooden spoon, toss to coat evenly, adding more pasta water if necessary. Add half of the Parmigiano-Reggiano and toss well.

5. Transfer to a large serving platter and sprinkle with remaining cheese. Serve immediately.

Variations

Substitute penne or cut ziti for the rigatoni.

Fusilli con la ricotta

Fusilli with Fresh Ricotta

Fusilli is corkscrew-shaped pasta, which is fun for kids. Fresh cow's-milk ricotta is sweet-tasting and quite different from cottage cheese. I encourage you to buy the best fresh whole-milk ricotta available (not the part-skim version, which can be dry and flat in flavor). The recipe calls for only ¼ cup (50 mL), so fat and calories are not an issue.

Serves 4 to 6

Tip

For best results grate the cheese yourself, but if time is at a premium, use already grated cheese. Whichever form you choose, just be sure to buy the very best Italian Parmigiano-Reggiano you can find and grate it finely to ensure you have the quantity called for in the recipe.

3 tbsp	extra-virgin olive oil	45 mL
1 tsp	thinly sliced garlic	5 mL
	Salt and freshly ground black pepper	
5	fresh unpeeled tomatoes, diced	5
6	hand-torn fresh basil leaves	6
1 tbsp	salt	15 mL
1 lb	dried fusilli (see Variations, below)	500 g
¼ cup	fresh ricotta	50 mL
6 tbsp	grated Parmigiano-Reggiano, divided	90 mL

1. In a covered pasta pot over high heat, bring water to a rapid boil.

2. In a large sauté pan, heat oil over medium heat. Add garlic and salt and pepper to taste and cook, stirring, until garlic is lightly browned, about 3 minutes. Using a slotted spoon, remove and discard garlic. Add tomatoes and basil. Reduce heat to low, cover and simmer until tomatoes are tender, about 5 minutes. Remove from heat and set aside.

3. While sauce is simmering, add salt and fusilli to the boiling water and cook, uncovered, over high heat until pasta is al dente. Scoop out about 1 cup (250 mL) of the pasta cooking water and set aside. Drain pasta.

4. Return sauté pan to high heat. Add 2 tbsp (25 mL) of the reserved pasta water and the ricotta and heat through. Add fusilli and, using a wooden spoon, toss to coat evenly, adding more pasta water if necessary. Add half of the Parmigiano-Reggiano and toss well.

5. Transfer to a large serving platter and sprinkle with remaining cheese. Serve immediately.

Variations

Substitute penne or cut ziti for the fusilli.

Farfalle con asparagi e mascarpone

Farfalle with Asparagus and Mascarpone

Farfalle ("butterflies" in Italian) are a fun shape for kids because they look like bow ties. Mascarpone is a rich, smooth, mild cheese that pairs well with asparagus. This is how we introduced our kids to asparagus — and it worked.

Serves 4 to 6

Tips

To prepare the asparagus for this recipe, cut off and discard the woody ends. Then cut in 2-inch (5 cm) lengths, starting from the tip ends so the tips remain intact.

For best results grate the cheese yourself, but if time is at a premium, use already grated cheese. Whichever form you choose, just be sure to buy the very best Italian Parmigiano-Reggiano you can find and grate it finely to ensure you have the quantity called for in the recipe.

3 tbsp	extra-virgin olive oil	45 mL
1 tsp	thinly sliced garlic	5 mL
	Salt and finely ground black pepper	
1½ cups	sliced (2 inches/5 cm) pencil-thin asparagus (see Tips, left)	375 mL
6	hand-torn fresh basil leaves	6
¼ cup	water	50 mL
1 tbsp	salt	15 mL
1 lb	dried farfalle (see Variations, below)	500 g
½ cup	mascarpone	125 mL
6 tbsp	grated Parmigiano-Reggiano, divided	90 mL

1. In a covered pasta pot over high heat, bring water to a rapid boil.

2. Meanwhile, in a large sauté pan, heat oil over medium heat. Add garlic and salt and pepper to taste and cook, stirring, until garlic is lightly browned, about 3 minutes. Using a slotted spoon, remove and discard garlic. Add asparagus, basil and water and stir. Reduce heat to low, cover and simmer until asparagus is tender, about 5 minutes. Remove from heat and set aside.

3. While sauce is simmering, add salt and farfalle to the boiling water and cook, uncovered, over high heat until pasta is al dente. Scoop out about 1 cup (250 mL) of the pasta cooking water and set aside. Drain pasta.

4. Return sauté pan to high heat. Add 2 tbsp (25 mL) of the reserved pasta water and the mascarpone. Stir. Add farfalle and, using a wooden spoon, toss to coat evenly, adding more pasta water if necessary. Add half of the Parmigiano-Reggiano and toss well.

5. Transfer to a large serving platter and sprinkle with remaining cheese. Serve immediately.

Variations

Substitute penne or garganelli for the farfalle.

Farfalle con broccoli

Farfalle with Broccoli

This is an easy way to help kids enjoy broccoli. Slicing it thinly helps to distribute it evenly throughout the pasta so it doesn't appear as big green clumps.

Serves 4 to 6

Tips

Always use a large pot and plenty of water when cooking pasta. To properly cook 1 pound (500 g) of pasta, you'll need a pot with a volume of at least 8 quarts (8 L) so that you can use 6 quarts (6 L) of water.

Never rinse pasta after draining it. The surface starch helps the sauce to cling and is important to producing the best-quality dish.

3 tbsp	extra-virgin olive oil	45 mL
1 tsp	thinly sliced garlic	5 mL
	Salt and freshly ground black pepper	
1½ cups	thinly sliced (vertically) broccoli florets	375 mL
6	hand-torn fresh basil leaves	6
¼ cup	water	50 mL
1 tbsp	salt	15 mL
1 lb	dried farfalle (see Variations, below)	500 g
2 tbsp	unsalted butter	25 mL
6 tbsp	grated Parmigiano-Reggiano, divided	90 mL

1. In a covered pasta pot over high heat, bring water to a rapid boil.

2. In a large sauté pan, heat oil over medium heat. Add garlic and salt and pepper to taste and cook, stirring, until garlic is lightly browned, about 3 minutes. Using a slotted spoon, remove and discard garlic. Add broccoli, basil and water and reduce heat to low. Cover and simmer until broccoli is tender, about 3 minutes. Remove from heat and set aside.

3. While sauce is simmering, add salt and farfalle to the boiling water and cook, uncovered, over high heat until pasta is al dente. Scoop out about 1 cup (250 mL) of the pasta cooking water and set aside. Drain pasta.

4. Return sauté pan to high heat. Add 2 tbsp (25 mL) of the reserved pasta water and the butter, stir and heat through. Add farfalle and, using a wooden spoon, toss to coat evenly, adding more pasta water if necessary. Add half of the Parmigiano-Reggiano and toss well.

5. Transfer to a large serving platter and sprinkle with remaining cheese. Serve immediately.

Variations

Substitute penne or cut ziti for the farfalle.

Fusilli con carote e pinoli

Fusilli with Carrots and Toasted Pine Nuts

Corkscrew pasta with orange carrots and little golden pine nuts is a very attractive combination. It looks pretty and tastes good too, and it's not only for children.

Serves 4 to 6

Tip

Toast pine nuts on an ungreased baking tray in a preheated 350°F (180°C) oven for 7 to 10 minutes. Check after 7 minutes, because they burn quickly. Remove from oven, spread on a plate lined with paper toweling and let cool.

3 tbsp	extra-virgin olive oil	45 mL
1 tsp	thinly sliced garlic	5 mL
	Salt and freshly ground pepper	
1½ cups	finely diced carrots	375 mL
6	hand-torn fresh basil leaves	6
½ cup	water	125 mL
1 tbsp	salt	15 mL
1 lb	dried fusilli (see Variations, below)	500 g
2 tbsp	unsalted butter	25 mL
6 tbsp	grated Parmigiano-Reggiano, divided	90 mL
3 tbsp	toasted pine nuts (see Tip, left)	45 mL

1. In a covered pasta pot over high heat, bring water to a rapid boil.

2. In a large sauté pan, heat oil over medium heat. Add garlic and salt and pepper to taste and cook, stirring, until garlic is lightly browned, about 3 minutes. Using a slotted spoon, remove and discard garlic. Add carrots, basil and water. Reduce heat to low, cover and simmer until carrots are tender, about 10 minutes. Remove from heat and set aside.

3. While sauce is simmering, add salt and fusilli to the boiling water and cook, uncovered, over high heat until pasta is al dente. Scoop out about 1 cup (250 mL) of the pasta cooking water and set aside. Drain pasta.

4. Return sauté pan to high heat. Add 2 tbsp (25 mL) of the reserved pasta water and the butter, stir and heat through. Add fusilli and, using a wooden spoon, toss to coat evenly, adding more pasta water if necessary. Add half of the Parmigiano-Reggiano and toss well.

5. Transfer to a large serving platter and sprinkle with remaining cheese and pine nuts. Serve immediately.

Variations

Substitute penne or cut ziti for the fusilli.

Garganelli alla salsa di pomodoro

Garganelli with Fresh Tomatoes and Basil

Here is a very simple cooked tomato sauce that kids themselves can sprinkle with cheese. It's easy to make and easy to eat, and the whole family can enjoy it. Garganelli are special pasta that look as if squares of pasta have been rolled up diagonally — like penne, only fancier.

Serves 4 to 6

Tips

Remember, when your pasta has finished cooking, you want it to be firm and supple, not soft and mushy. It will cook a bit more from the residual heat after it is drained, and also when you add it to the sauce.

I like to tear the basil leaves by hand rather than slicing them, because I think they look and taste better.

3 tbsp	unsalted butter	45 mL
3 cups	diced unpeeled Roma tomatoes	750 mL
¼ cup	finely diced carrot	50 mL
¼ cup	diced peeled celery	50 mL
¼ cup	diced onion	50 mL
	Salt and freshly ground black pepper	
6	hand-torn fresh basil leaves	6
1 tbsp	salt	15 mL
1 lb	dried garganelli (see Variations, below)	500 g
6 tbsp	grated Parmigiano-Reggiano, divided	90 mL

1. In a covered pasta pot over high heat, bring water to a rapid boil.

2. Meanwhile, in a large sauté pan, melt butter over low heat. Add tomatoes, carrot, celery and onion and stir well. Season to taste with salt and pepper and add basil. Raise heat to medium, cover and simmer until vegetables are very tender and sauce is slightly thickened, about 10 minutes. Remove from heat and set aside.

3. While sauce is simmering, add salt and garganelli to the boiling water and cook, uncovered, over high heat until pasta is al dente. Scoop out about 1 cup (250 mL) of the pasta cooking water and set aside. Drain pasta.

4. Return sauté pan to high heat. Add 2 tbsp (25 mL) of the reserved pasta water, stir and heat through. Add garganelli and, using a wooden spoon, toss to coat evenly, adding more pasta water if necessary. Add half of the Parmigiano-Reggiano and toss well.

5. Transfer to a large serving platter and sprinkle with remaining cheese. Serve immediately.

Variations

Substitute penne or cut ziti for the garganelli.

Making Fresh Pasta

Pasta Fresca

In Italy fresh pasta — *pasta fresca* — has coexisted alongside dried pasta for centuries. And, like dried pasta, it has regional variations. Often people assume that fresh pasta is somehow better than dried pasta. Not so. It is just different. They are equally good.

You can buy fresh pasta, but it's important to buy only the best. Fresh cut pasta and pasta sheets for making ravioli and lasagne (usually 12 by 9 inches/ 30 by 23 cm) are available in gourmet markets, but they vary widely in quality. To ensure the best products, I recommend that you seek out an Italian store, deli or pasta maker that specializes in fresh pasta, either in your area or online.

Buying Fresh Pasta

When buying good ready-made fresh pasta, these are the things to look for:

- It is made fresh daily.
- If shipped, it is shipped the same day it is made or frozen the day it is made, then shipped.
- It contains only eggs, flour (preferably Tipo 00 Italian flour) and salt — no additives of any kind, including preservatives.

The Joy of Homemade Pasta

Fresh pasta can be made at home by hand (or with a bare minimum of equipment) from flour (either finely milled Italian flour or all-purpose flour), eggs and salt. Making pasta is a skill, but one that can easily be mastered and enjoyed. In my opinion, homemade pasta is a simple luxury. It's a pleasure we rarely indulge in today because our lifestyles are so hectic. That's why I recommend making pasta on the weekend. Even my mother made pasta only on Sundays, when she had the time to do it. She would put a mound of flour on a wooden board, make a well in the center, add eggs and a little salt, mix it with a fork and work the dough until it came together. Then she would knead it, let it rest, roll it out with a wooden rolling pin and shape it. She made fabulous cavatelli and fettuccine. She also made a different and softer kind of fresh pasta sheet for filled pasta such as anolini, ravioli, tortelli, agnolotti, cappelletti and tortellini. This was a real luxury.

Compared to commercially produced dried pasta, fresh pasta that you make yourself is tender, delicate and worth the extra time and effort. This chapter includes two basic recipes for sheets of pasta dough that you can use to make cut pastas for sauce — tagliolini, tagliatelle, fettuccine, pappardelle, stracci, quadrati, maltagliati — and the baked pastas in the chapter Baked Pastas: Make Today, Bake Tomorrow.

This chapter also includes three recipes for fresh pasta dough to be filled: plain, red (from carrots and tomato) and green (from spinach). Fresh pasta dough for filling needs to be softer and more delicate than that used for boiling and baking. From any of these you can create the nine different shapes in the chapter Filled Pastas: Gift-Wrapped — anolini, agnolotti, fagottini, caramelle, ravioli, tortelli, tortellini, tortelloni and cappelletti. In theory, any of these doughs may be used with any of the fillings.

I have also included two recipes for fresh sweet pasta doughs — one plain and one chocolate — to be used in pasta desserts. Please consider these as alternatives to desserts for other meals, not as the dessert course in a meal that contains pasta. Too much of a good thing really can be too much!

Not in My Kitchen

An electric automatic pasta-making machine for the home kitchen — the kind where you put the eggs and flour in one end and shaped pasta is extruded out the other — will never give you the texture or flavor of well-made fresh pasta that has been stretched (by a rolling pin) or compressed (by a pasta machine with rollers). I do not recommend using one.

Making Pasta at Home

I suggest that you save your first fresh pasta-making occasion for a day when you have plenty of time. It's really very easy, but you can't rush the process. My Basic Pasta recipe (see page 222) calls for either very finely milled Tipo 00 Italian flour or unbleached all-purpose flour. I strongly recommend the Tipo 00 Italian flour, which you can buy online from a number of vendors; it gives the best flavor and texture for sauce to cling to. But you can still produce an excellent result using unbleached all-purpose flour. For those of you who are looking for whole-grain options, I have also included a recipe for Whole Wheat Pasta dough (see page 222).

Farina Tipo 00

Also called *doppio zero* ("double zero"), Tipo (type) 00 Italian flours are very finely milled and have the least fiber of any flours. There are two kinds of wheat, hard and soft, and many Italian mills use both to produce several different kinds of Tipo 00 flour. Flours milled from hard wheat are called *semola* or *grano duro*, whereas those made from soft wheat are known as *grano tenero* ("tender grain"). Tipo 00 flours milled from soft wheat have less protein, or gluten — 7% to 9% — than flours milled from hard wheat, which have a protein content of at least 11%. In my opinion, the best flour for making fresh pasta is Tipo 00 made from *grano tenero*. Tipo 00 flours can be purchased online.

Fresh Pasta For Cutting and Baking

I've included instructions for three basic ways to make pasta. Once you become comfortable with making fresh pasta, you'll find the method that works best for you. You can make the pasta one day, then lay it out on lightly floured parchment paper, cover it with a lint-free kitchen towel and cook it the next day. If you prefer the flavor and texture of whole grains, make my whole wheat pasta. For the proper texture it needs a little olive oil and water, which is added along with the eggs.

Tips

I like to mix pasta dough on a pastry board because it's the traditional way. However, you can also use marble, granite, stainless steel — in fact, any solid surface.

Until you're experienced, you may find that the eggs threaten to or actually break through the "walls" of the flour well. Placing your free hand on the outside of the flour wall can help to support it as you beat inside the well.

If you prefer, mix the dough in a mixing bowl, making a well in the center of the flour, then adding the remaining ingredients. After the dough comes together, transfer to a board to knead.

Basic Pasta

Makes about 1 lb (500 g) / 4 to 6 servings / 12 pasta sheets, each 12 by 4 inches (30 by 10 cm)

2⅓ cups	unbleached all-purpose flour or Tipo 00 Italian flour (see page 221), fluffed and leveled	575 mL
4	large eggs, beaten	4
1 tsp	salt	5 mL
	Water, optional	

Whole Wheat Pasta

Makes about 1 lb (500 g) / 4 to 6 servings / at least 12 pasta sheets, each 12 by 4 inches (30 by 10 cm)

3 cups	sifted whole wheat flour, fluffed and leveled	750 mL
3	large eggs, beaten	3
½ tsp	salt	2 mL
6 tbsp	water + additional, if necessary	90 mL
½ tsp	extra-virgin olive oil	2 mL

Hand Method

1. Place flour in the center of a pastry board or in a mixing bowl (see Tips, left). Make a well in the center. Add eggs and salt (and water and olive oil, if making whole wheat pasta) to well and, using your fingers or a fork, start to mix the flour inside the well into eggs. As you mix, gather and reinforce flour on outside of well so it doesn't allow eggs to leak out the sides. Continue to mix from the inside and reinforce well from the outside until dough forms a ball, using your hands to form the dough when it becomes too thick for the fork. Then, using your hands, shape dough into a ball.

2. Lightly dust work surface with flour and, using the heel of your hand, knead dough until smooth and elastic (not sticky), 5 to 8 minutes. Transfer to a plate dusted with flour, cover with plastic wrap and let rest for 1 hour.

3. After dough has finished resting, dust board lightly with flour and knead briefly until smooth and pliable, less than 1 minute. Divide dough into six equal pieces and flatten slightly. It is now ready to roll, cut and shape.

The stand mixer has the advantage of a powerful motor that turns the beater, paddle or dough hook much faster than a hand mixer, and it can handle stiff dough not suitable for hand mixers. The stand mixer also spares the cook labor.

Stand Mixer Method

1. In the bowl of a stand mixer, combine flour, eggs and salt (then water and olive oil, if making whole wheat pasta). Attach bowl and flat paddle to mixer. Mix at low speed until combined. Remove paddle and attach dough hook. Turn to speed 2 and mix until dough forms a ball, stopping to scrape down sides of bowl as necessary. Continue to mix dough for 5 minutes, adding water and/or flour by the tablespoon (15 mL) if necessary for proper consistency. Transfer to a lightly floured plate. Cover with plastic wrap and let rest for 1 hour.

2. After dough has finished resting, dust pastry board lightly with flour and knead dough briefly until smooth and pliable, less than 1 minute. Divide dough into six equal pieces and flatten slightly. It is now ready to roll, cut and shape.

Food Processor Method

1. In a large-capacity food processor fitted with a plastic dough blade, combine flour and salt. Pulse for 5 seconds. Add eggs (and water and olive oil, if making whole wheat pasta) and pulse just until a pasta ball forms, 1 minute or less, stopping the motor and scraping down the sides of the bowl as necessary. If necessary, add additional flour or water 1 tbsp (15 mL) at a time to form a dough. Transfer to a board and knead until dough comes together.

2. Transfer to a plate lightly dusted with flour, cover with plastic wrap and let rest for 1 hour.

3. After dough has finished resting, dust pastry board lightly with flour and knead dough briefly until smooth and pliable, less than 1 minute. Divide dough into six equal pieces and flatten slightly. It is now ready to roll, cut and shape.

This is the fastest, easiest method of all. Pasta dough made in a food processor does not have the same texture as dough made by hand or mixer. However, if time is of the essence, this is the way to go.

Tip

It is impossible to be precise about yields for fresh pasta, for a number of reasons. Depending on the weather, the ability of the flour to absorb water varies. Also, the size of eggs varies even among standardized sizes. And finally, more experienced cooks are able to roll the dough thinner, which produces larger sheets.

Hand mixing method
(flour well)

Rolling Fresh Pasta

Tip

I recommend that you keep a straight edge or ruler on hand so you can measure and cut the sheets to the size required in your recipes.

Using a Pastry Board

I like to mix and roll my pasta dough on a wooden pastry board, perhaps because that's how I watched my mother do it. Wood has been traditional for centuries. It is porous and "breathes," and it's warm, not cold like marble or granite. I recommend a standard wooden pastry board 24 by 18 inches (60 by 45 cm), but you can manage with a smaller standard-size (20 by 16 inches/50 by 40 cm) cutting board. After mixing my pasta on the board, I use a bench scraper to clean it off until it's smooth and dry. (Don't wash or even wet the board, because the flour and dough will stick.)

Hand Method

When you roll out pasta dough with a rolling pin, you are basically stretching the dough. Traditional Italian cooks believe that this produces the best texture.

- One piece at a time (keep remaining dough covered with plastic wrap to prevent it from drying out) on a lightly floured surface, roll dough into a rectangle a little larger than 12 by 8 inches (30 by 20 cm). It should be about $\frac{1}{8}$ inch (3 mm) thick. To prevent sticking, flour the surface of the dough lightly as you roll.

- If you plan to make pasta sheets for use in layered, baked or filled pasta recipes, measure and cut the size of sheets the recipe calls for and lay them out on a floured sheet of parchment paper.

- If you plan to make cut pasta, roll up the pasta sheet snugly in jelly-roll fashion, starting from the short side. Be careful not to roll so tightly that it sticks together. You are now ready to cut the dough.

Measuring Flour

Chefs weigh rather than measure flour. The reason is that 8 ounces (250 g) always weighs 8 ounces (250 g), but 1 cup (250 mL) of flour does not always weigh the same as another. That's because, after being packed and stored, flour can settle and become more compact. Also, it can absorb moisture in humid environments and lose moisture in dry air. For the home cook, who will likely be measuring rather than weighing, I strongly recommend placing the flour to be measured in a large bowl and "fluffing" it from the bottom with a large spoon. After it has been aerated, scoop it into a dry measure (a measuring cup with a level edge) and use a ruler or flat-edged spatula to level off the top. If you do that consistently, 1 cup (250 mL) will pretty much equal 1 cup (250 mL) — at least in your kitchen.

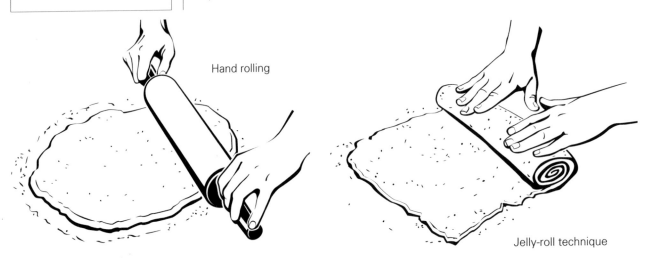

Hand rolling

Jelly-roll technique

Tips

If at any point while machine-rolling, the dough begins to stick, dust it very lightly on both sides with flour. If it tears because it is too wet, simply knead it again in a little flour and start over — nothing lost.

Remember, when making fresh pasta for filling, roll out the sheets one at a time and fill them before rolling out the next sheet. Otherwise your pasta is likely to become dry and brittle because it has been exposed to the air.

Machine Method

When you roll out pasta dough into sheets using mechanical rollers, you are basically compressing rather than stretching the dough. This produces perfectly good pasta and is much faster than the hand method. For all our recipes you can use either a hand-cranked pasta-rolling machine or the pasta-rolling attachment for a stand mixer.

- One piece at a time (keep remaining dough covered with plastic wrap to prevent it from drying out), flatten dough into a rectangle about ½ inch (1 cm) thick. Set the machine on its widest setting and roll each rectangle through twice. Repeat, reducing the width setting by 2 each time, until pasta reaches desired thickness. (For example, if your machine has settings from 1 through 8, roll on 1, 3, 5 and 7.) After it is rolled, using a ruler, trim to 12 inches (30 cm) long by 4 inches (10 cm) wide. Place the cut pasta sheets on sheets of floured parchment paper until ready to use. Cover with a second sheet of unfloured parchment to prevent the dough from drying out. If you fill up a whole sheet of parchment, place another floured sheet on top and continue the process, finishing with a sheet of unfloured parchment.

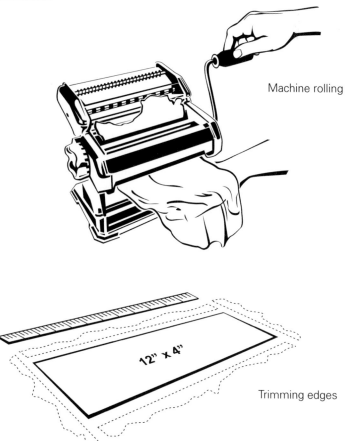

Machine rolling

12" x 4"

Trimming edges

Cutting Fresh Pasta

Hand cutting strand pasta

Laying out strands on floured parchment

Part of the pleasure of fresh pasta, like its dried counterpart, lies in its shapes. There are hundreds of traditional fresh pasta shapes, many of which, like my mother's cavatelli, are made by hand and require considerable skill. Here I have selected seven shapes that are easy to make by simply cutting flat pasta sheets by hand or using a pasta-cutting wheel or machine.

- To cut long strands of pasta dough by hand, snugly roll up the pasta sheet, starting from the short side. Be careful not to roll so tightly that it sticks together. Using a sharp knife, cut across the roll to the desired width. You may also be able to use a pasta-cutting wheel or an attachment that comes with your pasta-rolling machine. See specific instructions for types of cut pasta below.

- Once pasta is cut, shake it gently to separate the strands and lay on lightly floured sheets of parchment, each 16 by 12 inches (40 by 30 cm). If not using immediately, cover with a lint-free towel.

Making Strands

When cutting pasta for strands, I don't recommend using a ruler to mark out the width. I think it makes much more sense to just eyeball the dough. The beauty of hand-cut pasta is its slight irregularity. Also, the more you make, the quicker and more precise you'll become.

Strand Pasta

Tagliolini: Tagliolini are long, thin, delicate strands of pasta a little thicker than angel hair. To make tagliolini, using a sharp knife, cut rolled pasta sheet crosswise into very thin strips, each $1/16$ inch (1 mm) wide. As you cut, shake gently to separate strands. If you prefer, use the thinnest cutter on the standard attachment of a pasta-rolling/cutting machine (which is $1/8$ inch/3 mm wide) and substitute the resulting tagliatelle in any recipes calling for tagliolini.

Tagliatelle: Tagliatelle are long strands of pasta slightly wider than tagliolini. To make tagliatelle, using a sharp knife, cut rolled pasta sheet crosswise into thin strips, each $1/8$ inch (3 mm) wide. As you cut, shake gently to separate strands and transfer to lightly floured parchment. If you prefer, tagliatelle may be cut using the thinnest cutter on the standard attachment of a pasta-rolling/cutting machine.

Fettuccine: Fettuccine are slightly wider than tagliolini and tagliatelle. To make fettuccine, using a straight-edged pasta wheel or a sharp knife, cut rolled pasta sheet crosswise into strips, each $1/4$ inch (0.5 cm) wide. As you cut, shake gently to separate strands and transfer to lightly floured parchment. If you prefer, fettuccine may be cut using the second, thicker cutter on the standard attachment of a pasta-rolling/cutting machine.

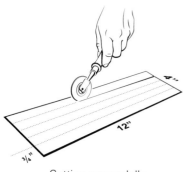

Cutting pappardelle

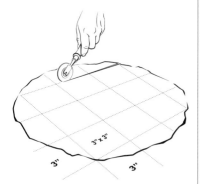

Cutting quadrati

Pappardelle: Pappardelle are long pasta ribbons. They can be cut from 12- by 4-inch (30 by 10 cm) sheets of pasta using a fluted or straight-edged pasta-cutting wheel. Place pasta sheet on a lightly floured board and cut lengthwise into strips approximately ¾ inch (1.5 cm) wide. Using a pasta wheel on the sheets is quicker and more accurate than a knife. If you prefer to use a knife, make sure it's sharp. Using a sharp knife, roll up each sheet of pasta dough from the short end and cut horizontally into ¾-inch (1.5 cm) strips. As you cut, shake gently to separate strands and transfer to lightly floured parchment.

Stracci: These are long, thick pasta ribbons 2 inches (5 cm) wide. They can be cut from 12- by 4-inch (30 by 10 cm) pasta sheets with a fluted or straight-edged pasta-cutting wheel, or they can be cut from rolled pasta sheets using a sharp knife. Follow the same procedure as for pappardelle, As you cut, shake gently to separate strands and transfer to lightly floured parchment.

Quadrati: Quadrati are large pasta squares cut from flat sheets of pasta using a straight-edged pasta-cutting wheel or sharp knife. Follow the method for pappardelle but cut 3-inch (7.5 cm) squares. Save the scraps of pasta, cut them irregularly and freeze for use in soups.

Maltagliati: Loosely translated, *maltagliati* means "badly cut." This pasta probably originated from irregularly cut unused pieces or scraps of fresh pasta sheets, which were used in soup. But there's an appeal to the irregular shapes, so maltagliati are often served with sauce just like other pastas. Maltagliati are cut from flat sheets of pasta. Use a straight-edged pasta-cutting wheel or sharp knife to cut quadrati diagonally in half, making slightly irregular triangles.

Cutting Attachments

Pasta machines have cutting attachments. The standard attachment has two settings, one thin (approximately ⅛ inch/0.25 cm) and one thicker (approximately ¼ inch/0.5 cm). You can also purchase additional cutting attachments for larger and smaller strand pastas. However, if you want to cut the pasta for the recipes that follow by machine, using the two standard settings, you can treat tagliolini as tagliatelle (see page 226) and use the wider attachment for fettuccine. The other shapes — pappardelle, stracci, quadrati, maltagliati, quadrati — must be cut by hand.

No Size Fits Everyone

Perhaps not surprisingly, there is wide disagreement among Italian food writers and cooks about the dimensions of pasta. For example, many say (as I do) that tagliatelle is thinner than fettuccine, but others say just the reverse. Some even say that the two pastas are interchangeable. Controversy surrounds almost all fresh, dried and filled pasta shapes. If nothing else, this proves only one thing: Italians are obsessed with ingredients, and most consider themselves not only the highest authority but the best judge of what is right and good when it comes to food.

Dough for Filled Pasta

This dough is prepared in the same way as the fresh pasta on pages 222–225. However, for the sake of uniformity, pasta for filling should be rolled out using a hand-cranked stainless steel pasta machine or the pasta-rolling attachment of a stand mixer. The sheets should measure 12 by 4 inches (30 by 10 cm) and should be about ⅛ inch (3 mm) thick. If you prefer, roll the dough out by hand with a wooden rolling pin, then use a ruler to measure the dimensions and cut it into sheets. Whether machine- or hand-rolled, the sheets should be cut straight at the sides and ends. Any dough scraps should not be gathered up, kneaded and rolled again, because the texture will not be the same.

Plain Pasta Dough for Filled Pasta (*La sfoglia*)

Makes about 1 pound (500 g) / 4 to 6 servings / 12 pasta sheets, each 12 by 4 inches (30 by 10 cm)

3 cups	unbleached all-purpose flour or Tipo 00 Italian flour, fluffed and leveled	750 mL
2	large eggs, beaten	2
8 tbsp	milk	120 mL
1 tsp	salt	5 mL

Hand Method

1. Place flour in center of a pastry board (see Using a Pastry Board, page 224) or in a mixing bowl. Make a well in the center. Add eggs, milk and salt to well and, using your fingers or a fork, start to mix flour inside well into eggs. As you mix, gather and reinforce flour on outside of well so it doesn't allow eggs to leak out the sides. Continue to mix from the inside and reinforce well from the outside until dough forms a ball, using your hands to form dough when it becomes too thick for the fork. Lightly dust work surface with flour and, using the heel of your hand, knead until smooth and elastic, about 5 to 8 minutes. Shape into a ball.

2. Transfer to a plate dusted with flour, cover with plastic wrap and let rest for 1 hour.

3. When dough has finished resting, dust work surface lightly with flour and knead dough briefly until smooth and pliable. Divide dough into 6 equal pieces and flatten slightly. Follow instructions for rolling out pasta with a pasta machine (see page 225), forming 12- by 4-inch (30 by 10 cm) rectangles that are about ⅛ inch (3 mm) thick. Cut edges straight.

Stand Mixer Method

1. In the bowl of a stand mixer, combine flour, eggs, milk and salt. Attach bowl and flat paddle to mixer. Mix at low speed until combined. Remove paddle and attach dough hook. Turn to speed 2 and mix until dough forms a ball, stopping to scrape down sides of bowl as necessary. Continue to mix dough for 5 minutes, adding milk and/or flour by the tablespoon (15 mL) if necessary for proper consistency. Continue with Steps 2 and 3.

Food Processor Method

1. In a large capacity food processor fitted with the plastic dough blade, combine flour and salt and pulse for 5 seconds. Add eggs and milk and pulse just until dough forms a ball. If necessary, add additional flour or milk 1 tbsp (15 mL) at a time to form a cohesive dough. You may need to stop the motor, open the lid and scrape down the sides once or twice. Remove dough from processor and knead on a floured surface for a few seconds. Continue with Steps 2 and 3.

Making Multicolored Dough

Italians create endless variety with many of the same basic ingredients. In pasta cuisine, variety is provided not only by shapes but also by colors — adding natural ingredients to fresh pasta dough to create red, green, orange, even black (using squid ink) dough. While these brightly colored pasta doughs don't add much flavor to a recipe, they give tremendous visual appeal to the finished dish.

You can make bi- or tricolored pasta dough by combining plain with red and/or green dough for filled pasta. Roll and trim pasta as per instructions. For bicolor dough, cut one pasta sheet in half lengthwise. Place a second half-sheet along its edge, slightly overlapping. Using red and green doughs will result in a sheet of pasta that is half red, half green. If you use a plain dough and a green dough, the result will be white and green. Roll the overlapped sheets through the pasta machine on the thin setting to fuse the two pieces into one bicolor sheet. For tricolor pasta dough, cut one sheet of each color in thirds, slightly overlap three different-colored pieces, and roll them through the pasta machine on the thin setting to fuse into one tricolor sheet.

Adding Flour and Liquid

Flour varies in production methods and batches and thus absorbs liquids differently. Even the time of year and humidity levels can affect absorption. Eggs also vary in size, even within the grade (extra-large, large, medium, small). So, when making dough, don't be afraid to add extra flour and/or milk in 1 tbsp (15 mL) increments to achieve the right consistency.

Dough for Filled Pasta *(continued...)*

This red dough, like most color-enhanced pasta dough, is made more for appearance than flavor. The flavor is very subtle, but the color, which comes from all-natural ingredients, creates a beautiful contrast with many fillings.

Fresh Red Dough for Filled Pasta *(La sfoglia rossa)*

Makes about 1 pound (500 g) / 4 to 6 servings / about 12 pasta sheets, each 12 by 4 inches (30 by 10 cm)

1 cup	diced peeled carrots	250 mL
2 tsp	salt, divided	10 mL
2 tbsp	tomato paste	25 mL
3 cups	all-purpose unbleached flour or Tipo 00 Italian flour, fluffed and leveled	750 mL
2	large eggs, lightly beaten	2
6 tbsp (approx.)	whole milk	90 mL

1. In a pot of boiling water, combine carrots and 1 tsp (5 mL) of the salt and cook over high heat until carrots are soft and tender. Drain. Return carrots to pot and add tomato paste. Cook over low heat, stirring, until carrots are quite dry, being careful not to brown or burn them, about 20 minutes.

2. Transfer carrot mixture to a food processor and pulse to finely purée, stopping and scraping down the sides of the work bowl as necessary. Transfer to a small bowl and let cool to room temperature.

Hand Method

3. Place flour in center of a pastry board or in a mixing bowl. Make a well in the center. Add carrot purée, eggs, milk and remaining 1 tsp (5 mL) salt to well and, using your fingers or a fork, start to mix flour inside well into wet ingredients. As you mix, gather and reinforce flour on outside of well so it doesn't allow wet ingredients to leak out the sides. Continue to mix from the inside and reinforce well from the outside until dough forms a ball, using your hands to form dough when it becomes too thick for the fork, adding more milk, if necessary. Knead until smooth and elastic, about 5 minutes. Then, using your hands, shape into a ball.

4. Transfer to a plate dusted with flour, cover with plastic wrap and let rest for 1 hour.

5. When dough has finished resting, dust work surface lightly with flour and knead dough briefly until smooth and pliable. Divide dough into 6 equal pieces and flatten slightly. Follow instructions for rolling out pasta using a pasta-rolling machine (see page 225), forming 12- by 4-inch (30 by 10 cm) rectangles that are about 1/8 inch (3 mm) thick. Cut edges straight.

Stand Mixer Method

Complete steps 1 and 2. In the bowl of a stand mixer, combine flour and remaining tsp (5 mL) salt, carrot purée, eggs and milk. Attach bowl and flat paddle to mixer. Mix at low speed until combined. Remove paddle and attach dough hook. Turn to speed 2 and mix until dough forms a ball, stopping to scrape down sides of bowl as necessary. Continue to mix dough for 5 minutes, adding milk or flour by the tablespoon (15 mL) if necessary for proper consistency. Continue with steps 4 and 5.

Food Processor Method

Complete steps 1 and 2. In a large capacity food processor fitted with the plastic dough blade, combine flour and remaining tsp (5 mL) salt. Pulse for 5 seconds. Add carrot purée, eggs and milk and pulse until dough forms a ball. If necessary, add additional flour 1 tbsp (15 mL) at a time to form a cohesive dough. You might need to stop the motor, open the lid and scrape down the sides once or twice. Remove dough from processor and knead on a floured surface for a few seconds. Continue with steps 4 and 5.

Fresh Spinach Dough for Filled Pasta *(La sfoglia verde)*

Green pasta, colored by spinach, is very traditional in Italy in both fresh and dried forms. It makes a striking contrast with the fillings and looks very appealing when cooked.

Makes about 1 pound (500 g) / 4 to 6 servings / about 12 pasta sheets, each 12 by 4 inches (30 by 10 cm)		
4 cups	stemmed fresh spinach	1 L
2 tsp	salt, divided	10 mL
3 cups	unbleached all-purpose flour or Tipo 00 Italian flour, fluffed and leveled	750 mL
2	large eggs, beaten	2
6 tbsp (approx.)	whole milk	90 mL

Hand Method

1. In a pot of boiling water, combine spinach and 1 tsp (5 mL) of the salt and cook over high heat just until leaves are wilted, less than 1 minute. Using a colander, drain and place under cold running water until spinach is at room temperature. Using your hands, squeeze excess moisture from spinach.

continued ...

Dough for Filled Pasta *(Fresh Spinach Dough continued...)*

Tip

Practice makes perfect. Once you have mastered the technique you will know just how thin to roll the dough, how much filling to add and how to seal and shape the dough. Do it once or twice and you will see that it's relatively uncomplicated.

2. Transfer spinach to a food processor and pulse to finely purée. Transfer to a small bowl and set aside.

3. Place flour in center of a pastry board or in a mixing bowl. Make a well in the center. Add spinach purée, eggs, milk and remaining 1 tsp (5 mL) salt to the well and, using your fingers or a fork, start to mix the flour inside well into wet ingredients. As you mix, gather and reinforce flour on outside of well so it doesn't allow eggs to leak out the sides. Continue to mix from the inside and reinforce well from the outside until dough forms a ball, using your hands to form dough when it becomes too thick for the fork, adding more milk, if necessary. Knead until smooth and elastic, about 5 minutes. Transfer to a lightly floured work surface.

4. Transfer to a plate dusted with flour, cover with plastic wrap and let rest for 1 hour.

5. When dough has finished resting, dust work surface lightly with flour and knead dough briefly until smooth and pliable. Divide dough into 6 equal pieces and flatten slightly. Follow instructions for rolling out pasta using a pasta machine (see page 225), forming 12- by 4-inch (30 by 10 cm) rectangles that are about $1/8$ inch (3 mm) thick. Cut edges straight.

Stand Mixer Method

Complete steps 1 and 2. In the bowl of a stand mixer, combine flour and remaining tsp (5 mL) salt, spinach purée, eggs and milk. Attach bowl and flat paddle to mixer. Mix at low speed until combined. Remove paddle and attach dough hook. Turn to speed 2 and mix until dough forms a ball, stopping to scrape down sides of bowl as necessary. Continue to knead dough for 5 minutes, adding milk and/or flour by the tablespoon (15 mL) if necessary for proper consistency. Continue with steps 4 and 5.

Food Processor Method

Complete steps 1 and 2. In a large capacity food processor fitted with the plastic dough blade, combine flour and remaining tsp (5 mL) salt. Pulse for 5 seconds. Add spinach purée, eggs and milk and pulse until dough forms a ball. If necessary, add additional flour 1 tbsp (15 mL) at a time to form a cohesive dough. You might need to stop the motor, open the lid and scrape down the sides once or twice. Remove dough from processor and knead on a floured surface for a few seconds. Continue with steps 4 and 5.

Fresh pasta shown at right (clockwise, from top left): spinach & plain fagottini, red tortellini, tortelloni and cappelletti, whole wheat quadrati, red & spinach ravioli, plain tagliatelle, red anolini and tortelli, plain cappelletti, spinach & plain caramelle, whole wheat pappardelle and red tagliatelle

Sweet Pasta Dough

Sweet pasta dough is made using equipment and techniques similar to those used for other fresh pastas. However, because it is the softest dough, it is the most difficult to handle. That's why I recommend you make it using a stand mixer.

Tip

Roll out dough one sheet at a time and use it sheet by sheet, covering the remainder with plastic to prevent it becoming dry and brittle. If you are going to cut the dough for long pasta, cut each sheet and lay the pasta strands on parchment paper lightly dusted with confectioner's sugar. If you are going to cut the dough into shapes for filled pasta, cut one sheet, fill and shape, and place on parchment paper dusted with confectioner's sugar. Then proceed with rolling and cutting, then filling and shaping, the second sheet.

Fresh Sweet Pasta Dough
(Pasta fresca al dolce)

Makes about 1 pound (500 g) / 6 to 8 servings / 12 pasta sheets, each 12 by 4 inches (30 by 10 cm)

- Stand mixer
- Dinner plate dusted with confectioner's (icing) sugar

3 cups	unbleached all-purpose flour or Italian Tipo 00 flour, fluffed and leveled	750 mL
¾ cup plus additional for dusting	confectioner's (icing) sugar	175 mL plus additional for dusting
¼ tsp	salt	1 mL
4	large eggs, lightly beaten	4

1. In bowl of stand mixer, combine flour, sugar and salt. Attach bowl and flat paddle to mixer. Mix at low speed until combined. Add eggs one at a time and mix until dough forms a ball and pulls away from sides of bowl, stopping to scrape down the sides as necessary, about 10 minutes. Knead until smooth and elastic.

2. Transfer to plate dusted with confectioner's sugar, cover with plastic wrap and let rest for 1 hour.

3. When dough has finished resting, dust a pastry board lightly with confectioner's sugar. Divide dough into 6 equal pieces. Follow instructions for rolling out pasta using a pasta-rolling machine (see page 225). Dusting as needed with confectioner's sugar, roll each piece into a 12- by 4-inch (30 by 10 cm) sheet that is ⅛ inch (3 mm) thick. Dough is now ready to use in recipes.

Variation: Hand Method

In a mixing bowl, combine flour, sugar and salt. Make a well in the center and add eggs. Working from the center out and using a wooden spoon, mix gently until dough becomes too hard to mix, then finish with hands. Knead until smooth and elastic. Continue with recipe.

This pasta dough can be used to make very festive Chocolate Cannelloni (see recipe, page 368) or Chocolate Stracci topped with ice cream and berries (see recipe, page 374).

Fresh Chocolate Pasta Dough
(Pasta fresca al cioccolato)

Makes about 1 pound (500 g) / 8 servings / 12 pasta sheets, each 12 by 4 inches (30 by 10 cm)

• Stand mixer

2 cups	sifted unbleached all-purpose flour or sifted Tipo 00 Italian flour, fluffed and leveled	500 mL
³⁄₄ cup	unsweetened cocoa powder, divided	175 mL
¹⁄₂ cup plus additional for dusting	confectioner's (icing) sugar	125 mL plus additional for dusting
¹⁄₄ tsp	salt	1 mL
4	large eggs, lightly beaten	4
	Milk	
	Unsweetened cocoa powder	

1. In bowl of stand mixer, combine flour, cocoa powder, sugar, salt and eggs. Attach bowl and flat paddle to mixer. Mix at low speed until combined. Remove paddle and attach dough hook. Turn to speed 2 and mix until dough forms a ball, stopping to scrape down sides of bowl as necessary. Continue to mix for 5 minutes, adding milk and/or flour by the tablespoon (15 mL) if necessary for proper consistency.

2. Transfer to a plate dusted with cocoa powder. Cover with plastic wrap and let rest for 1 hour.

3. When dough has finished resting, dust a pastry board lightly with cocoa powder. Divide dough into 6 equal pieces. Follow instructions for using a pasta-rolling machine (see page 225). Dusting as needed with cocoa powder, roll each piece into a 12- by 4-inch (30 by 10 cm) sheet that is ¹⁄₈ inch (3 mm) thick. Dough is now ready to use in recipes.

Variation: Hand Method

In a mixing bowl, combine flour, cocoa powder, sugar and salt. Make a well in the center and add eggs. Working from the center out and using a wooden spoon, mix gently until dough becomes too hard to mix, then finish with hands. Knead until smooth and elastic. Continue with recipe.

RISTORANTE

QUARTINO

PIZZERIA • WINE BAR

ARIA
ZIONATA

APERTURA
DALLE 15.00
ENGLISH SP

Simple Luxury: Fresh Pasta Tossed in Sauce

Gently Does It

For tossing cooked dried pasta in sauce, I recommend using tongs for the long strand pasta and a wooden spoon for the short pasta. However, fresh pasta is more delicate when cooked than dried pasta. Rather than using pasta tongs to toss the cooked fresh pasta, both strands and short cuts, I recommend using a wooden spoon — there's less chance of breaking the pasta while tossing.

When I was a boy, I had two favorite fresh pastas that my mother made: cavatelli and fettuccine. Cavatelli is about 1½ inches (4 cm) long and has a rolled edge; it looks like a short, narrow, irregular tube. My mother would cut the finished dough into ribbons, then cut each ribbon into lengths. She shaped the cavatelli by placing two fingers in the center of each piece and pressing and pulling quickly. This motion stretched the dough and caused it to roll back on itself to form a tube. Cavatelli (also called casarecci) is traditionally combined with a meat sauce, which is how my mother served it. Her meat ragù was very special. She used beef and pork shoulder — never ground meat — which she braised and added to a slow-simmering tomato sauce.

Once in a great while, when she was really short of time, my mother would make a quick tomato sauce from home-canned plum tomatoes. Every summer, from the end of July until the middle of August, my dad would buy bushels of ripe tomatoes, and together they would can them in 1-gallon (4 L) and half-gallon (2 L) Mason jars, tucking a sprig of fresh basil into every jar.

In contrast to the labor-intensive bold meat sauce my mother made for cavatelli, her fettuccine was simplicity itself. It was made from the same dough just cut into ribbons. After cooking it, she tossed the fettuccine with butter and cheese. Only three ingredients — well-made pasta, great butter and cheese — but it was delicious. That was one of my early lessons in the importance of good ingredients.

Cooking Fresh Pasta

As with dried pasta, when cooking fresh pasta, always use a large pot and plenty of rapidly boiling salted water. To properly cook 1 pound (500 g) of pasta, you'll need a pot with a volume of at least 8 quarts (8 L) so that you can use 6 quarts (6 L) of water. However, fresh pasta takes only 3 to 6 minutes to reach the al dente stage, depending on its shape and thickness. Experience will be your best teacher.

Tagliolini con pomodoro crudo e basilico

Tagliolini with Uncooked Tomatoes and Basil

The ideal time to enjoy this pasta is July, August and September, when tomatoes and basil are in season. This light and refreshing pasta involves a minimal amount of cooking. Macerating the tomatoes lets the flavors bloom and adding the hot pasta brings the flavor to its fullest.

Serves 4 to 6

Tips

Fresh pasta cooks very quickly. When you are ready to cook, have an 8-quart (8 L) pot of boiling water ready. Just lift up the parchment sheet with the fresh pasta on it and tip it into the boiling water, add the salt and stir once or twice gently with a wooden spoon.

Tearing basil by hand is quick and easy and lends itself to home cooking — so natural.

I prefer the flavor and texture of freshly grated cheese. However, when time is at a premium, by all means use already grated cheese. Just be sure to use the very best Italian Parmigiano-Reggiano you can find. If you're grating it yourself, be sure to grate it finely.

2 cups	halved cherry tomatoes	500 mL
1/4 cup	extra-virgin olive oil	50 mL
1 tsp	salt	5 mL
1/8 tsp	freshly ground white pepper	0.5 mL
1 cup	hand-torn fresh basil leaves	250 mL
1 tbsp	salt	15 mL
1 lb	fresh tagliolini (see page 226)	500 g
6 tbsp	grated Parmigiano-Reggiano (see Tips, left)	90 mL

1. In a large bowl combine tomatoes, olive oil, salt, pepper and basil. Toss well, cover and set aside at room temperature for 1 hour.

2. In a covered pasta pot over high heat, bring water to a rapid boil. Add salt and tagliolini and cook, uncovered, until pasta is al dente. Drain pasta.

3. Add pasta to tomato mixture and, using a wooden spoon, toss well.

4. Transfer to a large serving bowl and sprinkle with Parmigiano-Reggiano. Serve immediately.

Variation

Substitute tagliatelle for the tagliolini.

Tagliolini con le fave

Tagliolini with Fava Beans

Fresh fava beans in their pods are widely available in supermarkets in spring and summer. The smaller, younger beans are most tender. This dish calls for fresh beans that have been shelled and cooked. Half of them are left in their inner peel and half are peeled, making for an interesting contrast in texture.

Serves 4 to 6

Tips

To cook fresh fava beans, first shell them by opening the pods along the seams and popping out the beans. Add shelled beans to boiling salted water and cook for 15 minutes. Drain and plunge into a bowl of ice-cold water. Divide in half. When cool enough to handle, remove the skin from half of the beans. Leave the other half unpeeled.

Remember, when your pasta has finished cooking, you want it to be firm and supple, not soft and mushy. It will cook a bit more from the residual heat after it is drained, and also when you add it to the sauce.

3 tbsp	extra-virgin olive oil	45 mL
½ cup	cooked shelled fava beans (see Tips, left)	125 mL
½ cup	peeled cooked shelled young fava beans	125 mL
¼ cup	dry white Italian wine	50 mL
1 tbsp	salt	15 mL
1 lb	fresh tagliolini (see page 226)	500 g
¼ cup	unsalted butter	50 mL
	Salt and freshly ground white pepper	
¾ cup	grated Parmigiano-Reggiano, divided	175 mL

1. In a covered pasta pot over high heat, bring water to a rapid boil.

2. Meanwhile, in a large sauté pan, heat oil over medium heat. Add fava beans and sauté until sizzling hot. Add wine and cook until reduced by half. Remove pan from heat and set aside.

3. Add salt and tagliolini to the boiling water and cook, uncovered, over high heat until pasta is al dente. Scoop out about 1 cup (250 mL) of the pasta water and set aside. Drain pasta.

4. Return pan to medium heat. Add 2 tbsp (25 mL) of the reserved pasta water and the butter and heat through. Add tagliolini and, using a wooden spoon, toss to coat evenly, adding more pasta water if necessary. Season to taste with salt and pepper. Add half of the Parmigiano-Reggiano and toss well.

5. Transfer to a serving bowl and sprinkle with remaining cheese. Serve immediately.

Variations

If fresh fava beans are unavailable, substitute fresh lima beans or cut (1 inch/2.5 cm) green or yellow wax beans. I am not a fan of the flavor and texture of frozen fava beans, despite their convenience.

Substitute tagliatelle for the tagliolini.

Tagliolini with Asparagus

This is quick and easy and because the asparagus is cut into pieces, it looks like there are twice as many asparagus tips as there really are. Pencil-thin asparagus is easy to use because you never have to peel the stems, which is often the case with more mature asparagus. And the fiber in the skin is very healthy. Can you use larger asparagus? Of course — just trim off any woody ends and peel the stalks if they look tough and fibrous.

Serves 4 to 6

Tips

I usually season my sauces in the initial stages of cooking so the flavors have time to bloom. I always taste the final product and, if necessary, add more salt and pepper just before serving.

I always use unsalted butter because it adds fresh flavor but not extra salt to a dish.

3 tbsp	extra-virgin olive oil	45 mL
2 cups	sliced (2½ inches/6 cm) pencil-thin asparagus	500 mL
	Salt and freshly ground white pepper	
¼ cup	dry white Italian wine	50 mL
1 tbsp	salt	15 mL
1 lb	fresh tagliolini (see page 226)	500 g
4 tbsp	unsalted butter	60 mL
¾ cup	grated Parmigiano-Reggiano, divided	175 mL

1. In a covered pasta pot over high heat, bring water to a rapid boil.

2. Meanwhile, in a large sauté pan, heat oil over medium-high heat. Add asparagus and cook, stirring, until tender-crisp, about 3 minutes. Season to taste with salt and pepper. Add wine and cook until reduced by half. Remove from heat and set aside.

3. Add salt and tagliolini to the boiling water and cook, uncovered, over high heat until pasta is almost al dente. Scoop out about 1 cup (250 mL) of the pasta water and set aside. Drain pasta.

4. Return sauté pan to medium heat. Add 2 tbsp (25 mL) of the reserved pasta cooking water and the butter and heat through. Add tagliolini and, using a wooden spoon, toss to coat evenly, adding more pasta water if necessary. Season to taste with salt and pepper and remove from heat. Add half of the Parmigiano-Reggiano and toss well.

5. Transfer to a serving bowl and sprinkle with remaining cheese. Serve immediately.

Variation

Substitute tagliatelle for the tagliolini.

Tagliolini alla mozzarella

Tagliolini with Buffalo Mozzarella

Although I named this recipe for mozzarella di bufala, or buffalo mozzarella, the king of soft Italian cheeses (see below), it is an expensive ingredient. So use it only if you want to take this dish over the top. Otherwise, use fresh water-packed domestic cow's-milk mozzarella.

Serves 4 to 6

Tips

When mozzarella is referred to in Italy, it can mean only mozzarella di bufala, or buffalo-milk mozzarella. All other soft cheeses that are similarly produced must be called fiore di latte, not mozzarella.

One 7-oz (210 g) tub of water-packed mozzarella usually holds one ball (approx. 5 oz/150 g) of mozzarella, which yields 2¼ cups (550 mL) of diced mozzarella.

2¼ cups	diced buffalo or soft cow's-milk mozzarella (see Tips, left)	550 mL
¼ cup	diced unsalted butter	50 mL
	Salt and freshly ground white pepper	
1 tbsp	salt	15 mL
1 lb	fresh tagliolini (see page 226)	500 g
6 tbsp	grated Parmigiano-Reggiano	90 mL
½ cup	hand-torn fresh basil leaves	125 mL

1. In a covered pasta pot over high heat, bring water to a rapid boil.

2. Meanwhile, in a mixing bowl, combine mozzarella, butter and salt and pepper to taste. Stir to mix, and set aside.

3. Add salt and tagliolini to the boiling water and cook, uncovered, over high heat until pasta is al dente. Scoop out about 1 cup (250 mL) of the pasta water and set aside. Drain pasta.

4. Add tagliolini to mozzarella mixture, along with Parmigiano-Reggiano and basil. Using a wooden spoon, toss to coat evenly, adding 2 tbsp (25 mL) of the pasta water if necessary.

5. Transfer to a large serving bowl and serve immediately.

Variation

Substitute tagliatelle for the tagliolini.

Mozzarella

Mozzarella di bufala, the Rolls-Royce of mozzarellas, is a semi-soft white cheese made in Campagnia from the milk of water buffaloes. These intelligent, gentle animals (which are not even remotely related to the American bison) were brought to Italy from Asia in the seventh century. The cheese made from this milk is rich, soft and very flavorful. It is extremely perishable and is exported to a few specialty stores outside Italy in 8-ounce (250 g) balls, vacuum sealed to extend its lifespan. In Italy, buffalo-milk mozzarella also comes braided (treccia) and in small balls (bocconcini).

Mozzarella fior di latte is made from cow's milk. It has a mild, fresh taste but is not as soft as mozzarella di bufala and lacks its richness and distinctive flavor. It is widely produced in Italy and in the United States. Mozzarella affumicata is smoked soft mozzarella; it varies widely in quality and texture. Low-moisture mozzarella made from whole or part-skim milk is widely used in the food-service industry for pizza. It is waxy and mild.

Tagliolini con olive

Tagliolini with Oil-Cured Olives

Oil-cured olives are the least salty and least pungent because they are cured in oil, not salt brine. If you can't get authentic oil-cured olives (the jar or package will say "oil-cured"), use dry-cured olives that have been packed in oil. I prefer black rather than white pepper here because it goes very nicely with the dark olives.

Serves 4 to 6

Tips

Fresh pasta cooks very quickly. When you are ready to cook, have an 8-quart (8 L) pot of boiling water ready. Add the salt, then tip the fresh pasta off its parchment sheet into the boiling water. Stir gently once or twice with a wooden spoon.

For best results grate the cheese yourself, but if time is at a premium, use already grated cheese. Whichever form you choose, just be sure to buy the very best Italian Parmigiano-Reggiano you can find and grate it finely to ensure you have the quantity called for in the recipe.

½ cup	minced pitted oil-cured black olives	125 mL
¼ cup	extra-virgin olive oil	50 mL
¼ tsp	freshly ground black pepper	1 mL
1 tbsp	salt	15 mL
1 lb	fresh tagliolini (see page 226)	500 g
¾ cup	grated Parmigiano-Reggiano, divided	175 mL

1. In a covered pasta pot over high heat, bring water to a rapid boil.
2. Meanwhile, in a mixing bowl, combine olives, olive oil and pepper and mix well. Set aside.
3. Add salt and tagliolini to the boiling water and cook, uncovered, until pasta is al dente. Drain pasta.
4. Add tagliolini to olive mixture. Add half of the Parmigiano-Reggiano and, using a wooden spoon, toss to coat evenly.
5. Transfer to a large serving bowl and sprinkle with remaining cheese. Serve immediately.

Variation
Substitute tagliatelle for the tagliolini.

Tagliatelle con sugo di pollo

Tagliatelle with Chicken-Tomato Sauce

Although tagliatelle — long, slender threads of pasta — are typical of Emilia-Romagna, chicken sauce for pasta is not typical of Italian cooking. Traditionally chickens were not abundant and tended to be saved for roasting. But today there is a huge demand for chicken with pasta, so I have adapted. The cooking time for this sauce is much shorter than for bolognese ragù.

Serves 4 to 6

Tips

White onions are slightly sweeter and less pungent than yellow onions, although cooking tends to mellow both. I like to use white onions in this recipe to complement the mild flavor of the chicken.

Any dry white Italian wine will work well in this recipe, but an Italian wine will help to create a more authentic flavor. In this recipe I'd probably use Pinot Bianco, which is a good basic dry white wine for use in Italian cooking.

3 tbsp	extra-virgin olive oil	45 mL
1/4 cup	diced white onion (see Tips, left)	50 mL
1/4 cup	diced peeled celery	50 mL
1/4 cup	diced trimmed fennel bulb	50 mL
1 tsp	thinly sliced garlic	5 mL
	Salt and freshly ground black pepper	
6	boneless, skinless chicken thighs, diced (1/2 inch/1 cm)	6
1/4 cup	dry white Italian wine (see Tips, left)	50 mL
3 cups	canned crushed Italian tomatoes	750 mL
1 tbsp	salt	15 mL
1 lb	fresh tagliatelle (see page 226)	500 g
3/4 cup	grated Parmigiano-Reggiano, divided	175 mL

1. In a heavy saucepan or Dutch oven, heat oil over high heat. Add onion, celery, fennel and garlic and stir. Season to taste with salt and pepper. Cook, stirring, until vegetables are softened, about 5 minutes. Stir in chicken. Add wine, lower heat to medium and cook until wine is reduced by half. Add tomatoes, reduce heat to low and simmer over low heat for 25 minutes. The consistency should be thick enough to coat the back of a spoon. Using a potato masher or fork, mash chicken into shreds. Remove from heat and set aside.

2. Meanwhile, in a covered pasta pot over high heat, bring water to a rapid boil. Add salt and tagliatelle and cook, uncovered, until pasta is almost al dente. Scoop out about 1 cup (250 mL) of the pasta water and set aside. Drain pasta.

3. In a large sauté pan, heat 2 tbsp (25 mL) of the reserved pasta water over medium heat. Add chicken-tomato sauce and bring to a simmer. Add tagliatelle and, using a wooden spoon, toss to coat evenly, adding more pasta water if necessary. Add half of the Parmigiano-Reggiano and toss well.

4. Transfer to a large serving bowl and sprinkle with remaining cheese. Serve immediately.

Variation

Substitute fettuccine for the tagliatelle.

Tagliatelle al cavolfiore

Tagliatelle with Cauliflower

Because cauliflower is available year-round, you can enjoy this tasty, uncomplicated pasta whenever you wish.

Serves 4 to 6

Tips

Because the cauliflower cooking water is full of flavor, I use it in place of pasta cooking water to increase flavor in this recipe.

Always use a large pot and plenty of water when cooking pasta. To properly cook 1 pound (500 g) of pasta, you'll need a pot with a volume of at least 8 quarts (8 L) so that you can use 6 quarts (6 L) of water.

Never rinse pasta after draining it. The surface starch helps the sauce to cling and is important to producing the best-quality dish.

3 tbsp	extra-virgin olive oil	45 mL
2 cups	diced cauliflower florets	500 mL
1 tsp	thinly sliced garlic	5 mL
	Salt and freshly ground white pepper	
1½ cups	water	375 mL
1 tbsp	salt	15 mL
1 lb	fresh tagliatelle (see page 226)	500 g
¼ cup	unsalted butter	50 mL
¾ cup	grated Parmigiano-Reggiano, divided	175 mL

1. In a covered pasta pot over high heat, bring water to a rapid boil.

2. In a saucepan, heat oil over medium heat. Add cauliflower and garlic and stir. Season to taste with salt and pepper and cook, stirring, for 3 minutes. Add water, cover and simmer until cauliflower is very tender, about 7 minutes. Drain, reserving cooking water. Set cauliflower aside.

3. Add salt and tagliatelle to the boiling water and cook, uncovered, until pasta is almost al dente. Drain pasta.

4. In a large sauté pan over medium heat, combine cauliflower, 2 tbsp (25 mL) of the reserved cauliflower cooking water and the butter. Heat through. Add tagliatelle, season to taste with salt and pepper and, using a wooden spoon, toss to coat evenly, adding more pasta water if necessary. Continue to cook until pasta is al dente, 1 to 2 minutes. Add half of the Parmigiano-Reggiano and toss well.

5. Transfer to a large serving bowl and sprinkle with remaining Parmigiano-Reggiano. Serve immediately.

Variation

Tagliatelle is a long, thin strand pasta that is indigenous to Emilia-Romagna. According to legend it was created in 1487 by Maestro Afriano, a royal chef. He was inspired by the beautiful blonde hair of Lucrezia Borgia on the occasion of her marriage to the Duke of Ferrara, and created the pasta in its image. Substitute fettuccine if you prefer.

Tagliatelle ai porri

Tagliatelle with Leeks

I believe leeks are a great but underutilized ingredient. I love their flavor and vibrant color. In this recipe I use both the white and pale green parts for their color contrast. Why just put them in stocks — especially in spring, when they are abundant? Leeks elevate the flavor of onions. It's that simple luxury again.

Serves 4 to 6

Tip

Leeks can be gritty, so be sure to clean them well before using. To clean leeks, trim off and discard the root end. Cut off the top, leaving about 6 inches (15 cm) of leek. Trim off and discard the dark green outer leaves (use the white and pale green parts only). Cut trimmed leek into 2-inch (5 cm) lengths and cut pieces in half lengthwise. Immerse in a large bowl of cold water, separate leaves, and rinse well to remove sand and grit. Save the trimmings for making stock.

3 tbsp	extra-virgin olive oil	45 mL
1½ cups	diced (½ inch/1 cm) cleaned leeks (see Tip, left)	375 mL
¼ cup	dry white Italian wine	50 mL
	Salt and freshly ground white pepper	
1 tbsp	salt	15 mL
1 lb	fresh tagliatelle (see page 226)	500 g
¼ cup	unsalted butter	50 mL
¾ cup	grated Parmigiano-Reggiano, divided	175 mL

1. In a covered pasta pot over high heat, bring water to a rapid boil.

2. Meanwhile, in a large sauté pan, heat oil over medium heat. Add leeks and stir. Add wine, season to taste with salt and pepper and cook, stirring, until leeks are soft and tender, about 5 minutes. Remove from heat and set aside.

3. Add salt and tagliatelle to the boiling water and cook, uncovered, until pasta is al dente. Scoop out about 1 cup (250 mL) of the pasta water and set aside. Drain pasta.

4. Return sauté pan to medium heat. Add 2 tbsp (25 mL) of the reserved pasta water and the butter. Cook, stirring, until heated through, about 2 minutes. Add tagliatelle and, using a wooden spoon, toss to coat evenly, adding more pasta water if necessary. Add half of the Parmigiano-Reggiano and toss well.

5. Transfer to a large serving bowl and sprinkle with remaining cheese. Serve immediately.

Variation

Substitute fettuccine for the tagliatelle.

Tagliatelle alla bolognese
Tagliatelle with Bolognese Meat Ragù

Perhaps no other Italian ragù is as famous as bolognese sauce — or has so many non-Italian versions. That's not to say that in Italy bolognese is always the same. There are many different variations on the theme, and most Italians think their version (or their mother's or uncle's) is the best. That being said, a bolognese sauce should display certain basic characteristics: the ragù contains vegetables and a very small amount of cream; it calls for veal, pork and chicken livers; and it is braised, so it is not a quick recipe. You can double, triple or quadruple this recipe, portion it into meal sizes and freeze it for up to a month in doubled self-sealing plastic bags. In Italy bolognese is traditionally served with tagliatelle, not spaghetti — or any other kind of strand or string pasta.

Serves 4 to 6

• Preheat oven to 250°F (120°C)

2 tbsp	extra-virgin olive oil	25 mL
¼ cup	finely diced onion	50 mL
¼ cup	finely diced carrot	50 mL
¼ cup	finely diced peeled celery	50 mL
4 oz	lean medium ground veal	125 g
4 oz	trimmed pork shoulder, cubed (½ inch/1 cm)	125 g
¼ cup	diced prosciutto	50 mL
¼ cup	roughly chopped chicken livers	50 mL
	Salt and freshly ground black pepper	
¼ cup	dry Marsala wine	50 mL
1 cup	canned crushed Italian tomatoes	250 mL
3 cups	water	750 mL
¼ cup	heavy or whipping (35%) cream	50 mL
1 tbsp	salt	15 mL
1 lb	fresh tagliatelle (see page 226)	500 g
¾ cup	grated Parmigiano-Reggiano, divided	175 mL

1. In a heavy ovenproof 3-quart (3 L) saucepan or Dutch oven with a tight-fitting lid, heat oil over high heat. Add onion, carrot and celery and cook, stirring, until vegetables are soft and lightly golden, about 5 minutes. Add veal, pork, prosciutto and chicken livers and stir. Season to taste with salt and pepper. Lower heat and simmer for 20 minutes, stirring occasionally to prevent burning. Add Marsala and cook until wine is reduced by half. Add tomatoes and water and bring to a boil.

2. Cover and bake in preheated oven until ragù reduces slightly and is thick and rich, 1½ to 2 hours.

3. Remove from oven and place over low heat. Remove lid and, using two forks, shred the meat. Add cream and simmer slowly, uncovered, to thicken, about 10 minutes. Remove from heat.

4. Meanwhile, in a covered pasta pot over high heat, bring water to a rapid boil. Add salt and tagliatelle and cook, uncovered, until pasta is almost al dente. Scoop out about 1 cup (250 mL) of the pasta water and set aside. Drain pasta.

5. In a large sauté pan, heat 2 tbsp (25 ml) of the reserved pasta water over medium heat. Add ragù and bring to a simmer. Add tagliatelle and continue to cook for about 3 minutes, until pasta is al dente, using a wooden spoon to toss and coat evenly, and adding more pasta water if necessary. Add half of the Parmigiano-Reggiano and toss well.

6. Transfer to a large serving bowl and sprinkle with remaining cheese. Serve immediately.

Variation

Substitute fettuccine for the tagliatelle.

Tagliatelle con carciofi crudo

Tagliatelle with Raw Artichokes

Italians have been cultivating and eating artichokes for centuries. We love them, big and small. In this dish they are served raw, sliced paper-thin on a mandoline. The contrast of textures, flavors and temperature between the delicate cooked noodles and the crisp uncooked artichokes is among my favorites. In the restaurant we shave the baby artichokes directly onto the hot al dente pasta. At home it's easier to first marinate the artichokes in olive oil and lemon juice to keep them from discoloring rapidly.

Serves 4 to 6

Tips

When slices too thin to be made with a knife are called for, an inexpensive Japanese-made plastic mandoline with a steel blade and a safety guard does a fine job of slicing artichokes and other fruits and vegetables.

Artichokes are available year-round but are most flavorful from March to May and then again briefly in October.

1 lb	fresh baby artichokes (10 to 12)	500 g
½ cup	extra-virgin olive oil	125 mL
3 tbsp	fresh lemon juice	45 mL
1 tbsp	salt	15 mL
1 lb	fresh tagliatelle (see page 226)	500 g
¼ cup	unsalted butter	50 mL
	Salt and freshly ground white pepper	
6 tbsp	grated Parmigiano-Reggiano	90 mL

1. In a covered pasta pot over high heat, bring water to a rapid boil.

2. Meanwhile, rinse artichokes under cold running water and, using a sharp knife, slice ½ inch (1 cm) off the top of the cone. Remove the dark green outer leaves by peeling them back and snapping them off at the base. Peel down to the pale green tender layer. Using a sharp knife, trim the stem of any woody parts on the sides and end and trim the base where the outer leaves have been removed. You will be left with a tender pale green baby artichoke with its stem (there is a heart inside but no thistles, hence all is edible).

3. In a bowl, whisk olive oil and lemon juice. Place a mandoline directly over the bowl and slice artichokes paper-thin so that they fall into the bowl, stopping once or twice to toss with a wooden spoon to coat evenly (this prevents discoloring). Set aside.

4. Add salt and tagliatelle to the boiling water and cook, uncovered, over high heat, until pasta is almost al dente. Scoop out about 1 cup (250 mL) of the pasta water and set aside. Drain pasta.

5. In a large sauté pan, heat 2 tbsp (25 mL) of the reserved pasta water over medium heat. Add butter, tagliatelle and salt and pepper to taste. Using a wooden spoon, toss to coat evenly, adding more pasta water if necessary.

6. Transfer tagliatelle to a large serving bowl. Using a slotted spoon, lift artichokes from olive oil mixture, blot quickly on paper toweling to remove excess oil, and distribute evenly over tagliatelle. Sprinkle with Parmigiano-Reggiano and serve immediately.

Variation

Substitute fettuccine for the tagliatelle.

Baby Artichokes

Baby artichokes are not a separate variety but simply a smaller version of conventional artichokes. They don't grow as large and the fibrous central "choke" doesn't have time to develop. When properly trimmed, they are completely edible: the texture is tender and the taste more delicate than that of mature artichokes. Choose small artichokes with undeveloped chokes.

Fettuccine in bianco

Fettuccine with Cream and Parmigiano-Reggiano

Pasta with cream and cheese — what's not to like? This simple, very Italian dish has been widely misinterpreted in American restaurants, which tend to drench the pasta in a heavy cream (béchamel) or cream-and-cheese (Mornay) sauce. Here is a lighter, more authentically Italian interpretation of the dish.

Serves 4 to 6

Tips

I always use unsalted butter because it adds fresh flavor without adding extra salt to the recipe.

When you combine the pasta and the sauce, be sure to toss well and for as long as it takes to coat the pasta evenly with sauce. Don't be afraid to add more pasta water if you feel the results are too dry.

1 tbsp	salt	15 mL
1 lb	fresh fettuccine (see page 226)	500 g
¼ cup	unsalted butter	50 mL
¼ cup	heavy or whipping (35%) cream	50 mL
6 tbsp	grated Parmigiano-Reggiano	90 mL
	Salt and freshly ground white pepper	

1. In a covered pasta pot over high heat, bring water to a rapid boil. Add salt and fettuccine and cook, uncovered, until pasta is almost al dente. Scoop out about 1 cup (250 mL) of the pasta water and set aside. Drain pasta.

2. In a large sauté pan, heat 2 tbsp (25 mL) of the reserved pasta water and the butter, cream and cheese over medium heat. Cook until butter melts. Add fettuccine and, using a wooden spoon, toss to coat evenly, adding more pasta water if necessary. Season to taste with salt and pepper and toss well.

3. Transfer to a large serving bowl and sprinkle with additional freshly ground white pepper. Serve immediately.

Variation

Substitute tagliatelle for the fettuccine.

Fettuccine al radicchio

Fettuccine with Radicchio

● ●

Radicchio is another vegetable that I believe is underutilized. It's great grilled, makes a wonderful addition to salads and adds color, flavor and texture to pasta. So here's a vote of confidence in this colorful, tasty vegetable.

Serves 4 to 6

Tips

Any dry white Italian wine will work well in this recipe. Ideally I'd use Orvieto because, when possible, I like to use wine from the same region as the pasta. The wine region in which Orvieto is produced bridges both Umbria and Lazio, where fettuccine is traditional.

I always use unsalted butter because it adds fresh flavor without adding extra salt to the recipe.

1 tbsp	salt	15 mL
1 lb	fresh fettuccine (see page 226)	500g
3 tbsp	extra-virgin olive oil	15 mL
3 cups	diced cored radicchio	750 mL
¼ cup	dry white Italian wine (see Tips, left)	40 mL
	Salt and freshly ground white pepper	
½ cup	unsalted butter	125 mL
⅔ cup	grated Parmigiano-Reggiano, divided	150 mL

1. In a covered pasta pot over high heat, bring water to a rapid boil. Add salt and fettuccine and cook, uncovered, until pasta is almost al dente. Scoop out about 1 cup (250 mL) of the pasta water and set aside. Drain pasta.

2. In a large sauté pan, heat oil over medium heat. Add radicchio and cook, stirring, until crisp-tender, about 7 minutes. Add wine, season to taste with salt and pepper and cook, stirring constantly, to meld flavors, about 1 minute. Add ¼ cup (50 mL) of the reserved pasta cooking water and the butter and cook, stirring, until butter melts. Add fettuccine and, using a wooden spoon, toss to coat evenly, adding more pasta water if necessary. Add ½ cup (125 mL) of the Parmigiano-Reggiano and toss well.

3. Transfer to a large serving bowl and sprinkle with remaining cheese. Serve immediately.

Variations

Substitute tagliatelle or pappardelle for the fettuccine.

Fettuccine Alfredo

Fettuccine with Parmigiano-Reggiano and Butter

This is the true Fettuccine Alfredo, which was created in Rome. No cream, no heavy cooked cheese sauce — just fresh pasta tossed with butter and cheese. Enough said.

Serves 4 to 6

Tips

For best results grate the cheese yourself, but if time is at a premium, use already grated cheese. Whichever form you choose, just be sure to buy the very best Italian Parmigiano-Reggiano you can find and grate it finely to ensure you have the quantity called for in the recipe.

It's important to continue to cook the pasta while tossing it in the sauce (see More or Less Al Dente, page 12).

1 tbsp	salt	15 mL
1 lb	fresh fettuccine (see page 226)	500 g
¾ cup	unsalted butter	175 mL
2 cups + 2 tbsp	grated Parmigiano-Reggiano, divided	525 mL

Salt and freshly ground white pepper

1. In a covered pasta pot over high heat, bring water to a rapid boil. Add salt and fettuccine and cook, uncovered, until pasta is almost al dente. Scoop out about 1 cup (250 mL) of the pasta water and set aside. Drain pasta.

2. In a large sauté pan, heat 2 tbsp (25 mL) of the reserved pasta water and the butter over medium heat. Cook until butter is melted. Add 1¾ cups (425 mL) of the Parmigiano-Reggiano. Cook, stirring, adding more pasta water as needed in 2 tbsp (25 mL) increments, to make a smooth, thick sauce. Season to taste with salt and pepper.

3. Add fettuccine and continue to cook for about 3 minutes, until pasta is al dente, tossing with a wooden spoon to coat evenly, and adding more pasta water if necessary.

4. Transfer to a serving bowl and sprinkle with remaining cheese. Serve immediately.

Variations

Substitute tagliatelle or pappardelle for the fettuccine.

Fettuccine with Prosciutto and Peas

Fresh English peas in the pod come to market in spring and summer, and they are worth waiting for, especially when used with prosciutto and a little cream and cheese to dress fresh fettuccine. I like the color of frozen green peas, but the flavor and texture aren't the same as fresh. If you can't wait until spring you can use frozen peas, or you can substitute fresh pencil-thin asparagus.

Serves 4 to 6

Tip

If you are using fresh green peas, blanch them first. To blanch peas, cook in boiling, lightly salted water for 4 minutes. Drain, rinse under cold running water, then add to the dish according to directions. If you are using frozen peas, make sure they are defrosted.

12	paper-thin slices prosciutto	12
1 tbsp	salt	15 mL
1 lb	fresh fettuccine (see page 226)	500 g
¾ cup	unsalted butter	175 mL
1 cup	fresh green peas, blanched (see Tip, left), or defrosted frozen green peas	250 mL
½ cup	heavy or whipping (35%) cream	125 mL
	Freshly ground white pepper to taste	
1⅓ cups	grated Parmigiano-Reggiano, divided	325 mL
3	egg yolks, lightly beaten	3

1. Line a large platter, including rim, with prosciutto. Set aside.
2. In a covered pasta pot over high heat, bring water to a rapid boil. Add salt and fettuccine and cook, uncovered, until pasta is almost al dente. Scoop out about 1 cup (250 mL) of the pasta water and set aside. Drain pasta.
3. In a large sauté pan over medium heat, heat 2 tbsp (25 mL) of the reserved pasta water and the butter and peas. Cook, stirring, until butter melts. Add cream, white pepper and 1 cup (250 mL) of the Parmigiano-Reggiano and simmer for 1 minute. Remove from heat.
4. Ladle out about 2 tbsp (25 mL) of the cream mixture (without including peas) and transfer to a small bowl. Add egg yolks and whisk well. Set aside.
5. Add fettuccine to sauté pan and continue to cook for about 3 minutes, until pasta is al dente. Using a wooden spoon, toss to coat evenly, adding more pasta water if necessary. Remove from heat. Add reserved egg yolk mixture (do not return to heat or you will scramble the eggs), and toss to coat evenly while eggs cook in the residual heat.
6. Transfer to prosciutto-lined platter and sprinkle with remaining cheese. Serve immediately.

Variation

Substitute tagliatelle for the fettuccine.

Pappardelle with Pancetta and Fresh Ricotta

Pancetta, from cured pork belly, has a very pronounced and unique flavor, partly because it has been rubbed with black pepper. This dish uses the sweetness and creaminess of fresh ricotta to balance that flavor.

Serves 4 to 6

Tips

Any dry white Italian wine will work well in this recipe. I'd probably use Pinot Bianco, which is a good basic dry white wine for use in Italian cooking.

Remember, when your pasta has finished cooking, you want it to be firm and supple, not soft and mushy. It will cook a bit more from the residual heat after it is drained, and also when you add it to the sauce.

1 cup	fresh whole-milk ricotta	250 mL
4	egg yolks	4
	Salt and freshly ground white pepper	
1 tbsp	salt	15 mL
1 lb	fresh pappardelle (see page 227)	500 g
3 tbsp	extra-virgin olive oil	45 mL
½ cup	diced onion	125 mL
¾ cup	diced pancetta	175 mL
½ cup	dry white Italian wine (see Tips, left)	125 mL
¾ cup	grated Parmigiano-Reggiano, divided	175 mL

1. In a covered pasta pot over high heat, bring water to a rapid boil.

2. In a large bowl combine ricotta, egg yolks and salt and pepper to taste. Mix well and set aside.

3. Add salt and pappardelle to the boiling water and cook, uncovered, until pasta is al dente. Scoop out about 1 cup (250 mL) of the pasta water and set aside. Drain pasta.

4. In a large sauté pan, heat oil over medium heat. Add onion and pancetta and cook, stirring, until lightly browned, about 5 minutes. Add wine and cook until reduced by half. Add 2 tbsp (25 mL) of the reserved pasta water and heat through. Add pappardelle and, using a wooden spoon, toss to coat evenly, adding more pasta water if necessary. Add half of the Parmigiano-Reggiano and toss well. Add to bowl with ricotta mixture and toss well.

5. Transfer to a large serving bowl and sprinkle with remaining cheese. Serve immediately.

Variation

Substitute fettuccine for the pappardelle.

Pappardelle alle noci

Pappardelle with Walnuts

Cooks in Liguria traditionally use a variety of nuts in their sauces, the most famous of which is pesto alla genovese, the famous basil-based concoction, which includes pine nuts. Italians in general use a variety of nuts in sauces other than pesto. Here is a very simple pasta sauce using walnuts, butter and cheese.

Serves 4 to 6

Tips

I recommend using a prepared organic vegetable broth, because organic broths are usually high-quality. If possible, find one that is lower in sodium so you don't risk oversalting the recipe.

The good news is that walnuts are very high in healthy omega-3 fatty acids. The bad news is that these oils tend to go rancid quickly. If you're not using walnuts immediately, keep them in the refrigerator or freezer. Always buy them from a purveyor that has high turnover and taste them before purchasing. If they are bitter, look elsewhere.

3 tbsp	extra-virgin olive oil	45 mL
1 cup	diced walnut meats (see Tips, left)	250 mL
½ cup	dry white Italian wine	125 mL
½ cup	vegetable broth, preferably organic (see Tips, left)	125 mL
1 tbsp	salt	15 mL
1 lb	fresh pappardelle (see page 227)	500 g
¼ cup	unsalted butter	50 mL
	Salt and freshly ground white pepper	
¾ cup	freshly grated Parmigiano-Reggiano, divided	175 mL

1. In a covered pasta pot over high heat, bring water to a rapid boil.

2. Meanwhile, in a large sauté pan, heat oil over medium heat. Add walnuts and cook, stirring, until golden but not browned, about 4 minutes. Add wine and cook until reduced by half. Add broth, reduce heat to low and simmer until walnuts are tender but not brown. Remove from heat and set aside.

3. Add salt and pappardelle to the boiling water and cook, uncovered, until pasta is al dente. Scoop out about 1 cup (250 mL) of the pasta water and set aside. Drain pasta.

4. Return sauté pan to medium heat. Add 2 tbsp (25 mL) of the reserved pasta water and heat through. Add butter, season to taste with salt and pepper and cook until butter melts. Add pappardelle and, using a wooden spoon, toss to coat evenly, adding more pasta water if necessary. Add half of the Parmigiano-Reggiano and toss well.

5. Transfer to a large serving bowl and sprinkle with remaining cheese. Serve immediately.

Variation

Substitute fettuccine for the pappardelle.

Pappardelle con gamberi e piselli

Pappardelle with Shrimp and Peas

Pappardelle is Tuscan in origin, although neighboring regions will argue that they created this wide, ribbon-like pasta. The name comes from the verb pappare, *"to gobble up," which tells you how Italians feel about this pasta.*

Serves 4 to 6

Tips

Don't scrimp on ingredients. Always buy the best quality you can find and afford. It will make a big difference to the results you produce.

I always use unsalted butter because it adds fresh flavor but not extra salt to a recipe.

3 tbsp	extra-virgin olive oil	45 mL
1 tsp	thinly sliced garlic	5 mL
¾ cup	green peas, blanched if fresh, thawed if frozen	175 mL
½ cup	dry white Italian wine	125 mL
½ cup	vegetable broth, preferably organic	125 mL
½ cup	unsalted butter	125 mL
1 tbsp	salt	15 mL
1 lb	fresh pappardelle (see page 227)	500 g
8 oz	peeled, deveined medium shrimp, halved lengthwise	250 g
	Salt and freshly ground white pepper	

1. In a covered pasta pot over high heat, bring water to a rapid boil.
2. Meanwhile, in a large sauté pan, heat oil over medium heat. Add garlic and peas and sauté for 1 minute. Add wine and cook, stirring, until reduced by half. Add vegetable broth and butter, reduce heat to low and cook until peas are tender but not mushy, 1 to 2 minutes. Remove from heat and set aside.
3. Add salt and pappardelle to the boiling water and cook, uncovered, until pasta is al dente. Drain.
4. Return sauté pan to medium heat. Add shrimp and season to taste with salt and pepper. Cook, stirring, until shrimp turn opaque and are just cooked through. Add pappardelle and, using a wooden spoon, toss to coat evenly.
5. Transfer to a large serving bowl. Serve immediately.

Variations

Substitute sliced (2 inches/5 cm) asparagus or fresh fava beans for the peas.

Substitute fresh scallops or crabmeat for the shrimp.

Substitute fettuccine for the pappardelle.

Pappardelle al ragù di maiale

Pappardelle with Pork Ragù

This is a ragù similar to my mom's, but it is easier to make. To let the flavor ripen to its fullest, I recommend making it a day or two in advance, refrigerating it, and then reheating when you are ready to serve it with the pasta. You can double or triple the recipe, portion it into meal sizes and freeze it for one month in doubled self-sealing plastic bags.

Serves 4 to 6

Tip

Any dry red Italian wine will work well in this recipe. My wine of choice would be Primitivo because it comes from southern Italy, where you would also be likely to find this pasta and sauce.

• Preheat oven to 250°F (120°C)

3 tbsp	extra-virgin olive oil	45 mL
¼ cup	diced pancetta	50 mL
¼ cup	diced onion	50 mL
¼ cup	diced carrot	50 mL
¼ cup	diced peeled celery	50 mL
8 oz	cubed (1 inch/2.5 cm) trimmed pork shoulder	250 g
	Salt and freshly ground black pepper	
½ cup	dry red Italian wine (see Tip, left)	125 mL
1 cup	canned crushed Italian tomatoes	250 mL
3 cups	water	750 mL
1 tbsp	salt	15 mL
1 lb	fresh pappardelle (see page 227)	500 g
¾ cup	grated Parmigiano-Reggiano, divided	175 mL

1. In a heavy ovenproof 3-quart (3 L) saucepan or Dutch oven with a tight-fitting lid, heat oil over medium heat. Add pancetta, onion, carrot and celery and cook, stirring, until vegetables are soft and golden, about 7 minutes. Add pork, season to taste with salt and pepper and cook, stirring, until pork is cooked through, about 10 minutes. Add wine and cook until reduced by half. Add tomatoes and water and bring to a boil.

2. Cover and bake in preheated oven until ragù reduces slightly, 2 hours. Remove from oven, uncover and place on very low heat. Continue to simmer, stirring occasionally from the bottom, for 30 minutes, until ragù is thick and rich.

3. In a covered pasta pot over high heat, bring water to a rapid boil. Add salt and pappardelle and cook, uncovered, until pasta is almost al dente. Scoop out about 1 cup (250 mL) of the pasta water and set aside. Drain pasta.

4. Transfer ragù to a large sauté pan. Add 2 tbsp (25 mL) of the reserved pasta water and heat through over medium heat. Using a fork, tear meat into shreds. Add pappardelle and continue to cook for about 3 minutes, until pasta is al dente, using a wooden spoon to coat evenly and adding more pasta water if necessary. Add half of the Parmigiano-Reggiano and toss well.

5. Transfer to a large serving bowl and sprinkle with remaining cheese. Serve immediately.

Variation

Substitute fettuccine for the pappardelle.

Pappardelle with Spring Vegetables

The vegetables in this recipe have only one thing in common: they are all available in the spring. Feel free to substitute an equal quantity of any fresh vegetables, with the exception of beets, which turn everything red, and Swiss chard, which has a slightly bitter taste that is not compatible with the other flavors. Just keep the vegetables close in size or thickness so they cook evenly.

Serves 4 to 6

Tips

To blanch the vegetables for use in this recipe, cook in lightly salted boiling water for 3 minutes. Drain and rinse under cold running water.

Never rinse pasta after draining it. The surface starch helps the sauce to cling and is important to producing the best-quality dish.

3 tbsp	extra-virgin olive oil	45 mL
1 tsp	thinly sliced garlic	5 mL
½ cup	sliced (2 inches/5 cm) pencil-thin asparagus, blanched (see Tips, left)	125 mL
½ cup	green peas, blanched if fresh, thawed if frozen	125 mL
½ cup	shelled fresh fava beans, blanched and skinned	125 mL
½ cup	diagonally sliced baby carrots	125 mL
	Salt and freshly ground white pepper	
½ cup	dry white Italian wine	125 mL
1 tbsp	salt	15 mL
1 lb	fresh pappardelle (see page 227)	500 g
½ cup	unsalted butter	125 mL
¾ cup	grated Parmigiano-Reggiano, divided	175 mL

1. In a covered pasta pot over high heat, bring water to a rapid boil.

2. Meanwhile, in a large sauté pan, heat oil over medium heat. Add garlic, asparagus, peas, fava beans and carrots and sauté, stirring, until vegetables are tender but not browned, about 7 minutes. Season to taste with salt and pepper and cook, stirring, for 2 minutes to meld flavors. Add wine and cook until reduced by half. Remove from heat and set aside.

3. Add salt and pappardelle to the boiling water and cook until pasta is almost al dente. Scoop out about 1 cup (250 mL) of the pasta water and set aside. Drain pasta.

4. Return sauté pan to medium heat. Add 2 tbsp (25 mL) of the reserved pasta water and heat through. Add butter and season to taste with salt and pepper. Add pappardelle and, using a wooden spoon, toss to coat evenly, adding more pasta water if necessary. Add half of the Parmigiano-Reggiano and toss well.

5. Transfer to a large serving bowl and sprinkle with remaining cheese. Serve immediately.

Variations

Substitute fresh lima beans for the fava beans.

Substitute fettuccine for the pappardelle.

Stracci al profumo di menta

Stracci with Tomato-Mint Sauce

Although this recipe is traditionally Italian, it may seem exotic because it uses mint rather than basil. Mint is a souvenir of the Moors, who occupied parts of southern Italy for centuries. Mint is treated as a secondary herb in Western cooking and doesn't get the respect it deserves, but in this recipe, in combination with tomatoes, it takes the pasta to another dimension.

Serves 4 to 6

Tip

For best results grate the cheese yourself, but if time is at a premium, use already grated cheese. Whichever form you choose, just be sure to buy the very best Italian Parmigiano-Reggiano you can find and grate it finely to ensure you have the quantity called for in the recipe.

3 tbsp	extra-virgin olive oil	45 mL
1 tsp	thinly sliced garlic	5 mL
¼ cup	dry white Italian wine	50 mL
4 tbsp	mint leaves, divided	60 mL
1¼ cups	canned crushed Italian tomatoes	300 mL
	Salt and freshly ground black pepper	
1 tbsp	salt	15 mL
1 lb	fresh stracci (see page 227)	500 g
6 tbsp	grated Parmigiano-Reggiano	90 mL

1. In a covered pasta pot over high heat, bring water to a rapid boil.

2. Meanwhile, in a large sauté pan, heat oil over medium heat. Add garlic and cook, stirring, until translucent but not browned, 2 to 3 minutes. Add wine, half of the mint, and tomatoes. Reduce heat to low and cook, stirring, until sauce thickens slightly, about 10 minutes. Season to taste with salt and pepper. Remove from heat and set aside.

3. Add salt and stracci to the boiling water and cook, uncovered, until pasta is al dente. Drain pasta.

4. Return sauté pan to medium heat until sauce is heated through Add stracci and, using a wooden spoon, toss to coat evenly.

5. Transfer to a large serving bowl and sprinkle with Parmigiano-Reggiano and remaining mint. Serve immediately.

Variation

Substitute pappardelle for the stracci.

Stracci e ceci

Stracci with Chickpeas

This savory pasta depends on the synergy between the fresh vegetables and the dried tomatoes and beans for its comforting flavor. Canned chickpeas are convenient if you don't have time to soak and cook your own. Look for those with the least amount of sodium and no added flavors or ingredients, and be sure to rinse them well before using.

Serves 4 to 6

Tip

Use dry-packed, not oil-packed, sun-dried tomatoes, preferably imported from Italy. I prefer dry-packed because they don't add extra oil to the recipe. Usually sun-dried tomatoes need to be rehydrated in water, but in this recipe they rehydrate while they are cooking in the sauce.

3 tbsp	extra-virgin olive oil	45 mL
1 tbsp	thinly sliced garlic	15 mL
2 tbsp	diced white onion	25 mL
2 tbsp	diced peeled celery	25 mL
2 tbsp	diced carrot	25 mL
1 tbsp	minced sun-dried tomato	15 mL
2 tbsp	dry white Italian wine	25 mL
1½ cups	cooked chickpeas, rinsed and drained	375 mL
1 cup	water	250 mL
	Salt and freshly ground white pepper	
1 tbsp	salt	15 mL
1 lb	fresh stracci (see page 227)	500 g
6 tbsp	grated Parmigiano-Reggiano	90 mL

1. In a covered pasta pot over high heat, bring water to a rapid boil.

2. Meanwhile, in a large sauté pan, heat oil over medium heat. Add garlic, onion, celery, carrot and sun-dried tomato and cook, stirring, until vegetables are softened, about 7 minutes. Add wine, chickpeas and water. Reduce heat and simmer, stirring occasionally, until thick and stew-like, 10 to 12 minutes. Season to taste with salt and pepper. Remove from heat and set aside.

3. Add salt and stracci to the boiling water and cook, uncovered, until pasta is al dente. Drain pasta.

4. Return sauté pan to element and cook, stirring, until heated through. Add stracci and, using a wooden spoon, toss to coat evenly.

5. Transfer to a large serving bowl and sprinkle with Parmigiano-Reggiano. Serve immediately.

Variation

Substitute pappardelle for the stracci.

Stracci con cimi di rape

Stracci with Broccoli Rabe

Broccoli rabe, also called rapini, is a popular southern Italian vegetable with a pleasantly bitter flavor. When used in pasta, it is traditionally combined with orecchiette, but it makes an interesting combination with stracci. In this recipe, as the broccoli rabe cooks it loses some of its vibrant green color, but what it loses in color it gains in flavor.

Serves 4 to 6

Tips

The broccoli rabe ends up looking like it is very finely chopped, but slicing it gives a more uniform result than would chopping it on a cutting board.

The Italian red chile, which is medium hot and slightly sweet, is not available here, but a good substitute is the California-grown red finger chile (also called Dutch or Holland chile) or the red Fresno. In a pinch you can use a ripe red jalapeño or cayenne chile, both of which are much hotter. If you're using these, mince them and reduce the quantity to about ¼ tsp (1 mL).

3 tbsp	extra-virgin olive oil	45 mL
1 tbsp	thinly sliced garlic	15 mL
1 lb	broccoli rabe, trimmed and sliced horizontally ¼ inch (0.5 cm) thick (see Tips, left)	500 g
½ tsp	thinly sliced fresh red finger chile (see Tips, left)	2 mL
	Salt and freshly ground black pepper	
½ cup	water	125 mL
1 tbsp	salt	15 mL
1 lb	fresh stracci (see page 227)	500 g
¾ cup	freshly grated Parmigiano-Reggiano, divided	175 mL

1. In a covered pasta pot over high heat, bring water to a rapid boil.

2. Meanwhile, in a large sauté pan, heat oil over medium heat. Add garlic and cook until translucent but not browned, 2 to 3 minutes. Add broccoli rabe and chile, season to taste with salt and pepper and add water. Reduce heat to low and simmer until broccoli rabe is tender, about 7 minutes. Remove from heat and set aside.

3. Add salt and stracci to the boiling water and cook, uncovered, until pasta is al dente. Scoop out about 1 cup (250 mL) of the pasta water and set aside. Drain pasta.

4. Return sauté pan to medium heat. Add ¼ cup (50 mL) of the reserved pasta water and heat through. Add stracci and continue to cook while tossing with a wooden spoon to coat evenly, adding more pasta water if necessary. Add half of the Parmigiano-Reggiano and toss well.

5. Transfer to a large serving bowl and sprinkle with remaining cheese. Serve immediately.

Variation

Substitute pappardelle for the stracci.

Stracci alle vongole

Stracci with Clams

The clams eaten in Italy are usually thin-shelled, very small and tender, and take only moments to cook. In America our clams are thick-shelled, larger and good for soups and chowders. Because restaurant customers really want clams and pasta, we chefs adapt traditional recipes to suit the clams that are available. Outside of Italy that usually means using small littleneck clams. And please enjoy this without cheese.

Serves 4 to 6

Tips

Purchase clams with shells that are intact, not broken, cracked or chipped. Shells should be tightly closed. Store them in a cool area of the refrigerator, unwrapped so they can breathe. Just before cooking, soak the clams for 30 minutes in 2 tbsp (25 mL) salt dissolved in 2 quarts (2 L) water — this allows them to filter sand out of their shells. Lift out of the water, scrub shells with a strong brush and transfer to a colander. Rinse well under tap water.

It's imperative to get fresh clams from a reputable fish market. Purchase the smallest available, probably littleneck clams.

½ cup	extra-virgin olive oil, divided	125 mL
2 tbsp	thinly sliced garlic	25 mL
1 tbsp	thinly sliced red finger chile (see Tips, page 264)	15 mL
	Salt and freshly ground black pepper	
24	fresh clams, cleaned (see Tips, left)	24
2 cups	dry white Italian wine	500 mL
1 tbsp	salt	15 mL
1 lb	fresh stracci (see page 227)	500 g
2 tbsp	diced frozen clam meat, thawed	25 mL
1 tbsp	unsalted butter	15 mL
2 tbsp	roughly chopped Italian parsley leaves	25 mL

1. In a covered pasta pot over high heat, bring water to a rapid boil.

2. Meanwhile, in a large sauté pan, heat 6 tbsp (90 mL) of the oil over medium heat. Add garlic, chile and salt and pepper to taste and cook, stirring, until translucent but not browned, 2 to 3 minutes. Add fresh clams (in their shells) and wine. Cover and cook until clams have opened. Discard any clams that do not open. Remove from heat and set aside, covered.

3. Add salt and stracci to the boiling water and cook, uncovered, until pasta is almost al dente. Scoop out about 1 cup (250 mL) of the pasta water and set aside. Drain pasta.

4. Return sauté pan to medium heat. Add 2 tbsp (25 mL) of the reserved pasta water and heat through. Add clam meat, butter, remaining olive oil and parsley. Cook, stirring, until clam meat is cooked through, about 10 minutes. Add stracci and, using a wooden spoon, toss to coat evenly, adding more pasta water if necessary.

5. Transfer to a large serving bowl and sprinkle with additional freshly ground black pepper. Serve immediately.

Variations

Frozen clam meat is available from fish markets. If it is not available, substitute chopped drained canned clams.

Substitute pappardelle for the stracci.

Stracci with Oven-Roasted Mushrooms

Oven-roasted mushrooms have a deep and delicious flavor. This is especially true of portobello mushrooms. In this recipe you can substitute other mushrooms, such as white button, cremini or even the very expensive porcini, but please stay within the European market basket. Shiitake mushrooms are too Asian in flavor.

Serves 4 to 6

Tip

To prepare the mushrooms, remove all dirt and grit. Separate caps from stems and cut caps into quarters. Trim off and discard woody stem ends and cut stems vertically into 4 equal pieces.

- Preheat oven to 450°F (230°C)
- Rimmed baking sheet

½ cup	extra-virgin olive oil	125 mL
¼ cup	balsamic vinegar	50 mL
1 tbsp	thinly sliced garlic	15 mL
¼ tsp	salt	1 mL
⅛ tsp	freshly ground black pepper	0.5 mL
1 lb	fresh portobello mushrooms, trimmed and quartered (see Tip, left)	500 g
1 tbsp	salt	15 mL
1 lb	fresh stracci (see page 227)	500 g
¼ cup	unsalted butter	50 mL
¾ cup	Parmigiano-Reggiano, divided	175 mL

1. In a covered pasta pot over high heat, bring water to a rapid boil.

2. In a bowl combine olive oil, balsamic vinegar, garlic, salt and pepper. Whisk to blend. Add prepared mushrooms and toss to coat evenly. Using a slotted spoon, transfer to baking sheet and bake in preheated oven until mushrooms have darkened and released some of their juices, about 15 minutes. Remove from oven and let cool to room temperature. Slice into ¼-inch (0.5 cm) strips and set aside.

3. Meanwhile, add salt and stracci to the boiling water and cook until pasta is almost al dente. Scoop out about 1 cup (250 mL) of the pasta water and set aside. Drain pasta.

4. In a large sauté pan, heat ¼ cup (50 mL) of the reserved pasta water over medium heat. Add reserved mushrooms and cook, stirring, until heated through. Add stracci and, using a wooden spoon, toss to coat evenly, adding more pasta water if necessary. Add half of the Parmigiano-Reggiano and toss well.

5. Transfer to a large serving bowl and sprinkle with remaining cheese. Serve immediately.

Variation

Substitute pappardelle for the stracci.

Quadrati with Calamari Ragù

In terms of "doneness," calamari is a matter of personal preference. If you like it tender and just cooked through, the cooking time is very brief. But if you like it well-done, you must cook it for a very long time. In this recipe it is just cooked through. The flavors are bold — garlic, chile, tomato — and complement the flavor and color of the calamari.

Serves 4 to 6

Tips

If you prefer, use just calamari rings in this recipe rather than rings and tentacles.

If using frozen calamari rings, first defrost them completely.

5 tbsp	extra-virgin olive oil, divided	70 mL
1 tsp	thinly sliced garlic	5 mL
¼ tsp	thinly sliced red finger chile (see Tips, page 264)	1 mL
½ cup	dry white Italian wine, divided	125 mL
1½ cups	canned crushed Italian tomatoes	375 mL
	Salt and freshly ground black pepper	
1 tbsp	salt	15 mL
1 lb	fresh quadrati (see page 227)	500 g
8 oz	calamari tubes, cut into ½-inch (1 cm) rings, and tentacles (see Tips, left)	250 g
2 tbsp	hand-torn basil leaves	25 mL

1. In a covered pasta pot over high heat, bring water to a rapid boil.

2. Meanwhile, in a saucepan, heat 3 tbsp (45 mL) of the oil over medium heat. Add garlic and cook, stirring with a wooden spoon, until translucent but not brown, 2 to 3 minutes. Add chile and ¼ cup (50 mL) of the wine and simmer until wine is reduced by half. Reduce heat to low, add tomatoes and salt and pepper to taste and simmer until sauce is thick enough to lightly coat the back of a spoon. Remove from heat and set aside.

3. While sauce is simmering, add salt and quadrati to the boiling water and cook, uncovered, over high heat until pasta is almost al dente. Scoop out about 1 cup (250 mL) of the pasta water and set aside. Drain pasta.

4. In a large, heavy sauté pan, heat remaining 2 tbsp (25 mL) oil over medium heat. Add calamari and sauté for 1 minute. Add remaining ¼ cup (50 mL) wine and the basil and simmer for 1 minute. Add reserved tomato sauce and increase heat to high. Add quadrati and continue to cook for about 3 minutes, until pasta is al dente, using a wooden spoon to coat evenly, and adding more pasta water if necessary.

5. Transfer to a large serving bowl and serve immediately.

Variation

Substitute maltagliati for the quadrati.

Quadrati di pasta fresca alla peperonata

Quadrati with Pepper Ragù

This is a colorful, good-looking and good-tasting pasta. The peppers are not skinned, which is in keeping with the rustic nature of the dish.

Serves 4 to 6

Tip

When dicing the peppers, cut them small — about ½ inch (1 cm) — but don't worry about being precise. A slightly irregular cut is more pleasing in this recipe.

3 tbsp	extra-virgin olive oil	45 mL
1 tsp	thinly sliced garlic	5 mL
¼ cup	finely diced onion	50 mL
¼ cup	finely diced red bell pepper	50 mL
¼ cup	finely diced green bell pepper	50 mL
¼ cup	finely diced yellow bell pepper	50 mL
½ cup	dry white Italian wine	125 mL
1 cup	canned crushed Italian tomatoes	250 mL
2 tbsp	hand-torn basil leaves	25 mL
	Salt and freshly ground black pepper	
1 tbsp	salt	15 mL
1 lb	fresh quadrati (see page 227)	500 g
¾ cup	grated Parmigiano-Reggiano, divided	375 mL

1. In a covered pasta pot over high heat, bring water to a rapid boil.

2. In a large sauté pan, heat oil over medium heat. Add garlic, onion and bell peppers and cook, stirring, until vegetables are soft, about 7 minutes. Add wine, tomatoes and basil, reduce heat to low and simmer until mixture thickens slightly, about 10 minutes. Season to taste with salt and pepper. Remove from heat and set aside.

3. Add salt and quadrati to the boiling water and cook, uncovered, over high heat until pasta is almost al dente. Scoop out about 1 cup (250 mL) of the pasta water and set aside. Drain pasta.

4. Return sauté pan to heat and add 2 tbsp (25 mL) of the reserved pasta water. Simmer for 2 minutes. Add quadrati and continue to cook for about 3 minutes, until pasta is al dente, using a wooden spoon to coat evenly, and adding more pasta water if necessary. Add half of the Parmigiano-Reggiano and toss well.

5. Transfer to a large serving bowl and sprinkle with remaining cheese. Serve immediately.

Variation

Substitute maltagliati for the quadrati.

Bell Peppers

Although they are available all year round, bell peppers are most abundant in August and September. Green and purple bell peppers have a slightly bitter flavor. Red, orange and yellow peppers are fruity and sweeter. All are rich sources of vitamins C, A and B_6 and folic acid, and red peppers contain lycopene, a powerful antioxidant. Bell peppers originated in South America around 5000 B.C. and were carried throughout the world by Spanish and Portuguese explorers.

Quadrati di pasta fresca con lenticche

Quadrati with Lentils

This cold-weather dish reminds me of Umbria, where there is a culture of cooking and eating lentils. There they enjoy the tiny, tender lentils grown in Castelluccio that, although very delicate, still hold their shape during cooking.

Serves 4 to 6

Tips

If you can't get Italian lentils, use green or brown ones. Don't use red or yellow Indian lentils, which will not hold their shape.

Any dry red Italian wine will work well in this recipe. Here my wine of choice would be Chianti, because it comes from the same general area in north-central Italy as the lentils: Castelluccio lentils are grown in Umbria and Chianti is produced in neighboring Tuscany.

In this recipe the pasta is cooked to just under al dente because it will finish cooking in the sauce, which also helps meld the flavors.

3 tbsp	extra-virgin olive oil	45 mL
2 tbsp	diced pancetta	25 mL
¼ cup	finely diced onion	50 mL
¼ cup	finely diced peeled celery	50 mL
½ cup	dry red Italian wine (see Tips, left)	125 mL
1 cup	rinsed lentils, preferably Italian (see Tips, left)	250 mL
¼ tsp	chopped fresh rosemary leaves	1 mL
1 tbsp	tomato paste	15 mL
3 cups	water	750 mL
1 tbsp	salt	15 mL
1 lb	fresh quadrati (see page 227)	500 g
	Salt and freshly ground black pepper	
¾ cup	grated Pecorino Romano, divided	175 mL

1. In a covered pasta pot over high heat, bring water to a rapid boil.

2. In a large sauté pan, heat oil over medium heat. Add pancetta, onion and celery and cook, stirring, until vegetables are soft, about 5 minutes. Add wine and cook until reduced by half. Add lentils, rosemary, tomato paste and water. Reduce heat to low, cover and simmer until lentils are tender, 20 to 25 minutes. Remove from heat and set aside.

3. Meanwhile, add salt and quadrati to the boiling water and cook, uncovered, over high heat until almost al dente. Scoop out about 1 cup (250 mL) of the pasta water and set aside. Drain pasta.

4. Return sauté pan to medium heat and simmer until heated through, about 2 minutes. Add quadrati and continue to cook for about 3 minutes, until pasta is al dente, using a wooden spoon to toss and coat evenly, and adding more pasta water if necessary. Season to taste with salt and pepper. Add half of the Pecorino Romano and toss well.

5. Transfer to a large serving bowl and sprinkle with remaining cheese. Serve immediately.

Variation

Substitute maltagliati for the quadrati.

Quadrati di pasta fresca con cozze

Quadrati with Mussels

Restaurant customers really want pasta and mussels — it's one of the most popular pastas. If you cook at home with fresh mussels, it is essential to get the freshest you can buy. They have a short shelf life once they are harvested, so either buy them from a fish market you trust or buy frozen-in-the-shell mussels, which are processed quickly and ensure a safe food experience. Even if it's made with good frozen mussels, this dish is very tasty.

Serves 4 to 6

Tips

Purchase mussels with whole, unbroken, unchipped shells that are tightly closed. Store in a cool place in the refrigerator, uncovered so they can breathe (an oblong glass baking dish in the bottom of the refrigerator is fine). Mussels sometimes have byssal threads attached to their shell, known as the "beard"; these need to be removed before using. Brush any sand, barnacles or attachments from the shells with a stiff brush. Rinse under tap water.

If you can't find good fresh mussels, substitute ones that have been frozen in the shell. Defrost before adding to the recipe.

7 tbsp	extra-virgin olive oil, divided	100 mL
1 tbsp	thinly sliced garlic	15 mL
2 lbs	mussels, cleaned and scrubbed (see Tips, left)	1 kg
1½ cups	dry white Italian wine	375 mL
½ cup	drained canned diced Italian tomatoes	125 mL
	Salt and freshly ground black pepper	
1 tbsp	salt	15 mL
1 lb	fresh quadrati (see page 227)	500 g
2 tbsp	roughly chopped Italian parsley leaves	25 mL

1. In a covered pasta pot over high heat, bring water to a rapid boil.

2. Meanwhile, in a heavy 6-quart (6 L) sauté pan, heat 5 tbsp (75 mL) of the oil over medium heat. Add garlic and cook, stirring, until translucent but not browned, 2 to 3 minutes. Add mussels, wine, tomatoes and salt and pepper to taste. Cover and cook until mussels have opened. Discard any mussels that do not open. Remove from heat and set aside.

3. Add salt and quadrati to the boiling water and cook, uncovered, until pasta is al dente. Scoop out about 1 cup (250 mL) of the pasta water and set aside. Drain pasta.

4. Return sauté pan to high heat, add quadrati and continue to cook while tossing with a wooden spoon to coat evenly, adding more pasta water if necessary. Add remaining 2 tbsp (25 mL) oil and the parsley and toss well.

5. Transfer to a large serving bowl. Serve immediately.

Variation

Substitute maltagliati for the quadrati.

Quadrati di pasta fresca alla rucola con pecorino

Quadrati with Arugula and Pecorino

This dish calls for the second most widely used cheese in Italy — Pecorino Romano, a sheep's-milk cheese with a nutty flavor. It is aged for six months and is less expensive than Parmigiano-Reggiano, which is aged for a minimum of 18 months and sometimes as long as three years. Pecorino Romano has a sharper flavor, which complements the peppery arugula.

Serves 4 to 6

Tips

I like to use unsalted butter in my recipes because it contributes fresh flavor without adding extra salt.

Never rinse pasta after draining it. The surface starch helps the sauce to cling and is important to producing the best-quality dish.

3 tbsp	extra-virgin olive oil	45 mL
1 cup	halved cherry tomatoes	250 mL
	Salt and freshly ground white pepper	
1 tbsp	salt	15 mL
1 lb	fresh quadrati (see page 227)	500 g
¼ cup	unsalted butter	50 mL
2 cups	coarsely chopped fresh arugula	500 mL
¾ cup	grated Pecorino Romano, divided	175 mL

1. In a covered pasta pot over high heat, bring water to a rapid boil.
2. Meanwhile, in a large sauté pan, heat oil over medium heat. Add tomatoes and salt and pepper to taste. Cook, stirring, for 2 minutes, until tomatoes are soft. Remove from heat and set aside.
3. Add salt and quadrati to the boiling water and cook, uncovered, over high heat, until pasta is al dente. Scoop out about 1 cup (250 mL) of the pasta water and set aside. Drain pasta.
4. Return sauté pan to high heat. Add 2 tbsp (25 mL) of the reserved pasta water and the butter. Add quadrati and, using a wooden spoon, toss to coat evenly. Remove from heat. Add arugula and half of the Pecorino Romano and toss well.
5. Transfer to a large serving bowl and sprinkle with remaining cheese. Serve immediately.

Variation

Substitute maltagliati for the quadrati.

Maltagliati with Zucchini and Sun-Dried Tomatoes

The optimum time to make this recipe, even though it uses sun-dried tomatoes, is summer. That's because zucchini are small at that time of year and at their delicate, flavorful best.

Serves 4 to 6

Tips

If your zucchini is large, slice it open, cut out the coarse seeds and discard them before dicing.

I like to tear basil leaves by hand rather than slicing them, because I think they look and taste better.

1 tbsp	salt	15 mL
1 lb	fresh maltagliati (see page 227)	500 g
3 tbsp	extra-virgin olive oil	45 mL
2 tbsp	diced dry-packed sun-dried tomatoes	25 mL
1 cup	diced unpeeled young zucchini (see Tips, left)	250 mL
1/4 cup	hand-torn basil leaves	50 mL
	Salt and freshly ground black pepper	
1/4 cup	shaved Parmigiano-Reggiano	50 mL

1. In a covered pasta pot over high heat, bring water to a rapid boil. Add salt and maltagliati and cook, uncovered, over high heat until pasta is al dente. Scoop out about 1 cup (250 mL) of the pasta water and set aside. Drain pasta.

2. In a large sauté pan, heat oil over medium heat. Add sun-dried tomatoes and 1/2 cup (125 mL) of the reserved pasta cooking water. Simmer until tomatoes are tender and water has reduced by half. Add zucchini, basil and salt and pepper to taste and simmer for 1 to 2 minutes, until basil wilts and zucchini is soft. Add maltagliati and, using a wooden spoon, toss to coat evenly, adding more pasta water if necessary. Season to taste with salt if needed.

3. Transfer to a large serving bowl. Sprinkle Parmigiano-Reggiano shavings evenly over top and finish with a few turns of the pepper mill. Serve immediately.

Variation

Maltagliati means "badly cut" pasta. This roughly shaped pasta probably originated with leftover scraps of fresh pasta that frugal cooks saved and threw into soup. But the rustic shape had its own charm, so eventually they were badly cut on purpose. Substitute quadrati for the maltagliati.

Maltagliati with Egg Sauce and Ricotta

This is a simple but luxurious dish that is completely reliant on good ingredients. The silky egg-and-cheese sauce takes center stage — it's not even the costar. You may substitute mascarpone cheese for the ricotta.

Serves 4 to 6

Tips

If you don't have a double boiler, you can make the egg sauce in a medium stainless steel bowl set snugly over a pot.

Making an egg sauce takes practice. If you do scramble the eggs, strain the sauce through a very fine mesh sieve or re-emulsify it using a hand-held immersion blender. Then add the ricotta. Practice makes perfect.

6	large egg yolks, at room temperature	6
2 tbsp	water, at room temperature	25 mL
½ cup	heavy or whipping (35%) cream, heated almost to boiling point	125 mL
1 tbsp	grated Parmigiano-Reggiano	15 mL
1 tbsp	salt	15 mL
1 lb	fresh maltagliati (see page 227)	500 g
½ cup	fresh whole-milk ricotta (see Variations, below)	125 mL
	Salt and freshly ground white pepper	

1. In a covered pasta pot over high heat, bring water to a rapid boil.

2. Meanwhile, in a double boiler over simmering water, combine egg yolks and water. Whisk constantly until mixture thickens.

3. Add cream and Parmigiano-Reggiano, whisking constantly until mixture coats the back of a spoon. (If the heat is too high, the eggs will coagulate like scrambled eggs; see Tips, left.) Remove from heat and transfer to a 3-quart (3 L) bowl. Set aside.

4. Add salt and maltagliati to the boiling water and cook, uncovered, over high heat until pasta is al dente. Drain pasta.

5. Add maltagliati to egg sauce. Add ricotta and salt to taste. Using a wooden spoon, toss to coat evenly.

6. Transfer to a large serving bowl and sprinkle with pepper. Serve immediately.

Variations

Substitute an equal quantity of mascarpone for the ricotta.

Substitute quadrati for the maltagliati.

Maltagliati with White Beans

This is a simple rustic bean stew. Almost any dried white beans will do — great Northern, cannellini, chickpeas, even dried favas. Don't use black-eyed peas, because they come from outside the Italian market basket and have the wrong flavor profile.

Serves 4 to 6

Tips

Use canned beans instead of cooking your own. Look for those that are low in sodium, and drain and rinse well before using.

Work like a chef. Have all your ingredients ready to go before you actually start to cook (see *Mise en Place*, page 15).

3 tbsp	extra-virgin olive oil	45 mL
1 tbsp	thinly sliced garlic	15 mL
2 tbsp	finely diced onion	25 mL
2 tbsp	finely diced peeled celery	25 mL
2 tbsp	finely diced carrot	25 mL
1 tbsp	finely diced dry-packed sun-dried tomato	15 mL
1 tsp	chopped fresh rosemary leaves	5 mL
	Salt and freshly ground black pepper	
½ cup	dry white Italian wine	125 mL
1 cup	water	250 mL
1½ cups	cooked white beans (see Tips, left)	375 mL
1 tbsp	salt	15 mL
1 lb	fresh maltagliati (see page 227)	500 g
2 tbsp	grated Parmigiano-Reggiano	25 mL

1. In a covered pasta pot over high heat, bring water to a rapid boil.

2. In a large sauté pan, heat oil over medium heat. Add garlic, onion, celery, carrot, sun-dried tomato, rosemary and salt and pepper to taste. Cook, stirring, until vegetables are soft, about 7 minutes. Add wine and simmer until it is almost evaporated. Add water and beans and simmer until slightly thickened, 5 to 10 minutes. Remove from heat and set aside.

3. Add salt and maltagliati to the boiling water and cook, uncovered, over high heat until pasta is al dente. Drain pasta.

4. Return sauté pan to medium heat. Add maltagliati and, using a wooden spoon, toss to coat evenly. Add Parmigiano-Reggiano and toss well.

5. Transfer to a large serving bowl and serve immediately.

Variation

Substitute quadrati for the maltagliati.

Maltagliati al mascarpone rosa

Maltagliati with Tomato-Mascarpone Cream

This combination of ingredients produces a rich, silky sauce that is a pleasant alternative to the standard tomato-and-pasta combination. Mascarpone is a double- or triple-cream cows'-milk cheese, originally from the Lombardy region of Italy and available today in most supermarkets. It appears most often in the infamous dessert tiramisu. But I like to think of mascarpone as the Italian crème fraîche, which is how I use it in this recipe.

Serves 4 to 6

Tips

I like to tear the basil leaves by hand rather than slicing them, because I think they look and taste better.

I always use unsalted butter because it adds fresh flavor without adding extra salt to a recipe.

2 tbsp	extra-virgin olive oil	25 mL
¼ cup	finely diced white onion	50 mL
¼ cup	dry white Italian wine	50 mL
½ cup	canned crushed Italian tomatoes	125 mL
1 tbsp	unsalted butter	15 mL
2 tbsp	mascarpone	25 mL
	Salt and freshly ground white pepper	
1 tbsp	salt	15 mL
1 lb	fresh maltagliati (see page 227)	500 g
6 tbsp	unsalted butter	90 mL
3 tbsp	hand-torn basil leaves	45 mL
½ cup	grated Parmigiano-Reggiano, divided	125 mL

1. In a covered pasta pot over high heat, bring water to a rapid boil.

2. In a saucepan, heat oil over medium heat. Add onion and cook, stirring, until translucent but not browned, 2 to 3 minutes. Add wine, tomatoes and 1 tbsp (15 mL) butter and simmer until sauce thickens slightly, about 5 minutes. Stir in mascarpone and season to taste with salt and pepper. Remove from heat and set aside, stirring often until cool enough to purée in a food processor. Transfer to food processor and process to a creamy consistency. Return to saucepan and keep warm over the lowest possible heat.

3. Add salt and maltagliati to the boiling water and cook, uncovered, over high heat until pasta is al dente. Scoop out about 1 cup (250 mL) of the pasta water and set aside. Drain pasta.

4. Meanwhile, in a large sauté pan, heat 2 tbsp (25 mL) of the reserved pasta water and the butter, basil and 2 tbsp (25 mL) of the Parmigiano-Reggiano over medium heat. Add pasta and, using a wooden spoon, toss to coat evenly.

5. Transfer to a large serving bowl and spoon the warm tomato-mascarpone cream on top. Sprinkle with remaining cheese and serve immediately.

Variation

Substitute quadrati for the maltagliati.

Maltagliati con pomodorini al forno

Maltagliati with Oven-Roasted Cherry Tomatoes

Although cherry tomatoes are now available year-round, in my opinion, in the dead of winter their flavor is not quite as full as it is during the summer. Roasting the tomatoes intensifies their natural flavor — this is true in summer as well. I like to leave them whole because I prefer the texture.

Serves 4 to 6

Tips

Always use a large pot and plenty of water when cooking pasta. To properly cook 1 pound (500 g) of pasta, you'll need a pot with a volume of at least 8 quarts (8 L) so that you can use 6 quarts (6 L) of water.

Never rinse pasta after draining it. The surface starch helps the sauce to cling and is important to producing the best-quality dish.

- Preheat oven to 375°F (190°C)
- Rimmed baking sheet lined with parchment paper

1½ pints	cherry tomatoes	750 mL
¼ cup	extra-virgin olive oil	50 mL
2 tbsp	thinly sliced garlic	25 mL
2 tbsp	chopped Italian parsley leaves	25 mL
2 tbsp	salt, divided	25 mL
1 tsp	freshly ground black pepper	5 mL
1 lb	fresh maltagliati (see page 227)	500 g
3 tbsp	hand-torn basil leaves	45 mL
6 tbsp	freshly grated Parmigiano-Reggiano	90 mL

1. In a covered pasta pot over high heat, bring water to a rapid boil.

2. In a large mixing bowl combine tomatoes, olive oil, garlic, parsley, 1 tbsp (15 mL) of the salt and the pepper and toss well. Place on prepared baking sheet and bake in preheated oven until tomatoes are soft, wrinkled and brown in places, about 25 minutes.

3. Meanwhile, add remaining 1 tbsp (15 mL) of salt and maltagliati to the boiling water and cook, uncovered, over high heat until pasta is al dente. Scoop out about 1 cup (250 mL) of the pasta water and set aside. Drain pasta and transfer to a large mixing bowl.

4. Add roasted tomatoes, basil and Parmigiano-Reggiano to pasta and, using a wooden spoon, toss to coat evenly.

5. Transfer to a large serving bowl and serve immediately.

Variation

Substitute quadrati for the maltagliati.

Baked Pastas: Make Today, Bake Tomorrow

If you like to cook and you like a challenge, then baked pasta is right up your alley. Some baked pastas — using dried pasta — are simple and easy. Others — using fresh homemade pasta — are time-consuming. That being said, nothing else comes close to the aroma, flavor and impact of a freshly baked pasta such as lasagne just out of the oven. It's great for a party and, because people perceive baking as laborious, it looks as though you have been slaving over a hot stove all day. In actual fact, you did most of the work the day before, when you prepared, assembled and refrigerated the lasagne. Baking the next day was a snap.

Year-Round Casseroles

My mom made baked pastas all the time. She was more than a native Italian who brought the cooking traditions of her country with her when she came to America. She was also a great cook, one who became better and better as time went by. Her lasagne was like a pasta pie. It was about 2 inches (15 cm) deep and had five layers of thin homemade pasta sheets interspersed with delicious sauce, meat or vegetables, and cheese. When it came out of the oven, the top was deep golden brown and the air above rippled with residual heat. We could hardly wait for it to become cool enough to eat. She baked it in an earthenware dish the same day she made it.

My mom always made baked pastas in fall and winter. Today ingredients such as cherry tomatoes, eggplant and zucchini — formerly seasonal vegetables — are available year-round, which means you can make many of these recipes whenever the mood strikes. While I am still in favor of using vegetables close to their source and in season, because they have the best flavor, I also think that every now and again it is a welcome indulgence to make something different and unexpected. That would include dishes such as Baked Penne with Shrimp and Peas (see page 294) in late spring, Baked Rigatoni with Radicchio (see page 291) in fall and Baked Fusilli with Creamed Lettuce (see page 292) in the winter.

Low Cost, High Impact

Baked pastas by and large are low-cost and high-impact, which is to say they make a great impression whenever they are served. They are great for parties or as part of a buffet. With a few exceptions (noted in the recipes) I recommend that you prepare and assemble the dish the day before you intend to serve it, then cover, wrap and refrigerate it overnight. When you're ready to serve, just pop it in the oven.

I have arranged the recipes in this chapter in order of difficulty, placing the quickest and easiest first. All can be made with dried pasta, but some can also be made using fresh homemade pasta sheets.

Not Quite Al Dente

All the pasta in these recipes is cooked to almost al dente, because it will continue cooking in the oven as the pasta bakes.

Using Fresh Pasta

Using fresh pasta dough is more time-consuming but the results are well worth it. Is that to say that fresh pasta is better and dried pasta a compromise? Not at all. Dried pasta is a wonderful alternative to labor-intensive fresh pasta sheets, but fresh pasta has the most tender texture and delicate flavor. In the end only you can decide how to spend your time. But I hope you will spend some of it making pasta *al forno* — from the oven.

Refrigerator-to-Oven Baking Dishes

To refrigerate pasta prepared the day before you want to bake it, you will need an ovenproof casserole that can go from cold to hot without breaking. There are many well-designed heavy stainless steel baking dishes on the market, and these are the safest choice. Enameled cast iron is also a good choice because it is attractive and can go from oven to table. However, the manufacturer of one well-known brand informs me that in order to avoid thermal shock and cracking of the enamel surface, you should remove the casserole from the refrigerator and let it sit at room temperature for 30 minutes before placing it in a hot oven. I do not recommend glass, ceramic or earthenware dishes unless you are planning to bake the dish the same day it is assembled.

If you're making lasagne, conchiglione (giant shells), cannelloni or pasta rolls, you will need a rectangular 13- by 9-inch (3 L) baking dish with sides that are 2 inches (5 cm) deep. The gratins and other baked dried pastas require a pan that holds a full pound (500 g) of pasta plus additional ingredients. A 13- by 9-inch (3 L) pan will do, as will any shallow but perhaps different-shaped pan that can hold 14 cups (3.5 L).

Fusilli alla napoletana

Baked Fusilli alla Napoletana

Easy, flavorful and fun, baked fusilli with tomatoes, olives and cheese produces a visually appealing bubbling casserole that makes a particularly good buffet dish. To serve, just dig in with a great big spoon the minute it comes out of the oven. Or bring it to the table and let people help themselves.

Serves 4 to 6

Tips

Approximately 6 oz (175 g) drained mozzarella yields ¾ cup (175 mL).

Cook pasta for baked dishes to almost (that is, firmer than) al dente, because the pasta will continue to cook in the oven with the other ingredients when it is baked.

- Preheat oven to 375°F (190°C)
- 13- by 9- by 2-inch (3 L) baking dish, lightly greased with butter

3 tbsp	extra-virgin olive oil	45 mL
¼ cup	diced onion	50 mL
	Salt and freshly ground black pepper	
1 cup	halved cherry tomatoes, cut horizontally	250 mL
¼ cup	chopped pitted oil-cured black olives	50 mL
3 tbsp	fresh oregano leaves	45 mL
1 tbsp	salt	15 mL
1 lb	dried fusilli	500 g
⅔ cup	grated Parmigiano-Reggiano, divided	150 mL
¾ cup	diced fresh cow's-milk mozzarella or mozzarella di bufala (see Tips, left)	175 mL

1. In a covered pasta pot over high heat, bring water to a rapid boil.

2. Meanwhile, in a large sauté pan, heat oil over medium heat. Add onion and cook, stirring, until soft, about 2 minutes. Season to taste with salt and pepper. Add tomatoes, olives and oregano and cook until tomatoes are soft, about 3 minutes. Remove from heat and set aside.

3. Add salt and fusilli to the boiling water and cook, uncovered, over high heat until pasta is almost al dente. Scoop out about 1 cup (250 mL) of the pasta cooking water and set aside. Drain pasta.

4. Return sauté pan to low heat, add 2 tbsp (25 mL) of the reserved pasta water and the fusilli and, using a wooden spoon, toss to coat evenly, adding more pasta water if necessary. Add 6 tbsp (90 mL) of the Parmigiano-Reggiano and, using a wooden spoon, toss to coat evenly.

5. Sprinkle prepared dish with 2 tbsp (25 mL) of the Parmigiano-Reggiano. Add fusilli mixture and sprinkle remaining Parmigiano-Reggiano and mozzarella evenly over top.

6. Bake in preheated oven until heated through and top is golden brown, about 30 minutes. Remove from oven and serve immediately.

Make Ahead

Complete steps 1 through 5. Cover with plastic wrap and refrigerate overnight. When you're ready to serve, bake in preheated oven, adding 10 to 15 minutes to the baking time.

Maccheroni ai porri con Gorgonzola

Baked Maccheroni with Leeks and Gorgonzola

Imagine macaroni and cheese with the added sweetness of leeks and the rich flavors of melted Italian blue cheese and fresh mozzarella. That's a good description of this sophisticated version of mac and cheese. Toss a salad, open a bottle of good Pinot Bianco and invite some friends.

Serves 4 to 6

Tips

Gorgonzola piccante is aged Gorgonzola. You may substitute regular soft Gorgonzola dolce.

Leeks can be gritty, so be sure to clean them well before using. To clean leeks, trim off and discard the root end. Cut off top, leaving about 6 inches (15 cm) of leek. Trim off and discard dark green outer leaves. Use the white and pale green parts only. Cut trimmed leeks into 2-inch (5 cm) lengths and cut in half vertically. Immerse in a large bowl of cold water, separate leaves, and rinse well to remove sand and grit. Save the trimmings for making stock.

Follow Make Ahead instructions on page 283.

- Preheat oven to 375°F (190°C)
- 13- by 9- by 2-inch (3 L) baking dish, lightly greased with butter

3 tbsp	extra-virgin olive oil	45 mL
¼ cup	diced onion	50 mL
1 cup	diced leeks (see Tips, left)	250 mL
	Salt and freshly ground black pepper	
1 cup	dry white Italian wine	250 mL
½ cup	heavy or whipping (35%) cream	125 mL
¾ cup	Gorgonzola piccante, at room temperature (see Tips, left)	175 mL
1 tbsp	salt	15 mL
1 lb	dried maccheroni (see Variation, below)	500 g
⅔ cup	grated Parmigiano-Reggiano, divided	150 mL
¾ cup	diced fresh cow's-milk mozzarella or mozzarella di bufala	175 mL

1. In a covered pasta pot over high heat, bring water to a rapid boil.

2. In a large sauté pan, heat oil over medium heat. Add onion and leeks cook, stirring, until soft and tender, about 5 minutes. Add salt and pepper to taste. Add wine and cook, stirring, until reduced by half. Reduce heat to low, add cream and simmer for 5 minutes, until slightly thickened. Add Gorgonzola and stir until almost melted. Remove from heat and set aside.

3. Meanwhile, add salt and maccheroni to the boiling water and cook, uncovered, over high heat until pasta is almost al dente. Scoop out about 1 cup (250 mL) of the pasta cooking water and set aside. Drain pasta.

4. Return sauté pan to low heat, add 2 tbsp (25 mL) of the reserved pasta water and maccheroni and, using a wooden spoon, toss to coat evenly, adding more pasta water if necessary. Add 6 tbsp (90 mL) of the Parmigiano-Reggiano and, using wooden spoon, toss to coat evenly.

5. Sprinkle prepared dish with 2 tbsp (25 mL) of the Parmigiano-Reggiano. Add maccheroni mixture and sprinkle remaining Parmigiano-Reggiano and mozzarella evenly over top.

6. Bake in preheated oven until top is golden brown, about 30 minutes.

Variation

Substitute penne for the maccheroni.

Rigatoni integrale con le melanzane al forno

Baked Whole Wheat Rigatoni with Eggplant

Whole wheat pasta and eggplant is a good combination because both have hearty flavor. The highest-quality whole wheat pasta holds up best to baking (see Tips, below).

Serves 4 to 6

Tips

You can recognize high-quality whole wheat pasta by its ingredients — durum whole wheat semolina and salt. It is usually imported from Italy and is, of course, slightly more expensive than domestic whole wheat pasta. It is available in gourmet Italian groceries and online.

Cook pasta for baked dishes to almost (that is, firmer than) al dente, because the pasta will continue to cook in the oven with the other ingredients when it is baked.

- Preheat oven to 375°F (190°C)
- 13- by 9- by 2-inch (3 L) baking dish, lightly greased with butter

6 tbsp	extra-virgin olive oil	90 mL
¼ cup	diced onion	50 mL
1 cup	halved cherry tomatoes	250 mL
2 cups	diced peeled eggplant	500 mL
2 tbsp	hand-torn fresh basil leaves	25 mL
	Salt and freshly ground black pepper	
1 tbsp	salt	15 mL
1 lb	dried whole wheat rigatoni (see Variations)	500 g
⅔ cup	grated Parmigiano-Reggiano, divided	150 mL
¾ cup	diced fresh cow's-milk mozzarella or mozzarella di bufala	175 mL

1. In a covered pasta pot over high heat, bring water to a rapid boil.

2. Meanwhile, in a large sauté pan, heat oil over medium heat. Add onion and tomatoes and cook, stirring, until onion is soft and tender, about 3 minutes. Add eggplant and basil and cook, stirring, until eggplant is soft and tender, about 5 minutes. Season to taste with salt and pepper. Remove from heat and set aside.

3. Add salt and rigatoni to the boiling water and cook, uncovered, over high heat until pasta is almost al dente. Scoop out about 1 cup (250 mL) of the pasta cooking water and set aside. Drain pasta.

4. Return sauté pan to low heat, add 2 tbsp (25 mL) of the reserved pasta water and rigatoni and, using a wooden spoon, toss to coat evenly, adding more pasta water if necessary. Add 6 tbsp (90 mL) of the Parmigiano-Reggiano and toss well.

5. Sprinkle prepared dish with 2 tbsp (25 mL) of the Parmigiano-Reggiano. Add rigatoni mixture and sprinkle remaining Parmigiano-Reggiano and mozzarella evenly over top.

6. Bake in preheated oven until top is golden brown, about 30 minutes. Serve immediately.

Variations

Substitute whole wheat penne or fusilli for the rigatoni.

Make Ahead

Complete steps 1 through 5. Cover with plastic wrap and refrigerate overnight. When you're ready to serve, bake in preheated oven, adding 10 to 15 minutes to the baking time.

Spaghetti al gratin con pomodorini e olive

Baked Spaghetti with Cherry Tomatoes and Oil-Cured Olives

This dish has only three main ingredients: ripe red cherry tomatoes, salty black olives and white pasta. Baked together, they come out of the oven bubbling in a marriage of sweet and salty flavors.

Serves 4 to 6

Tip

Cook pasta for baked dishes to almost (that is, firmer than) al dente, because the pasta will continue to cook in the oven with the other ingredients when it is baked.

- Preheat oven to 375°F (190°C)
- 13- by 9- by 2-inch (3 L) baking dish, lightly greased with butter

6 tbsp	extra-virgin olive oil	90 mL
¼ cup	diced onion	50 mL
1 cup	halved cherry tomatoes	250 mL
½ cup	chopped pitted oil-cured black olives	125 mL
2 tbsp	hand-torn fresh basil leaves	25 mL
	Salt and freshly ground black pepper	
1 tbsp	salt	15 mL
1 lb	dried spaghetti (see Variations, below)	500 g
¼ cup	dry white Italian breadcrumbs, divided	50 mL

1. In a covered pasta pot over high heat, bring water to a rapid boil.

2. Meanwhile, in a large sauté pan, heat oil over medium heat. Add onion and tomatoes. Cook, stirring, until onion is soft, about 3 minutes. Add olives and basil and cook, stirring, to meld flavors, about 2 minutes. Season to taste with salt and pepper. Remove from heat and set aside.

3. Add salt and spaghetti to the boiling water and cook, uncovered, over high heat until pasta is almost al dente. Scoop out about 1 cup (250 mL) of the pasta cooking water and set aside. Drain pasta.

4. Return sauté pan to low heat. Add 2 tbsp (25 mL) of the reserved pasta water and spaghetti and, using pasta tongs, toss to coat evenly, adding more pasta water if necessary.

5. Coat prepared dish with half of the breadcrumbs. Add spaghetti mixture and sprinkle with remaining breadcrumbs.

6. Bake in preheated oven until top is golden brown, about 30 minutes. Serve immediately.

Variations

Substitute perciatelli, bucatini or thick spaghetti for the spaghetti.

Make Ahead

Complete steps 1 through 5. Cover with plastic wrap and refrigerate overnight. When you're ready to serve, bake in preheated oven, adding 10 to 15 minutes to the baking time.

Spaghetti Gratin with Calamari

To keep it tender, calamari need to be cooked either very briefly or for a considerable time. That makes them ideal for a baked pasta casserole, where they are baked after simmering briefly in a tomato sauce. Like all seafood dishes, this casserole is best made and served on the same day, because reheating diminishes the flavor and texture of seafood.

Serves 4 to 6

Tips

Unless you live by the sea, almost all the calamari you buy have been previously frozen. If you're using previously frozen calamari, make sure to purchase them from a quality fish market. Frozen calamari (rings, or rings and tentacles) are widely available in fish markets and at supermarkets, and these are also an acceptable product. Defrost before using in a recipe.

I recommend using good-quality unsalted butter, because it adds flavor but not extra salt to a recipe.

- Preheat oven to 375°F (190°C)
- 13- by 9- by 2-inch (3 L) baking dish, lightly greased with butter

5 tbsp	extra-virgin olive oil, divided	75 mL
1 tsp	thinly sliced garlic	5 mL
1 tsp	thinly sliced red finger chile (see Tips, page 264)	5 mL
1½ cups	calamari rings and tentacles or frozen calamari rings, defrosted	375 mL
1 cup	dry white Italian wine	250 mL
1 cup	canned crushed Italian tomatoes	250 mL
2 tbsp	hand-torn basil leaves	25 mL
	Salt and freshly ground black pepper	
1 tbsp	salt	15 mL
1 lb	dried spaghetti (see Variations, below)	500 g
	Salt and freshly ground black pepper	
¼ cup	dry white Italian breadcrumbs	50 mL

1. In a covered pasta pot over high heat, bring water to a rapid boil.

2. Meanwhile, in a large sauté pan, heat oil over medium heat. Stir in garlic and chile. Add calamari and wine and cook until reduced by half. Add tomatoes and basil and season to taste with salt and pepper. Stir well and reduce heat to low. Simmer slowly until sauce thickens, about 10 minutes. Remove from heat and set aside.

3. While sauce is simmering, add salt and spaghetti to the boiling water and cook, uncovered, over high heat until pasta is almost al dente. Scoop out about 1 cup (250 mL) of the pasta cooking water and set aside. Drain pasta.

4. Return sauté pan to low heat. Add ¼ cup (50 L) of the pasta cooking water and spaghetti and, using pasta tongs, toss to coat evenly, adding more pasta water if necessary. Add remaining 2 tbsp (25 mL) olive oil and season to taste with salt and pepper.

5. Sprinkle prepared dish with half of the breadcrumbs. Add spaghetti mixture and sprinkle with remaining breadcrumbs.

6. Bake in preheated oven until top is golden brown, about 30 minutes. Serve immediately.

Variations

Substitute perciatelli, bucatini or thick spaghetti for the spaghetti.

Perciatelli con zucchini al forno

Baked Perciatelli with Zucchini

Here's a baked pasta dish that can be prepared in late summer, when fresh tomato and zucchini season is coming to an end and both vegetables are ripe and still abundant. Enjoy it on a day when the first nip of fall is in the air.

Serves 4 to 6

Tips

I like to grease the dish with fresh unsalted butter for the flavor it imparts.

Cook pasta for baked dishes to almost (that is, firmer than) al dente, because the pasta will continue to cook in the oven with the other ingredients when it is baked.

- Preheat oven to 375°F (190°C)
- 13- by 9- by 2-inch (3 L) baking dish, lightly greased with butter

6 tbsp	extra-virgin olive oil	90 mL
¼ cup	diced onion	50 mL
1 cup	halved cherry tomatoes	250 mL
2 cups	diced unpeeled zucchini	500 mL
2 tbsp	hand-torn fresh sage leaves	25 mL
	Salt and freshly ground black pepper	
1 tbsp	salt	15 mL
1 lb	dried perciatelli (see Variation, below)	500 g
⅔ cup	grated Parmigiano-Reggiano, divided	150 mL
¾ cup	diced fresh cow's-milk mozzarella or mozzarella di bufala	175 mL

1. In a covered pasta pot over high heat, bring water to a rapid boil.

2. Meanwhile, in a large sauté pan, heat oil over medium heat. Add onion and tomatoes. Cook, stirring, until onion is soft and tender, about 3 minutes. Add zucchini and sage and cook, stirring, until zucchini is soft, about 5 minutes. Season to taste with salt and pepper. Remove from heat and set aside.

3. Add salt and perciatelli to the boiling water and cook, uncovered, over high heat until pasta is almost al dente. Scoop out about 1 cup (250 mL) of the pasta cooking water and set aside. Drain pasta.

4. Return sauté pan to low heat, add 2 tbsp (25 mL) of the reserved pasta water and perciatelli and, using pasta tongs, toss to coat evenly, adding more pasta water if necessary. Add 6 tbsp (90 mL) of the Parmigiano-Reggiano and, using pasta tongs, toss to coat evenly.

5. Sprinkle prepared dish with 2 tbsp (25 mL) of the Parmigiano-Reggiano. Add perciatelli mixture and sprinkle remaining Parmigiano-Reggiano and mozzarella evenly over top.

6. Bake in preheated oven until top is golden brown, about 30 minutes. Remove from oven and serve immediately.

Variation

Substitute thick spaghetti for the perciatelli.

Make Ahead

Complete steps 1 through 5. Cover with plastic wrap and refrigerate overnight. When you're ready to serve, bake in preheated oven, adding 10 to 15 minutes to the baking time.

Baked Capellini with Fresh Ricotta

Delicate in texture, smooth and rich in flavor, this baked pasta is easy to prepare and will appeal to a wide variety of tastes. Capellini are thin strands of pasta, thinner than spaghettini but slightly thicker than angel hair.

Serves 4 to 6

Tip

The beaten eggs are strained through a fine mesh sieve to remove the cordlike white strand (the chalaza) that anchors the yolk in the egg's center. This rarely gets completely emulsified when beaten, and when cooked, it ends up as a tiny firm, gelatinous lump.

- Preheat oven to 375°F (190°C)
- 13- by 9- by 2-inch (3 L) baking dish, lightly greased with butter

1 tbsp	salt	15 mL
1 lb	dried capellini (see Variations, below)	500 g
4 cups	Besciamella Sauce (see recipe, page 289), divided	1 L
9 tbsp	grated Parmigiano-Reggiano, divided	135 mL
	Salt and freshly ground white pepper	
4	large eggs, beaten and strained (see Tip, left)	4
3 tbsp	whole milk	45 mL
¾ cup	fresh whole-milk ricotta	175 mL

1. In a covered pasta pot over high heat, bring water to a rapid boil. Add salt and capellini and cook, uncovered, until pasta is almost al dente. Scoop out about 1 cup (250 mL) of the pasta cooking water and set aside. Drain pasta.

2. In a large sauté pan over low heat, combine ⅓ cup (75 mL) of the reserved pasta water and 2 cups (500 mL) of the besciamella sauce. Bring to a simmer. Add capellini and, using pasta tongs, toss to coat evenly. Add 3 tbsp (45 mL) of the Parmigiano-Reggiano and toss well. Season to taste with salt and pepper.

3. Remove from heat. Add eggs and toss to mix well.

4. Sprinkle prepared dish with 3 tbsp (45 mL) of the Parmigiano-Reggiano. Add capellini mixture. Whisk milk into remaining besciamella sauce and spread evenly on top of capellini. Distribute ricotta equally over top and sprinkle with remaining Parmigiano-Reggiano.

5. Bake in preheated oven until top is golden, about 35 minutes. Serve immediately.

Variations

Substitute vermicelli or thin spaghetti for the capellini.

Besciamella Sauce

Salsa besciamella, or béchamel sauce, appears often in Italian recipes. How did a French sauce become integral to Italian cooking? Italians claim it as their invention, brought to France in 1533 by Caterina de Medici when she married Henry of Orleans, who became king of France. Caterina brought Tuscan cooks, pastry makers and Italian culinary arts and recipes to France with her, among them *salsa besciamella*. The French, of course, claim béchamel sauce as their own, created by the famous French chef François-Pierre de La Varenne (1615-78).

Salsa besciamella

Besciamella Sauce

Besciamella sauce is used in several of my baked pasta recipes, including lasagne. When making besciamella, it is important to cook the flour and butter together but not to brown them, because the finished sauce should be white, delicate in flavor and creamy. After the milk is added, the sauce needs to cook long enough not just to thicken but also to ensure that the flour is completely cooked and no raw flour taste remains. This recipe makes 4 cups (1 L), enough for all the recipes but more than enough for some. You can refrigerate unused besciamella for up to three days. Simply transfer to a glass container and place plastic wrap directly on the surface. Rewarm on the stovetop and use it to create your own versions of crespelle (see page 359) by adding besciamella to fillings you improvise and spooning it on top to bake the crespelle.

Makes about 4 cups (1 L)

¼ cup	clarified butter (see below)	50 mL
½ cup	all-purpose flour, sifted	125 mL
4 cups	whole milk, heated (see Tips, below)	1 L
¾ tsp	salt	3 mL
½ tsp	freshly ground white pepper	2 mL
¼ tsp	freshly grated nutmeg	1 mL

1. In a heavy saucepan, melt clarified butter over medium heat. Gradually add flour, stirring constantly. Reduce heat to low and cook until flour absorbs butter and starts to foam, about 3 minutes. Do not brown.

2. Remove from heat. Whisk in all the milk at once and return to medium-high heat. Season with salt, pepper and nutmeg and cook, stirring constantly, until sauce is fully thickened, up to 25 minutes. Remove from heat and set aside.

Clarified Butter

Why clarify butter? The milk solids present in butter tend to burn at high heat, which means that when unclarified butter is used in cooking, it is subject to burning. To clarify butter, heat 8 oz (250 g) or 1 cup (250 mL) unsalted butter in a small saucepan over medium-low heat until melted. Remove from heat. Allow the milk solids to settle to the bottom and the foam to rise to the top. Let sit for 10 minutes undisturbed. Using a spoon, carefully skim the foam off the top and discard. Pour the clear liquid butter from the middle into a glass container. Discard the milk solids on the bottom. Cover and refrigerate any surplus for up to one week. Makes about ⅔ cup (150 mL).

Tips

When making besciamella, I like to sift the flour after measuring, because it helps to make a smoother sauce.

Heating the milk before adding it to the roux speeds up the cooking. Heat it just until scalded (bubbles form around the edges) either in a microwave over high heat, stirring occasionally to ensure the bottom doesn't burn.

To thin besciamella, whisk in milk or pasta-cooking water in 1 tbsp (15 mL) increments until the desired texture is reached.

Maccheroni con cavolfiore gratinate

Gratin of Maccheroni with Cauliflower

Maccheroni is white, besciamella sauce is white, cauliflower is white and Parmigiano-Reggiano is whitish. However, four whites don't make a wrong in this casserole, because each element has its own flavor. The besciamella is creamy and neutral, the cauliflower (which has the most subtle flavor in the cabbage family) is sweet and savory, and the Parmigiano is sharp and salty. It's a great combination.

Serves 4 to 6

Tip

For best results grate the cheese yourself, but if time is at a premium, use already grated cheese. Whichever form you choose, just be sure to buy the very best Italian Parmigiano-Reggiano you can find and grate it finely to ensure you have the quantity called for in the recipe.

- Preheat oven to 375°F (190°C)
- 13- by 9- by 2-inch (3 L) baking dish, lightly greased with butter

3 tbsp	extra-virgin olive oil	45 mL
¼ cup	diced onion	50 mL
3 cups	sliced (lengthwise, ¼ inch/0.5 cm) cauliflower florets	750 mL
½ cup	dry white Italian wine	125 mL
1 cup	water	250 mL
	Salt and finely ground white pepper	
3 cups	Besciamella Sauce (see recipe, page 289), divided	750 mL
1 tbsp	salt	15 mL
1 lb	dried maccheroni (see Variations, below)	500 g
⅔ cup	grated Parmigiano-Reggiano, divided	150 mL

1. In a covered pasta pot over high heat, bring water to a rapid boil.

2. Meanwhile, in a large sauté pan, heat oil over medium heat. Add onion and cook, stirring, until translucent, about 3 minutes. Add cauliflower, wine and water and cook until cauliflower is tender. Add 2 cups (500 mL) of the besciamella sauce and cook, stirring, until heated through. Remove from heat and set aside.

3. Add salt and maccheroni to the boiling water and cook, uncovered, over high heat until pasta is almost al dente. Scoop out about 1 cup (250 mL) of the pasta cooking water and set aside. Drain pasta.

4. Return pan to low heat, add 2 tbsp (25 mL) of the reserved pasta water and toss to coat evenly, adding more pasta water if necessary. Add 3 tbsp (45 mL) of the Parmigiano-Reggiano and toss well.

5. Sprinkle prepared dish with 3 tbsp (45 mL) of the cheese. Add maccheroni mixture. Thin remaining besciamella with 4 tbsp (60 mL) pasta water. Spread sauce over top and into the corners of the baking dish. Sprinkle with remaining cheese.

6. Bake in preheated oven until top is golden brown, about 30 minutes. Serve immediately.

Variations

Substitute penne or rigatoni for the maccheroni.

Make Ahead

Complete steps 1 through 5. Cover with plastic wrap and refrigerate overnight. When you're ready to serve, bake in preheated oven, adding 10 to 15 minutes to the baking time.

Rigatoni con radicchio al forno

Baked Rigatoni with Radicchio

The radicchio used in this recipe is the widely available round, bright maroon variety, Chioggia, which resembles a small ruby-colored head lettuce. Although radicchio loses its vibrant color when cooked, cooking actually enhances its flavor, mellowing some of the natural bitterness.

Serves 4 to 6

Tip

Any dry white Italian table wine will work well in this recipe. Here I'd probably use Pinot Bianco, which is a good basic dry white wine for use in Italian cooking.

- Preheat oven to 375°F (190°C)
- 13- by 9- by 2-inch (3 L) baking dish, lightly greased with butter

3 tbsp	extra-virgin olive oil	45 mL
¼ cup	diced onion	50 mL
4 cups	diced cored radicchio	1 L
½ cup	dry white Italian wine	125 mL
	Salt and freshly ground white pepper	
3 cups	Besciamella Sauce (see recipe, page 289), divided	750 mL
1 tbsp	salt	15 mL
1 lb	dried rigatoni (see Variations, below)	500 g
⅔ cup	grated Parmigiano-Reggiano, divided	150 mL

1. In a covered pasta pot over high heat, bring water to a rapid boil.
2. Meanwhile, in a large sauté pan, heat oil over medium heat. Add onion and cook, stirring, until translucent, about 3 minutes. Add radicchio and wine and cook, stirring, until wine is almost evaporated. Season to taste with salt and pepper. Add 2 cups (500 mL) of the besciamella sauce and cook, stirring, until heated through. Remove from heat and set aside.
3. Add salt and rigatoni to the boiling water and cook, uncovered, over high heat until pasta is almost al dente. Scoop out about 1 cup (250 mL) of the pasta cooking water and set aside. Drain pasta.
4. Return sauté pan to low heat. Stir in 2 tbsp (25 mL) of the reserved pasta water. Add rigatoni and, using a wooden spoon, toss to coat evenly, adding more pasta water if necessary. Add 3 tbsp (45 mL) of the Parmigiano-Reggiano and toss well.
5. Sprinkle prepared dish with 3 tbsp (45 mL) of the Parmigiano-Reggiano. Add rigatoni mixture. Thin remaining besciamella sauce with 4 tbsp (50 mL) reserved pasta water. Spread sauce evenly over top and sprinkle with remaining cheese.
6. Bake in preheated oven until top is golden brown, about 30 minutes. Serve immediately.

Variations

Substitute penne or maccheroni for the rigatoni.

Make Ahead

Complete steps 1 through 5. Cover with plastic wrap and refrigerate overnight. When you're ready to serve, bake in preheated oven, adding 10 to 15 minutes to the baking time.

Fusilli con lattuga al forno

Baked Fusilli with Creamed Lettuce

Say "lettuce" and we think salad. But tender, darker green lettuces such as Boston Bibb have their own distinct flavors, which stand up to cooking. I believe you will enjoy the lettuce in this baked pasta dish.

Serves 4 to 6

Tips

Cook pasta for baked dishes to almost (that is, firmer than) al dente, because the pasta will continue to cook in the oven with the other ingredients when it is baked.

Any dry white Italian table wine will work well in this recipe. Here I'd probably use Pinot Bianco, which is a good basic dry white wine for use in Italian cooking.

- Preheat oven to 375°F (190°C)
- 13- by 9- by 2-inch (3 L) baking dish, lightly greased with butter

3 tbsp	extra-virgin olive oil	45 mL
¼ cup	diced onion	50 mL
4 cups	diced cored Boston or Bibb lettuce	1 L
½ cup	dry white Italian wine	125 mL
	Salt and freshly ground white pepper	
3 cups	Besciamella Sauce (see recipe, page 289), divided	750 mL
1 tbsp	salt	15 mL
1 lb	dried fusilli (see Variations, below)	500 g
⅔ cup	grated Parmigiano-Reggiano, divided	150 mL

1. In a covered pasta pot over high heat, bring water to a rapid boil.

2. Meanwhile, in a large sauté pan, heat oil over medium heat. Add onion and stir until translucent, about 3 minutes. Add lettuce and wine. Cook, stirring, until wine evaporates. Season to taste with salt and pepper. Add 1½ cups (375 mL) of the besciamella sauce, reduce heat to low and cook, stirring, until heated through, about 5 minutes. Remove from heat and set aside.

3. Add salt and fusilli to the boiling water and cook, uncovered, over high heat until pasta is almost al dente. Scoop out about 1 cup (250 mL) of the pasta cooking water and set aside. Drain pasta.

4. Return sauté pan to medium-low heat and add 2 tbsp (25 mL) of the reserved pasta water. Add fusilli and, using a wooden spoon, toss to coat evenly, adding more pasta water if necessary. Add 4 tbsp (60 mL) of the Parmigiano-Reggiano and toss well.

5. Sprinkle prepared dish with 2 tbsp (25 mL) of the Parmigiano-Reggiano and add fusilli mixture. Thin remaining besciamella sauce with 4 tbsp (60 mL) reserved pasta water. Spread sauce evenly over pasta from side to side and end to end, filling corners of baking dish. Sprinkle with remaining cheese.

6. Bake in preheated oven until top is golden brown, about 30 minutes. Serve immediately.

Variations

Substitute rotini or cavatappi for the fusilli.

Make Ahead

Complete steps 1 through 5. Cover with plastic wrap and refrigerate overnight. When you're ready to serve, bake in preheated oven, adding 10 to 15 minutes to the baking time.

Penne con funghi al forno

Baked Penne with Mushrooms

Cremini mushrooms are immature portobellos. They are simpler to prepare because they are smaller and easier to handle than their large relatives. They are very flavorful and add a savory, meaty dimension to this simple baked pasta.

Serves 4 to 6

Tips

To prepare cremini mushrooms for cooking, leave the stems on but trim off and discard any woody ends. Brush mushrooms clean with a soft brush or paper toweling.

Use finely grated, not shredded, Parmigiano-Reggiano cheese. The fine teeth on a standard box grater produce nicely grated cheese for cooking. In the interests of time, particularly when making recipes from this chapter, purchase good-quality pre-grated cheese.

- Preheat oven to 375°F (190°C)
- 13- by 9- by 2-inch (3 L) baking dish, lightly greased with butter

3 tbsp	extra-virgin olive oil	45 mL
¼ cup	diced onion	50 mL
2 cups	quartered cremini mushrooms	500 mL
½ cup	dry white Italian wine	125 mL
	Salt and freshly ground white pepper	
3 cups	Besciamella Sauce (see recipe, page 289), divided	750 mL
1 tbsp	salt	15 mL
1 lb	dried penne (see Variations, below)	500 g
⅔ cup	grated Parmigiano-Reggiano, divided	150 mL

1. In a covered pasta pot over high heat, bring water to a rapid boil.

2. Meanwhile, in a large sauté pan, heat oil over medium heat. Add onion and cook, stirring, until translucent, about 3 minutes. Add mushrooms and wine and cook, stirring, until wine is almost evaporated. Season to taste with salt and pepper. Stir in 2 cups (500 mL) of the besciamella sauce and cook just to heat through. Remove from heat and set aside.

3. Add salt and penne to the boiling water and cook, uncovered, over high heat until pasta is almost al dente. Scoop out about 1 cup (250 mL) of the pasta cooking water and set aside. Drain pasta.

4. Return sauté pan to low heat. Stir in 2 tbsp (25 mL) of the reserved pasta water. Add penne and, using a wooden spoon, toss to coat evenly. Add 3 tbsp (45 mL) of the Parmigiano-Reggiano and toss well

5. Sprinkle prepared dish with 3 tbsp (45 mL) of the Parmigiano-Reggiano. Add penne. Thin remaining besciamella sauce with ¼ cup (50 mL) reserved pasta water. Spread sauce evenly over the top from side to side and end to end, filling corners of baking dish. Sprinkle with remaining cheese.

6. Bake in preheated oven until top is golden brown, about 30 minutes. Serve immediately.

Variations

Substitute pennette, cut ziti or maccheroni for the penne.

Make Ahead

Complete steps 1 through 5. Cover with plastic wrap and refrigerate overnight. When you're ready to serve, bake in preheated oven, adding 10 to 15 minutes to the baking time.

Penne al gratin con gamberetti e piselli

Baked Penne with Shrimp and Peas

Pink shrimp and green peas look and taste good together. When you slice the shrimp in half vertically, it helps them cook evenly and it is also easier to distribute them throughout the pasta.

Serves 4 to 6

Tips

I recommend using organic peas, because they are free of chemicals and pesticide residues.

I like to use medium (41 to 50 per pound/500 g) shrimp in this recipe. When they are halved lengthwise, they can be evenly distributed throughout the pasta, giving an impression of abundance. However, you may use larger shrimp, also cut in half lengthwise.

I do not recommend refrigerating this recipe and baking it the following day. It is best made and enjoyed on the same day, because the flavor and texture of seafood diminish when it is reheated.

- Preheat oven to 375°F (190°C)
- 13- by 9- by 2-inch (3 L) baking dish, lightly greased with butter

6 tbsp	extra-virgin olive oil	90 mL
¼ cup	diced onion	50 mL
1 cup	halved cherry tomatoes	250 mL
1 cup	blanched fresh peas or frozen peas, defrosted (see Tips, left)	250 mL
2 tbsp	hand-torn fresh basil leaves	25 mL
	Salt and freshly ground black pepper	
1½ cups	halved (lengthwise) peeled, deveined medium shrimp, heads and tails off (12 oz/375 g)	375 mL
½ cup	dry white Italian wine	125 mL
1 tbsp	salt	15 mL
1 lb	dried penne (see Variations, below)	500 g
¼ cup	dry white Italian breadcrumbs, divided	50 mL

1. In a covered pasta pot over high heat, bring water to a rapid boil.

2. In a large sauté pan, heat oil over medium heat. Add onion and tomatoes and cook, stirring, until onion is soft and tender, about 3 minutes. Add peas and basil and cook, stirring, until vegetables are soft and tender, about 5 minutes. Season to taste with salt and pepper. Add shrimp and wine, stir and cook until shrimp are half-cooked (barely opaque). Remove from heat and set aside.

3. Add salt and penne to the boiling water and cook, uncovered, over high heat until pasta is almost al dente. Scoop out about 1 cup (250 mL) of the pasta cooking water and set aside. Drain pasta.

4. Return sauté pan to low heat. Add 2 tbsp (25 mL) of the reserved pasta water and penne and, using a wooden spoon, toss to coat evenly, adding more pasta water if necessary.

5. Sprinkle prepared dish with half of the breadcrumbs. Add penne mixture and sprinkle with remaining breadcrumbs.

6. Bake in preheated oven until top is golden brown, about 35 minutes. Serve immediately.

Variations

Substitute pennette, cut ziti or fusilli for the penne.

Cannelloni con spinaci e besciamella

Baked Cannelloni with Spinach and Béchamel

Although many people don't like spinach, they do like it when it is served creamed. Here fresh spinach is combined with fresh ricotta, rich mascarpone and sharp, salty Parmigiano, all bound in besciamella sauce, stuffed into cannelloni and baked until golden brown on top. It doesn't get much creamier or more luscious than this. You can use dried manicotti tubes or you can make fresh pasta sheets and then form the cannelloni rolls. The choice is yours.

Serves 4 to 6

Tip

Work like a chef. Have all your ingredients ready to go before you actually start to cook (see *Mise en Place*, page 15).

- Preheat oven to 375°F (190°C)
- 13- by 9- by 2-inch (3 L) baking dish, lightly greased with butter

1 lb	fresh spinach leaves, stems removed	500 g
1 cup	fresh whole-milk ricotta	250 mL
⅔ cup	grated Parmigiano-Reggiano, divided	150 mL
1	large egg, beaten	1
½ cup	mascarpone	125 mL
	Salt and freshly ground white pepper	
	Freshly grated nutmeg	
1 tbsp	salt	15 mL
12	fresh 6- by 4-inch (15 by 10 cm) pasta sheets (see Tips, 297)	12
	OR	
12 oz	dried manicotti/cannelloni shells	375 g
1½ cups	Besciamella Sauce (see recipe, page 289)	375 mL
3 tbsp	whole milk	45 mL

1. In a covered pasta pot over high heat, bring water to a rapid boil.

2. Meanwhile, in another large pot of lightly salted boiling water, cook spinach just until wilted. Drain in a colander and hold under cold running water to cool and set the color. Once it is cool, squeeze spinach dry, using your hands. On a cutting board, chop spinach medium-fine.

3. Transfer spinach to a mixing bowl. Add ricotta, ¼ cup (50 mL) of the Parmigiano-Reggiano, egg and mascarpone. Mix well. Season to taste with salt, pepper and nutmeg. If not using right away, cover with plastic wrap and refrigerate.

4. Add salt and pasta to the boiling water and cook, uncovered, over high heat until pasta is almost al dente. Drain pasta. Transfer to a baking tray and set aside until cool enough to handle. If you're using fresh pasta sheets, drain in a colander, remove sheets gently one by one and place on a dinner plate with plastic wrap between each sheet.

The recipes for Basic Pasta
and Whole Wheat Pasta
(see page 222) yield at
least 12 sheets of pasta,
each 12 by 4 inches (30 by
10 cm). If you are using
fresh pasta, make half a
recipe and cut each 12- by
4-inch (30 by 10 cm) sheet
in half horizontally to get
the quantity required for
this recipe.

When cutting the pasta
sheets for this recipe,
save some larger pieces of
leftover "scrap" pasta. Add
these to the boiling water
along with the sheets and
use them to test whether
the pasta is cooked. That
way your pasta sheets will
remain whole for use in
the recipe.

If you're using dried
manicotti, do what chefs
do: spoon the filling into a
pastry tube fitted with the
largest tip and squeeze into
the pasta shells.

To serve, use a long, thin
cake spatula to separate
cannelloni on the sides,
then lift them out by sliding
the spatula underneath.

5. Sprinkle prepared dish with 3 tbsp (45 mL) of the Parmigiano-Reggiano. Divide spinach mixture into 12 equal portions, each about $\frac{1}{4}$ cup (50 mL). If using fresh pasta sheets, lay them one at a time on a clean work surface, shorter side nearest you. Place one portion of spinach mixture across center of sheet, parallel to shorter side, and roll pasta up to form a tube. Place seam-side-down in dish. If using prepared shells, fill using a small spoon or pastry tube (see Tips, left).

6. Add milk to besciamella sauce, stir well and spread evenly over top of cannelloni from end to end and side to side, into corners of the baking dish. Sprinkle with remaining Parmigiano-Reggiano.

7. Bake in preheated oven until golden brown on top, about 30 minutes if using fresh pasta, 35 to 40 minutes if using dried. Serve immediately.

Variation

Substitute 12 crespelle (see recipe, page 359) for the fresh pasta sheets or dried manicotti.

Make Ahead

Complete steps 1 through 6. Cover with plastic wrap and refrigerate overnight. When you're ready to serve, bake in preheated oven, adding 10 to 15 minutes to the baking time.

Cannelloni

Cannelloni as we know them today — fresh pasta sheets rolled around a filling, covered with a béchamel or tomato sauce, then baked — are said to have been invented in 1907 by Chef Salvatore Coletta at the restaurant La Favorita (known as 'o Parrucchiano) in Sorrento, Italy. They were previously known as *strascinati* because the pasta sheets used to make them were rolled out and stretched with a rolling pin. Outside Italy cannelloni are sometimes confused with manicotti, the pre-shaped dried pasta tubes. For that reason commercially produced dried pasta tubes often carry both names.

Cannelloni al ragù manzo

Baked Cannelloni with Beef Ragù

This is exactly the kind of baked stuffed pasta my mother used to make with fresh homemade pasta sheets, and it is very labor-intensive. It is also amazingly delicious. To ease preparation, prepare and cook the beef ragù and the besciamella sauce the day before you intend to serve this. Cover and refrigerate both overnight. You can also use dried manicotti tubes, which will reduce your workload considerably.

Serves 4 to 6

Tip

Cook pasta for baked dishes to almost (that is, firmer than) al dente, because the pasta will continue to cook in the oven with the other ingredients when it is baked.

- Preheat oven to 300°F (150°C)
- 13- by 9- by 2-inch (3 L) baking dish, lightly greased with butter

3 tbsp	extra-virgin olive oil	45 mL
¼ cup	diced thinly sliced pancetta	50 mL
¼ cup	diced onion	50 mL
¼ cup	finely diced carrot	50 mL
¼ cup	diced peeled celery	50 mL
6 oz	boneless beef shoulder, trimmed of excess fat and cubed (1 inch/2.5 cm)	175 g
	Salt and freshly ground black pepper	
1 cup	dry red Italian wine	250 mL
1 cup	canned crushed Italian tomatoes	250 mL
½ cup	water	125 mL
2	large eggs	2
½ cup	grated Parmigiano-Reggiano, divided	125 mL
	Freshly grated nutmeg	
1 tbsp	salt	15 mL
12	fresh 6- by 4-inch (15 by 10 cm) pasta sheets (see Tips, right)	12
	OR	
12 oz	dried manicotti/cannelloni shells	375 g
1½ cups	Besciamella Sauce (see recipe, page 289)	375 mL
3 tbsp	whole milk	45 mL

1. In a heavy ovenproof 3-quart (3 L) saucepan or Dutch oven with a tight-fitting lid, heat oil over high heat. Add pancetta, onion, carrot and celery and cook, stirring occasionally, until vegetables are soft, about 7 minutes. Stir in beef and season to taste with salt and pepper. Add wine and cook until reduced by half. Add tomatoes and water and bring to a boil.

2. Cover and bake in preheated oven until ragù reduces slightly, 1½ to 2 hours. Remove from oven, uncover, place on very low heat and continue to simmer, stirring occasionally from the bottom, until ragù is thick and rich, about 30 minutes. Using a dinner fork or potato masher, mash meat into fine shreds. Transfer to a bowl and refrigerate until cool enough to handle.

3. When ragù has cooled, drain excess liquid (save for use in soups or stews). Add eggs and 2 tbsp (25 mL) of the Parmigiano-Reggiano. Mix well and season to taste with salt, pepper and nutmeg. Set aside. (If you plan to complete the pasta the next day, cover ragù with plastic wrap and refrigerate until needed.)

Tips

The recipes for Basic Pasta and Whole Wheat Pasta (see page 222) yield at least 12 sheets of pasta, each 12 by 4 inches (30 by 10 cm). If you are using fresh pasta, make half the recipe and cut each 12- by 4-inch (30 by 10 cm) sheet in half horizontally to get the quantity required for this recipe.

An enameled cast iron pot is ideal for making this ragù because it heats slowly and evenly and the heavy bottom helps prevent burning.

To serve, use a long, thin cake spatula to separate cannelloni along the sides, then lift them out by sliding the spatula underneath.

4. In a covered pasta pot over high heat, bring water to a rapid boil. Add salt and pasta to the boiling water and cook, uncovered, over high heat until pasta is almost al dente. Drain pasta. Transfer to a baking tray and set aside until cool enough to handle. If you're using fresh pasta sheets, drain in a colander, remove sheets gently one by one and place them on a dinner plate with plastic wrap between them.

5. Sprinkle prepared dish with 3 tbsp (45 mL) of the Parmigiano-Reggiano. Divide filling into 12 portions. If using pasta sheets, lay them one at a time on a clean work surface, shorter side nearest you. Place one portion of ragù mixture across center of sheet, parallel to shorter side and roll pasta up to form a tube. If using prepared tubes, fill them using a small spoon. Place filled tubes seam-side-down in prepared dish.

6. Add milk to besciamella sauce and stir well. Spread sauce evenly over top of cannelloni from end to end and side to side and into corners of the dish. Sprinkle with remaining cheese.

7. Bake in preheated oven until golden brown on top, about 30 minutes if using fresh pasta, 40 minutes if using dried. Serve immediately.

Variation

Substitute 12 crespelle (see recipe, page 359) for the pasta sheets or dried manicotti.

Make Ahead

Complete steps 1 through 6. Cover with plastic wrap and refrigerate overnight. When you're ready to serve, bake in preheated oven, adding 10 to 15 minutes to the baking time. Or you can simply make the ragù and refrigerate it (steps 1 through 3).

Too Much Liquid?

When you finish making this beef ragù, you will find it is quite liquid, and I ask you to drain it. Why, you wonder, didn't I specify less liquid to begin with? Because when you make a long-, slow-cooking ragù, ample liquid is necessary to keep the pot from boiling dry and burning, thus ruining the ragù and wasting hours of work. The excess broth from a ragù can be refrigerated, skimmed of hard surface fat, and used to enrich soups and stews. It can even be frozen for later use.

Lasagne alla Bolognese

Lasagne alla bolognese

When lasagne is mentioned, most people think of lasagne alla bolognese. If they are not Italian, chances are they think of versions they have eaten in restaurants, not the lasagne bolognese that Italians make at home. If you prepare this dish just once and enjoy it, I believe you will never order it at a restaurant again. I recommend that you make the meat and besciamella sauces ahead of time and cover and refrigerate them until ready to use. You can assemble the lasagne and bake it the next day. Using the widely available no-boil lasagna noodles will reduce preparation time considerably.

Serves 4 to 6

- Preheat oven to 300°F (150°C)
- 13- by 9- by 2-inch (3 L) baking dish, lightly greased with butter

3 tbsp	extra-virgin olive oil	45 mL
½ cup	diced thinly sliced pancetta	125 mL
½ cup	diced onion	125 mL
½ cup	finely diced carrot	125 mL
½ cup	diced peeled celery	125 mL
	Salt and freshly ground white pepper	
4 oz	cubed boneless beef shoulder, trimmed of excess fat	125 g
4 oz	cubed boneless veal shoulder, trimmed of excess fat	125 g
4 oz	cubed boneless pork shoulder, trimmed of excess fat	125 g
2 oz	chopped chicken livers	60 g
1 cup	dry red Italian wine	250 mL
1 cup	canned crushed Italian tomatoes	250 mL
½ cup	water	125 mL
1 tbsp	salt	15 mL
12	fresh 6- by 4-inch (15 by 10 cm) pasta sheets (see Tips, right)	12
	OR	
12	dried no-boil lasagna sheets (8 oz/250 g)	12
2 cups	Besciamella Sauce (see recipe, page 289)	500 mL
¼ cup	whole milk	50 mL
1 cup	grated Parmigiano-Reggiano, divided	250 mL

1. In a heavy ovenproof 3-quart (3 L) saucepan or Dutch oven with a tight-fitting lid, heat oil over medium heat. Add pancetta, onion, carrot and celery and season to taste with salt and pepper. Cook, stirring occasionally, until vegetables are soft, about 7 minutes. Add beef, veal, pork and chicken livers. Cook, stirring, until meats are cooked through, about 10 minutes. Add wine and cook until reduced by half. Add tomatoes and water and bring to a boil.

2. Cover and bake in preheated oven until ragù reduces slightly, 1½ to 2 hours. Remove from oven, uncover, place on very low heat and continue to simmer, stirring occasionally from the bottom, for 30 minutes, until ragù is thick and rich. Using a dinner fork or potato masher, mash meat into fine shreds. Transfer to a bowl and refrigerate until cool enough to handle. When ragù has cooled, drain excess liquid (save for use in soups or stews).

3. Meanwhile, if using fresh pasta sheets, in a covered pasta pot over high heat, bring water to a rapid boil. Add salt and pasta to the boiling water and cook, uncovered, over high heat until pasta is almost al dente. Drain in a colander, remove sheets gently one by one and place them on a dinner plate with plastic wrap between each sheet.

4. In a bowl combine besciamella sauce and milk. Mix well and set aside.

5. Preheat oven to 350°F (180°C). Using a ladle, spread a thin layer of ragù over bottom of prepared dish and sprinkle with about 3 tbsp (45 mL) of the Parmigiano-Reggiano. Cover with 3 sheets of pasta or no-boil lasagna noodles. Add a thin layer of ragù and one of besciamella sauce (about 1/4 cup/50 mL). Sprinkle with cheese. The object is to keep the layers of ragù, besciamella and Parmigiano-Reggiano as thin as possible. Top with 3 more pasta sheets and add another thin layer each of ragù and besciamella; sprinkle with cheese (you now have 2 layers of pasta, 6 sheets in total). Top with 3 more pasta sheets and add another thin layer each of ragù and besciamella; sprinkle with cheese. (You now have 3 layers of pasta, 9 sheets in total). Top with 3 more pasta sheets (making 12 in total) and top this last layer with remaining ragù and besciamella. Spread besciamella sauce from side to side and end to end, filling corners of the dish. Sprinkle with remaining Parmigiano-Reggiano.

6. Transfer to preheated oven. If using fresh pasta, bake uncovered until top is deep golden and edges are bubbling and crispy and have shrunken away from the baking dish, about 45 minutes. If using no-boil lasagna noodles, cover dish with aluminum foil that has been lightly sprayed with cooking spray and bake for 1 hour. Remove from oven, let rest for 10 minutes and serve.

Variation

If you prefer, substitute 12 crespelle (see recipe, page 359) for the lasagna noodles. Lay them over the prepared pan, slightly overlapping to form successive layers.

Lasagne con verdure di primavera

Spring Vegetable Lasagne

While lasagne alla bolognese is typical of Bologna, in Emilia-Romagna, spring vegetable lasagne is a familiar dish in the neighboring region of Toscana (Tuscany). It is equally delicious and takes less time because there is no long-cooking ragù. You can make and assemble this lasagne the day before you intend to serve it, then wrap and refrigerate and bake the following day. Why do I blanch the vegetables? To set their color and preserve their flavor during baking.

Serves 4 to 6

- Preheat oven to 375°F (190°C)
- 13- by 9-inch (3 L) baking dish, greased with butter

3 tbsp	extra-virgin olive oil	45 mL
¾ cup	diced onion	175 mL
¾ cup	diced unpeeled Yukon Gold potato, blanched (see Tips, right)	175 mL
¾ cup	blanched fresh peas or frozen peas, defrosted	175 mL
¾ cup	sliced (1 inch/2.5 cm) asparagus, blanched	175 mL
¾ cup	peeled fava beans or fresh lima beans, blanched	175 mL
1 cup	chopped (1 inch/2.5 cm) green beans, blanched	250 mL
	Salt and freshly ground white pepper	
1 cup	water	250 mL
1 tbsp	salt	15 mL
12	fresh 6- by 4-inch (15 by 10 cm) pasta sheets (see Tips, right)	12
	OR	
12	dried no-boil lasagna sheets (8 oz/250 g)	12
2 cups	Besciamella Sauce (see recipe, page 289)	500 mL
¼ cup	milk	50 mL
1 cup	grated Parmigiano-Reggiano, divided	250 mL

1. In a large sauté pan, heat oil over medium heat. Add onion, potato, peas, asparagus, fava beans and green beans. Stir and season to taste with salt and pepper. Add water and cook until vegetables are soft, about 10 minutes. Transfer vegetables to a baking sheet and cool to room temperature.

2. Meanwhile, if using fresh pasta sheets, in a covered pasta pot over high heat, bring water to a rapid boil. Add salt and pasta to the boiling water and cook, uncovered, over high heat, until pasta is almost al dente. Drain in a colander, remove sheets gently one by one and place them on a dinner plate with plastic wrap between each sheet.

3. In a bowl combine besciamella sauce and milk. Mix well and set aside.

Tips

To blanch vegetables, bring a large, wide-mouthed pot of lightly salted water to a boil. Add vegetables and boil for 3 minutes. Transfer to a colander and rinse under running tap water until cold. Drain well.

The recipes for Basic Pasta and Whole Wheat Pasta (see page 222) yield at least 12 sheets of pasta, each 12 by 4 inches (30 by 10 cm). If you are using fresh pasta, make half the recipe and cut each 12- by 4-inch (30 by 10 cm) sheet in half horizontally to get the quantity required for this recipe.

4. Line bottom of prepared dish with a thin layer of blanched vegetables. Sprinkle with about 3 tbsp (45 mL) of the Parmigiano-Reggiano. Add a layer of pasta (3 sheets or noodles), one of vegetables and one of besciamella sauce (about ¼ cup/50 mL); sprinkle with Parmigiano-Reggiano. Repeat twice. Add a final layer of pasta and top with remaining vegetables. Spread remaining besciamella sauce from side to side and end to end, filling the corners of the dish. Sprinkle with remaining cheese.

5. Transfer to preheated oven. If using fresh pasta, bake uncovered until top is golden brown and sides are crispy and have shrunk away from the dish, about 35 minutes. If using no-boil noodles, cover dish with aluminum foil that has been lightly sprayed with nonstick cooking spray and bake for 45 minutes. Remove from oven, let rest for 10 minutes, covered, and serve.

Variation

If you prefer, substitute 12 crespelle (see recipe, page 359) for the lasagna noodles. Lay them over the prepared pan, slightly overlapping to form successive layers.

Lasagna or Lasagne?

Lasagna is singular: one pasta sheet. Lasagne is plural: several sheets of pasta. Therefore, a lasagna is a noodle. A dish composed of several layers of noodles is a lasagne.

Filled Pasta: Gift-Wrapped

I like to think of filled pastas as tasty morsels gift-wrapped in fresh homemade pasta and presented on a plate. If you have ever prepared authentic Italian filled pasta from start to finish, you certainly know that it is a real gift from the cook. More than a labor of love, it is also a work of art. Filled pasta requires more skill and takes more time to make than any other kind, and it is the most elaborate style of pasta gastronomy.

I grew up eating the filled pastas that my mother made, and believe me when I say there is no comparison between filled pasta freshly made in the home and the ravioli served by most restaurants. Restaurant ravioli, except in the finest gourmet or smallest family-owned-and-operated Italian restaurants, is rarely made there. The ravioli and other filled pastas on most restaurant menus are either purchased premade from a pasta manufacturer or else purchased frozen. All the restaurant does is cook or reheat it, sauce it and serve it. It may be good, but it's not great. Homemade filled pasta can be great.

The aristocrats of pasta cuisine have a long history. These stuffed, shaped pasta packets probably originated in north and central Italy: Emilia-Romagna, Lombardia, Piedmont and Veneto. Historically, these regions were relatively wealthy — the aristocracy had cooks — somewhat industrialized, and active in trade. Chefs who were given the means and the time added inspiration, which produced interesting culinary creations such as filled pasta. Filled pasta spread from these regions throughout Italy. In southern Italy, where people were poorer and worked harder for sustenance, the filled pasta were much less elaborate.

Of all the possible ways to prepare pasta, filled pasta is the most challenging and the most exciting and unusual. Most cooked pasta (fresh or dried) has flavor added in the form of sauce. Filled pasta has another layer of flavor — the filling on the inside. Another difference: you need only a fork to twirl long pasta on or eat short pasta. Filled pastas (in Italian, *paste*) are the only pastas you cut while eating. That being said, this is Italian cooking, and for every rule there is an exception or two. So, you may cut the larger filled pastas in order to eat them, but not necessarily the smallest ones.

There are more than a hundred filled pasta shapes, with regional variations, and of course different names depending on the size and the region of Italy where they are eaten or considered indigenous. And there is endless controversy in Italy as to which region is the birthplace of which filled pasta and why the pastas of other regions are either inferior or not authentic. Ravioli is prepared not only in different shapes — square, round, half-moon — but also in different sizes — large, medium, small. And each variation has a different name. The hundreds of fillings can also be divided into meatless (for days of abstinence) and those with meat.

In this chapter I have taken liberties with traditional Italian filled pastas and fillings because my goal is to simplify them for the non-Italian cook. In so doing I hope to make your experience a pleasant one. These recipes do not pretend to replicate precisely the regional filled pastas you would find in Italy. On the other hand, once you have made them, I believe you will find them superior to what you will find in most restaurants. They are true to the spirit of authentic Italian cooking.

So if you enjoy a challenge, this chapter is for you. Here you will find nine shapes — five easy ones and four that are more challenging, 17 flavorful fillings, and an illustrated chart for all nine shapes. When you have time, you can make these filled pastas and freeze them for later use. I'm a big fan of spending one or two days preparing and filling pasta, then freezing it for up to 30 days so you can cook and sauce it at the last minute. There is very little difference in taste and texture. Even as a chef, I can taste the difference only if I have pasta filled the same day and cooked frozen filled pasta side by side.

Basic Cheese and Butter Sauce for Filled Pasta

This simple sauce works well with all of the filled pastas. Simply combine 3 tbsp (45 mL) grated Parmigiano-Reggiano, 2 tbsp (25 mL) butter and 2 tbsp (25 mL) reserved pasta water in a large sauté pan. Add the filled pasta and toss gently to coat.

A parting thought: practice makes perfect. Once you have mastered the technique you will know just how thin to roll the dough, how much filling to use, and how to seal and shape the dough. Do it once or twice and you will see that it's relatively uncomplicated.

Filled pasta speaks directly to Italian culture. We start with something simple — basic pasta dough — and we turn it into something extravagant. I hope I can encourage you to give it a try.

Filled Pasta Simplified

In the recipes I suggest you roll the dough $\frac{1}{8}$-inch (3 mm) thick, because that is fairly easy. As you become more experienced I believe you will begin to roll the dough even thinner, about $\frac{1}{16}$-inch (1.5 mm). This will, of course, increase the yield slightly.

As for sauces, I like to keep it simple — a little butter, a little cheese and the occasional fresh herb or vegetables. However, please feel free to sauce all the filled pastas with cheese and butter if you prefer.

Freezing Filled Pasta

Place filled pasta in a single layer on parchment-lined baking sheets lightly dusted with flour. Freeze until solid. Transfer to resealable plastic bags, date and label the bags, and keep pasta frozen for up to one month. Keep frozen until ready to cook. Drop frozen pasta directly into boiling water and allow an extra 2 or 3 minutes for cooking compared to the freshly made version.

Interchanging Fillings

Although I have specified fillings to use in specific shapes — usually these are traditional — you may consider all the fillings interchangeable. Choose your shape and choose your filling and sauce them with a basic cheese and butter sauce (see recipe, page 306).

Filled Pasta: A Four-Step Process

Making filled pasta is a four-step process:

- Make the filling
- Make the pasta dough
- Fill and shape the pasta
- Cook and sauce the pasta

I suggest that you make the filling first and refrigerate it, make the pasta next, and complete the assembly last, rolling out and filling the sheets one at a time. At that point you are ready to poach the filled pasta in lightly salted water and toss it in a simple cheese and butter sauce. If you prefer, freeze the filled pasta (see Freezing Filled Pasta, above, left).

Nine Filled Pasta Shapes: Cutting, Filling and Forming

The dimensions of the pasta shapes below are based on dough that has been rolled to ⅛ inch (3 mm) thick using a standard stainless steel hand-cranked pasta machine with rollers about 6 inches (15 cm) wide. Pasta sheets should be trimmed to 4 inches (10 cm) wide and cut to the standard length of 12 inches (30 cm).

    Anolini, caramelle, fagottini, ravioli and tortelli are the easiest shapes to make. Agnolotti, cappelletti, tortellini and tortelloni are more challenging, but mastering the technique can be lots of fun.

Freezing Leftovers

After cutting and trimming pasta shapes, gather up leftover dough scraps, cut into appropriate shapes and sizes and let air-dry on floured parchment paper. Freeze in resealable plastic bags for use in soups and stews.

---

1. Anolini (small half-moon shapes)

Cut: Place one pasta sheet (12 by 4 inches/30 by 10 cm) on a clean work surface, longer side nearest you. Using a 1½-inch (4 cm) diameter round straight-edged cookie cutter, cut out circles of pasta. Transfer to a small plate. Using a small pastry brush, brush exposed side with water.

Fill: Using 2 spoons, place ⅛ to ¼ tsp (0.5 to 1 mL) filling in center of each circle. Fold into a half-moon.

Seal: Using fingertips, press edges down and seal well.

2. Caramelle (resemble candies wrapped in paper)

Cut: Place one pasta sheet (12 by 4 inches/30 by 10 cm) on a clean work surface, longer side nearest you. Using a ruler and a straight-edged pasta wheel or sharp knife, trim 1 inch (2.5 cm) off the long side, creating a strip of dough 3 inches (7.5 cm) wide by 12 inches (30 cm) long. Cut strip into 3-inch (7.5 cm) squares, setting aside excess dough for another use. You will get four squares from each sheet of pasta. Holding the square of dough at a diagonal, brush the far corner with water.

Fill: Place ½ tsp (2 mL) filling in the center of each square.

Seal and shape: Keeping filling in the middle, twist both ends like a candy wrapper as you roll toward the dampened corner. Pinch to seal.

3. Fagottini (pouch shapes, also known as "beggars' pouches")

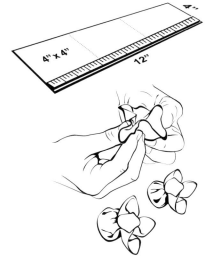

Cut: Place one pasta sheet (12 by 4 inches/30 by 10 cm) on a clean work surface, longer side nearest you. Using a ruler and a straight-edged pasta wheel or sharp knife, make two cuts 4 inches (10 cm) apart to form three 4-inch (10 cm) squares. Brush each square with water.

Fill: Place $^{1}/_{2}$ to 1 tsp (2 to 5 mL) filling in center of each square.

Seal and shape: Using fingers, gather up all four corners of the pasta and pinch them together in the middle. Press gathered edges together firmly to seal well.

4. Ravioli (square packets with fluted edges)

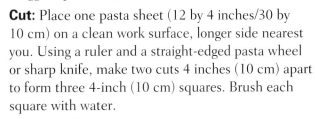

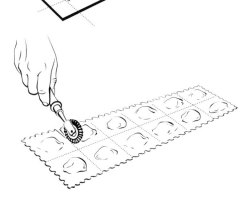

Fill: Place one pasta sheet (12 by 4 inches/30 by 10 cm) on a clean work surface, longer side nearest you. Using a pastry brush, brush entire sheet with water. Beginning in the lower left-hand corner, 1 inch (2.5 cm) from bottom edge, place 6 dollops of filling (each about 1 tsp/5 mL) equidistant from each other and lined up parallel to the edges of the pasta sheet. Repeat 1 inch (2.5 cm) from top edge, making another row. The sheet of pasta should have 12 equidistant dollops of filling.

Seal and cut: Place a second pasta sheet on top. Gently press down with fingertips between the dollops of filling to seal edges well. Using a fluted pasta wheel, cut between the rows in both directions to make 12 ravioli.

5. Tortelli (medium-sized half-moon shapes)

Cut: Place one pasta sheet (12 by 4 inches/30 by 10 cm) on a clean work surface, longer side nearest you. Using a 2-inch (5 cm) diameter round straight-edged cookie cutter, cut out 12 circles. Brush each with water.

Fill and seal: Place about ½ tsp (2 mL) filling in center of each circle. Fold in half to make a half-moon. Press down with fingertips to seal well.

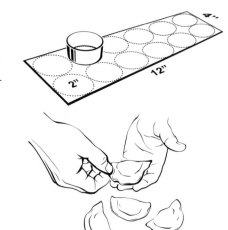

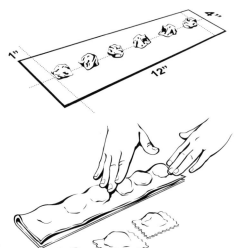

6. Agnolotti (square "pillows" folded over with three fluted edges)

Fill and seal: Place one pasta sheet (12 by 4 inches/30 by 10 cm) on a clean work surface, longer side nearest you. Brush with water. Place 1 tsp (5 mL) filling in the middle of the sheet, 2 inches (5 cm) from the bottom and 1 inch (2.5 cm) from the left side, and then every 2 inches (5 cm) thereafter, for a total of 6 dollops of filling in a row. (You will have filling at 1, 3, 5, 7, 9 and 11 inches/2.5, 7.5, 12.5, 18, 23 and 28 cm). Fold pasta sheet in half to cover filling completely. Using your fingertips, gently press down between and around each dollop of filling to create individual agnolotti.

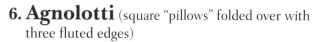

Cut: Using a fluted pasta wheel, cut between the fillings to make 6 squares. Run the pasta wheel along the other sealed edges to flute them, but not along the one that is folded over.

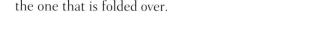

7. Cappelletti (small triangular cap shapes)

Cut: Place one pasta sheet (12 by 4 inches/30 by 10 cm) on a clean work surface, longer side nearest you. Using a ruler and straight-edged pasta wheel or sharp knife, cut sheet in half lengthwise, then crosswise every 2 inches (5 cm) to make 12 squares. Brush each square with water.

Fill: Place ⅛ tsp (0.5 mL) filling in center of each square.

Seal and shape: Fold corner-to-corner to form a triangle. Using fingertips, press down on edges to seal. Wrap filled triangle around index finger with filled portion resting on fingernail. Wet two ends of triangle and join them around finger, overlapping slightly, and press firmly to seal. Then push tip of triangle on top of finger back and up to create a "brim" on the cap.

8. Tortellini (medium-sized round cap shapes)

Cut: Place one pasta sheet (12 by 4 inches/30 by 10 cm) on a clean work surface, longer side nearest you. Using a 2-inch (5 cm) diameter round straight-edged cookie cutter, cut out circles. Brush each with water.

Fill: Place ¼ tsp (1 mL) filling in center of each circle.

Seal and shape: Fold edges over into a half-moon. Using fingertips, press down to seal edges well. Wrap filled half-moon around index finger with filled portion resting on fingernail. Wet ends and join around finger, slightly overlapping. Pinch ends together and gently slide off your finger.

9. Tortelloni (large tortellini)

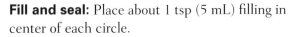

Cut: Place one pasta sheet (12 by 4 inches/30 by 10 cm) on a clean work surface, longer side nearest you. Using a 3½-inch (8.5 cm) diameter round straight-edged cookie cutter, cut out circles. Brush each with water.

Fill and seal: Place about 1 tsp (5 mL) filling in center of each circle.

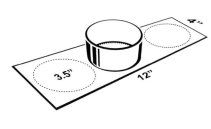

Seal and shape: Fold edges over to form a half-moon. Using fingertips, press down to seal edges well. Wrap filled pasta around index finger with filled portion resting on fingernail. Wet ends and join around finger, slightly overlapping. Pinch ends together and gently slide off your finger.

Fagottini di barbabietole con burro, salvia e limone

Fagottini Filled with Roasted Beets and Lemon-Sage Butter

Fagottini, also known as "beggars' pouches," are easy and fun to make. They resemble the square-tied bundles that beggars would carry fastened on a sturdy stick or pole. You place the filling in the center of the pasta square, then pull up all four corners and pinch to seal. Because beets color whatever they come in contact with, I like to use Fresh Red Dough for Filled Pasta (see recipe, page 230) in this recipe.

Makes 4 to 6 servings/ 36 fagottini

Tip

Since beets will stain your hands red, it's a good idea to wear disposable plastic gloves when peeling them.

• Preheat oven to 400°F (200°C)

Filling

2 cups	water	500 mL
1¼ lbs	fresh whole beets, washed, tops and bottoms trimmed (see Tip, left)	625 g
2	garlic cloves, peeled	2
1	bay leaf	1
	Salt and freshly ground black pepper	
10 tbsp	grated Parmigiano-Reggiano, divided	150 mL
1	large egg	1
	Freshly grated nutmeg	
1 tbsp	salt	15 mL

Pasta

12	fresh pasta sheets for filled pasta (see Tips, right)	12

Sauce

3 tbsp	extra-virgin olive oil	45 mL
3 tbsp	fresh sage leaves	45 mL
2 tbsp	fresh lemon juice	25 mL
2 tbsp	unsalted butter	25 mL

1. *Filling:* In a roasting pan combine water, beets, garlic, bay leaf, and salt and pepper to taste. Cover tightly with aluminum foil and bake in preheated oven until beets are tender, about 1½ hours. Let cool to room temperature and peel.

2. Transfer beets to a food processor fitted with a metal blade and purée. Transfer to a small mixing bowl. Add 4 tbsp (60 mL) of the Parmigiano-Reggiano, egg and nutmeg and mix well. Set aside or cover and refrigerate until ready to use.

3. *Fagottini:* Place one pasta sheet on a clean work surface, longer side nearest you. Using a ruler and a straight-edged pasta wheel or a sharp knife, make two cuts 4 inches (10 cm) apart to form three 4-inch (10 cm) squares. Brush each square with water. Place 1 tsp (5 mL) filling in center of each square. Using fingers, gather up all four corners of the pasta and pinch together in the middle. Press gathered edges firmly together to seal well. Place completed fagottini on floured parchment sheets (do not let them touch). Repeat until all the pasta has been fully used. Cover and refrigerate unused filling for later use (see Tips, right).

Tips

This recipe uses one full recipe of Dough for Filled Pasta (see recipes, pages 228–232), but there will be leftover filling. If you want to make extra fagottini you can double the pasta recipe to make enough additional sheets. You can cut and freeze any extra pasta sheets the same way you freeze pasta trimmings for soup or stew (see Tip, page 229). As always, when rolling out the dough, roll out one sheet at a time and fill it, keeping the unrolled dough covered.

Use extra filling to fill different shapes of pasta or crespelle, or as topping for Polenta Crostini (see recipe, page 353). Since this filling contains raw egg, be sure to broil or bake the crostini long enough to cook the egg, about 15 minutes in a preheated 350°F (180°C) oven.

4. In a covered pasta pot over high heat, bring water to a rapid boil. Add salt and fagottini and cook until pasta is al dente and filling is heated through, 3 to 4 minutes. Scoop out about 1 cup (250 mL) of the pasta water and set aside. Drain pasta.

5. *Sauce:* In a large sauté pan, heat oil and sage over medium heat. Cook, stirring, until sage begins to crackle and pop. Add lemon juice and simmer for 1 minute. Add 4 tbsp (60 mL) of the reserved pasta water, fagottini, butter and 3 tbsp (45 mL) of the Parmigiano-Reggiano and cook until sauce is lightly thickened, about 3 minutes, using a wooden spoon to toss gently and coat evenly, and adding more pasta water as necessary.

6. Transfer to a large serving platter and sprinkle with remaining cheese. Serve immediately.

Variations

Substitute cheese and butter sauce (see recipe, page 306) for the sage sauce.

Although I have specified fillings to use in specific shapes — usually these are traditional — you may consider all the fillings interchangeable.

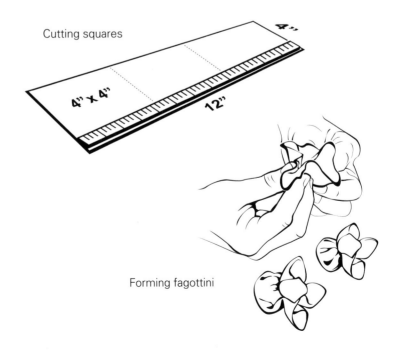

Cutting squares

4"

4" × 4"

12"

Forming fagottini

Fagottini d'asparagi
Fagottini with Asparagus

These pasta pouches are filled with puréed asparagus flavored with onions, cheese and a pinch of nutmeg. To complement this filling I suggest plain or spinach dough.

Makes 4 to 6 servings / 36 fagottini

Tips
I like to use unsalted butter in my recipes because it contributes fresh flavor without adding extra salt.

Filling

3 tbsp	extra-virgin olive oil	45 mL
½ cup	diced onion	125 mL
2 cups	sliced (1 inch/2.5 cm) pencil-thin asparagus	500 mL
3 cups	water	750 mL
	Salt and freshly ground black pepper	
4 tbsp	grated Parmigiano-Reggiano	60 mL
1	large egg	1
	Freshly grated nutmeg	

Fagottini

12	fresh pasta sheets for filled pasta (see Tips, right)	12
1 tbsp	salt	15 mL

Sauce

3 tbsp	extra-virgin olive oil	45 mL
1 cup	diagonally sliced (1 inch/2.5 cm) pencil-thin asparagus	250 mL
6 tbsp	Parmigiano-Reggiano, divided	90 mL
2 tbsp	unsalted butter	25 mL

1. *Filling:* In a saucepan over medium heat, heat oil, onion, asparagus, water and salt and pepper to taste. Cook until asparagus is tender, about 5 minutes. Drain and transfer to a food processor fitted with a metal blade. Purée.

2. Transfer purée to a mixing bowl and add Parmigiano-Reggiano, egg and nutmeg to taste. Stir well. Set aside or cover and refrigerate until ready to use.

3. *Fagottini:* Place one pasta sheet on a clean work surface, longer side nearest you. Using a ruler and a straight-edged pasta wheel or a sharp knife, make two cuts 4 inches (10 cm) apart to form three 4-inch (10 cm) squares. Brush each square with water. Place 1 tsp (5 mL) filling in center of each square. Using fingers, gather up all four corners of the pasta and pinch together in the middle. Press gathered edges firmly together to seal well. Place completed fagottini on floured parchment sheets (do not let them touch). Repeat until all the pasta has been fully used. Cover and refrigerate unused filling for later use.

4. In a covered pasta pot over high heat, bring water to a rapid boil. Add salt and fagottini and cook until pasta is al dente and filling is heated through, 3 to 4 minutes. Scoop out about 1 cup (250 mL) of the pasta water and set aside. Drain pasta.

5. *Sauce:* In a large sauté pan, heat oil over medium heat. Add asparagus and cook, stirring, until tender, about 3 minutes. Add 4 tbsp (60 mL) of the reserved pasta water, fagottini, 3 tbsp (45 mL) of the Parmigiano-Reggiano and butter and cook until sauce is lightly thickened, about 3 minutes, using a wooden spoon to toss gently and coat evenly, and adding more pasta water if necessary.

6. Transfer to a large serving platter and sprinkle with remaining cheese. Serve immediately.

Variation

Substitute cheese and butter sauce (see recipe, page 306) for the asparagus sauce.

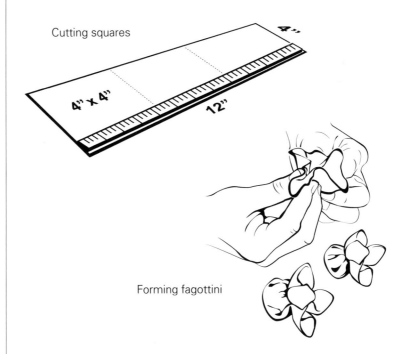

Cutting squares

4" x 4"

12"

4"

Forming fagottini

Caramelle di ricotta dolce al pomodoro

Caramelle Filled with Sweet Ricotta and Tomatoes

Caramelle, as the name suggests, look like pasta-wrapped candies with the ends twisted. These caramelle are filled with sweet fresh ricotta flavored with a hint of cinnamon. The cooked caramelle are tossed in a simple fresh tomato sauce.

Makes 4 to 6 servings / 48 caramelle

Tips

Work like a chef. Have all your ingredients ready to go before you actually start to cook (see *Mise en Place*, page 15.)

For best results grate the cheese yourself, but if time is at a premium, use already grated cheese. Whichever form you choose, just be sure to buy the very best Italian Parmigiano-Reggiano you can find and grate it finely to ensure you have the quantity called for in the recipe.

Filling

1 cup	fresh whole-milk ricotta	250 mL
2 tbsp	granulated sugar	25 mL
4 tbsp	grated Parmigiano-Reggiano	60 mL
1	large egg	1
¼ tsp	ground cinnamon	1 mL
	Salt and freshly ground black pepper	

Caramelle

12	fresh pasta sheets for filled pasta (see Tips, right)	12
1 tbsp	salt	15 mL

Sauce

3 tbsp	extra-virgin olive oil	45 mL
1 cup	chopped ripe Italian tomatoes, preferably peeled	250 mL
2 tbsp	fresh basil leaves, packed	25 mL
6 tbsp	grated Parmigiano-Reggiano, divided	90 mL
2 tbsp	unsalted butter	25 mL

1. *Filling:* In a mixing bowl, combine ricotta, sugar, Parmigiano-Reggiano, egg, cinnamon, and salt and pepper to taste. Mix well. Cover and refrigerate until ready to use.

2. *Caramelle:* Place one pasta sheet on a clean work surface, longer side nearest you. Using a ruler and a straight-edged pasta wheel or sharp knife, trim 1 inch (2.5 cm) off the long side, creating a strip of dough 3 inches (7.5 cm) wide by 12 inches (30 cm) long. Cut strip into four 3-inch (7.5 cm) squares, setting aside excess dough for another use. With the square of dough at a diagonal, brush the far corner with water. Place ½ tsp (2 mL) filling in center of each square. Keeping filling in the middle, twist both ends like a candy wrapper as you roll toward the dampened corner. Pinch to seal.

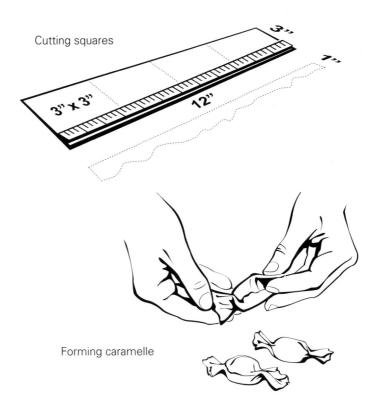

Tips

This recipe uses one full recipe of Dough for Filled Pasta (see recipes, pages 228–232), but there will be leftover filling. Use extra filling to fill different shapes of pasta or crespelle, or as topping for Polenta Crostini (see recipe, page 353). Since this filling contains raw egg, be sure to broil or bake the crostini long enough to cook the egg, about 15 minutes in a preheated 350°F (180°C) oven.

These look nice made with plain, red or spinach dough. And they look especially nice if you combine two or three doughs for a candy-striped effect.

3. In a covered pasta pot over high heat, bring water to a rapid boil. Add salt and caramelle and cook, uncovered, over high heat until pasta is al dente and filling is cooked, 3 to 4 minutes. Scoop out about 1 cup (250 mL) of the pasta water and set aside. Drain pasta.

4. *Sauce:* In a large sauté pan, heat oil, tomatoes and basil over medium heat. Cook, stirring, until tomatoes are tender, about 5 minutes. Stir in 4 tbsp (60 mL) of the reserved pasta water. Add caramelle, 3 tbsp (45 mL) of the Parmigiano-Reggiano and butter. Cook until sauce is slightly thickened, using a wooden spoon to toss gently and coat evenly, about 3 minutes, adding more pasta water if necessary.

5. Transfer to a large serving platter and sprinkle with remaining Parmigiano-Reggiano. Serve immediately.

Variation

Substitute cheese and butter sauce (see recipe, page 306) for the tomato sauce.

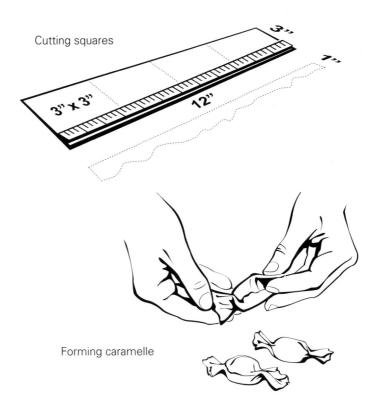

Cutting squares

3"

1"

3" x 3"

12"

Forming caramelle

Caramelle alla salsiccia d'anatra e uva passa

Caramelle Filled with Duck Sausage and Raisins

●●

This duck sausage filling takes about two minutes to mix, and at that point it's ready to cook. It has the advantage of being very flavorful and completely natural — no preservatives or chemicals. The sweet spices are a legacy of the Moors in Italy, as is the touch of sweetness from the raisins and grapes in the sauce.

Makes 4 to 6 servings / 48 caramelle

Filling

⅛ tsp	freshly grated nutmeg	0.5mL
⅛ tsp	ground coriander	0.5 mL
⅛ tsp	ground cinnamon	0.5 mL
⅛ tsp	ground mace	0.5 mL
⅛ tsp	smashed fennel seeds	0.5 mL
⅛ tsp	coarsely ground black pepper	0.5 mL
⅛ tsp	salt	0.5 mL
½ tsp	red wine vinegar	5 mL
8 oz	ground duck (leg or thigh meat, see Variation)	250 g
4 tbsp	grated Parmigiano-Reggiano	60 mL
1	large egg	1

Caramelle

12	fresh pasta sheets for filled pasta (see Tips, right)	12
1 tbsp	salt	15 mL

Sauce

½ cup	seedless green grapes, puréed in food processor	125 mL
¼ cup	dark raisins, packed	50 mL
¼ cup	golden raisins, packed	50 mL
2 tbsp	red wine vinegar	25 mL
6 tbsp	grated Parmigiano-Reggiano, divided	90 mL
2 tbsp	unsalted butter	25 mL

1. *Filling:* In a mixing bowl combine nutmeg, coriander, cinnamon, mace, fennel, pepper, salt, vinegar and duck. Mix well. Add Parmigiano-Reggiano and egg and mix well. Cover and refrigerate until ready to use.

2. *Caramelle:* Place one pasta sheet on a work surface, longer side nearest you. Using a ruler and a straight-edged pasta wheel or sharp knife, trim 1 inch (2.5 cm) off the long side, creating a strip of dough 3 inches (7.5 cm) wide by 12 inches (30 cm) long. Cut strip into four 3-inch (7.5 cm) squares, setting aside excess dough for another use. With the square of dough at a diagonal, brush the far corner with water. Place ½ tsp (2 mL) filling in center of each square. Keeping filling in the middle, twist both ends like a candy wrapper as you

roll toward the dampened corner. Pinch to seal. Place on floured parchment paper sheets (do not allow to touch). Repeat until pasta has been used up. Cover and refrigerate any unused filling for later use.

3. In a covered pasta pot over high heat, bring water to a rapid boil. Add salt and caramelle and cook, uncovered, over high heat until pasta is al dente and filling is cooked through, 3 to 4 minutes. Scoop out about 1 cup (250 mL) of the pasta water and set aside. Drain pasta.

4. *Sauce:* In a large sauté pan over medium heat, combine grape purée, raisins and vinegar. Cook, stirring, until reduced by half. Add 4 tbsp (60 mL) of the reserved pasta water, caramelle, 3 tbsp (45 mL) of the Parmigiano-Reggiano and butter and cook until sauce is lightly thickened, about 3 minutes, using a wooden spoon to toss gently and coat evenly, and adding more pasta water if necessary.

5. Transfer to a large serving platter and sprinkle with remaining cheese. Serve immediately.

Variation

Substitute ground turkey for the duck.

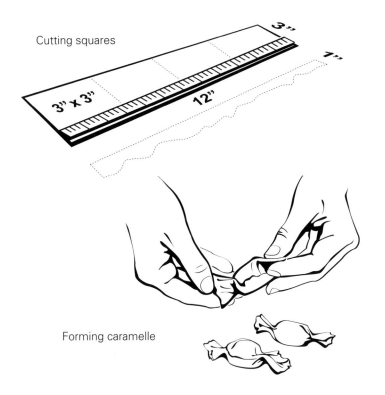

Cutting squares

3" x 3"

12"

3"

1"

Forming caramelle

Anolini con salsiccia di tacchino

Anolini with Turkey Sausage Filling

The turkey sausage here is homemade and all natural (no preservatives or additives), but it has a nice level of spice. It makes quite a tasty morsel wrapped in plain, spinach or red pasta.

Makes 8 to 12 servings / 144 anolini

Tips

This recipe uses one full recipe of Dough for Filled Pasta (see recipes, pages 228–232), but there will be leftover filling. See Tips, page 319, for ideas on how to use it up.

Don't forget, when rolling out pasta dough for filling, roll out the sheets one at a time, then fill, keeping the remaining dough covered. Otherwise the pasta sheets will dry out and become brittle.

Transfer pasta rounds to a small plate before brushing with water, to keep your pastry board dry. Use two spoons to scoop up the filling. It will keep your fingers clean.

Filling

1/8 tsp	ground allspice	0.5 mL
1/8 tsp	ground cloves	0.5 mL
1/8 tsp	ground cinnamon	0.5 mL
1/8 tsp	grated nutmeg	0.5 mL
1/8 tsp	cayenne	0.5 mL
1/8 tsp	freshly ground black pepper	0.5 mL
1/8 tsp	salt	0.5 mL
2 tbsp	dry white Italian wine	25 mL
8 oz	ground turkey	250 g
1/4 cup	grated Parmigiano-Reggiano	50 mL
1	large egg, beaten	1
	Salt and freshly ground black pepper	

Anolini

12	fresh pasta sheets for filled pasta (see Tips, left)	12
1 tbsp	salt	15 mL

Sauce

1/4 cup	unsalted butter	50 mL
6 tbsp	grated Parmigiano-Reggiano, divided	90 mL

1. *Filling:* In a bowl, combine allspice, cloves, cinnamon, nutmeg, cayenne, pepper, salt, wine and turkey. Mix well. Add Parmigiano-Reggiano and egg. Season lightly with additional salt and pepper and mix well. Cover and refrigerate until ready to use.

2. *Anolini:* Place one pasta sheet on a clean work surface, longer side nearest you. Using a 1 1/2-inch (4 cm) diameter straight-edged round cookie cutter, cut out circles of pasta. Using a small pastry brush, brush exposed side with water. Place 1/8 to 1/4 tsp (0.5 to 1 mL) filling in center of each circle and fold into a half-moon. Using fingertips, press edges down and seal well. Place on floured parchment paper sheets (do not let them touch). Repeat until all the pasta is used. Cover and refrigerate any unused filling for later use.

3. Meanwhile, in a covered pasta pot over high heat, bring water to a rapid boil. Add salt and anolini and cook, uncovered, until pasta is al dente and filling is cooked through, 3 to 4 minutes. Scoop out about 1 cup (250 mL) of the pasta water and set aside. Drain pasta.

4. *Sauce:* In a large sauté pan over medium heat, combine 2 tbsp (25 mL) of the reserved pasta water, butter, anolini and 3 tbsp (45 mL) of the Parmigiano-Reggiano. Using a wooden spoon, toss gently to coat evenly, adding more pasta water if necessary.

5. Transfer to a large serving platter and sprinkle with remaining cheese. Serve immediately.

Agnolotti con ricotta e spinaci

Agnolotti with Ricotta and Spinach Filling

This filling is traditional for agnolotti. Agnolotti are a specialty of the Piedmont region of Italy, where they come with a variety of meat and vegetable fillings. They are larger than anolini and square or rectangular with fluted edges.

Makes 4 to 6 servings / 72 agnolotti

Filling

1 tbsp	salt	15 mL
1 lb	stemmed spinach	500 g
1 cup	whole-milk ricotta	250 mL
¼ cup	grated Parmigiano-Reggiano	50 mL
1	large egg, beaten	1
½ cup	mascarpone	125 mL
	Salt and freshly ground white pepper	
	Freshly grated nutmeg	

Agnolotti

12	fresh pasta sheets for filled pasta (see Tips, right)	12
1 tbsp	salt	15 mL

Sauce

¼ cup	unsalted butter	50 mL
⅓ cup	grated Parmigiano-Reggiano, divided	75 mL

1. *Filling:* In a pot of boiling water, combine salt and spinach. Cook until spinach is wilted, about 3 minutes. Drain in a colander and place under cold running water until spinach is at room temperature. Using hands, squeeze spinach dry by handfuls.

2. Place spinach on a wooden cutting board and chop into small pieces about 1½ inches (4 cm) square, transferring to a bowl as completed. Add ricotta, Parmigiano-Reggiano, egg and mascarpone and mix well. Season to taste with salt, pepper and nutmeg.

3. *Agnolotti:* Place one pasta sheet on a clean work surface, longer side nearest you. Brush with water. Place 1 tsp (5 mL) filling in middle of sheet 2 inches (5 cm) from bottom and 1 inch (2.5 cm) from left side, and every 2 inches (5 cm) thereafter, for a total of 6 dollops of filling. (You will have filling at 1, 3, 5, 7, 9 and 11 inches/2.5, 7.5, 12.5, 18, 23 and 28 cm). Fold pasta sheet in half to cover filling completely. Using fingertips, gently press down between and around each dollop of filling to create individual agnolotti. Using a fluted pasta wheel, cut between fillings to make 6 squares and along other sealed edges to flute them. Place completed agnolotti on floured parchment paper sheets (do not let them touch). Repeat until all the pasta has been used. Cover and refrigerate any unused filling for later use.

Tips

This recipe uses one full recipe of Dough for Filled Pasta (see recipes, pages 228–232), but there will be leftover filling. Use extra filling to fill different shapes of pasta or crespelle, or as topping for Polenta Crostini (see recipe, page 353). Since this filling contains raw egg, be sure to broil or bake the crostini long enough to cook the egg, about 15 minutes in a preheated 350°F (180°C) oven.

Don't forget, when rolling out pasta dough for filling, roll out the sheets one at a time, then fill, keeping the remaining dough covered. Otherwise the pasta sheets will dry out and become brittle.

4. Meanwhile, in a covered pasta pot over high heat, bring water to a rapid boil. Add salt and agnolotti and cook, uncovered, until pasta is al dente and filling is cooked through, 3 to 4 minutes. Scoop out about 1 cup (250 mL) of the pasta water and set aside. Drain pasta.

5. *Sauce:* In a large sauté pan over medium heat, combine 2 tbsp (25 mL) of the reserved pasta water, butter, agnolotti and ¼ cup (50 mL) of the Parmigiano-Reggiano. Using a wooden spoon, toss gently to coat evenly, adding more pasta water if necessary.

6. Transfer to a large serving platter and sprinkle with remaining cheese. Serve immediately.

Agnolotti al plin

Agnolotti are native to Piedmont and come in many varieties and several shapes, including square and rectangular. They are made by folding the dough over the stuffing and pinching (*plin* means "pinch") between the mounds of filling to seal each filled pasta.

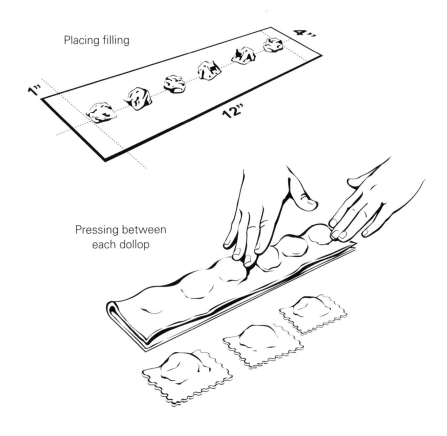

Placing filling

4"

1"

12"

Pressing between each dollop

Ravioli di melanzane al burro

Ravioli with Eggplant and Butter

In this recipe, sautéed eggplant is mixed with sweet ricotta, salty Parmigiano-Reggiano and rich, velvety mascarpone for a filling that tastes even better than the sum of its parts. Any of the fresh pasta doughs would complement this filling: plain, red or spinach. I like these with a simple cheese and butter sauce.

Makes 6 to 8 servings / 72 ravioli

Tip

Fresh ricotta is a whey cheese with a texture similar to cottage cheese but lighter. While low-fat and part-skim versions are available, they are not suitable for my recipes, because the flavor is diminished and the texture tends to be dry.

Filling

2 tbsp	extra-virgin olive oil	25 mL
½ cup	diced onion	125 mL
2 cups	finely diced peeled eggplant	500 mL
¼ cup	dry white Italian wine	50 mL
½ cup	fresh whole-milk ricotta	125 mL
1	large egg, beaten	1
¼ cup	grated Parmigiano-Reggiano	50 mL
¼ cup	mascarpone	50 mL
	Salt and freshly ground white pepper	
	Freshly grated nutmeg	

Ravioli

12	fresh pasta sheets for filled pasta (see Tips, right)	12
1 tbsp	salt	15 mL

Sauce

6 tbsp	grated Parmigiano-Reggiano, divided	90 mL
2 tbsp	unsalted butter	25 mL

1. *Filling:* In a large sauté pan, heat oil over medium heat. Add onion and cook, stirring, until soft, about 3 minutes. Add eggplant and cook, stirring, until soft, about 5 minutes. Add wine and simmer until almost evaporated. Remove from heat and let cool to room temperature.

2. Transfer eggplant mixture to a mixing bowl. Add ricotta, egg, Parmigiano-Reggiano and mascarpone. Mix well. Season to taste with salt, pepper and nutmeg. Cover and refrigerate until ready to use.

3. *Ravioli:* Place one pasta sheet on a work surface, longer side nearest you. Using a pastry brush, brush entire sheet with water. Place 1 tsp (5 mL) filling in lower left-hand corner, 1 inch (2.5 cm) from edges. Repeat every 2 inches (10 cm) to form a row of 6 dollops parallel with the longer side. Beginning in the upper left-hand corner, repeat to form a second row above the first. The sheet of pasta should have 12 equidistant dollops of filling. Place a second pasta sheet on top. Gently press down with fingertips between dollops of filling to seal edges well. Using a fluted pasta wheel, cut straight lines between dollops to make 12 ravioli. Place completed ravioli on floured parchment sheets (do not let them touch). Repeat until all the pasta has been used. Cover and refrigerate unused filling.

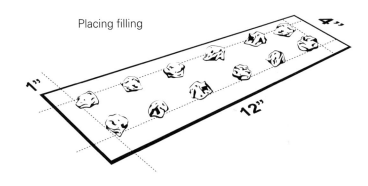

Tips

This recipe uses one full recipe of Dough for Filled Pasta (see recipes, pages 228–232), but there will be leftover filling. Use extra filling to fill different shapes of pasta or crespelle, or as topping for Polenta Crostini (see recipe, page 353). Since this filling contains raw egg, be sure to broil or bake the crostini long enough to cook the egg, about 15 minutes in a preheated 350°F (180°C) oven.

Don't forget, when rolling out pasta dough for filling, roll out the sheets one at a time, then fill, keeping the remaining dough covered. Otherwise the pasta sheets will dry out and become brittle.

4. In a covered pasta pot over high heat, bring water to a rapid boil. Add salt and ravioli and cook, uncovered, over high heat until ravioli are al dente and filling is cooked, 3 to 4 minutes. Scoop out about 1 cup (250 mL) of the pasta water and set aside. Drain pasta.

5. *Sauce:* In a sauté pan over medium heat, add ¼ cup (50 mL) of the reserved pasta water. Add ravioli, 3 tbsp (45 mL) of the Parmigiano-Reggiano and butter. Cook until heated through, using a wooden spoon to toss gently and coat evenly, adding more pasta water if necessary.

6. Transfer to a large serving platter and sprinkle with remaining Parmigiano-Reggiano. Serve immediately.

Placing filling

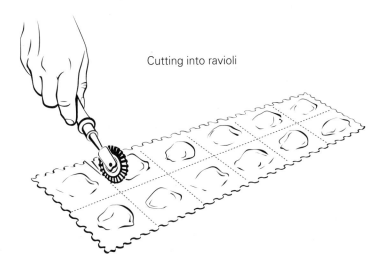

Cutting into ravioli

Ravioli Filled with Peas

This filling of fresh spring peas and creamy cheese works best with plain or spinach pasta dough. Fresh mint leaves, a classic combination with peas, are added to the sauce, which is very quick to make.

Makes 6 to 8 servings / 72 ravioli

Tip

Mascarpone is a double- to triple-cream cow's milk cheese that is rich and delicious. Technically it's not really a cheese because it's not thickened with rennet. The cream is coagulated and then drained to thicken it even more. The finished cheese has a texture similar to very dense crème fraîche or clotted cream. In Italian cooking it is often used in savory sauces to thicken and enrich.

• Rimmed baking sheet

Filling

3 tbsp	extra-virgin olive oil	45 mL
½ cup	finely diced onion	125 mL
1½ cups	shelled fresh peas (see Tips, right)	375 mL
¼ cup	dry white Italian wine	50 mL
2 cups	water	500 mL
	Salt and freshly ground white pepper	
½ cup	fresh whole-milk ricotta	125 mL
¼ cup	grated Parmigiano-Reggiano	50 mL
1	large egg, beaten	1
¼ cup	mascarpone	50 mL
	Freshly grated nutmeg	

Ravioli

12	fresh pasta sheets for filled pasta (see Tips, right)	12
1 tbsp	salt	15 mL

Sauce

6 tbsp	freshly grated Parmigiano-Reggiano, divided	90 mL
2 tbsp	unsalted butter	25 mL
3 tbsp	fresh mint leaves	45 mL

1. *Filling:* In a saucepan, heat oil over medium heat. Add onion and cook, stirring, until soft, about 3 minutes. Add peas and cook, stirring, for 2 minutes, until they soften. Add wine and cook until reduced by half. Add water and cook until peas are soft and tender, about 10 minutes. Season to taste with salt and pepper. Using a slotted spoon, strain and transfer to baking sheet. Let cool to room temperature.

2. In a food processor fitted with a steel blade, purée peas. Transfer to a mixing bowl. Add ricotta, Parmigiano-Reggiano, egg and mascarpone. Mix well. Season to taste with salt, pepper and nutmeg. Cover and refrigerate until ready to use.

Tips

Substitute frozen peas for fresh and reduce cooking time by half.

This recipe uses one full recipe of Dough for Filled Pasta (see recipes, pages 228–232), but there will be leftover filling. Use extra filling to fill different shapes of pasta or crespelle, or as topping for Polenta Crostini (see recipe, page 353). Since this filling contains raw egg, be sure to broil or bake the crostini long enough to cook the egg, about 15 minutes in a preheated 350°F (180°C) oven.

Don't forget, when rolling out pasta dough for filling, roll out the sheets one at a time, then fill, keeping the remaining dough covered. Otherwise the pasta sheets will dry out and become brittle.

3. *Ravioli:* Place one pasta sheet on a work surface, longer side nearest you. Using a pastry brush, brush entire sheet with water. Place 1 tsp (5 mL) filling in lower left-hand corner, 1 inch (2.5 cm) from edges. Repeat every 2 inches (10 cm) to form a row of 6 dollops parallel with the longer side. Beginning in the upper left-hand corner, repeat to form a second row above the first. The sheet of pasta should have 12 equidistant dollops of filling. Place a second pasta sheet on top. Gently press down with fingertips between dollops of filling to seal edges well. Using a fluted pasta wheel, cut straight lines between dollops to make 12 ravioli. Place completed ravioli on floured parchment sheets (do not let them touch). Repeat until all the pasta has been used. Cover and refrigerate unused filling.

4. In a covered pasta pot over high heat, bring water to a rapid boil. Add salt and ravioli. Cook, uncovered, until ravioli are al dente and filling is cooked, 3 to 4 minutes. Scoop out about 1 cup (250 mL) of the pasta water and set aside. Drain pasta.

5. *Sauce:* In large sauté pan over medium heat, add ¼ cup (50 mL) of reserved pasta water. Add ravioli, 3 tablespoons (45 mL) of the Parmigiano-Reggiano, butter and mint and, using a wooden spoon, toss gently to coat evenly, adding more pasta water if necessary.

6. Transfer to a large serving platter and sprinkle with remaining Parmigiano-Reggiano. Serve immediately.

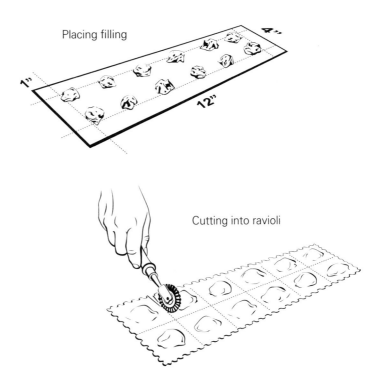

Placing filling

Cutting into ravioli

Ravioli alle zucchine

Ravioli with Zucchini

When making this recipe, my preference is to use locally grown ripe summer zucchini rather than some that have spent time in cold storage, because I think you can tell the difference in taste. If zucchini are not in season, you could substitute 2 cups (500 mL) of a cold-weather vegetable such as broccoli, broccoli rabe, kale, cabbage or Brussels sprouts, and use a simple cheese and butter sauce (see recipe, page 306).

Makes 6 to 8 servings / 72 ravioli

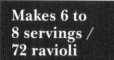

Tip

Fresh ricotta is a whey cheese with a texture similar to cottage cheese but lighter. While low-fat and part-skim versions are available, they are not suitable for my recipes, because the flavor is diminished and the texture tends to be dry.

Filling

3 tbsp	extra-virgin olive oil	45 mL
½ cup	finely diced onion	125 mL
2¾ cups	finely diced unpeeled zucchini, divided	675 mL
¼ cup	dry white Italian wine	50 mL
	Salt and freshly ground white pepper	
½ cup	fresh whole-milk ricotta	125 mL
2 tbsp	grated Parmigiano-Reggiano	25 mL
1	large egg	1
¼ cup	mascarpone	50 mL
	Freshly ground nutmeg	

Ravioli

12	fresh pasta sheets for filled pasta (see Tips, right)	12
1 tbsp	salt	15 mL

Sauce

2 tbsp	unsalted butter	25 mL
6 tbsp	grated Parmigiano-Reggiano, divided	90 mL

1. *Filling:* In a large sauté pan, heat oil over medium heat. Add onion and cook, stirring until soft, about 3 minutes. Add 2 cups (500 mL) of the zucchini and cook until tender, about 7 minutes. Add wine and cook until almost evaporated. Season to taste with salt and pepper. Remove from heat and transfer to a baking tray. Let cool to room temperature.

2. Transfer zucchini to a mixing bowl. Add ricotta, Parmigiano-Reggiano, egg and mascarpone. Mix well. Season to taste with salt, pepper and nutmeg. Cover and refrigerate until ready to use.

3. *Ravioli:* Place one pasta sheet on a work surface, longer side nearest you. Using a pastry brush, brush entire sheet with water. Place 1 tsp (5 mL) filling in lower left-hand corner, 1 inch (2.5 cm) from edges. Repeat every 2 inches (10 cm) to form a row of 6 dollops parallel with the longer side. Beginning in the upper left-hand corner, repeat to form a second row above the first. The sheet of pasta should have 12 equidistant dollops of filling. Place a second pasta sheet on top. Gently press down with fingertips between dollops of filling to seal edges well. Using a fluted pasta wheel, cut straight lines between dollops to make 12 ravioli. Place completed ravioli on floured parchment sheets (do not let them touch). Repeat until all the pasta has been used. Cover and refrigerate unused filling.

Tips

This recipe uses one full recipe of Dough for Filled Pasta (see recipes, pages 228–232), but there will be leftover filling. See Tips, page 327, for ideas on how to use it up.

Don't forget, when rolling out pasta dough for filling, roll out the sheets one at a time, then fill, keeping the remaining dough covered. Otherwise the pasta sheets will dry out and become brittle.

To freeze: Place filled ravioli on parchment-lined baking sheets lightly dusted with flour. Place in freezer until solid. Transfer to resealable plastic bags, date and label bags and keep frozen for up to 30 days. Freeze until ready to cook. Drop frozen ravioli directly into boiling water but allow 2 to 3 additional minutes for cooking.

4. In a covered pasta pot over high heat, bring water to a rapid boil. Add salt and ravioli and cook over high heat until ravioli are al dente and filling is cooked, 3 to 4 minutes. Scoop out about 1 cup (250 mL) of the pasta water and set aside. Drain pasta.

5. *Sauce:* To a large sauté pan over medium heat, add $1/2$ cup (125 mL) of the reserved pasta water. Add ravioli, butter and remaining zucchini. Cook until zucchini is soft, about 5 minutes. Add 3 tbsp (45 mL) of the Parmigiano-Reggiano and, using a wooden spoon, toss gently to coat evenly.

6. Transfer to a large serving platter. Sprinkle with remaining Parmigiano-Reggiano and serve immediately.

Variations

Substitute 2 cups (500 mL) broccoli, broccoli rabe, kale, cabbage or Brussels sprouts for the zucchini.

Substitute a cheese and butter sauce (see recipe, page 306) for the zucchini sauce.

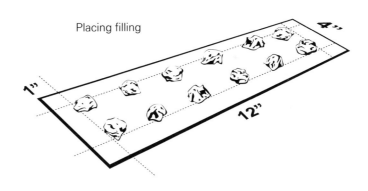

Placing filling

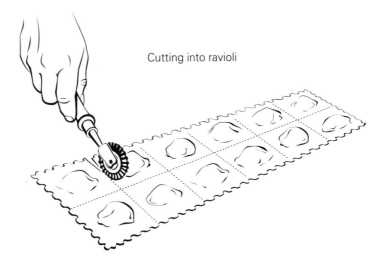

Cutting into ravioli

Tortelli Filled with Cauliflower

Tortelli are similar to anolini — half-moon in shape but larger — a good example of how a size difference of less than an inch results in a different name. Cauliflower, despite its pale color, is very rich in flavor and makes a delicious savory filling. This recipe makes a lot of tortelli; I recommend that you freeze half.

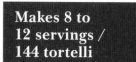

Makes 8 to 12 servings / 144 tortelli

Tips

This recipe uses one full recipe of Dough for Filled Pasta (see recipes, pages 228–232), but there will be leftover filling. See Tips, page 327, for ideas on how to use it up.

To slice cauliflower paper-thin, use a mandoline.

Filling

3 tbsp	extra-virgin olive oil	45 mL
1/4 cup	diced onion	50 mL
2 1/2 cups	cauliflower florets, divided	625 mL
3 cups	water	750 mL
	Salt and freshly ground while pepper	
1/4 cup	grated Parmigiano-Reggiano	50 mL
2 tbsp	fresh whole-milk ricotta	25 mL
1	large egg, beaten	1

Tortelli

12	fresh pasta sheets for filled pasta (see Tips, left)	12
1 tbsp	salt	15 mL

Sauce

2 tbsp	unsalted butter	25 mL
6 tbsp	grated Parmigiano-Reggiano, divided	90 mL

1. *Filling:* In a saucepan, heat oil over medium heat. Add onion, 2 cups (500 mL) of the cauliflower and water. Season to taste. Cover and cook until cauliflower is tender, about 10 minutes. Drain and let cool for 5 minutes. Purée in a food processor.

2. Transfer to a bowl. Add Parmigiano-Reggiano, ricotta and egg. Mix well. Adjust seasoning. Cover and refrigerate until ready to use.

3. *Tortelli:* Lay out one pasta sheet on a work surface, longer side nearest you. Using a 2-inch (5 cm) diameter straight-edged round cookie cutter, cut out 12 circles. Brush each with water. Place 1/2 tsp (2 mL) filling in the center of each and fold in half to make a half-moon. Press down with fingertips to seal well. Place completed tortelli on lightly floured parchment sheets (do not let them touch). Repeat until all pasta is used.

4. Meanwhile, in a covered pasta pot over high heat, bring water to a rapid boil. Add salt and tortelli and cook, uncovered, until tortelli are al dente and filling is cooked, 3 to 4 minutes. Scoop out about 1 cup (250 mL) of the pasta water and set aside. Drain pasta.

5. *Sauce:* In a large sauté pan over medium heat, combine 1/4 cup (50 mL) of the reserved pasta water, tortelli and butter. Simmer until water evaporates. Add 3 tbsp (45 mL) of the Parmigiano-Reggiano and, using a wooden spoon, toss gently to coat evenly, adding more pasta water if necessary.

6. Transfer to a large serving platter. Slice remaining cauliflower paper-thin. Sprinkle over tortelli. Sprinkle with remaining cheese and serve immediately.

Tortelli con le fave

Tortelli Filled with Fava Beans

In Italy fava beans are more than just popular — they are doted on. This filling is easier than most fava bean preparations because the beans don't have to be peeled; they are puréed instead. Although the beans in the sauce are peeled, you can always opt for a simple cheese and butter sauce. This filling would be suitable for plain, red or green fresh pasta dough. This recipe makes a lot of tortelli; I recommend that you freeze half. They're great to have on hand.

Makes 8 to 12 servings / 144 tortelli

Tips

This recipe uses one full recipe of Dough for Filled Pasta (see recipes, pages 228–232), but there will be leftover filling. See Tips, page 327, for ideas on how to use it up.

To freeze: Place filled tortelli on parchment-lined baking sheets lightly dusted with flour. Place in freezer until solid. Transfer to resealable plastic bags, date and label bags and keep frozen for up to 30 days. Freeze until ready to cook. Drop frozen tortelli directly into boiling water, allowing an extra 2 to 3 minutes to cook.

Filling

3 tbsp	extra-virgin olive oil	45 mL
1/4 cup	diced onion	50 mL
2 cups	fresh fava or lima beans, unpeeled	500 mL
3 cups	water	750 mL
	Salt and freshly ground black pepper	
1/4 cup	grated Parmigiano-Reggiano	50 mL
2 tbsp	fresh whole-milk ricotta	25 mL
1	large egg, beaten	1

Tortelli

12	fresh pasta sheets for filled pasta (see Tips, left)	12
1 tbsp	salt	15 mL

Sauce

1/2 cup	cooked, peeled fava beans, optional	125 mL
2 tbsp	unsalted butter	25 mL
6 tbsp	grated Parmigiano-Reggiano, divided	90 mL

1. *Filling:* In a saucepan over medium heat, combine olive oil, onion, fava beans and water. Season to taste with salt and pepper and cook, uncovered, until beans are soft and tender, about 10 minutes. Drain. Let cool 5 minutes and transfer to a food processor fitted with a steel blade. Purée.

2. Transfer purée to a mixing bowl and add Parmigiano-Reggiano, ricotta and egg. Mix well and adjust seasoning. Cover and refrigerate until ready to use.

3. *Tortelli:* Lay out one pasta sheet on a work surface, longer side nearest you. Using a 2-inch (5 cm) diameter straight-edged round cookie cutter, cut out 12 circles. Brush each with water. Place 1/2 tsp (2 mL) filling in the center of each and fold in half to make a half-moon. Press down with fingertips to seal well. Place completed tortelli on lightly floured parchment sheets (do not let them touch). Repeat until all pasta is used.

4. Meanwhile, in a covered pasta pot over high heat, bring water to a rapid boil. Add salt and tortelli and cook, uncovered, until tortelli are al dente and filling is cooked, 3 to 4 minutes. Drain pasta.

5. *Sauce:* In a large sauté pan over medium heat, combine 1/4 cup (50 mL) of the reserved pasta water, tortelli, peeled fava beans and butter. Add 3 tbsp (45 mL) of the Parmigiano-Reggiano and, using a wooden spoon, toss gently to coat evenly.

6. Transfer to a large serving platter and sprinkle with remaining cheese. Serve immediately.

Tortellini con quattro formaggi

Tortellini with Four Cheeses

● ●

Ideal for tortellini, this four-cheese filling will also work in simpler shapes such as ravioli, caramelle and fagottini. Tortellini are small cap-shaped pastas similar to cappelletti, but these are made from rounds rather than squares of dough. This recipe makes a lot, so I recommend that you freeze half.

Makes 8 to 10 first-course servings / 144 tortellini

Tips

This recipe uses one full recipe of Dough for Filled Pasta (see recipes, pages 228–231), but there will be leftover filling. See Tips, page 327, for ideas on how to use it up.

To freeze: Place filled tortellini on parchment-lined baking sheets lightly dusted with flour. Place in freezer until solid. Transfer to resealable plastic bags, date and label bags and keep frozen for up to 30 days. Freeze until ready to cook. Drop frozen tortellini directly into boiling water, allowing an extra 2 to 3 minutes to cook.

Filling

½ cup	fresh whole-milk ricotta	125 mL
1 cup	grated Parmigiano-Reggiano	250 mL
½ cup	grated Pecorino Romano	125 mL
¼ cup	mascarpone	50 mL
1	large egg, beaten	1
	Salt and freshly ground white pepper	

Tortellini

12	fresh pasta sheets for filled pasta (see Tips, left)	12
1 tbsp	salt	15 mL

Sauce

¼ cup	unsalted butter	50 mL
¼ cup	Pecorino Romano	50 mL

1. *Filling:* In a bowl combine ricotta, Parmigiano-Reggiano, Pecorino Romano, mascarpone and egg. Using a stiff whisk or a rotary beater, mix well. Season to taste with salt and pepper. Transfer to a bowl and set aside.

2. *Tortellini:* Place one pasta sheet on a work surface, longer side facing you. Using a 2-inch (5 cm) diameter straight-edged round cookie cutter, cut out circles. Brush each with water and place ¼ tsp (1 mL) filling in center. Fold edges over into a half-moon. Using fingertips, press down to seal edges well. Wrap filled half-moon around index finger with filled portion resting on fingernail. Wet ends of half-moon and join around finger, slightly overlapping. Pinch ends together and gently slide off your finger. Place completed tortellini on floured parchment paper sheets (do not let them touch). Repeat until all the pasta has been used. Cover and refrigerate any unused filling for later use.

3. Meanwhile, in a covered pasta pot over high heat, bring water to a rapid boil. Add salt and tortellini and cook, uncovered, until pasta is al dente and filling is cooked through, 3 to 4 minutes. Scoop out about 1 cup (250 mL) of the pasta water and set aside. Drain pasta.

4. *Sauce:* In a large sauté pan over medium heat, combine 2 tbsp (25 mL) of the reserved pasta water, butter, tortellini and Pecorino Romano. Using a wooden spoon, toss gently to coat evenly, adding more pasta water if necessary.

5. Transfer to a large serving platter and serve immediately.

Tortellini con pesto di noci e pomodori secchi

Tortellini with Sun-Dried Tomato and Walnut Pesto

This rich pesto, traditionally a good filling for tortellini, would complement Fresh Red Dough (see recipe, page 230), but plain or Fresh Spinach doughs (see recipes, pages 228 and 231) would also work well. Tortellini come from Emilia-Romagna, and the regional cities of Bologna and Modena both claim to be the birthplace of this filled pasta. When you make this recipe, I suggest that you freeze half.

Makes 8 to 10 first-course servings / 144 tortellini

Tips

Work like a chef. Have all your ingredients ready to go before you actually start to cook (see *Mise en Place*, page 15.)

For best results grate the cheese yourself, but if time is at a premium, use already grated cheese. Whichever form you choose, just be sure to buy the very best Italian Parmigiano-Reggiano you can find and grate it finely to ensure you have the quantity called for in the recipe.

Filling

1 cup	dry-packed sun-dried tomatoes, rehydrated and drained, soaking liquid reserved	250 mL
½ cup	walnut halves	125 mL
2 tbsp	minced garlic	25 mL
2 tbsp	extra-virgin olive oil	25 mL
¼ cup	grated Parmigiano-Reggiano	50 mL
1	large egg	1
	Freshly ground black pepper	

Tortellini

12	fresh pasta sheets for filled pasta (see Tips, right)	12
1 tbsp	salt	15 mL

Sauce

¼ cup	unsalted butter	50 mL
¼ cup	grated Parmigiano-Reggiano, divided	50 mL

1. *Filling:* In a food processor fitted with a metal blade, combine sun-dried tomatoes, walnuts and garlic. Pulse to chop (do not purée), adding a bit of the soaking liquid if necessary. Leaving machine running, pour oil through feeder tube in a slow, steady stream. Add Parmigiano-Reggiano and egg and season to taste with pepper. Pulse just to mix. Transfer to a bowl and set aside or cover and refrigerate until ready to use.

2. *Tortellini:* Place one pasta sheet on a work surface, longer side facing you. Using a 2-inch (5 cm) diameter straight-edged round cookie cutter, cut out circles of pasta. Brush each with water and place ¼ tsp (1 mL) filling in center. Fold edges over into a half-moon. Using fingertips, press down to seal edges well. Wrap filled half-moon around index finger with filled portion resting on fingernail. Wet ends of half-moon and join around finger, slightly overlapping. Pinch ends together and gently slide off your finger. Place completed tortellini on floured parchment paper sheets (do not let them touch). Repeat until all the pasta has been used. Cover and refrigerate any unused filling for later use.

Tips

To rehydrate sun-dried tomatoes, place them in a bowl and add boiling water to cover. Place a small plate on top to keep tomatoes submerged, and set aside for 30 minutes. Drain, reserving the liquid for soups. Tomatoes are now ready to use.

This recipe uses one full recipe of Dough for Filled Pasta (see recipes, pages 228–232), but there will be leftover filling. See Tips, page 327, for ideas on how to use it up.

Don't forget, when rolling out pasta dough for filling, roll out the sheets one at a time, then fill, keeping the remaining dough covered. Otherwise the pasta sheets will dry out and become brittle.

3. Meanwhile, in a covered pasta pot over high heat, bring water to a rapid boil. Add salt and tortellini and cook, uncovered, until pasta is al dente and filling is cooked through, 3 to 4 minutes. Scoop out about 1 cup (250 mL) of the pasta water and set aside. Drain pasta.

4. *Sauce:* In a large sauté pan over medium heat, combine 2 tbsp (25 mL) of the reserved pasta water, butter, tortellini and 2 tbsp (25 mL) of the Parmigiano-Reggiano. Using a wooden spoon, toss gently to coat evenly, adding more pasta water if necessary.

5. Transfer to a large serving platter and sprinkle with remaining cheese. Serve immediately.

Placing filling

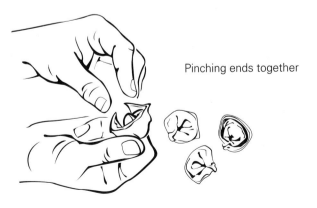

Pinching ends together

Tortelloni with Tuscan Kale

A good filling for tortelloni, this hearty Tuscan kale also works well with ravioli, fagottini and caramelle. Use a simple cheese and butter sauce (see recipe, page 306) for the finished pasta. Tortelloni are a larger version of tortellini.

Makes 4 to 6 servings / 36 tortelloni

Tip

For best results grate the cheese yourself, but if time is at a premium, use already grated cheese. Whichever form you choose, just be sure to buy the very best Italian Parmigiano-Reggiano you can find and grate it finely to ensure you have the quantity called for in the recipe.

Filling

2 tbsp	extra-virgin olive oil	25 mL
¼ cup	diced pancetta	50 mL
¼ cup	diced onion	50 mL
2½ cups	diced stemmed Tuscan kale (see Tips, right and Variation)	625 mL
¾ cup	dry white Italian wine	175 mL
1 cup	grated Parmigiano-Reggiano	250 mL
1	large egg	1
	Salt and freshly ground black pepper	

Tortelloni

12	fresh pasta sheets for filled pasta (see Tips, right)	12
1 tbsp	salt	15 mL

Sauce

¼ cup	butter	50 mL
¼ cup	grated Parmigiano-Reggiano, divided	50 mL

1. *Filling:* In a saucepan over medium heat, combine oil, pancetta and onion. Cook, stirring, until onion is soft and pancetta is cooked through. Add kale and reduce heat to low. Cook, stirring, until tender, about 10 minutes. Add wine and cook until almost dry. Remove from heat and let cool to room temperature.

2. In a food processor fitted with a metal blade, combine kale mixture, Parmigiano-Reggiano and egg. Pulse until mixture is chopped medium-fine (do not purée). Season to taste with salt and pepper. Transfer filling mixture to a bowl. Set aside or cover and refrigerate until ready to use.

3. *Tortelloni:* Place one pasta sheet on a work surface, longer side nearest you. Using a 3½-inch (8.5 cm) diameter straight-edged round cookie cutter, cut out circles of pasta. Brush each with water and place 1 tsp (5 mL) filling in center. Fold edges over to form a half-moon. Using fingertips, press down to seal edges. Wrap half-moon around index finger with filled portion resting on fingernail. Wet ends and join them around finger, slightly overlapping. Pinch ends together and gently slide off your finger. Place completed tortelloni on floured parchment paper sheets (do not let them touch). Repeat until all the pasta has been used. Cover and refrigerate any unused filling for later use.

Tips

Tuscan kale is dark green, almost black. It is also called black kale or dinosaur kale.

This recipe uses one full recipe of Dough for Filled Pasta (see recipes, pages 228–232), but there will be leftover filling. See Tips, page 327, for ideas on how to use it up.

Don't forget, when rolling out pasta dough for filling, roll out the sheets one at a time, then fill, keeping the remaining dough covered. Otherwise the pasta sheets will dry out and become brittle.

4. Meanwhile, in a covered pasta pot over high heat, bring water to a rapid boil. Add salt and tortelloni and cook, uncovered, until pasta is al dente and filling is cooked through, 3 to 4 minutes. Scoop out about 1 cup (250 mL) of the pasta water and set aside. Drain pasta.

5. *Sauce:* In a large sauté pan over medium heat, combine 2 tbsp (25 mL) of the reserved pasta water, butter, tortelloni and 2 tbsp (25 mL) of the Parmigiano-Reggiano. Using a wooden spoon, toss gently to coat evenly, adding more pasta water if necessary.

6. Transfer to a large serving platter and sprinkle with remaining cheese. Serve immediately.

Variation

Substitute Savoy cabbage for the kale.

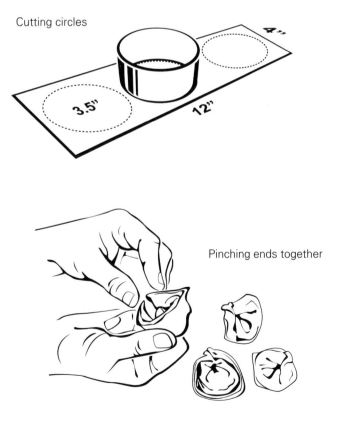

Cutting circles

4"

3.5"

12"

Pinching ends together

Cappelletti con Broccoli

Cappelletti with Broccoli Filling

This broccoli filling is usually found in cappelletti, which are small triangular cap-shaped pastas hand-shaped from small squares of dough. They are traditional in the Modena area of Emilia-Romagna in northern Italy and are often cooked in broth. This recipe makes lots of cappelletti, so I recommend that you freeze half.

Makes 8 to 10 servings / 144 cappelletti

Filling

2 tbsp	extra-virgin olive oil	25 mL
¼ cup	diced onion	50 mL
1 tbsp	minced garlic	15 mL
1½ cups	broccoli florets	375 mL
¼ cup	dry white Italian wine	50 mL
¼ cup	grated Parmigiano-Reggiano	50 mL
1	large egg, beaten	1
	Salt and freshly ground black pepper	
	Freshly grated nutmeg	

Cappelletti

12	fresh pasta sheets for filled pasta (see Tips, right)	12
1 tbsp	salt	15 mL

Sauce

¼ cup	unsalted butter	50 mL
⅓ cup	grated Parmigiano-Reggiano, divided	75 mL

1. *Filling:* In a sauté pan over medium heat, combine oil, onion, garlic and broccoli. Cook, stirring, until vegetables are soft and tender, about 7 minutes. Add wine and simmer until reduced by half. Remove from heat and let cool to room temperature.

2. Transfer broccoli mixture to a food processor fitted with a metal blade and pulse to chop. Add Parmigiano-Reggiano and egg. Season to taste with salt, pepper and nutmeg and pulse to blend. Transfer to a bowl.

3. *Cappelletti:* Place one pasta sheet on a work surface, longer side nearest you. Using a ruler and a straight-edged pasta wheel or sharp knife, cut sheet in half lengthwise into 2 strips each 12 by 2 inches (30 by 5 cm). Then cut each strip into six 2-inch (5 cm) squares, making 12 squares per pasta sheet. Brush each square with water and place ⅛ tsp (0.5 mL) filling in center. Fold corner-to-corner into a triangle. Using fingertips, press down on edges to seal. Wrap filled triangle around index finger with filled portion resting on fingernail. Wet ends of triangle and join around finger, overlapping slightly, and press firmly to seal. Then push tip of triangle back to create "brim" on "cap." Place completed cappelletti on floured parchment paper sheets (do not let them touch). Repeat until all pasta has been used. Cover and refrigerate any unused filling for later use.

Tips

This recipe uses one full recipe of Dough for Filled Pasta (see recipes, pages 228–232), but there will be leftover filling. Use extra filling to fill different shapes of pasta or crespelle, or as topping for Polenta Crostini (see recipe, page 353). Since this filling contains raw egg, be sure to broil or bake the crostini long enough to cook the egg, about 15 minutes in a preheated 350°F (180°C) oven.

Don't forget, when rolling out pasta dough for filling, roll out the sheets one at a time, then fill, keeping the remaining dough covered. Otherwise the pasta sheets will dry out and become brittle.

4. Meanwhile, in a covered pasta pot over high heat, bring water to a rapid boil. Add salt and cappelletti and cook, uncovered, until pasta is al dente and filling is cooked through, 3 to 4 minutes. Scoop out about 1 cup (250 mL) of the pasta water and set aside. Drain pasta.

5. *Sauce:* In a large sauté pan over medium heat, combine 2 tbsp (25 mL) of the reserved pasta water, butter, cappelletti and ¼ cup (50 mL) of the Parmigiano-Reggiano. Using a wooden spoon, toss gently to coat evenly, adding more pasta water if necessary.

6. Transfer to a large serving platter and sprinkle with remaining cheese. Serve immediately.

Broccoli

Italians have been eating broccoli for thousands of years. Broccoli, a member of the cabbage family, descends from wild cabbage that grew along the Mediterranean coast and was domesticated by the first century A.D. Thomas Jefferson planted broccoli at Monticello in 1767, but it remained a gardening curiosity. According to some sources, Italian immigrants brought broccoli with them to North America in the early nineteenth century, but it didn't become popular until the following century. In 1923 Stephano and Andrea D'Arrigo — two brothers who had emigrated from Messina, Italy, and started a produce business in San Jose, California — planted broccoli and shipped a few crates to the Italian community in Boston's North End. Their broccoli business, named Andy Boy after Stephano's two-year-old son, boomed. And so did the vegetable's popularity. From a nutritional standpoint broccoli is considered a superhero, providing a wide range of nutrients.

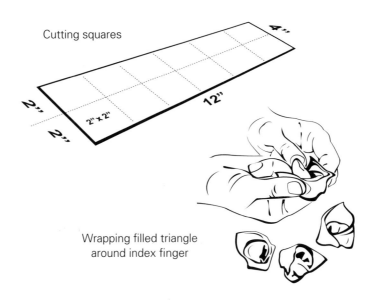

Cutting squares

Wrapping filled triangle around index finger

Gnocchi, Polenta and Crespelle: Cooking Cousins

Gnocchi (little dumplings), polenta (cornmeal mush) and crespelle (thin, savory pancakes) are not pasta, but they are prepared in so many of the same ways that I consider them cooking cousins of pasta. Like fresh pasta, they are mixed from scratch. Like fresh and dried pasta, they can be served with sauce or baked in the oven. Crespelle can even be filled, sauced and baked like fresh pasta. In fact you can substitute crespelle for the fresh pasta sheets called for in any of the baked pasta recipes.

In several ways gnocchi, polenta and crespelle are more versatile than pasta. They can all be prepared in advance and refrigerated or frozen for final cooking at a later time. They are less labor-intensive to make than fresh pasta. And they all have multiple applications. Gnocchi and polenta can be served as a side dish with roasted or grilled meats, poultry and fish in place of potatoes and rice. Polenta — the most versatile of the three — can be served warm and plain, warm with a sauce, fried or baked. It can even be cut into small crostini and fried, or topped with dozens of different savory toppings and served as hors d'oeuvres.

Gnocchi

Gnocchi are actually dumplings, but because they are frequently served and sauced like pasta, recipes for this Italian treat are often found in the fresh pasta section of cookbooks. They can be made from semolina, bread, cornmeal or potatoes. The most traditional gnocchi are made from potatoes (*gnocchi di patate*). Gnocchi dough is easier and quicker to mix than pasta dough. It doesn't need to be rolled out, requires minimal shaping and cooks quickly. In my opinion, gnocchi give you a lot of bang for your buck. My recipe for basic gnocchi calls for Yukon Gold potatoes, which give the gnocchi a golden color and full flavor — full enough to stand up to the five sauce recipes that accompany them. However, you may use russet or all-purpose white potatoes instead.

Polenta

Polenta is so traditional in the north of Italy that southern Italians call people from Lombardy, Trentino, the Veneto and Friuli *polentoni* — "polenta eaters." Polenta is slow-cooked cornmeal, but that description doesn't do it justice. It is not difficult to prepare but does require time and patience. The result is worth the effort. Cooked correctly, polenta is creamy, hearty and even more versatile than pasta. It can be served soft and hot as a side dish or as a main dish with many different sauces: cheese, vegetable, sausage, game, meat, seafood. Polenta can be chilled until set, then cut into shapes and fried, grilled or baked. For example, Polenta Gnocchi Roman Style (see recipe, page 354) is gnocchi made from chilled polenta cut into shapes and baked with butter and cheese. Although buckwheat flour is sometimes used in Italy to make polenta, the most common types are made with either finely ground white cornmeal or coarsely ground bright yellow cornmeal. From this one basic recipe you can prepare five different dishes.

Crespelle

Crespelle — traditional thin, savory pancakes — are easy to make and easy to fill, roll and bake. They can be made a day ahead and stacked, wrapped and refrigerated for filling and baking the next day. And once you get the hang of making crespelle, you can easily improvise your own fillings. Just fill and roll, place in a prepared baking pan, lightly nap with besciamella sauce and bake until bubbly. Crespelle make a nice appetizer or first course, or an entrée for supper.

Gnocchi di patate

Potato Gnocchi

Any floury or mealy potatoes, such as all-purpose white or russet potatoes, will work in this recipe, but don't use waxy potatoes. I like to use Yukon Gold potatoes for their rich color and flavor. Be aware that the potatoes should be cooked the day before you intend to make gnocchi and refrigerated overnight.

Makes about 1 lb (500 g) / 4 to 6 servings

Tip
If you are using a food mill to process the potatoes, use the coarsest blade.

- Potato ricer or food mill
- Stand mixer and dough hook

3	medium Yukon Gold potatoes, unpeeled	3
¾ cup	unbleached all-purpose flour or Tipo 00 Italian flour (see Tips, right)	175 mL
1	large egg	1
1 tbsp	grated Parmigiano-Reggiano	15 mL
¼ tsp	salt	1 mL
¼ tsp	freshly ground white pepper	1 mL
	Flour for dusting	

1. Place potatoes in a large pot. Add water to cover and bring to a boil over medium heat. Reduce heat and simmer until potatoes are easily pierced with a fork. Drain and let cool to room temperature. Then place in a self-sealing plastic bag and refrigerate overnight. The next day, using a paring knife, scrape off and discard skins and any eyes or blemishes. Put potatoes through ricer. Measure out 12 ounces (375 g), or 2 slightly rounded cups (510 mL).

2. Using stand mixer fitted with beaters or the paddle attachment, place potatoes in mixer bowl. Mix on slowest speed for 1 minute, to a relatively smooth consistency. Gradually add flour, egg, Parmigiano-Reggiano and salt and pepper. Remove beaters or paddle and attach dough hook. On speed 2, knead, scraping sides of bowl as necessary, until dough is firm and pliable, about 3 minutes.

3. Divide dough into 4 equal pieces. Dust a clean work surface lightly with flour. With lightly floured hands, shape each piece of dough by rolling into a long rope the thickness of an index finger. Using a sharp knife or bench scraper, cut dough into pieces about ½ inch (1 cm) long. Dust lightly with flour or roll them lightly in flour on your work surface. If you prefer indentations in your gnocchi, which help the sauce to cling, place a fork on work surface and press each gnocchi against the tines. You can also press them against the smallest holes of a cheese grater. Transfer to a plate dusted with flour. The gnocchi are now ready for use in your favorite recipe.

Tips

To measure flour, place in a large bowl and fluff with a large spoon. Then scoop into a flat-topped measuring cup and level with a straight-edged ruler or spatula.

Once gnocchi are made, you must cook them immediately. After they are cooked you can put them away for future use (see Cooking, Storing and Freezing Gnocchi, right).

Cooking, Storing and Freezing Gnocchi

Like their pasta relatives, gnocchi should be cooked in a large pot (at least 8 quarts/8 L) in about 6 quarts (6 L) of well salted (about 1 tbsp/15 mL) rapidly boiling water. Use a flat bench scraper to scoop up gnocchi and drop into the boiling water. Gnocchi are cooked to the al dente stage (about 6 minutes) and drained. Because they are tender, drain with care. Lift from water with a spider or large, shallow perforated scoop and transfer to a colander. If pouring directly into a colander, pour slowly and gently. Reserving some of the cooking water allows you to adjust sauces to the proper consistency, very much as you would use reserved pasta cooking water.

After gnocchi are cooked you can serve them immediately with your choice of sauce. If you prefer to use them later, place on a lightly greased baking sheet and let cool to room temperature. Once they are cooled, cover with plastic wrap and refrigerate for several hours or overnight. When you're ready to serve them, add cooked gnocchi to warm sauce and, using a nonstick spatula, toss gently to coat evenly.

If you prefer, you can place the pans of gnocchi in the freezer. Once frozen, transfer gnocchi to a resealable plastic bag lightly sprayed with vegetable oil on the inside. Gnocchi will keep, frozen, for up to 1 month. Before using, defrost in the refrigerator overnight or at room temperature.

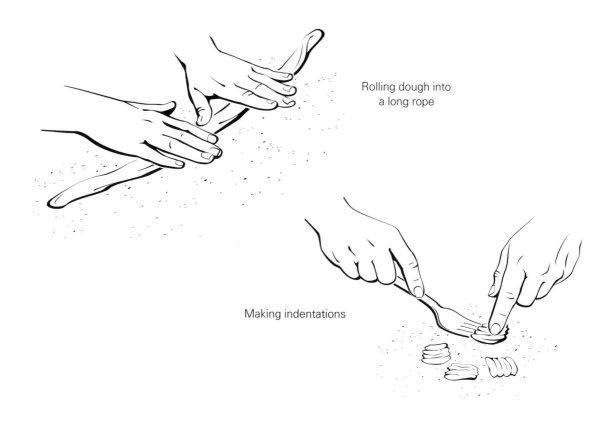

Rolling dough into a long rope

Making indentations

Gnocchi al pomodoro e basilico

Gnocchi with Tomato and Basil

This is a simple, straightforward way to serve gnocchi. It's a very approachable recipe and certainly an approachable dish.

Serves 4 to 6

Tips

Gnocchi are very tender. To coat gently with sauce without breaking them, use a thin nonstick spatula instead of a wooden spoon to lift and turn them in the sauce.

Gnocchi take about 6 minutes to reach the al dente stage.

Any dry white Italian table wine will work well in this recipe. Here I'd probably use Pinot Bianco, which is a good basic dry white wine for use in Italian cooking.

3 tbsp	extra-virgin olive oil	45 mL
1 tsp	thinly sliced garlic	5 mL
¼ cup	dry white Italian wine (see Tips, left)	50 mL
1½ cups	canned crushed Italian tomatoes	375 mL
¼ cup	hand-torn basil leaves	50 mL
	Salt and freshly ground black pepper	
1 tbsp	salt	15 mL
1 recipe	Potato Gnocchi (see page 344)	1 recipe
¾ cup	grated Parmigiano-Reggiano, divided	175 mL

1. In a covered pasta pot over high heat, bring water to a rapid boil.

2. Meanwhile, in a heavy 3-quart (3 L) pot, heat oil over medium heat. Add garlic and cook, stirring, until translucent but not browned, 2 to 3 minutes. Add wine and cook until reduced by half. Add tomatoes, basil and salt and pepper to taste. Reduce heat to low and simmer, stirring occasionally, until sauce is thick enough to coat the back of a spoon. Remove from heat and set aside, if necessary.

3. While sauce is simmering, add salt and gnocchi to the boiling water and cook, uncovered, over high heat until gnocchi are al dente. Scoop out about 1 cup (250 mL) of the cooking water and set aside. Drain gnocchi.

4. In a heavy 6-quart (6 L) sauté pan over medium heat, heat 2 tbsp (25 mL) of the reserved cooking water. Add tomato-basil sauce, stir and simmer for 1 to 2 minutes. Add gnocchi and, using a nonstick spatula (see Tips, left), toss gently to coat evenly. Simmer until sauce thickens slightly. Add half of the Parmigiano-Reggiano and swirl to coat well.

5. Transfer to a large serving platter and sprinkle with remaining cheese. Serve immediately.

Gnocchi alla Gorgonzola e noci

Gnocchi with Gorgonzola and Walnuts

Gorgonzola, one of Italy's most famous cheeses, comes in two forms: dolce and piccante. The piccante is firmer, with a more assertive flavor that goes particularly well with the walnuts in this recipe.

Serves 4 to 6

Tips

You can always find soft Gorgonzola at supermarkets, but you may have to go to a cheese shop for the firmer version, Gorgonzola piccante. If you can't find it, use soft Gorgonzola. You could also use other blue cheeses, but bear in mind that the farther you move away from good-quality Italian ingredients, the less authentic your pasta will become.

Walnuts are widely cultivated and very popular in Italy. Just make sure they are fresh. Walnuts are highly perishable because they contain a large amount of healthful omega-3 fatty acids. Buy them from a purveyor with high turnover, or taste before you buy. Walnuts that aren't fresh have an unpleasant rancid taste.

1½ cups	dry white Italian wine	375 mL
1 tsp	minced garlic	5 mL
2 tbsp	heavy or whipping (35%) cream	25 mL
8 oz	Gorgonzola piccante, at room-temperature, broken into chunks (see Tips, left)	250 g
	Salt and freshly ground white pepper	
1 tbsp	salt	15 mL
1 recipe	Potato Gnocchi (see page 344)	1 recipe
¼ cup	chopped walnut meats (see Tips, left)	50 mL

1. In a covered pasta pot over high heat, bring water to a rapid boil.

2. Meanwhile, in a heavy 3-quart (3 L) stainless steel pot over medium heat, bring wine and garlic to a boil. Cook until reduced to ¼ cup (50 mL). Add cream, lower heat and simmer, stirring, until slightly thickened. Add Gorgonzola and cook, stirring, until melted and smooth. Whisk to a smooth consistency as cheese melts. Season to taste with salt and pepper. Remove from heat and set aside.

3. Add salt and gnocchi to the boiling water and cook, uncovered, over high heat until gnocchi are al dente. Scoop out about 1 cup (250 mL) of the cooking water and set aside. Drain gnocchi.

4. In a large sauté pan, heat 2 tbsp (25 mL) of the reserved cooking water over medium heat. Add Gorgonzola sauce. Simmer, stirring, until smooth and thick. Add gnocchi and, using a nonstick spatula, toss gently to coat evenly.

5. Transfer to a large platter and sprinkle with walnuts. Serve immediately.

Gnocchi al pesto genovese

Gnocchi with Pesto

Pesto is a classic preparation that comes from Liguria, a region of Italy located near France. France has pistou, an uncooked basil-based sauce that is similar to the Italian pesto. Traditionally both were made by hand in a mortar and pestle. The secret when using modern equipment such as a blender or food processor is just to pulse so that you produce an uneven purée.

Serves 4 to 6

Tips

Gnocchi are very tender. To coat gently with sauce, use a thin nonstick spatula to lift and turn the gnocchi in the sauce without breaking them.

One of the cheeses used in this dish is Pecorino Sardo, a sheep's-milk cheese from Sardinia. It comes in two forms: soft, or dolce (it has a green emblem on the package), and hard, or maturo (it has a blue emblem). The hard cheese is used for grating.

I usually season my sauces in the initial stages of cooking so the flavors have time to bloom. I always taste the final product and, if necessary, add more salt and pepper just before serving.

Pesto

30	fresh basil leaves (no stems)	30
2	cloves garlic	2
3 tbsp	pine nuts	45 mL
½ cup	grated Parmigiano-Reggiano	125 mL
½ cup	grated Pecorino Sardo (see Tips, left)	125 mL
3 tbsp	extra-virgin olive oil	45 mL
	Salt and freshly ground black pepper	

Gnocchi

1 tbsp	salt	15 mL
1 recipe	Potato Gnocchi (see page 344)	1 recipe
3 tbsp	grated Parmigiano-Reggiano	45 mL

1. In a covered pasta pot over high heat, bring water to a rapid boil.

2. *Pesto:* In a blender or food processor fitted with a steel blade, combine basil, garlic, pine nuts, Parmigiano-Reggiano and Pecorino Sardo. Pulse for 3 seconds. Add olive oil and continue to pulse until mixture is roughly puréed. Add salt and pepper to taste and pulse once. Set aside or cover and refrigerate for up to 4 days.

3. *Gnocchi:* Add salt and gnocchi to the boiling water and cook, uncovered, over high heat until gnocchi are al dente, about 6 minutes. Scoop out about 1 cup (250 mL) of the cooking water and set aside. Drain gnocchi.

4. In a large sauté pan, heat 2 tbsp (25 mL) of the reserved cooking water, reserved pesto and Parmigiano-Reggiano. Over medium heat and using a nonstick spatula, toss gently to coat evenly.

5. Transfer to a large serving platter and serve immediately.

Gnocchi con broccoli

Gnocchi with Broccoli

This dish is a bit different because we are used to seeing broccoli with pasta, not gnocchi — but it is very easy to make. American domestic broccoli is popular and widely available; the finished dish depends on good-quality ingredients.

Serves 4 to 6

Tip

Gnocchi are very tender. To coat gently with sauce, use a thin nonstick spatula to lift and turn the gnocchi in the sauce without breaking them.

3 tbsp	extra-virgin olive oil	45 mL
1 lb	broccoli florets (about 6 cups/1.5 L, packed)	500 g
	Salt and freshly ground white pepper	
4 cups (approx.)	water	1 L
1 tbsp	salt	15 mL
1 recipe	Potato Gnocchi (see page 344)	1 recipe
¾ cup	grated Parmigiano-Reggiano, divided	175 mL

1. In a covered pasta pot over high heat, bring water to a rapid boil.

2. Meanwhile, in a large sauté pan, heat oil over medium heat. Add broccoli and salt and pepper to taste and cook, stirring, until broccoli changes color to intensely green, about 5 minutes. Add ¼ cup (50 mL) water and cook, stirring, until evaporated. Continue cooking and stirring, adding water ¼ cup (50 mL) at a time, until broccoli is soft and tender, about 10 minutes. Remove from heat and set aside.

3. Add salt and gnocchi to the boiling water and cook, uncovered, over high heat until gnocchi are al dente. Drain.

4. Return sauté pan to medium heat. Add gnocchi and, using a thin nonstick spatula, toss gently to coat evenly. Add half of the Parmigiano-Reggiano and toss well.

5. Transfer to a large platter and sprinkle with remaining cheese. Serve immediately.

Gnocchi con zucca e salvia

Gnocchi with Butternut Squash and Sage

Butternut squash and fresh sage make a classic combination in Italian cooking. Squash-stuffed ravioli with brown butter and sage is a particularly popular dish. This is my interpretation of the combination.

Serves 4 to 6

Tips

Gnocchi are very tender. To coat gently with sauce, use a thin nonstick spatula to lift and turn the gnocchi in the sauce without breaking them.

For best results grate the cheese yourself, but if time is at a premium, use already grated cheese. Whichever form you choose, just be sure to buy the very best Italian Pecorino Romano you can find and grate it finely to ensure you have the quantity called for in the recipe.

3 tbsp	extra-virgin olive oil	45 mL
1½ cups	diced butternut squash	375 mL
	Salt and freshly ground white pepper	
2 tbsp	chopped fresh sage leaves	25 mL
1 cup (approx.)	water, divided	250 mL
1 tbsp	salt	15 mL
1 recipe	Potato Gnocchi (see page 344)	1 recipe
¾ cup	grated Pecorino Romano, divided	175 mL

1. In a covered pasta pot over high heat, bring water to a rapid boil.

2. Meanwhile, in a large sauté pan, heat oil over medium heat. Add squash and stir. Season with salt and pepper to taste. Add sage and cook, stirring, until squash is lightly browned, about 9 minutes. Add ¼ cup (50 mL) water and cook, stirring, until reduced by half. Continue cooking and stirring, adding water ¼ cup (50 mL) at a time, until squash is extremely soft and water is absorbed. Remove pan from heat and set aside.

3. Add salt and gnocchi to the boiling water and cook, uncovered, over high heat, until gnocchi are al dente. Drain.

4. Return sauté pan to medium heat. Add gnocchi and, using a nonstick spatula, toss gently to coat evenly. Add half of the Pecorino Romano and swirl pan and toss again to coat well.

5. Transfer to a large serving platter and sprinkle with remaining cheese. Serve immediately.

Basic Polenta

Polenta is as versatile as if not more so than pasta. You can serve it hot as a side dish or top it with a variety of sauces. You can chill and slice it, or mold it, then bake or fry. I have shown each way to use this delicious dish in the recipes that follow. Polenta does take time to cook and develop its full flavor. And, as with many Italian dishes, various cooks and chefs assert that theirs is the best — perhaps the only — way to prepare it, from cooking it for 3 hours to microwaving it for 12 minutes to baking it slowly in the oven. The following stovetop recipe is the most widely used method. It will give you a good result, so long as your cornmeal is freshly milled, not old and stale. Can you use the so-called instant or quick-cooking versions of polenta that are available? Of course. And you can even use the bland packed precooked polenta — just open and heat. But I recommend you try this method first so you will have a basis for taste comparison. Polenta is a great accompaniment to chicken and fish.

Serves 4 to 6

4 cups	water, divided	1 L
1 cup	coarse yellow cornmeal, preferably stone-ground	250 mL
1 tsp	salt	5 mL
2 tbsp	unsalted butter	25 mL
1/3 cup	grated Parmigiano-Reggiano	75 mL

1. In a medium saucepan over high heat, bring 3 cups (750 mL) of the water to a boil. In a small bowl whisk together cornmeal, salt and remaining 1 cup (250 mL) water until smooth. Add to boiling water, whisking constantly until it returns to a boil. Reduce heat to low (see Tips, below). Cook, uncovered, until polenta is thick and creamy, about 40 minutes, stirring every 10 minutes to prevent lumps from forming. If polenta becomes too thick, add more water. Remove from heat.

2. Stir in butter and cheese. Transfer to a serving bowl and serve immediately or use to make Polenta Crostini (see recipe, page 353).

Variation

I'm a big fan of making polenta with milk instead of water, because it has a richer flavor. Simply substitute an equal quantity of milk for the water in the recipe. If you really want to notch up the flavor, infuse the milk with a couple of sprigs of fresh rosemary or sage before using. Just add the herbs to the milk and bring it to a boil, then remove from heat and let it steep. When milk reaches room temperature, strain and discard the herbs.

Tips

If necessary, use a "heat tamer" under the pot to keep the heat low enough to prevent polenta from splattering.

You can prepare polenta up to an hour before serving. Transfer to a stainless steel bowl or the top of a double boiler, cover and keep warm over barely simmering water. Stir in butter and cheese just before serving.

If polenta becomes too thick during cooking because the heat is too high, stir in more water 1/4 cup (50 mL) at a time until desired consistency is reached.

Crostini di polenta

Polenta Crostini

Polenta crostini are easy to make and great platforms for toppings such as caponata, tapenade, sautéed finely diced mushrooms, tiny shrimp, pâté, cheese, chopped tomatoes — almost anything you would put on crackers or bruschetta. You can serve them as appetizers or canapés.

Makes 48 crostini

Tips

Wiping the pan with a damp towel helps the plastic to stick.

To yield 48 crostini, cut 6 rows along the shorter side of the pan and 8 rows along the longer side. The pieces will be almost square. You can also cut the crostini into diamond or rectangle shapes, or into small circles using a straight-edged cookie cutter. The circles can be cut in half to form half-moons. Squares, diamonds and rectangles utilize the polenta fully; circles create some waste.

If you are not going to cook the cut crostini, you can freeze them on a lightly oiled pan, covered with plastic wrap, until solid, then transfer to a resealable plastic bag lightly sprayed on the inside with vegetable oil to prevent sticking. Freeze for up to 1 month.

• 13- by 9- by 2-inch (3 L) baking dish or jelly-roll pan

1 recipe	Basic Polenta (see page 352)	1 recipe
	Extra-virgin olive oil	

1. Wipe pan with a damp clean towel, then line with a large piece of plastic wrap at least twice the length of the pan, pressing it down so it sticks and making sure corners are covered. Using a spatula, spread warm polenta evenly over plastic, taking care to fill the corners. Bring ends of plastic wrap up to cover entire surface.

2. Using a spatula, flatten polenta to level it. Let cool to room temperature, then refrigerate, covered, for at least 6 hours or up to 3 days.

3. When you're ready to cook, cut crostini (see Tips, left) and make baked or fried polenta crostini.

Baked Polenta Crostini

• Preheat oven to 400°F (200°C)

Brush polenta shapes with olive oil. Place on a greased baking sheet and bake in preheated oven for 30 minutes, turning once.

Fried Polenta Crostini

In a large sauté pan, heat oil or butter to a depth of 1 inch (2.5 cm) over medium-high heat. Add polenta pieces in batches and cook until golden brown on both sides, turning once, about 5 minutes a side. Serve warm or at room temperature, spread with your choice of topping.

Gnocchi di polenta alla romana

Polenta Gnocchi Roman Style

· ·

When it comes to eating polenta, some Italians like it soft and creamy, some like it fried, some like it baked, and some like it shaped into dumplings. Long ago, people in the province of Lazio, where Rome is located, developed this, their favorite method of baking polenta, which is an easy two-day project. They make it into (in this case, round) gnocchi-like dumplings — that's why this recipe has been dubbed alla romana, *or "Roman style."*

Serves 4 to 6

- 13- by 9- by 2-inch (3 L) baking dish or jelly-roll pan
- 12-cup (3 L) shallow baking dish, lightly greased with butter

3 cups	whole milk	750 mL
1 cup	cold water	250 mL
1 tsp	salt	5 mL
1⅜ cups	fine yellow cornmeal, preferably stone-ground	325 mL
¼ tsp	freshly ground white pepper	1 mL
¼ cup	unsalted butter, at room temperature	50 mL
1 cup	grated Parmigiano-Reggiano, divided	250 mL

1. *Day One:* In a heavy saucepan over medium heat, combine milk, water and salt. Bring to a simmer. Gradually add cornmeal in a steady stream, stirring constantly as polenta thickens. Once all of the cornmeal has been added to the pot, reduce heat to very low (place a "heat tamer" under the pot if necessary) and cook, stirring every 10 minutes, until polenta is soft and creamy, about 30 minutes.

2. Add pepper, butter and ⅔ cup (150 mL) of the Parmigiano-Reggiano. Stir, remove from heat and set aside.

3. Wipe pan with a damp clean towel, then line with a piece of plastic wrap at least twice the length of the pan, pressing down so that it sticks and making sure corners are covered. Using a spatula, spread warm polenta evenly over plastic, taking care to fill the corners. Bring ends of plastic wrap up to cover entire surface.

4. Using a spatula, flatten polenta to level it. Let cool to room temperature, then refrigerate, covered, overnight.

5. *Day Two:* When you're ready to cook, preheat oven to 350°F (180°C). Cut polenta into circles using a straight-sided 1-inch (2.5 cm) or 1½-inch (4 cm) diameter cookie cutter. Sprinkle bottom and sides of prepared 12-cup (3 L) baking dish with half the remaining cheese. Layer polenta gnocchi, slightly overlapping, in the dish. Sprinkle with remaining cheese. Bake until gnocchi are hot and lightly browned, about 1 hour. Serve immediately.

Polenta e patate arrostide

Polenta and Roasted Potatoes

Potatoes and polenta baked together is a familiar combination in central Italy, where it is traditionally served as a pasta course. It also makes a great side dish. The addition of onions and aromatic rosemary enhances the flavor. You can make the polenta gnocchi a day or two in advance and refrigerate, then make the potatoes and assemble the dish for baking the day you are going to eat it.

Serves 4 to 6

- Preheat oven to 350°F (180°C)
- Ovenproof sauté pan with lid
- 12-cup (3 L) shallow baking dish, liberally greased with butter

3	potatoes, preferably Yukon Gold, peeled and patted dry	3
¼ cup	extra-virgin olive oil	50 mL
	Salt and freshly ground black pepper	
1	onion, halved lengthwise, then horizontally and thinly sliced	1
1 tsp	fresh rosemary leaves	5 mL
6 tbsp	grated Parmigiano-Reggiano, divided	90 mL
½ recipe	Polenta Gnocchi Roman Style (see recipe, page 354)	½ recipe

1. Cut each potato in half and each half into quarters. In a large sauté pan, heat oil over medium heat. Add potatoes and season to taste with salt and pepper. Cook until well browned, turning once, about 10 minutes (8 minutes on the first side, 2 minutes on the second). Cover and place in preheated oven for 15 minutes to crisp and continue browning. Remove from oven.

2. Add onion and rosemary to potatoes and mix well, distributing evenly. Return to oven and bake, uncovered, for 10 minutes. Remove from oven and set aside.

3. Sprinkle prepared baking dish with 3 tbsp (45 mL) of the Parmigiano-Reggiano. In a single layer, arrange polenta gnocchi alternately with potato wedges, overlapping. Sprinkle with remaining cheese. Return to oven and bake until gnocchi have begun to turn golden, about 1 hour. Serve immediately.

Polenta con polpette di vitello

Soft Polenta with Veal Meatballs

Serves 4 to 6

Tip

I usually season my sauces
in the initial stages of
cooking so the flavors have
time to bloom. I always
taste the final product and,
if necessary, add more salt
and pepper just before
serving.

Classic Tomato Sauce

2 tbsp	extra-virgin olive oil	25 mL
1 tsp	thinly sliced garlic	5 mL
	Salt and freshly ground black pepper	
1 cup	canned crushed Italian tomatoes	250 mL
1 tbsp	hand-torn basil leaves	15 mL
½ tsp	granulated sugar (see Tips, right)	2 mL

Meatballs

8 oz	ground veal, divided	250 g
2	slices (1 inch/2.5 cm) Italian bread, crusts removed and torn into chunks	2
1	large egg, whisked	1
1 tsp	finely chopped Italian parsley leaves	5 mL
½ tsp	minced garlic	2 mL
1 tbsp	grated Parmigiano-Reggiano	15 mL
	Freshly grated nutmeg	
	Salt and freshly ground black pepper	
2 tbsp	extra-virgin olive oil	25 mL

Polenta

1 recipe	Basic Polenta (see page 352)	1 recipe
¼ cup	unsalted butter	50 mL
¼ cup	grated Parmigiano-Reggiano	50 mL

1. *Classic Tomato Sauce:* In a large saucepan, heat oil, garlic and salt and pepper to taste over medium heat. Cook, stirring, until garlic is translucent but not browned, 2 to 3 minutes. Add tomatoes, basil and sugar, reduce heat to low and simmer until thick enough to coat the back of a spoon, about 30 minutes. Remove from heat and set aside.

2. *Meatballs:* Meanwhile, in a food processor, combine half of the veal, bread, egg, parsley, garlic, cheese and nutmeg, salt and pepper to taste. Pulse several times. Transfer to a chilled mixing bowl. Add remaining veal and mix well. Shape into 12 small meatballs, placing on a tray as completed.

When mixing the veal in the food processor, be sure not to overprocess, or the meat will overheat, which will damage the texture.

Granulated white refined sugar is labeled either "granulated sugar" or "granulated cane sugar." Granulated sugar can be made from beets, but granulated cane sugar can be made only from sugar cane. It has, in my opinion, a better, cleaner flavor than granulated beet sugar.

3. In a large, heavy sauté pan, heat olive oil over medium heat until it ripples. Add meatballs, in batches if necessary, and brown on all sides, about 10 minutes. As meatballs brown, transfer them to tomato sauce. When all have been added, return saucepan to medium-low heat and simmer for 30 minutes, until meatballs are cooked through and flavors meld.

4. *Polenta:* Add butter and Parmigiano-Reggiano to polenta and stir well (polenta should be creamy).

5. To serve, transfer prepared polenta to a warm platter and top with meatballs and tomato sauce. Serve immediately.

Soft Polenta with Poached Egg

On a cold winter's day, especially when it is snowing outside, this is one of my favorite dishes for lunch or dinner.

Serves 4 to 6

Tips

To infuse milk with rosemary, add a couple of sprigs of fresh rosemary to the milk, bring it to a boil, remove from heat and let it steep. When it reaches room temperature, strain and discard the rosemary. You could also make the polenta using sage-infused milk, in which case substitute sage for the rosemary.

Don't scrimp on ingredients. Always buy the best quality you can find and afford. It will make a big difference to the results you produce.

Any dry white Italian table wine will work well in this recipe. Here I'd probably use Pinot Bianco, which is a good basic dry white wine for use in Italian cooking.

1 recipe	Basic Polenta (see page 352) made with rosemary-infused milk (see Tips, left)	1 recipe
¼ cup	unsalted butter	50 mL
¼ cup	grated Parmigiano-Reggiano	50 mL
8 cups	water	2 L
¼ cup	dry white Italian wine	50 mL
2 tbsp	Italian white wine vinegar	25 mL
1 tsp	salt	5 mL
4 to 6	large eggs	4 to 6
¼ cup	shaved Parmigiano-Reggiano	50 mL

1. Add butter and grated Parmigiano-Reggiano to polenta and stir well (polenta should be creamy). Set aside and keep warm.

2. In a saucepan over high heat, bring water, wine, vinegar and salt to a rapid boil. Reduce heat to medium-low so water just simmers.

3. One at a time, crack eggs into simmering water. Meanwhile, transfer polenta to serving plates. Poach eggs to desired degree of doneness and, using a slotted spoon, place on top of polenta.

Crespelle

The French call them crêpes, but Italians call thin, savory pancakes crespelle. Italians also insist that crespelle were introduced to France by 14-year-old Caterina de Medici when she came from Florence — with her Tuscan chefs and recipes — to marry Henri of Orleans (later Henri II of France). In any event, crespelle are easy to make. They can also be cooked in advance and stacked, then stuffed and baked later.

Makes 15 crespelle

- 8-inch (20 cm) nonstick skillet or crepe pan, lightly brushed or sprayed with olive oil

1 cup	all-purpose flour	250 mL
2	large eggs	2
1 cup	whole milk	250 mL
1 tbsp	melted unsalted butter	15 mL
½ tsp	salt	2 mL
½ tsp	freshly ground white pepper	2 mL
1 tsp	extra-virgin olive oil or olive oil cooking spray	5 mL

1. In a blender, combine flour, eggs, milk, butter, salt and pepper. Blend at high speed to make a smooth batter, stopping and scraping down sides as necessary. Transfer to a bowl, cover and let rest at room temperature for 1 hour. Whisk before using.

2. Place prepared pan over medium heat and heat until a drop of water sizzles. Using a ladle, pour 2 tbsp (25 mL) batter into pan, tilting until batter evenly covers bottom of pan. Cook until firm on top, with no uncooked spots, and light brown on bottom, about 1 minute. Using a small spatula, turn and cook for about 10 seconds more. Transfer to a large plate and cover with a clean napkin. Repeat until all the batter is used up, stacking crespelle under napkin as they are cooked and spraying or brushing the pan with oil as necessary. Crespelle are now ready to be filled. If not using immediately, remove napkin, wrap plate with plastic and refrigerate for several hours or overnight.

Variations

Crespelle can be used in place of cannelloni in Baked Cannelloni with Beef Ragù (see recipe, page 298) and Baked Cannelloni with Spinach and Béchamel (page 296). When substituting crespelle for cannelloni, fill and roll as for fresh pasta sheets.

Crespelle can be used in place of fresh lasagna sheets in Lasagne alla Bolognese (see recipe, page 300) and Spring Vegetable Lasagne (see recipe, page 302). When substituting crespelle for fresh pasta sheets in these recipes, lay them out flat, overlapping them to fit the pan.

Crespelle al petto di pollo e verza

Baked Crespelle with Chicken Breast and Cabbage

Serves 4 to 6		

Tip

For best results grate the cheese yourself, but if time is at a premium, use already grated cheese. Whichever form you choose, just be sure to buy the very best Italian Parmigiano-Reggiano you can find and grate it finely to ensure you have the quantity called for in the recipe.

- Preheat oven to 375°F (190°C)
- 13- by 9- by 2-inch (3 L) baking dish, lightly greased with butter

3 tbsp	extra-virgin olive oil	45 mL
¼ cup	finely diced pancetta	50 mL
¼ cup	finely diced onion	50 mL
1½ cups	finely diced deribbed Savoy cabbage	375 mL
1½ cups	diced boneless, skinless chicken breast	75 mL
	Salt and freshly ground white pepper	
1 cup	dry white Italian wine	250 mL
⅔ cup	grated Parmigiano-Reggiano, divided	150 mL
3 cups	Besciamella Sauce, divided (see recipe, page 289)	750 mL
12	crespelle (see recipe, page 359)	12
3 tbsp	whole milk	45 mL

1. In a large sauté pan, heat oil over medium heat. Add pancetta and onion and cook, stirring, until onion is translucent, about 3 minutes. Add cabbage and chicken and season to taste with salt and pepper. Cook, stirring, until cabbage is tender and chicken is cooked through, about 10 minutes. Add wine and cook over medium-high heat until almost evaporated. Remove from heat, transfer to a mixing bowl and let cool to room temperature.

2. When cabbage mixture has cooled, add ¼ cup (50 mL) of the Parmigiano-Reggiano and half of the besciamella sauce. Mix well.

3. Sprinkle prepared dish with 3 tbsp (45 mL) of the Parmigiano-Reggiano. One at a time, place crespelle on a work surface. Spoon about ¼ cup (50 mL) filling along center and roll to form a tube, keeping filling in the middle. Transfer filled crespelle, seam-side-down, to prepared dish. Add milk to remaining besciamella sauce and stir well. Ladle over crespelle and sprinkle with remaining cheese.

4. Bake in preheated oven until top is golden brown, about 30 minutes. Serve immediately.

Make Ahead

Complete steps 1 through 3. Cover with plastic wrap and refrigerate overnight. When you're ready to serve, bake in preheated oven, adding 10 to 15 minutes to the baking time.

Crespelle al ragù di merluzzo

Baked Crespelle with Cod Ragù

Merluzzo *is what Italians call nasello (hake), a fish very similar to the North American cod. Mild white cod makes a perfect filling for the tender, delicate crespelle. You can make the filling and the crespelle a day ahead and refrigerate, but I recommend that you assemble, bake and enjoy the cod-filled crespelle on the same day.*

Serves 4 to 6

Tip

To serve crespelle, use a thin 10-inch (25 cm) cake spatula to separate each crepe at the sides and lift them out by sliding the spatula underneath.

- Preheat oven to 375°F (190°C)
- 13- by 9- by 2-inch (3 L) baking dish, lightly greased with butter

3 tbsp	extra-virgin olive oil	45 mL
2 tbsp	diced onion	25 mL
2 tbsp	diced peeled celery	25 mL
2 tbsp	diced fennel bulb	25 mL
1½ cups	diced boneless, skinless cod	375 mL
1 cup	dry white Italian wine	250 mL
	Salt and freshly ground white pepper	
3 cups	Besciamella Sauce, divided (see recipe, page 289)	750 mL
3 tbsp	whole milk	45 mL
⅔ cup	dry white Italian breadcrumbs, divided	150 mL
12	crespelle (see recipe, page 359)	12

1. In a large sauté pan, heat oil over medium heat. Add onion, celery and fennel and cook, stirring, until vegetables are soft, about 5 minutes. Add cod and wine and cook until wine is almost evaporated. Season to taste with salt and pepper. Remove from heat, transfer to a mixing bowl and let cool to room temperature.

2. When mixture has cooled, add half of the besciamella sauce and stir well.

3. Sprinkle ¼ cup (50 mL) of the breadcrumbs evenly over prepared dish. One at a time, place crespelle on a work surface. Spoon about ¼ cup (50 mL) filling along center and roll to form a tube, keeping filling in the middle. Transfer filled crespelle, seam-side-down, to prepared dish. Add milk to remaining besciamella sauce and stir well. Spread evenly over top and sprinkle with remaining breadcrumbs.

4. Bake in preheated oven until top is golden brown, about 35 minutes. Serve immediately.

Make Ahead

Complete step 2 and cover and refrigerate overnight. Make crespelle, wrap with plastic and refrigerate. When you're ready to cook, complete the recipe.

Pasta Desserts: For the Sweet Tooth

The Italian dessert kitchen is immensely elaborate, a result of centuries of regional traditions. In my opinion, Italian desserts are as complex as those for which the French and Swiss are known. Traditional Italian desserts include cakes, tarts, tortes, sweet breads, pastries, cookies, creams and puddings, fried pastries and fruit desserts, not to mention frozen desserts such as gelato, granita and semifreddo. Pasta, however, is used sparingly in the Italian dessert kitchen. But because this book is about pasta, I have created some recipes to satisfy those with a sweet tooth.

Six of the desserts call for dried pasta and are rather simple to make. In the chapter Making Fresh Pasta, I have included two recipes for sweet pasta dough, one plain and one chocolate. From these two doughs you can make four very special finales to a festive — non-pasta — meal.

Budino di fusilli con ricotta al miele

Fusilli Pudding with Ricotta and Honey

This resembles a baked noodle pudding, with curly fusilli standing in for the noodles. Creamy ricotta is flavored with citrus and cinnamon, and after baking, the top is drizzled with honey. Because honey is the crowning touch, I encourage you to find excellent artisanally produced honey rather than using a generic blend. I think the taste will be a pleasant surprise.

Serves 8

Tip

I prefer the texture, taste and appearance of dried breadcrumbs made from crustless Italian bread. An Italian bakery is the best source for these, or you can make them yourself from Italian bread, crusts removed, by pulsing it in a food processor.

- Preheat oven to 350°F (180°C)
- 12-cup (3 L) shallow baking dish, greased with butter

1 tbsp	salt	15 mL
1 lb	dried fusilli (see Variation, below)	500 g
1½ tbsp	finely grated orange zest	22 mL
1½ tbsp	finely grated lemon zest	22 mL
½ tsp	ground cinnamon	2 mL
2 tbsp	confectioner's (icing) sugar	25 mL
1 cup	fresh whole-milk ricotta	250 mL
½ cup	heavy or whipping (35%) cream	125 mL
3	large eggs, lightly beaten	3
1 tbsp	unsalted butter	15 mL
4 tbsp	dry white Italian breadcrumbs (see Tip, left)	60 mL
¼ cup	honey, preferably Italian	50 mL
	Vanilla gelato or ice cream, optional	
	Lightly sweetened vanilla-flavored whipped cream, optional (see Tip, page 372)	

1. In a covered pasta pot over high heat, bring water to a rapid boil. Add salt and fusilli and cook, uncovered, until pasta is slightly more than al dente. Drain and transfer to a mixing bowl.

2. Add orange and lemon zest, cinnamon, sugar, ricotta, cream and eggs. Mix well and set aside for 10 minutes.

3. Cover bottom and sides of prepared dish with breadcrumbs. Add fusilli mixture and use a plastic spatula level the top. Bake in preheated oven until pudding is firm to the touch and a tester inserted in the middle comes out clean, 30 to 35 minutes.

4. Remove from oven and drizzle honey over top. Serve immediately. If desired, top each serving with a scoop of vanilla ice cream or gelato or a large dollop of whipped cream.

Variation

Substitute rotini for the fusilli.

Budino di maccheroni con mele e mandorle

Maccheroni Pudding with Apple and Almonds

Consider this a sweet Italian version of kugel, or noodle pudding. It is not cloyingly sweet, but just sweet enough. Serve it with a very large spoon so everyone at the table gets some of the sugar-dusted top in their dish.

Serves 8

Tip

If your baking dish is attractive, place it on the dining table on top of a trivet or large plate. Serve with a very large spoon.

Mace

Mace tastes similar to nutmeg, and here's why. Mace is a lacy red membrane that covers the nutmeg seed. When the membrane is dried, it turns orange-yellow. Usually sold ground, mace tastes sharper than nutmeg. Warm and aromatic, it can flavor both sweet and savory foods. If you don't have it, substitute an equal quantity of nutmeg, allspice or cinnamon.

- Preheat oven to 350°F (180°C)
- 12-cup (3 L) shallow baking dish, greased with butter

1 tbsp	salt	15 mL
1 lb	dried maccheroni	500 g
3 cups	diced peeled Granny Smith apples	750 mL
1/4 cup	dark raisins	50 mL
1/4 cup	golden raisins	50 ml
1/2 tsp	ground mace	2 mL
1/4 cup	confectioner's (icing) sugar, plus additional for dusting	50 mL
1 cup	heavy or whipping (35%) cream	250 mL
4	large eggs, lightly beaten	4
1 tbsp	unsalted butter	15 mL
1/4 cup	dry white Italian breadcrumbs	50 mL
1/2 cup	thinly sliced almonds	125 mL
	Vanilla gelato or ice cream, optional	
	Lightly sweetened vanilla-flavored whipped cream, optional (see Tip, page 372)	

1. In a covered pasta pot over high heat, bring water to a rapid boil. Add salt and maccheroni and cook, uncovered, until pasta is slightly softer than al dente. Drain and transfer to a mixing bowl.

2. Add apple, raisins, mace, sugar, cream and eggs. Mix well and set aside for 10 minutes.

3. Cover bottom and sides of prepared dish with breadcrumbs. Add maccheroni mixture and use a plastic spatula to level the top. Sprinkle with almonds. Bake in preheated oven until pudding is firm to the touch and a tester inserted in the middle comes out clean, 30 to 35 minutes.

4. Remove from oven and dust top generously with confectioner's sugar. Serve immediately. If desired, top each serving with a scoop of gelato or ice cream or a dollop of whipped cream.

Variation

Substitute penne for the maccheroni.

Ditalini con crema di Nutella

Ditalini with Chocolate Hazelnut Cream

Ditalini ("little thimbles") are a small ridged tubular pasta cut so that its width roughly equals its length. Chocolate hazelnut spread, a delicious combination of hazelnuts, honey and cocoa, has been called Italian peanut butter. This pudding is served immediately or it can be chilled and then served.

Serves 8

Tip

Always use a large pot and plenty of water when cooking pasta. To properly cook 1 pound (500 g) of pasta, you'll need a pot with a volume of at least 8 quarts (8 L) so that you can use 6 quarts (6 L) of water.

- Rimmed baking sheet

1 tbsp	salt	15 mL
1 lb	dried ditalini	500 g
¾ cup	mascarpone	175 mL
1 cup	chocolate hazelnut spread	250 mL
1 cup	heavy or whipping (35%) cream, stiffly whipped	250 mL
¼ cup	chopped hazelnuts	50 mL
	Lightly sweetened vanilla-flavored whipped cream, optional (see Tip, page 372)	

1. In a covered pasta pot over high heat, bring water to a rapid boil. Add salt and ditalini and cook, uncovered, until pasta is slightly softer than al dente. Drain. Transfer to baking sheet and let cool to room temperature.

2. In a mixing bowl, combine mascarpone and chocolate hazelnut spread and mix well. Gently fold in whipped cream. Add cooled ditalini and mix gently.

3. Transfer to a serving dish and top with hazelnuts. Serve immediately, topped with a large dollop of whipped cream, if using. To serve later, refrigerate, covered, until chilled, and top with whipped cream just before serving, if using.

Variation

Substitute 1 cup (250 mL) imported Italian apricot jam for the chocolate hazelnut spread.

Nutella

Nutella is the brand name of the sweet chocolate hazelnut spread invented by an Italian company in the 1940s. It is now available in more than 75 countries. The amount of sugar in the recipes varies from country to country — in Italy Nutella contains less sugar than the version sold in France.

Tripolini con frutti secchi e pistacchi

Tripolini with Dried Fruits and Pistachios

●●●

Tripolini are tiny bow-tie shapes. In this dessert they are combined with a variety of minced dried fruits that have been marinated in dry Marsala wine.

Serves 6 to 8

- Rimmed baking sheet

¼ cup	finely minced dried apricots	50 mL
¼ cup	finely minced dried cherries	50 mL
¼ cup	finely minced dark raisins	50 mL
¼ cup	finely minced golden raisins	50 mL
¼ cup	finely minced dried figs	50 mL
1 cup	dry (secco) Marsala wine	250 mL
⅛ tsp	ground dried juniper berries	0.5 mL
1 tbsp	salt	15 mL
1 lb	dried tripolini	500 g
¼ cup	chopped pistachios	50 mL
	Lightly sweetened vanilla-flavored whipped cream, optional (see Tip, page 372)	

1. In a mixing bowl, combine dried fruit, Marsala and juniper berries. Stir well and set aside.

2. In a covered pasta pot over high heat, bring water to a rapid boil. Add salt and tripolini and cook, uncovered, until pasta is slightly softer than al dente. Drain and spread out on baking sheet and let cool to room temperature.

3. Add tripolini to fruit-wine mixture and mix well to coat pasta evenly.

4. Transfer to a serving bowl and top with chopped pistachios. Serve immediately, topping each serving with a large dollop of whipped cream, if using.

Variations

Substitute orzo for the tripolini.

Substitute ground allspice or cinnamon for the juniper berries.

Juniper Berries

Edible dried juniper berries are actually the tiny cones produced by a handful of juniper trees, among them *Juniperus communis*. (Some juniper tree berries are too bitter to eat and a few are even toxic.) The berries are green when young and purple-black when mature. Dried mature berries are used in cooking, while fresh green berries are used to flavor gin. It is best to buy the freshest dried whole berries and grind them just before using. Once crushed, the flavor rapidly diminishes.

Cannelloni al cioccolato con ricotta e arancia

Chocolate Cannelloni Filled with Sweet Ricotta and Oranges

* * *

This cannelloni shell is made of sweet fresh chocolate pasta and filled with sweet ricotta flavored with orange and lemon zest. The cannelloni are baked on a bed of orange slices and served warm topped with fresh ripe orange segments. It takes a bit of effort, but I believe the results are well worth it.

Serves 6

Tips

Slice peeled oranges crosswise with a sharp knife into thin rounds, ⅛ to ¼ inch (0.25 to 0.5 cm) thick.

To easily segment oranges, first slice about ¼ inch (0.5 cm) off the top and bottom of the orange. Next, using a sharp chef's knife, cut off the peel and pith in sections from top to bottom. The flesh of the orange, without any pith or peel, should be exposed. Next, take a thin, sharp paring knife and separate the segments by cutting in toward the center between the membranes on each side.

- Preheat oven to 350°F (180°C)
- 12-cup (3 L) shallow baking dish, greased with butter

1¼ cups	fresh whole-milk ricotta	300 mL
3 tbsp	confectioner's (icing) sugar, divided	45 mL
2 tbsp	finely grated orange zest	25 mL
1 tbsp	finely grated lemon zest	15 mL
¼ cup	granulated sugar	50 mL
5	peeled, seeded ripe oranges (preferably blood, clementine or mandarin), sliced paper-thin (see Tips, left)	5
12	sheets (6- by 4-inch/15 by 10 cm each) Fresh Chocolate Pasta Dough (½ recipe, see page 235)	12
2 tsp	salt	10 mL
1 cup	orange segments, seeded (see Tips, left)	250 mL
	Confectioner's (icing) sugar in a shaker	

1. In a mixing bowl, combine ricotta, 2 tbsp (25 mL) of the confectioner's sugar and orange and lemon zest. Mix well and set aside.

2. Sprinkle prepared baking dish with granulated sugar to cover bottom and sides. Arrange orange slices evenly over bottom, overlapping shingle style. Set aside.

3. In a covered pasta pot over high heat, bring water to a rapid boil. Add salt and pasta sheets to the boiling water and cook, uncovered, over high heat until pasta is almost al dente. Drain in a colander. Remove gently one by one, using tongs or a spatula, or empty colander onto a lint-free clean kitchen towel and then separate pasta sheets. Place on a dinner plate with sheets of plastic wrap between them.

4. Divide ricotta mixture into 12 equal portions. One at a time, lay out pasta sheets on a clean work surface, shorter side nearest you. Place one portion of ricotta mixture across center of sheet and roll up to form a tube. Place seam-side-down over oranges in baking dish. Cover with aluminum foil and bake in preheated oven until cannelloni are soft and tender, about 35 minutes. Remove from oven and let rest, covered, for 5 minutes.

5. In a small bowl combine orange segments with remaining 1 tbsp (15 mL) confectioner's sugar. Toss gently to mix. Remove foil from baking dish, top with orange segments and dust generously with confectioner's sugar. Serve immediately.

Frittata dolci di fideo con uva e pinoli

Sweet Frittata of Fideo with Grapes and Pine Nuts

Fideo is a short (about 2 inches/5 cm), thin pasta that is slightly curved. It is often used in Italian and Spanish cookery. Because it is fine in texture it is perfect for a baked frittata topped with grapes and pine nuts. Think of it as a custard pie topped with fruit.

Serves 8

Toasting Pine Nuts

Pine nuts have a high oil content and burn quickly. To toast them, spread on an ungreased baking sheet and bake in a preheated 350°F (180°C) oven for 7 to 10 minutes. Check after 7 minutes and remove from oven if nuts are already golden.

- Preheat oven to 325°F (160°C)
- Rimmed baking sheet
- 10-inch (25 cm) round nonstick cake or deep-dish pie pan, sprayed with vegetable oil

1 tbsp	salt	15 mL
8 oz	dried fideo	250 g
1/3 cup	confectioner's (icing) sugar	75 mL
1/4 cup	whole milk	50 mL
6	large eggs	6
1/4 cup	sliced (crosswise) seedless green grapes	50 mL
1/4 cup	sliced (crosswise) seedless red grapes	50 mL
2 tbsp	pine nuts, roasted	25 mL
	Lightly sweetened vanilla-flavored whipped cream, optional (see Tip, page 372)	

1. In a covered pasta pot over high heat, bring water to a rapid boil. Add salt and fideo and cook, uncovered, over high heat until slightly softer than al dente. Drain. Spread on baking sheet and let cool to room temperature.

2. In a mixing bowl combine sugar, milk and eggs. Whisk until sugar is dissolved and eggs are blended. Add fideo and mix to coat evenly.

3. Transfer to prepared pan. Place pan inside a small roasting pan and add boiling water halfway up the sides, being careful not to splash frittata. Bake until firm to the touch, about 30 minutes.

4. Remove from oven and lift out of hot water bath. Let cool for 10 minutes. Run a thin-bladed spatula around edges to loosen. Cover pan with a large serving plate, flip and unmold frittata onto plate.

5. Sprinkle top with grapes and pine nuts. Cut into 8 equal pieces with a sharp serrated knife and serve immediately. If desired, garnish each slice with a dollop of whipped cream.

Variation

Substitute angel hair pasta (capellini) for the fideo.

Orzo con crema di Gorgonzola dolce, pere e noci

Orzo with Sweet Gorgonzola Cream, Pear and Walnuts

Cheese, fruit and nuts are a traditional after-dinner course. Here they are combined in a savory pudding. Gorgonzola dolce is the readily available young, soft variety of the cheese, as opposed to Gorgonzola piccante, the firmer, aged variety.

Serves 8

• Rimmed baking sheet

1 tbsp	salt	15 mL
1 lb	dried orzo	500 g
1¼ cups	Gorgonzola dolce	300 mL
½ cup	mascarpone	125 mL
1 cup	heavy or whipping (35%) cream, stiffly whipped	250 mL
¾ cup	diced unpeeled fresh pear	175 mL
¼ cup	chopped walnuts	50 mL

1. In a covered pasta pot over high heat, bring water to a rapid boil. Add salt and orzo and cook, uncovered, until pasta is slightly softer than al dente. Drain and spread out on baking tray and let cool to room temperature.

2. In a mixer bowl, combine Gorgonzola and mascarpone. Using electric mixer, mix on low until creamy. Increase speed to high and beat for 1 minute. Gently fold in whipped cream. Add orzo and fold gently to mix.

3. Transfer to a serving bowl and sprinkle with pear and walnuts. Serve immediately.

Mascarpone

This double- to triple-cream cow's-milk cheese from Lombardy is rich and delicious. Technically it is not really a cheese, because rennet is not used to thicken it. The cream is coagulated using citric or tartaric acid and the resulting product is drained to thicken it even more. The finished cheese has a fat content between 70% and 75% and a texture similar to very dense crème fraîche or clotted cream. It is also used with fruit and in desserts such as the infamous tiramisu.

Paglia e fieno al dolce

Sweet "Straw and Hay" Tagliatelle

"Straw and hay" is a traditional savory pasta dish in which plain and spinach tagliatelle are cooked together. In this dessert recipe, the plain sweet pasta dough is the straw and the chocolate dough is the hay.

Serves 6 to 8

Tip

To make whipped cream for this recipe, beat ½ cup (125 mL) heavy (35%) cream until soft peaks form. With mixer running, sprinkle 1 tbsp (15 mL) sugar and ½ tsp (2 mL) vanilla extract into the cream and continue beating until stiff peaks form.

1 tbsp	salt	15 mL
½ recipe	Fresh Sweet Pasta Dough, rolled and cut into tagliatelle (see pages 234 and 226)	½ recipe
½ recipe	Fresh Chocolate Pasta Dough, rolled and cut into tagliatelle (see pages 235 and 226)	½ recipe
2 tbsp	unsalted butter	25 mL
1½ cups	diced peeled Granny Smith apples	375 mL
2 tbsp	confectioner's (icing) sugar plus additional for dusting	25 mL
	Lightly sweetened vanilla-flavored whipped cream, optional (see Tip, left)	

1. In a covered pasta pot over high heat, bring water to a rapid boil. Add salt and two types of tagliatelle and cook, uncovered, over high heat until pasta is al dente. Scoop out about 1 cup (250 mL) of the pasta cooking water and set aside. Drain pasta.

2. In a large sauté pan over medium heat, bring ¼ cup (50 mL) of the reserved pasta water to a simmer. Add butter and raise heat to high. Add apple and sugar and cook until apple is tender, about 10 minutes. Add another ¼ cup (50 mL) of reserved pasta water and tagliatelle and, using a wooden spoon, toss to coat evenly.

3. Transfer to a large serving platter and sprinkle generously with confectioner's sugar. Serve immediately. If desired, top each serving with a large dollop of whipped cream.

Ravioli ripieni con albicocche e rosmarino

Apricot Ravioli with Rosemary

In Italy jams are made from fresh ripe fruit in season and cooked with sugar, using little or no water, until the fruit reduces to a thick, intensely fruity preserve. This filling for ravioli, which is made from dried apricots, has an intense flavor. The addition of rosemary provides another dimension. I recommend that you prepare the jam the day before you intend to make the ravioli.

Makes 8 to 9 servings / 36 ravioli

Tip

Cut the recipe for Fresh Sweet Pasta Dough (page 234) in half to get this quantity.

1½ tbsp	fresh rosemary leaves	22 mL
1	bay leaf	1
8 oz	dried apricots	250 g
2½ cups	apple juice, divided	625 mL
½ cup	water	125 mL
¼ cup	granulated sugar	50 mL
6	sheets Fresh Sweet Pasta Dough (see recipe, page 234)	6
3 tbsp	confectioner's (icing) sugar	45 mL
1 tbsp	salt	15 mL
	Confectioner's (icing) sugar for dusting	

1. In a square of cheesecloth, tie rosemary and bay leaf into a bouquet garni. Place in a heavy-bottomed saucepan. Add apricots, 2 cups (500 mL) of the apple juice, water and granulated sugar. Cook, uncovered, over medium heat, stirring occasionally and lowering heat as necessary to maintain a steady simmer, until very thick, about 2 hours. Remove from heat, discard bouquet garni and cool to room temperature. Transfer to a food processor and purée.

2. Lay out one pasta sheet on a wooden board, longer side nearest you. Using a pastry brush, brush sheet with water. Place 1 tsp (5 mL) apricot filling in lower left-hand corner, 1 inch (2.5 cm) from each edge. Repeat every 2 inches (5 cm) to form a row of 6 dollops. Beginning in the upper left-hand corner, repeat to form a second row above. Carefully lay a second sheet of pasta onto the first, covering the fillings completely. Using fingertips, gently press down pasta between dollops of filling to seal. Using a fluted pasta wheel, cut between rows in straight lines to make 12 ravioli, each 2 inches (5 cm) square. Place completed ravioli on parchment sheets dusted with confectioner's sugar (do not let them touch). Repeat until all the pasta has been used.

3. In a covered pasta pot over high heat, bring water to a rapid boil. Add salt and ravioli and cook, uncovered, until ravioli are al dente, 3 to 4 minutes. Drain.

4. In a sauté pan over medium heat, combine 2 tbsp (25 mL) of the apricot purée and remaining ½ cup (125 mL) of apple juice. Bring to a simmer, stirring. Add ravioli and cook, stirring gently, until sauce thickens slightly, about 5 minutes. Transfer to a large serving platter and dust with confectioner's sugar. Serve immediately.

Variation

Substitute Fresh Chocolate Pasta Dough (see recipe, page 235) for the Fresh Sweet Pasta Dough.

Stracci al cioccolato con gelato e fragole al menta

Chocolate Stracci with Vanilla Ice Cream and Minted Strawberries

Stracci, meaning "rags," are well suited to this sweet chocolate pasta dish. It is served warm, topped with vanilla ice cream and strawberries with a hint of mint.

Serves 8

Tip
You'll need one recipe of Fresh Chocolate Pasta Dough (see page 235) to make this quantity.

2 cups	quartered fresh strawberries	500 mL
2 tbsp	confectioner's (icing) sugar	25 mL
2 tbsp	julienned mint leaves, lightly packed	25 mL
1 tbsp	salt	15 mL
12	sheets Fresh Chocolate Pasta Dough (see Tips, left)	12
8	medium scoops vanilla gelato	8
½ cup	white chocolate shavings	125 mL
8	mint sprigs	8
	Confectioner's (icing) sugar in a shaker	

1. In a mixing bowl, combine strawberries, confectioner's sugar and mint. Mix well and set aside.

2. Using a straight-edged pasta cutting wheel or sharp knife, cut each sheet of pasta dough horizontally into strips 2 inches (5 cm) wide by 4 inches (10 cm) long. You should get 6 strips of stracci from each sheet.

3. In a covered pasta pot over high heat, bring water to a rapid boil. Add salt and stracci and cook, uncovered, over high heat until almost al dente. Drain. Add to strawberry mixture and, using pasta tongs, toss to coat evenly.

4. Transfer to a large serving platter and top with vanilla gelato at even intervals. Sprinkle with white chocolate shavings, garnish with mint sprigs and dust with confectioner's sugar. Serve immediately.

Variation

Divide the stracci-strawberry mixture equally among 8 large, shallow rimmed bowls. Top each bowl with a scoop of gelato, a mint sprig and a sprinkling of white chocolate shavings. Dust with confectioner's sugar and serve at once.

Library and Archives Canada Cataloguing in Publication

Coletta, John
   250 true Italian pasta dishes : easy & authentic recipes : inspired by
Quartino ristorante, pizzeria, wine bar / John Coletta with Nancy Ross Ryan.

Includes index.
ISBN 978-0-7788-0221-1

   1. Cookery (Pasta). 2. Cookery, Italian. I. Ryan, Nancy Ross II. Title.
III. Title: Two hundred fifty true Italian pasta dishes.

TX809.M17C64 2009   641.8′22   C2009-902217-6

Index